One Million Deaths and a Black Man... One in a Billion ! The Odds of Amazing Modern Prophecies

- Hillary Clinton a Dictator?
- Barak Obama and a Million Deaths?
- The Complete Destruction of America.
- And Many Others...

By R Scott Giberti

Published in the United States by
First Stone Publishing, Inc., 8987 E. Tanque Verde #309 Box 392, Tucson, Arizona 85703 - Or visit our website: www.firststonellc.com

First Stone book titles may be purchased in bulk for education, business, fundraising, or sales promotional use. For information, please email sales@firststonellc.org or tlc@dakotacom.net

Library of Congress Catalog-in-Publication Data

Giberti, R. Scott.
One Million Deaths and a Black Man… One in a Billion! The Odds of Amazing Modern Prophecies / R. Scott Giberti.
p.cm.
Includes bibliographical references.
ISBN 13: **978-0-578-01460-9** (pbk.)
1. Bible—Prophecies. 2. Prophecy—Christian. 3. Historical—Religious. I. Title. II. Title: One Million Deaths. III. Title: One in a Billion.

Library of Congress Control Number: 2009902397

Printed in the United States of America
06 07 08 09 10 RRD 9 8 6 7 5 4 3 2

First Edition

Dedication

This book is written in memory of Reverend William Branham, a humble, Christian minister that demonstrated the outstanding qualities necessary to being a chosen instrument of God.

Disclaimer

The use of either the term "Black man," "Colored" or "Negro" by the author or the Reverend William Branham in the title or through this literary work is not meant to be pejorative; rather, they denote the generally accepted social and political appellation(s) of their day.

Acknowledgments

I would like to start with a special acknowledgement for the encouragement and support given by my wife Tina, my sons Silas and Scott and my daughter Alison, all whom I love dearly and am extremely thankful for and proud of.

This book would not have been possible without my father-in-law, who provided the initial inspiration to compile a book of prophecy, *America, You Will Be Destroyed! Thus Saith the Lord*, which I wrote in 2007.

Finally, I would like to acknowledge and especially thank the following individuals for their contributions of oral history, research, editing, page layout, and other support:

Dale Knight

Gerard & Rebecca Washburn

Reverend Pearry Green

Reverend Billy Wiggins

Connie Sabo-Walker (1940-2008)

To God be all the glory,

R Scott Giberti – December 2008

About the Author

Born in Long Island, New York in 1962, R Scott Giberti has formed and run several successful businesses and not-for-profit corporations. R Scott Giberti began his helping career in 1982, in the post Viet Nam-era Marine Corps. Having had a life-altering spiritual experience a year or so earlier, he felt compelled to provide religious education and training to his fellow Marines. His continued desire to help others led him to religious and psychological studies resulting in a Master's Degree in Counseling from Chapman University and nearly two decades of providing pastoral and clinical support.

He is an energetic man of vision and deep spirituality with an unusual ability to communicate spiritual truths. R Scott Giberti, a sought-after speaker known for his gritty, practical, down-to-earth approach to successful Christian living, has helped change countless lives. His educational and humanitarian efforts have taken him to over thirty countries.

Today, R Scott Giberti lives in Tucson, Arizona, with his lovely and talented wife and two college-age children. His oldest son is an Army Scout, a combat veteran of Operation Iraqi Freedom and Multi-National Force-Iraq. R Scott Giberti is the author of several books, including:

America - You Will Be Destroyed! - Thus Saith the Lord; *Unlocking the King James Bible's Common Words & Phrases*, and; the soon to be released *An Exposition of the Seven Church Ages*. Research is being conducted on the ancient Babylonian religious system, for a historical novel entitled *A Cage of Hateful Birds*.

Table of Contents

Hillary the demagogue – going, going, gone? After Obama's January 20th, 2009 Presidential Inauguration, with Bidden as his Vice-Presidential running mate, are Hillary's aspirations of power gone?

Not Likely.

Ladies and Gentleman, introducing Madam Secretary...

1

A Woman Dictator?
Hillary Rodham Clinton

"Madame Secretary" - Hillary Rodham Clinton

On December 1st, 2008 President-elect Barack Obama selected the New York senator, Senate Armed Services Committee member, former presidential contender and former first lady for secretary of state[A]

[A] In accordance with the United States Constitution, the Secretary performs such duties as the President requires. These include negotiating with foreign representatives and instructing U.S. embassies or consulates abroad. The Secretary also serves as a principal adviser to the President in the determination of U.S. foreign policy and, in recent decades, has become responsible for overall direction, coordination, and supervision of interdepartmental activities of the U.S. Government overseas, excepting certain military activities.

As the highest-ranking member of the cabinet, the Secretary of State is fourth in line to succeed the Presidency, coming after the Vice President, the Speaker of the House of Representatives, and the President pro tempore of the Senate.

- an appointment that will go a long way toward healing the wounds left by their bruising Democratic primary.

Obama waited until after Thanksgiving before officially announcing the nomination because the full national security team was still being worked out, and he wanted to have all the members in place first.

After it was evident that Clinton would not have the necessary votes to secure the Democratic nomination, her aides and legions of supporters began to campaign for other top positions in the Obama administration. Clinton had much to offer, politically, as well as influencing the outcome of Obama's bid for the Presidency. Her millions of loyal supporters, especially women, Hispanics and blue collar crowd were critical to ensure Obama's victory.

Once the decision to drop out of the Presidential race was made, Hillary quickly and aggressively campaigned for Obama's election. For the past eight years Hillary has shown this type of middle-of-the-road diplomacy within the US Senate, garnering bi-partisan praise repetitively. As fellow New Yorker Donald Trump might say, she knows the art of the deal – remain flexible and think big, really big.

Clinton had aggressively pursued the secretary of state slot and mounted an all-out sales campaign amid fears the job might be slipping away. Former Clinton campaign aides and some of her inner-circle advisers - aka *Hillaryland* - were part of a coordinated effort to win her the top State Department post. These Clinton allies were e-mailing and working the phones with Obama contacts, appearing on cable TV and leaking optimistic scenarios to the media. All you had to do was pay attention and see how they were operating, and it looked like a planned-out campaign.

By Thursday, November 20th, 2008, reports were coming in that Obama had vetted and reassured Clinton that as secretary of state she would have direct access to him and could select her own staff.

"She feels like she's been treated very well in the way she's been asked," said a close associate of Clinton, who like most others interviewed asked for anonymity because the nomination would not be formally announced until after Thanksgiving, November 27, 2008. Confidants to Clinton said Friday that she had decided to give up her Senate seat to become secretary of state in the Obama administration.

Her appointment would be yet another vertical direction in the unlikely journey of a former political spouse in Arkansas who went on to build a political base of her own and become a symbol of achievement to many women. "At long last, the feminist icon would represent the feminist ideal of getting a room of her own, all on her own."[1]

The role, though a supporting one, would make her one of the most influential players on the international stage, and it would represent at least one more act for one of the nation's most prominent public families, as former President Bill Clinton would also become an ad hoc member of the Obama team.

As Secretary, Hillary will perform such duties as negotiating with foreign representatives, negotiating treaties and agreements with foreign governments and in general, serve as the President's principal advisor in the determination of U.S. foreign policy.

In the Obama-Clinton relationship, advisers say, the relatively smooth nature of their talks about the secretary of state job indicate that both, for now, have a working chemistry. The advisers say that Obama was clearly interested in bringing a rival under his wing, and that he also recognized that Clinton had far more discipline and focus than her husband.

At the same time, Obama's advisers said, he had the self-confidence to name a global brand as his emissary to the world. He recognizes, they said, that he will have to build the kind of relationship that ensures that foreign leaders know that when Clinton speaks, she is speaking directly for him.

When Hillary speaks, she will be speaking as the President.

A Woman Dictator? - Hillary Rodham Clinton

Warning others of danger is not easy. *Chicken Little*[2] [3] had an acorn fall on her head and believed it was the sky itself falling. She saw danger where none truly existed and her foolish ranting, rather than being helpful, actually caused hurt to others. *The Boy That Cried Wolf*[4] warned of danger so often, that when real danger arose, no one believed his warning. And in *The Emperor's New Clothes*[5] the young lad that spoke up about what he saw, told the King the truth about his condition, faced humiliation and possibly worse consequences – all for his forth-telling.

Despite the oft knee-jerk reactions by some conservatives (remember the tirades about Tele-Tubbies[6] [7] and Sponge Bob[8] being pro-gay?), when they warn of perils that Hillary Clinton may cause our nation, maybe they have it right this time. Perhaps for the wrong reasons, but they still might be correct in saying she will bring the nation to ruin.

Hillary Clinton is an inspiration for this book; she has also been the villain, the bogey-man, the Tonton-Macoute, and the black hat of the religious right and typically conservative moral majority[9].

With all the inaccurate, sensationalized diatribes about the end-of-the-world and/or the Middle East "crisis," possibly nobody is listening anymore.[10] [11] What a sad irony, the world at large perishes because both the secular and religious communities commissioned to warn us have prophesied falsely for so long (for their own gain), that our hearing has grown dull.

Jesus prophesied that after he left the earth false prophets and false christs would come - and both would *"deceive many."* (Matthew 24:23-28) What is a "christ?" The term *christ*, *christos*, the Greek equivalent of the Hebrew *Messias*, means "anointed." Today the term would be equivalent to charismatic, energetic, goal-driven, zealous, enthusiastic etc. Those terms could be applied to every modern leader, ruler, or religious authority that promises change, reforms or a better way of life.

> "Is Hillary Clinton a *christ?*"

By definition, Steve Jobs could be considered as a "christ." – Is Hillary Clinton a "christ?" Both are dynamic and charismatic leaders extremely proficient in the keeping of public opinion. Now, I do not personally know these two, but I can see them on television, hear them on the radio or audio files, and I can say they are visionary pioneers. Each has very loyal, "never surrender, never-say-die" followers.

As I said, I may not know them personally, nor have experienced a one-on-one meeting or encounter with them, but I can certainly see their effects upon the masses. In the Fall of 1993 I heard Hillary Clinton in person at the Augusta Civic Center, when she was pitching her health care reform program and her "it takes a village" approach to family and child rearing. Why did I go? I had heard about an obscure prophecy made by William Branham in 1933 and I thought to myself...maybe, just maybe...

The prophesy went like this:

"I said, 'Remember, in that day, before the end time comes, before the end time comes, that a woman... Now, you all keep this wrote down. There'll be a great powerful woman raise up, either be President, or dictator, or some great powerful woman in this United States. And [America] she'll sink under the influence of women. Now, you remember; that's THUS SAITH THE LORD.'" [12]

The prophecy describes this woman as cruel in heart, cold, and calculating. It says that her time of leadership might go beyond high cabinet post influence, that she would behave more like a dictator. Her presence would signal the end and would perhaps contribute to the cataclysmic destruction of the United States (a different prophecy – see Chapters 9 & 10) during the "Last Days."

I thought, "Which woman has a personality and power base to be or do this?" Former U.S. Secretary of State Condoleezza Rice, Geraldine Ferraro, Dianne Feinstein, Oprah Winfrey, Sarah Palin (just kidding – I couldn't resist), or U.S. House of Representatives Speaker Nancy Pelosi? All of these are successful and talented women; each a little hard or harsh at times (except Palin), but none carried enough clout or had enough popularity to rule America, especially like a dictator. But, Hillary Rodham Clinton... So I went to hear her, to see her, to experience her presence – for it would take more than words or sound bites to draw people under her spell. Nearly all contemporary leaders have been powerful public speakers, swaying people with the magic of their anointed words and believable unswerving conviction.

I went and I was conquered...until the end. Hillary held her audience spellbound; she had the audience in that large, packed indoor stadium swept up in her enthusiasm. It was not the health-care reforms (though that was and is an important issue), the magic was in *her belief* in the health care issue. She seemed crazed, angry, and passionate; she was a believer, she was anointed – she was a *christ.*

What snapped me back to reality were her actions, her ruthless behavior, and through extension, the audience's behavior towards a *non-politico* mother that questioned Clinton's "it takes a village" diatribe. This woman from the unwashed masses dared challenge *the Hillary*. She calmly, but clearly disagreed with Hillary in the open, public forum of Q & A after the speech. Hillary shut the woman down and turned all her angry zeal upon this mother that felt the family, not the community or the state was the better caretaker. Whew! It was not pretty, not presidential – it looked and felt dictatorial.

At that moment I could close my eyes and imagine Idi Amin, or Hitler or any other ruler that truly cannot stand being opposed. I know that is strong and harsh and maybe unwarranted, but it is how I felt at the moment and all that I read currently and objectively leads me to believe she has the temperament and potential to fulfill this prophecy.

The Need to Believe

I think it is in our nature to believe in something, and in someone. We want to believe in our parents, our civic and religious leaders, a God or Higher Power. It is such a deep instinct that for most people it takes a lot of associated negative events to shake us from a belief or from believing in a person or an institution. Even when our "faith" is shaken, we do not stop "believing"-period. No, our loyalties simply change.

If my PC computer crashes too many times, or Microsoft comes out with one too many version updates and I really get fed up, I will switch to Apple and become a Mac convert. I will swear by the un-crashable Mac OS system, tell how even the "Windows" and other graphical aspects of the user interface (UI) was an Apple idea (true).[13] [14] I will talk about the freshness and relativity of Apple products (the iPod and the iPhone etc.), and I will point you to my helmsman, the charismatic visionary and *christ* Steve Jobs.

Yes, we not only *want* to believe, I think we *need* to believe.

"The human spirit glows from that small inner light of doubt whether we are right, while those that believe with complete certainty that they possess the right are dark inside and darken the world outside with cruelty, pain, and injustice."

Is Hillary Clinton evil, like say, Hitler or Pol Pot was evil? No, I do not think so. But is she cruel-hearted, calculated, obsessive, vindictive, domineering, and possibly unscrupulous in her progress to achieve her quest? In my opinion – Yes! Emphatically, Yes!

Hitler had a platform that pandered to only a few people or a certain group, many of his ideas and delusions were beyond bizarre. Why did people believe him? Simply, *he believed*, and therefore was believable.
Mark Twain said "The most outrageous lies that can be invented will find believers if a man only tells them with all his might."[15] It is classic, basic psychology of human behavior, much like the story *Chicken Little.* "The sky is falling, the sky is falling" said Chicken Little with complete conviction. She believed, and soon she had a following.

"We believe whatever we want to believe."[16]

Mass hysteria is not solely isolated to past history; there are plenty of modern occurrences as well. The Jewish Question, the Salem Witch Trials, The Stanford Prison Experiment, the original "War of the Worlds" broadcast, and more recently the Duke Lacrosse gang-rape frenzy – all examples of mass action based on erroneous or harmful beliefs. It is not too difficult to visualize the current Hillary Rodham Clinton or Barak Obama for President Movements.

The Influence of Hillary Clinton

How will Hillary Clinton ruin or destroy America? I really cannot specifically say. Some say that she concurred with much, if not all of the executive decisions made by her husband and former President Bill Clinton. If that is so, then she will continue what some believe to have been a conspiracy by her husband, to systematically weaken the nation though the *1991 Presidential Nuclear Initiative*,[17] [18] by:

- Eliminating the entire inventory of ground-launched non-strategic nuclear weapons (nuclear artillery and Lance surface-to-surface missiles).
- Removing all nonstrategic nuclear weapons from surface ships, attack submarines and land-based naval aircraft bases.
- Removing strategic bombers from alert.
- Standing down the Minuteman II ICBMs scheduled for deactivation under Start I.
- Terminating the mobile Peacekeeper and mobile small ICBM programs.
- Terminating the SCRAM-II nuclear short-range attack missile.
- Limiting B-2 production to 20 bombers.
- Cancelling the entire small ICBM program.
- Ceasing production of W-88 Trident SLBM (submarine-launched missile) warheads.
- Halting purchases of advanced cruise missiles.
- And stopping new production of Peacekeeper missiles (our biggest MIRV-warhead ICBM).

A conspiracy? Research (detailed later in this section) indicates that the Clinton *presidencies* (plural) were planned, and therefore by definition is a conspiracy. Not necessarily a conspiracy in legal terms, but when people plan, plot, scheme or enter into a semi-secret accord, it is a *conspiracy*.

Despite Hillary's flat, cold, even off-putting demeanor, on January 20, 2009, many believed and feared that Hillary Rodham Clinton would be sworn in as the 44th President of the United States. Though that will not happen in 2009, she will keep her ambitions alive and her chances even greater by becoming Obama's Secretary of State. Her future Presidential election will be due to her Machiavellian determination to surmount all the obstacles between her and the Oval Office, by any means necessary. She will continue to reinvent herself as much and as often as necessary to insure political survival and her run for the presidency.

In the introduction of *Her Way* - a new biography on Hillary Clinton by Jeff Gerth and Don Van Natta[19] - the authors report:

More than three decades ago, in the earliest days of their romance, Bill and Hillary struck a plan, one that would become both the foundation and the engine of their relationship. They agreed to work together to revolutionize the Democratic Party and ultimately make the White House their home. Once their "twenty-year project" was realized, with Bill's victory in 1992, their plan became even more ambitious: eight years as president for him, then eight years for her. Their audacious pact has remained a secret until now.

What is the source for this claim? According to the authors, it is renowned historian Taylor Branch:

By the summer of 1993, the ways of Washington, sometimes, called Potomac fever, had not dissuaded Bill or Hillary. According to one of their closest friends, Taylor Branch, they still planned two terms in the White House for Bill and, later, two for Hillary. Branch described the plan to two Washington friends, John Henry and Ann Crittenden, over a barbeque dinner at a rodeo in Aspen, Colorado, that summer.

One reviewer of the book *The Vast Right-wing Conspiracy's Dossier on Hillary Clinton*[20] said, "Hillary and her sponsors want to install her as ruler of America."

Later Taylor Branch back-pedaled, "did a crawdad" or just plain lied, when asked by The Washington Post to verify this remark.[21] He did what most politicians do, the infamous *2-step Potomac Shuffle* – privately saying one thing, publically stating another. It appears that someone remembered a candid conversation made in private from which Mr. Branch wanted to distance himself. That sounds vaguely familiar to "Senator, I have no recollection of that!" "No recollection" is typically invoked by governmental officials during sworn testimony to the U.S. Congress denying potentially damaging -- political and/or criminal -- behavior.

What more obvious of a sign could God give in warning America and even the world than a woman rising to power in a patriarchal society, with an all-male presidential club? It is so unique, it catches your attention, and it forces you to think.

Did that prophecy by William Branham suggest that a woman might raise up that could be a *dictator*? Can you imagine how preposterous that must have sounded in 1933? Morality and conventionality were still the norm - During the 1930's, in many parts of the country men were arrested for indecent exposure for going bare-chested in public.[22] [23] The majority of women did not even work outside of the home, still wore dresses, not pants or shorts or their underwear outside of their clothes.[24] [25]

Women were for the most part considered someone's daughter, wife or mother[26] [27] – not leaders of nations, especially not having such power and authority to become a dictator! During this time even the Motion Picture Association lived by a code (The Hays Code)[28] that strongly restricted immorality, indecency, profanity and even forbad taking God's name in vain. It also forbad any behavioral representation that might denigrate or injure the "institution of marriage and the home."[29]

A Gallup Poll was taken in 1937 asking Americans if "a qualified woman ran for office, would you vote her?" Only 33% said they would.[30]

How could a prophecy like this be made, except were it not for the inspiration and direction of the Spirit of God? The Almighty provided a warning that would be needed at a later time and in a day of such moral breakdown.

Hillary Clinton may directly destroy America or she may only be one insignificant piece of the Last Days puzzle. Her presidency could be one event in a series of events that act like a chain reaction. *What more obvious of a sign could God give in warning America and even the world than a woman rising to power in a patriarchal society, with an all-male presidential club? It is so unique, it catches your attention, and it forces you to think.*

This is not 1933 or 1937 - Seventy years have transpired since the initial prophecy and a massive shift in popular opinion has occurred. Our politicians are no longer held to a high standard of morality, nor are the norms of a traditional Judea-Christian nation observed. Seventy years have erased the 33% polling opinion and in two recent polls conducted, nearly ninety percent (90%) of respondents today said they would vote for a woman commander in chief.[31] [32]

"There'll be a great powerful woman raise up, either be President, or dictator, or some great powerful woman in this United States... Now, you remember; that's THUS SAITH THE LORD."

Wm. Branham
1933

William Branham said that God had been warning America since 1933 and that America had "rejected" God in 1956.[33] It has been fifty years since that time. Fifty years in the Bible represented a *Jubilee.*[34] A jubilee was when all slaves were offered their freedom, they had the choice to go free or remain slaves. Yes, they could actually choose to remain slaves! If they chose to remain with their "master" a ceremony took place where the slave was taken to a wooden post and an awl (or sharp nail) pierced through an earlobe. This symbolized that the slave could no longer "hear" any future calls for freedom. The slave would remain a slave forever.[35]

Is God offering this great nation an opportunity to be set free, only to have her refuse His freedom, to remain servants of sin and to corrupt systems and institutions? Hillary Clinton's selection as secretary of state signifies an acceptance of an immoral leadership and lifestyle and a rejection of morality, integrity and ultimately God; and it would appear America through her choice, is setting a course for her own destruction.

Interestingly, there are many people today from diverse camps that are writing about Hillary Clinton as a Dictator, Empress and the like, either directly through factual analysis or indirectly as the subject for a fictional character. In Chuck Slate's book, *Caution! Hillary – America's First Dictator* he says that he had done extensive research into the dynamics of dictatorships and felt that the actions and character of Hillary Clinton were suggestive of a dictator. He says; "DO NOT underestimate the tenacity, the ruthlessness, the need for power and the lack of conscience of Hillary Clinton!" (emphasis by author). He goes on to say that she has "the backbone" for a dictatorship. The works of Carl Limbacher (*Hillary's Scheme*) and Anne Coulter (*Treason*) provide additional reference material and a factual basis to Mr. Slate's assertions of a pending dictatorship.[36]

Look what others in the political realm say about Hillary Clinton:

"She's the most calculating person in modern politics..."[37]

"[Voters] are likely to see her for what she is: an aggressive, calculating, insincere, opportunistic, and exceptionally liberal woman."[38]

"She's cold, scarily calculating…"[39]

When I say a dictatorship, it is not meant to imply the establishment of one person through the use of force. Rather a quasi-totalitarian dictatorship form of government; a dictatorship by and of someone that can wield the power of Head of State with unyielding inflexibility and myopia.

In her book *The Vast Right-Wing Conspiracies Dossier on Hillary Clinton* and during both a *Hannity & Colmes* interview (October 13, 2006)[40] and *The Big Story with John Gibson* on Fox News (October 16, 2006)[41] author Amanda Carpenter describes the abuses of power Hillary and Bill Clinton participated in during his White House years, as well as their post-Presidency years. In the October 13, 2006 interview, guest host and *National Review* editor Rich Lowry makes this observation; "Everything she [Hillary Clinton] does seems so calculated."

The Clintons have been in government most of their adult lives and are experts at playing the political system. None of their machinations seems to have "just happened" by accident. As Peggy Noonan wrote, "they have learned a number of things in their life in politics, but one of the biggest is this: They can do anything."[42] They have learned that if they are willing to let any dirty secret be aired out publically, after a short while people forget. They have learned the key to modern political survivability. Hillary put all her hard-earned lessons into use for her failed presidential election, and subsequent bid for Secretary of State. Her campaigns always have the look and feel of something meticulously planned, long ago, at the highest levels. Franklin Roosevelt is attributed to saying, *"If anything happens in politics, you can bet it was planned that way in a smoke-filled room".*[43]

How far will Hillary Clinton go in obtaining the presidency? In a fictional work, Dr. Richard Little, author of *The Empress Project*, says "An American woman, guided to evil by Satan, secretly becomes the willing agent of the Red Chinese, infiltrates and subverts the American Government at the highest levels, and with active guidance and assistance of her Chinese Communist masters plots to completely take over America's government from within and become the Empress of America."[44] How far will she go? As far as she needs to and, according to Dr. Little, she'll even sell her soul to the devil if need be.

> Dominant personalities enjoy the power to direct others and to evoke obedience and respect from them. They tend to be tough and unsentimental, and derive satisfaction from acts that ***dictate*** and direct the lives of others.

Though *The Empress Project* is a fictionalization of the influences that shape contemporary political figures, it has the breadth of an op-ed essay well versed in political affairs at the national and international level. It provides in-depth fly-on-the-wall characterizations of pivotal contemporary events affecting our nation at its core; the author weaves a plausible scenario that leaves the reader stunned and wanting to know more. At one level the book operates as a crime novel played out on the grand stage of Presidential politics, and at another level the book provides a study in the psychoanalysis of deceit. After reading this book one would have to say that Thomas Jefferson was correct – "eternal vigilance"[45] against the excesses of tyrants is fully warranted.

One reviewer (Christopher N. Hatley)[46] says this about *The Empress Project*; "a must read for any American who wants to know about the inner workings of the Hillary Clinton political machine." Mr. Hatley says that he has conversed with the author Dr. Little and that his work was offered as fiction for several reasons. The answer is because those who provided him with his information based it on their intimate/firsthand knowledge of that which Hillary and her cronies have been doing.

Thus, the author's contributors are unwilling to put their names into the public forum, in association with this project, for fear of retribution or retaliation. Once you read the book, you will understand that their apprehensions are not only justified but also very prudent.

However, it is readily obvious, if you know anything about the events of the Clintons' continuing rise to power (namely Hillary's), that there is very little of a fictitious nature in what Richard Little conveys to the reader. The author stated to Mr. Hatley that, "The book is probably about 95% fact."[47]

Edward Gibbons, said in his *History of the Decline and Fall of the Roman Empire*, the major reason for the fall of the 1,200-year-old Roman Empire was a secret conspiracy within government itself. All the while the conspirators were wreaking their damage, they masterfully deceived the citizens of the Empire through lies, scoffing at the stupidity of anyone who would dare suggest conspiracy.[48] Ms. Clinton has been very vocal in diverting attention away from herself and accusing others, especially the "Right-Wing Conspiracy groups" of trying to damage her and her husband's reputation.[49]

She certainly appears to have the personality to fit the characteristics of this cruel, cold-hearted, dictator-like leader.

Researchers at Saint John's University and the College of Saint Benedict performed an indirect personality assessment on Hillary Clinton in April 2000 using the Millon Inventory of Diagnostic Criteria and identified her primary personality patterns to be "Ambitious/superior and Dominant/controlling," she also has had some situation-specific "Contentious and Distrusting features." Her major personality strengths in a political role are her "confident assertiveness and commanding presence". Her major personality-based shortcomings are a "lack of empathy and congeniality, uncompromising assertiveness, and cognitive inflexibility".[50]

Theodore Millon, the distinguished contemporary personality theorist, asserts that dominant personalities enjoy the power to direct others and to evoke obedience and respect from them. They tend to be tough and unsentimental, and derive satisfaction from acts that ***dictate*** and direct the lives of others. Millon's theory illuminates the darker recesses of Clinton's dominant, controlling character type: a penchant for perceptual and cognitive distortion; a demeaning of cooperative behavior and affection.

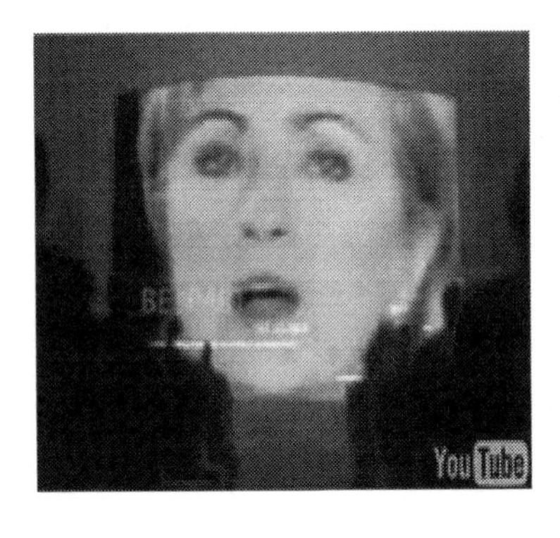

Hillary Clinton as the Dictator in YouTube Spoof (from Apple's 1984 commercial)[51]

This video is a spoof of Apple's famous 1984 Super Bowl ad, this time with Hillary Clinton portrayed as the monotonous dictator droning on and on. In the end, the video plugs Barack Obama.

Despite that Jacob Weisberg said Hillary faces a genuine electability[52] issue due to her off-putting personality, she has repeatedly been elected to significant posts and positions within our government. In her four years in the Senate, Hillary has proven herself to be capable, diligent, formidable, effective, and shrewd. She can make Republican colleagues sound like star-struck teenagers. As hard as she tries, Hillary has little facility for connecting with ordinary folk, for making them feel that she understands, identifies, and is at some level one of them. You may admire and respect her. But it is hard not to find Hillary a bit inhuman. Whatever she may be like in private, her public persona is calculating, clenched, relentless—and a little robotic. But none of this seems to matter.

Then how does one explain the fact that despite her many, many documented faults and flaws, Hillary Clinton at one point was the Democratic frontrunner and the candidate to beat from both major Parties; Or that in her quest for the 2008 presidency she was able to garner the support of millions of primary voters and win 23 states? Or on a much more recent note, how does she go from being a junior Senator with little actual experience or personal accomplishment, to being fourth in line to the presidency?

I know she has tremendous press corps connections and a vast network of political savvy supporters. I know she is a political survivor and a political chameleon. But, the only explanation I can offer that fully accounts for her ascendancy to the pinnacle of our political system is that a spiritual blindness is upon the hearts and minds of the populace.

Our culture is riddled with deception. It is everywhere, as illustrated by outlandish advertising claims like diet loss programs, wrinkle removers, sexual enhancers, "how to play the piano instantly"[53], etc. Sometimes it is easy to see through the falsehood (as in the claim that one can play the piano instantly). Unfortunately, however, most deception is not quite so easy to detect.

Satan deceived Eve by causing her to make her decision based on what she could see and on what her emotions and her flawed reasoning told her to be right, even though it was not established with facts or actually truthful.

Deception was....and still is....crucial to Satan's strategy. According to Jesus, it is the devil's very nature to deceive:

[The devil] was a murderer from the beginning, not holding to the truth, for there is no truth in him. When he lies, he speaks his native language, for he is a liar and the father of lies. (John 8:44 NIV)

For reasons we cannot fully understand, Satan chose to target the woman for his strategy of deception. Twice in the New Testament the apostle Paul points out that it was the woman who was deceived: *"The serpent beguiled Eve through his subtilty"* (2 Corinthians 11:3); "*Adam was not the one deceived; it was the woman who was deceived*" (1 Timothy 2:14 NIV).

Some theologians believe there was something in the way Eve was created that made her more vulnerable to deception....that she was inherently more "tempt-able," or "seducible." Others suggest that because God had given her a specific role within the male-female relationship and after her fall had placed her under the authority of her husband, once she stepped out from under that spiritual covering and away from authority, she was more easily deceived.

Regardless, the point is that women seem to be primary targets of Satan's deception. Remember that he did not first approach the man; he deliberately approached and deceived the woman. It was the woman who led her husband into sin, and together they led the whole human race into sin (though Adam, as head or leader, was held ultimately responsible). I believe there is something significant about that progression and that, to this day, there is a unique sense in which Satan targets women for deception. This is part of his strategy. He knows that if women accept his deception, they can then influence the men (and other women) around them towards wrong and harmful things, and those choices will set a pattern for subsequent generations to follow.

De Dubby, he de Smoove-Tongue Raskill…(The Devil is a Liar)

Sometimes, as was the case with Eve, Satan deceives directly. Sometimes, however, he uses other people as instruments of deception.

In the fifth chapter of Ephesians, Paul warns, "*Let no one deceive you with empty words*" (v. 6). Repeatedly, he challenges God's people to speak truth to one another. When we are not honest with each other, we actually do Satan's work for him, acting as his agents, deceiving and destroying each other.

There are no harmless lies. We cannot expose ourselves to the world's false, deceptive way of thinking and come out unscathed. Eve's first mistake was not eating the fruit from the tree of knowledge; her first mistake was listening to the Serpent, a.k.a. the Devil.

Listening to counsel or ways of thinking that are not truthful is the first step in developing wrong beliefs that will ultimately impact our behaviors. Hillary Clinton employs a similar strategy as Joseph Goebbels, Hitler's propaganda director did; "Tell a lie big enough and keep repeating it, people will eventually come to believe it."[54] Once we have listened to a lie enough, we can begin to believe it and then we are on the road to mental and oftentimes spiritual slavery.

Believe the lie and finally we become damned. This is how the Bible describes the chain of consequences for believing lies. More specifically this passage describes key events in what many Christians call "The Last Days" or "End Times."

2 Thessalonians 2: 7-12

For the mystery of iniquity doth already work: only he who now letteth will let, until he be taken out of the way. And then shall that Wicked be revealed, whom the Lord shall consume with the spirit of his mouth, and shall destroy with the brightness of his coming: Even him, whose coming is after the working of Satan with all power and signs and lying wonders, And with all deceivableness of unrighteousness in them that perish; because they received not the love of the truth, that they might be saved.

And for this cause God shall send them strong delusion, that they should believe a lie: That they all might be damned who believed not the truth...

I am not implying that Hillary Clinton is THE Antichrist. Her career happens to co-exist with a powerful spiritual influence prevalent in the earth to believe lies, and a deception that clouds mankind's reasoning. She benefits from this spirit of deception upon the world. This spirit is inevitably and ultimately going to deceive the majority of the world's inhabitants to believe in a grand and final leader who promises peaceful solutions to conflicts, famine and other major calamities.

Surprisingly, believing lies is easier than you might imagine. Dr. Anthony P. Young, national president of the Association of Black Psychologists and a specialist in forensic psychology, says "Individuals construct reality in their own mind. If you believe something is true, it becomes true regardless of what the facts are."

He says that lies are often more believable than the truth because people have a huge capacity for denial. "It's easier for a person to accept something when it is similar to what they believe. Individuals tend to deny certain facts which contradict what they want to believe." [55]

For a long time our society has held the belief that women are the gentler, nurturing, more caring gender of the human species. To believe the truth that women lie, cheat, steal, and molest statistically as often as men and commit crimes as often as men[56] does not fit our stereotype and thus we change the truth and believe a lie – citing research bias or newspaper slant etc. Current research indicates that not only do women have the capacity to break the law, but they are keeping pace with men in criminal activity other than violent crimes (murder and rape).

When compared to men, women seem to be committing the crimes of embezzlement, fraud, forgery, and larceny at a rate comparable to men.[57] Though women generally commit less violent crimes than men, they certainly do commit them, and at a rate of one out of every five.[58] [59] In 2006 alone, that twenty percent would account for seventy-one thousand violent crimes – a violent crime was committed by a woman every ten minutes in America.[60]

"Counter-attitudinal advocacy"[61] – that is what dissonance researchers call the ancient practice of self deception, and its name implies we have to work to change our attitudes before we can accept a lie. Our society does not want to believe that Hillary Clinton or women in general are liars, thieves and cold-blooded criminals. So we believe her lies and her handlers' lies, rather than accept the truth about her reported and documented criminality.

External and internal misinformation is precisely why people find lies believable, contends Dr. Bette J. Dickerson:

"When people are bombarded with false information by the gate keepers and power brokers of information, such as the media, people will start believing it," argues Dickerson, chair of the Department of Sociology at American University in Washington, D.C. "If we get enough false information, myths and untruths long enough, which we do, we will come to believe it because that's all we know. What we believe, though false, will become true in its consequences."[62]

She says that many people stray from challenging lies just to keep the peace:

"In our learning how to live, we're not educated to question, challenge or even `revolt' against pieces of false information that disrupt the status quo. This is because that allows us to avoid controversial issues. Few human beings want lives filled with drama. People will resist change in long-held established beliefs that are based on falsehood because it maintains a `proper order, proper functioning.'[63] So the beat goes on, and 'Hillary for President' with it."

After interviewing many of Clinton's associates for a *New Yorker* article, Connie Bruck concluded, "In the end, the sureness about her own judgment—at its extreme, a sense that she alone is wise—is probably Hillary's cardinal trait."[64]

Childhood nicknames sometimes provide a useful index of an individual's ingrained, central personality traits. Among their mock predictions for seniors, Hillary Rodham's high school newspaper proclaimed that Hillary's destiny was to become a nun named "Sister Frigidaire." As Gail Sheehy has commented, "Empathy was not characteristic of Hillary."[65]

The urge to save humanity is almost always a false front for the urge to rule.

- H. L. Mencken

In 1957, during a message entitled *God Keeps His Word* William Branham reiterates the prophecy he made in 1933; He says "And I seen a woman lying, vulgar as she was, and dominated the country. And I predict that a woman will either be President, or do, or come into great power of some sort in the United States before the total annihilation of the world. Keep that in mind, and I have said it. Notice, now, what takes place? Jezebel, she ruled Ahab."[66]

The Slippery Slope Argument

A slippery slope argument is a kind of argument that warns you if you take a first step, you will find yourself involved in a sticky sequence of consequences from which you will be unable to extricate yourself, and eventually you will wind up speeding faster and faster towards some disastrous outcome. Given a favorable climate of social acceptance, one first step, if taken, may trigger a contagious sequence of steps, ultimately leading to a parade of horrors such as gay marriage, abortion on demand or a police state.

> *If Hillary Clinton is the one, the object in and of the prophecy, she will knowingly or unwittingly fulfill events that lead our country and the world to the brink of destruction.*

The slippery slope arguments depend on a strong presumption in favor of the status quo, and thus are invoked only when someone advocates departing from the status quo (extending marriage rather than preserving it).

Some believe if we reduce diligence, that reduction in civil liberties in order to combat terrorism will result in dictatorship, or relaxation in our sexual conventions will lead to abandon and lasciviousness. The slippery slope argument is therefore a warning not to abandon the legal and moral conventions on which our Country was founded, or we will find ourselves sliding in the direction of an immoral police state within a modern Babylon.

Some "steps" or events may not even be obvious or easily recognizable as "bad" or "evil" or "treasonous" to the average citizen. Hitler's torture and extermination of Jews, Gypsies, the aged and the mentally ill was evidently cruel and evil, yet many events and indoctrination seemed logical and justified to many individuals. More importantly, the policy that was discussed and eventually put into force was innocuous and innocent and on its face. Few could have foretold the dire consequences of such a doctrine or policy.

Consider the Balfour Doctrine, the American policy of non-intervention; Recall Britain's decision to sack Churchill and install the weak, pandering Prime Minister Neville Chamberlain who would eventually collude with Hitler and bargain away Hungary and Poland - or even the subservient mentality that developed in the American citizenry through the Great Depression and Roosevelt's socialization by and of the government. Each of these had far-reaching consequences and collectively factored into the horrible events perpetrated by Germany during World War Two.

> "Most do not realize that it was American and Canadian doctrine that provided the inspiration and justification of Germany's policies of sterilization and genocide."

Most do not realize that it was American and Canadian doctrine that provided the inspiration and justification of Germany's policies of sterilization and genocide. From its inception eugenics was supported by prominent people, including Alexander Graham Bell, George Bernard Shaw, Winston Churchill and Adolf Hitler. Eugenics was an academic discipline at many colleges and universities. Funding was provided by prestigious sources such as the Rockefeller Foundation, the Carnegie Institute of Washington, and the Harriman family.[67]

One of the first acts by Adolf Hitler after achieving total control over the German state was to pass the Law for the Prevention of Hereditarily Diseased Offspring (*Gesetz zur Verhütung erbkranken Nachwuchses*) in July 1933. [The law was signed in by Hitler himself, and over 200 eugenic courts were created specifically as a result of the law.] Under the German law, any doctor in the Reich was required to report patients of theirs who were mentally retarded, mentally ill (including schizophrenia and manic depression), epileptic, blind, deaf, or physically deformed, and a steep monetary penalty was imposed for any patients who were not properly reported.

Individuals suffering from alcoholism or Huntington's Chorea could also be sterilized. The individual's case was then presented in front of a court of Nazi officials and public health officers who would review their medical records, take testimony from friends and colleagues, and eventually decide whether or not to order a sterilization operation performed on the individual, using force if necessary. Though not explicitly covered by the law, 400 mixed-race "Rhineland Bastards" were also sterilized beginning in 1937.[68]

By the end of World War II, over 400,000 individuals were sterilized under the German law and its revisions, most within its first four years of being enacted. When the issue of compulsory sterilization was brought up at the Nuremberg trials after the war, many Nazis defended their actions on the matter by indicating that it was the United States itself from whom they had taken inspiration.

The first country to concertedly undertake compulsory sterilization programs for the purpose of eugenics was the United States. The principal targets of the American program were the mentally retarded and the mentally ill, but also targeted under many state laws were the deaf, the blind, the epileptic, and the physically deformed. Native Americans were sterilized against their will in many states, often without their knowledge, while they were in a hospital for some other reason (e.g. after giving birth). Some sterilization also took place in prisons and other penal institutions, targeting criminality, but they were in the relative minority. In the end, over 65,000 individuals were sterilized in 33 states under state compulsory sterilization programs in the United States.[69]

California sterilized more people than any other state by a wide margin, and was responsible for over a third of all sterilization operations. Information about the California sterilization program was produced into book form and widely disseminated by eugenicists E.S. Gosney and Paul B. Popenoe, which was said by the government of Adolf Hitler to be of key importance in proving that large-scale compulsory sterilization programs were feasible.[70]

California later apologized and eventually paid restitution to those forced to undergo compulsory sterilization. But could California or eugenicists Gosney & Popenoe ever have imagined that it was their ideas and policy that set in motion the annihilation of one third of the world's Jews and up to 42 million total people killed? No.

But when the history books were written by the victors, it was expeditious to place the full blame on Hitler and the Nazi regime. Little, if anything is ever taught in schools about America's part in the Nazi's genocide campaigns. Santayana said, "Those who cannot remember the past are condemned to repeat it."[71]

The problem we have today is that not only do most people not remember history; they probably never accurately learned it to begin with. Additionally, a new generation has arisen in the midst of an informational boom, a deluge of irrelevant knowledge that vies with truth. History has been "dumbed-down" and sanitized; it must pass the test of the "PC" (politically correct) enforcers before it reaches the desks of the schools and universities today. By the time "history" is taught, it has been spun, diluted and politicized so as the hard lessons are never learned.

Better Suited to Lead

After the ratification of the Constitution, a philosophical feud developed between two of the leading architects of the American Revolution and the new nation: Alexander Hamilton and Thomas Jefferson. Jefferson believed that the "common man" [meaning farmers and tradesmen] were best suited to lead. On the other hand, Hamilton favored a nation led by "elitist," whom he considered better educated and better suited to rule.

Two hundred years ago Hamilton was widely known to have favored a highly centralized government, and a near-dictatorial executive branch. Fast-forward to Washington, DC 2008 -- the imperial presidency, judicial activism, the Federal Reserve System's institutionalized counterfeiting and fraud, the ever-metastasizing government debt, the expanding ranks of tax-subsidized corporate welfare parasites, the reduction of the states to docile administrative units of a national regime -- were inspired by, and are the fulfillment of, Hamilton's designs.

Though Hillary may dress-up like a Jeffersonian, she acts like a Hamiltonian. It is this author's opinion that Hillary Clinton truly believes that the government (read: Hillary Clinton) is more qualified to govern your life and your family's life than you are. In 1977 Hillary was part of the Carnegie Council for Children, which made this statement, "What would matter in the future of children was not the family structure, but the larger village of teachers, pediatricians, and social workers who would socialize the task of raising, supporting, and nurturing children."[72] In Hillary's world, parents would be subordinates to lawyers, judges, social workers and bureaucrats, which she believes are the true experts in child-rearing.

Hillary truly believes that children are in a "dependency relationship"[73] similar to that of earlier slaves and akin to the Indian reservation system. Children therefore are in need of governmental protection and emancipation as necessary to ensure their rights. Despite strong opposition to her ideas, years later she continued to defend her position. She said that it was not her interest for the government to interfere in mundane squabbles like taking out the trash or washing dishes, rather governmental intervention would involve important matters about "motherhood and abortion, schooling, cosmetic surgery, treatment of venereal disease, or employment." The *important* decisions should be made by the child with the government's help, and not left for parents to make "unilaterally."[74]

Why does this ideology matter? Set aside her belief that children should have the right to make their own decisions apart from their parents (which would translate to mean the right to abort their babies at will, or go to work in a saloon or brothel) – what is truly frightening is not the ideology but the reality of children's right run amok. Her ideas are tangible today, lived out in courtrooms across America where the rights of parents and individual adults are overridden and even trampled on to advance legal advocates perceptions of the health and safety of the child. Given the overabundance of attorneys, a law-suit crazed society and the natural tendency of children to chafe at parental limits and discipline – children will and have already sued their parents over trivial issues. Taking out the trash as "involuntary servitude" is not too far away.

The Parent-Child bond will become defendant and plaintiff. The financial cost alone of one lawsuit will bankrupt the average family. In our country, and under the current conditions of a law-suit crazy society, if children are given the full rights of adults to sue, families as we know them will be destroyed in and by the adversarial legal system. Just as it had been prophesied 2000 years ago in Luke 12:53,

The father shall be divided against the son, and the son against the father; the mother against the daughter, and the daughter against the mother; the mother in law against her daughter in law, and the daughter in law against her mother in law.

A Cautionary Tale

June 14 of 2006, in Oaxaca, Mexico, that state's despot governor Ulises Ruiz attacked a peaceful encampment of thousands of striking schoolteachers and their supporters. He sent 3,000 police in at dawn, as the protesters slept, with bullets, nightsticks and teargas canisters shot from the ground and dropped from a helicopter. It was only the latest incident in a violent and repressive chain. Only this time, the public, armed with nothing but sticks and stones and strength in numbers, regrouped and chased the police out of the city. They established their own government by popular assembly, set up locally-organized and volunteer-staffed barricades in each neighborhood, and the governor's security forces were unable to enter - although they had tried on multiple occasions - for five months after that.

A 37-year-old reporter by the name of Brad Will, went to Oaxaca in early October 2006 to videotape the story. On October 27, 2006, he filmed gunmen loyal to the despot governor attacking one of the blockades and shooting their guns directly at him. It was believed that some of the attackers were plainclothes police. Will died during that attack, with his camera in his hand.[75]

Brad, a constituent of New York's Junior United States Senator Hillary Clinton (D-New York) from 2001 until his death, continues to provide a lurid example of the consequences of violent regimes and US policy that protects certain foreign government at all costs as long as they toe the line on trade, drug policy, and other matters.

Brad's family and friends have sought justice now for several years; even some members of the New York Congressional delegation - like US Rep. Jose Serrano (D-Bronx) - have taken up the cause of seeking justice in that case.

But multiple and sustained efforts by Friends of Brad Will in New York to convince Senator Clinton to use her international "experience" and influence to help bring justice and closure to the case have gone unanswered.

Recently, some of them sat in front of Senator Clinton's New York office, at 780 Third Avenue in midtown Manhattan, and fasted to appeal for her assistance to her late constituent, his family and friends.

According to one report, Senator Clinton was physically present in the office on at least one of those days, but avoided responding to or speaking with those fasting out in front, much less writing the letters and making the public statements to bring justice to the case that any authentic advocate of human rights would do, especially if it involved a constituent.

There are those who claim that Senator Clinton is a "champion" of human rights, based on a solitary speech she gave in September of 1995 to the UN Conference on Women in Beijing, China, because her most quoted sound-bite from that speech was "women's rights are human rights."

Nobody, takes issue with her statement, *Women's rights are human rights*, as are men's rights, children's rights, minority rights, and everybody else's. But if a politician doesn't have a basic understanding of *what human rights are* to begin with, and has shrunk from the duty to defend them time and time again even when they have hit close to home, that politician is not going to be able and ready to extend them to any gender or demographic.

So much happens, day in, day out, in so many lands... so many daily attacks on dissidents, community organizers, and others who dare speak and act to improve lives... that no US president could possibly micro-manage the situation and take preemptive action on each pending atrocity from the Oval Office. That's what the Secretary of State and a State Department is for, to handle the constant communications that are necessary with other governments.

And since US President Barack Obama recently installed someone as the next Secretary of State who has shown zero understanding of, much less passion and action for, human rights in Mexico, Colombia and elsewhere (except in isolated cases where the same mass media has turned a particular case into an international cause célèbre), we're going to see more of the same terrible stories happen over and over again.

If you can't get somebody to act to defend human rights when she's your own local elected representative, do you really believe that such a person would begin to do so if she suddenly represented the entire country before the world?

During the editing of this chapter, I realized that though Clinton seems to be the most likely candidate to fulfill this prophecy of a woman dictator, someone other than Clinton, who has been "flying under the radar" may actually end up to be "the one." Why do I say this? From our review of history incidents [Hitler, Balfour, Eugenics, etc.] and the subject of deception, betrayal is often perpetrated by seemingly unsuspecting sources. *"Take heed that no man deceive you. For many shall come in my name saying, 'I am the Christ,' and shall deceive many."*[76]

In the beginning, Adam and Eve were first seduced, then deceived into forfeiting their Kingdom by the cunning *Old Serpent*[77] (a.k.a. The Devil, Satan, Great Dragon) described as the most subtle of all the creatures under Adam's dominion. What started off as subtle and cunning became proud, boastful and violent.

Despite our longing for peace, mankind's warring and fighting is not finished. The Bible describes a time of horrendous warfare and bloodshed, precipitated by an influx of demons/fallen angels that pour from their dimension into ours. The battle that once began in the Heavenly realms will continue upon the Earth through the period known as the *End of Days*, and the *Battle of Armageddon*.

"And the great dragon was cast out, that old serpent, called the Devil, and Satan, which deceives the whole world: he was cast out into the earth, and his angels were cast out with him."[78]

Hillary Clinton appears conciliatory, cooperative and an enthusiastic team player *for now*, but it may not be long before her raging, bullying, dictatorial side asserts itself.

"The beast was given a mouth to utter proud words and blasphemies and to exercise his authority for forty-two months. He opened his mouth to blaspheme God, and to slander his name and his dwelling place and those who live in heaven. He was given power to make war against the saints and to conquer them. And he was given authority over every tribe, people, language and nation."[79]

Forty-two months. Three and half years. This describes near perfectly the duration of one Presidential term of office. Who could wield such power? Realistically, only someone from within the government of the United States of America – the President, the Secretary of State and the Secretary of Homeland Security all are potential de-facto dictators (see Chapter 9 – *Preparing the Way for an American Dictator*).

Over the next four years, either Secretary of State Hillary Clinton or even Secretary of Homeland Security Janet Napolitano may become America's first dictator, and thus fulfill the awful and terrible prophecy uttered by William Branham in 1933.

Therefore, having this knowledge, will we as a Nation learn the kind of lessons that will help us escape destruction? - Sadly, no. Not according to the prophecies given by Wm. Branham in 1933. Will Hillary Clinton or another "great powerful woman in this United

States" rise up, as President, Secretary of State, Secretary of Homeland Security, De-facto Dictator or some other power broker and contribute to the events that lead to that destruction? – Sadly, yes. Hillary Clinton being this leader/dictator really is not the point, the point is, if it is not her, it will be another like her – that is "THUS SAITH THE LORD."

2 So Dark the Con of Man

So Dark the Con of Man – Could this Woman be a Church?

Despite the assertions by Dan Brown that his novel The DaVinci Code is historically accurate[80], both historians and theologians have exposed his fraud as a Great Con of Man. Certainly not *the* Dark Con of Man, but nonetheless, it is an elaborate gotcha.

In Brown's novel Jacques Saunière was a curator at the Louvre Museum in France, and the Grand Master of the Priory of Sion and therefore knew the hidden location of the "keystone", which leads to the Holy Grail and documents which would shake the foundation of Christianity and the Church.

In an opening scene, Saunière has been murdered, but before he dies he leaves a series of cryptic message-clues for his granddaughter to help her piece together the mystery behind the secrets he guarded. At the Louvre, on the glass over the Mona Lisa, Saunière wrote the message "So dark the con of Man" with a curator's pen that can only be read in ultra-violet light. This clue was an anagram for *Madonna of the Rocks*, another DaVinci painting hanging nearby. The clue was to lead the main characters all over Europe, where they would discover that the Great Con of Man was a secret bloodline from the union of Jesus Christ and Mary Magdalene.

Brown writes that the Great Con was conducted by the Catholic Church to keep this secret from being disclosed to the public. Brown wasn't too far off. To his credit, Brown actually describes the formation of the Roman Catholic Church during the Nicene Council of 325 AD. The *Great Cons* they say are 99% true.

The Great Con of Man was not conducted by the Priory of Sion, it wasn't conducted by the Knights Templar, it wasn't even conducted by the Catholic Church – **the Great Con of Man *is* the Roman Catholic Church.**

William Branham's 1933 Prophecy: A Woman or possibly the Catholic Church?

One of God's ways to communicate with His servants is through a vision. In a natural sense, "vision" is defined as a "sense of sight." In scripture it refers to a supernatural sense of sight that goes beyond the "natural" realm, allowing the believer to see what is unfolding in a spiritual dimension – a dimension in which the Lord may show His servants things in the past, the present, and the future.

In June of 1933, William Branham, who in the 1940's & 50's became the leading voice of healing revivals, revealed seven events that were shown to him through a vision, which were to be fulfilled before the return of Jesus Christ. Five of these have already been fulfilled, it's interesting to note the two that remain unfulfilled are: #6 - a woman will raise up in the United States who will be president, dictator or a wield great power, and #7 – America destroyed and left a smoldering heap of ruins.

In the sixth vision, a woman rose to great power in America. William Branham was not sure whether the "Woman" in this vision was a physical woman, or a religious power such as the Catholic Church. This chapter addresses both the rise of women, and the rise of the Catholic Church in America.

In 1958, he recounts the vision: *And I said, "Remember, in that day, before the end time comes, before the end time comes, that a woman... Now, you all keep this wrote down. There'll be a great powerful woman raise up, either be President, or dictator, or some great powerful woman in this United States. And she'll sink under the influence of women. Now, you remember; that's THUS SAITH THE LORD."*[81]

1960 – November
"Ever time the Lord speaks to me I place it down, and then watch it, and bring it to the people, and show them how it comes to pass. I picked up a prophecy, and I didn't... And I was a pastor of the Baptist church there. I didn't even know what a vision meant, and now, them things that happened I'd calling it falling into a trance. I didn't know to call it a vision. At that time I was just a boy: 1933, on June.
I said, "It will come to pass before the end time comes that there will be a great woman stand up in the United States, because the United States is marked woman. Her number is thirteen, and she'll rise up, either be president, or (I put it in parentheses) perhaps the woman being beautiful and attractive will be the Catholic church but cruel at heart, and she'll lead the nation to pollution."[82]

1960 – November
"I was quoting last night a prophecy that was given me back in 1933 of seven things that'd take place... the coming of the control of a woman in the United States to take over, maybe a church to take over to rule... Watch. It's THUS SAITH THE LORD."[83]

1956 – October
"In the United States, the woman's the head of the house here. This is a woman's country. The woman is the god of America. I predict that before the coming of the Lord that a woman will be a great ruler in the United States."[84]

1960 – November
"I seen a great woman rise up in the United States, well-dressed and beautiful, but cruel in heart. She will either guide or lead this nation to ruination. I've got in parenthesis 'perhaps the Catholic church."[85]

1960- December
"Now, and it said in there, 'At that time, there'd be a great woman stand up in the United States.' And she was dressed and beautiful, but

she was cruel in heart. And I got a parenthesis on the vision, even yellow paper, said, 'perhaps the Catholic church.'"[86]

1961- August

"Now, that brings us then to the election of President Kennedy, and this car coming on the--on the scene, bringing five things out of the seven that has happened exactly.

Now, I predicted and said, 'I saw a great woman stand up, beautiful looking, dressed in real highly royals like purple', and I got little parenthesis down here, 'She was a great ruler in the United States, perhaps the Catholic church.' A woman, some woman... I don't know her to be the Catholic church. I don't know. I can't say. Only thing I seen, I seen the woman; that was all."[87]

The Rise of the Catholic Church in America

In 1785, at the end of the American Revolution, less than 1% of Americans were Catholic.[88] As Protestant America opened its arms to immigrants from all corners of the world, it also accepted their religions. By 1910, as the result of huge number of Irish, German, Italian, Polish, French Canadian, and Eastern European immigrants, 14.6 Million Americans (16.4% of the population) were Catholic.

In 1850, New York Archbishop John Hughes made the following statement:

> *Everybody should know that we have for our mission to convert the world - including the inhabitants of the United States - the people of the cities, and the people of the country, the Officers of the Navy and the Marines, commander of the Army, the legislatures, the Senate, the Cabinet, the President and all.*[89]

In 1926, one million Catholics gathered in Chicago for the 28th International Eucharist Congress; it was seen as a "kind of formal debut for the American Church." The running of Catholic governor Al Smith for President in 1928 sparked a sense of alarm among Protestants, and his defeat to Herbert Hoover was widely seen as a rejection of his religion.

The 1940's saw an abundance of positive Catholic images coming out of Hollywood. Movies regularly featured strong, sensitive priests or nuns directly involved in the lives of ordinary people. The most popular U.S. television show in the mid-1950's was *Life Is Worth Living*, a 30 minute lecture by the charismatic Bishop Fulton Sheen. It quickly took the number one spot from the *Texaco Comedy Hour*, which aired at the same time. At the height of his career, Sheen had a regular audience of 30 million.[90]

In 1960, the first Catholic president, John F. Kennedy, was elected. Still, Kennedy sought to distance himself from the Catholic Church to assure Protestant voters that his religion would not influence his political decisions. By 2008 President George Bush had eclipsed Kennedy's association with Rome, evidenced by his enthusiastic welcome of Pope Benedict XVI onto U.S. soil. In an article entitled *A Catholic Wind in the White House*, the Washington Post discussed the extent of Catholic influence on America policy, concluding that Bush has "*wedded Catholic intellectualism with evangelical political savvy to forge a powerful electoral coalition* and that *the key to understanding Bush's domestic policy is to view it through the lens of Rome.*"[91]

A Church Represents a Woman in Biblical Metaphor

"Be ye followers of me, as I also am of Christ. Now I praise you, brethren, that in all things you are mindful of me: and keep my ordinances as I have delivered them to you. But I would have you know, that the head of every man is Christ; and the head of the woman is the man; and the head of Christ is God." (1 Corinthians 11:1-16)

This facial reading is entirely clear. St. Paul begins by explaining that "the head of every man is Christ; and the head of the woman is the man; and the head of Christ is God." Here he is drawing an analogy, a classic analogy that has been used throughout the History of the Church, particularly in explaining the marriage: that man is to woman as Christ is to the Church. The head of man, St. Paul tells us, is Christ; the head of woman is man. He further tells us that man "is the image and glory of God; but the woman is the glory of man."

Indeed, St. Paul is hated by modern feminists because of this doctrinal principle laid out in his Epistle to the Ephesians. There St. Paul makes the analogy much more explicitly, but it can easily be recognized as the same analogy all the same:

"Let women be subject to their husbands, as to the Lord: Because the husband is the head of the wife, as Christ is the head of the church, He is the saviour of his body. Therefore as the church is subject to Christ, so also let the wives be to their husbands in all things. Husbands, love your wives, as Christ also loved the church, and delivered himself up for it." (Ephesians 5:22–25)

The imagery and symbolism of marriage is applied to Christ and the body of believers known as the church. These are those who have trusted in Jesus Christ as their personal savior and have received eternal life. In the New Testament, Christ, the Bridegroom, has sacrificially and lovingly chosen the church to be His bride (Ephesians 5:25-27). Just as there was a betrothal period in biblical times during which the bride and groom were separated until the wedding, so is the bride of Christ separate from her Bridegroom during the church age. Her responsibility during the betrothal period is to be faithful to Him (2 Corinthians 11:2; Ephesians 5:24). At the Second Coming of Christ, the church will be united with the Bridegroom, the official "wedding ceremony" will take place and, with it, the eternal union of Christ and His bride will be actualized (Revelation 19:7-9; 21:1-2).

At that time, all believers will inhabit the heavenly city known as New Jerusalem, also called "the holy city" in Revelation 21:2 and 10. The New Jerusalem is not the church, but it takes on the church's characteristics. In his vision of the end of the age, the Apostle John sees the city coming down from heaven adorned "as a bride," meaning that the inhabitants of the city, the redeemed of the Lord, will be holy and pure, wearing white garments of holiness and righteousness. Some have misinterpreted verse 9 to mean the holy city is the bride of Christ, but that cannot be because Christ died for His people, not for a city. The city is called "the bride" because it encompasses all who are the bride, just as all the students of a school are sometimes called "the school."

As believers in Jesus Christ, we who are the bride of Christ wait with great anticipation for the day when we will be united with our Bridegroom. Until then, we remain faithful to Him and say with all the redeemed of the Lord, "Come, Lord Jesus!" (Revelation 22:20).

"Let us be glad and rejoice, and give honour to him: for the marriage of the Lamb is come, and his wife hath made herself ready." And to her was granted that she should be arrayed in fine linen, clean and white: for the fine linen is the righteousness of saints. (Revelation 19:7-8)

1. The bride will be presented as a **pure virgin** to him (2 Corinthians 11:2).

2. The bride will be known for her **righteous acts** (Revelation 19:7-8).

3. The bridal church will be made holy, blameless, without blemish through **washing/cleansing of "the Word"** (Ephesians 5:25-27).

4. The bride will have a sincere and pure **devotion to Christ** (2 Corinthians 11:3).

5. The bride will be **watchful and prayerful** (Luke 21:36).

6. The bride will have been **pressing for perfection** (2 Corinthians 13:9,11).

7. The bride will be given, **endowed with glory** (1 Corinthians 11:7, 15).

8. The bride will live in a state of **readiness** to meet the bridegroom (Matthew 25:10; Luke 12:35; Revelation 19:7).

9. The Bride will be **submitted to the bridegroom** and will recognize Him as her "Lord." (1 Corinthians 11:2-5).

St. Paul equates fidelity and loyalty to Christ, with both the belief and keeping of doctrinal/scriptural purity. He writes to the church in Galatia, *"I marvel that ye are so soon removed from him that called you into the grace of Christ, unto another gospel."* (Galatians 1:6) To adhere to "another" or tainted gospel is to commit spiritual adultery.

This principle is elaborated on in a letter to the Corinthians. Once again Paul uses the husband-wife, Christ-Church analogy, but adds the word-seed analogy to convey the truth that doctrinal purity is equated with marital fidelity. Doctrines are like seeds, they can impregnate our minds for better or worse – for spiritual life or death.

"I am jealous over you with godly jealousy: for I have espoused you to one husband, that I may present you as a chaste virgin to Christ. But I fear, lest by any means, as the serpent beguiled Eve through his subtilty, so your minds should be corrupted from the simplicity that is in Christ. For if he that cometh preacheth another Jesus, whom we have not preached, or if ye receive another spirit, which ye have not received, or another gospel, which ye have not accepted, ye might well bear with him." (2 *Corinthians 11:2-4)*

The Apostle warns that our minds could become corrupted, our thoughts perverted by accepting a perverted gospel. This truth is so important that millions of Christians have been willing to become martyrs rather than compromise in what they believed to be the truth.

The characteristics of God's true bride stand in stark contrast to the characteristics of the false bride, which are the Catholic Church and her daughters[B] [92]. From history we see that any religious group that claims Jesus as its head, yet believes and acts contrary to His Word is a usurper of His authority.

"How much she hath glorified herself, and lived deliciously, so much torment and sorrow give her: for she saith in her heart, I sit a queen, and am no widow, and shall see no sorrow." (Revelation 18:7)

[B] The various Denominations who nearly all have also strayed from doctrinal purity, rendering them as spiritual "harlots." See Endnote 92 for fuller explanation.

The Seven Hills of Rome

Give glory to the LORD your God, before he cause darkness, and before your feet stumble upon the dark mountains, and, while ye look for light, he turn it into the shadow of death, [and] make [it] gross darkness. (Jeremiah 13:16)

And there came one of the seven angels which had the seven vials, and talked with me, saying unto me, Come hither; I will shew unto thee the judgment of the great whore that sitteth upon many waters: **2** *With whom the kings of the earth have committed fornication, and the inhabitants of the earth have been made drunk with the wine of her fornication.* **3** *So he carried me away in the spirit into the wilderness: and I saw a woman sit upon a scarlet coloured beast, full of names of blasphemy, having seven heads and ten horns.* **4** *And the woman was arrayed in purple and scarlet colour, and decked with gold and precious stones and pearls, having a golden cup in her hand full of abominations and filthiness of her fornication:* **5** *And upon her forehead was a name written, MYSTERY, BABYLON THE GREAT, THE MOTHER OF HARLOTS AND ABOMINATIONS OF THE EARTH.* **6** *And I saw the woman drunken with the blood of the saints, and with the blood of the martyrs of Jesus: and when I saw her, I wondered with great admiration. 7 And the angel said unto me, Wherefore didst thou marvel? I will tell thee the mystery of the woman, and of the beast that carrieth her, which hath the seven heads and ten horns. (Revelation 17:1-7)*

And here is the mind which hath wisdom. The seven heads are seven mountains, on which the woman sitteth. (Revelation 17:9)

And the woman which thou sawest is that great city, which reigneth over the kings of the earth. (Revelation 17:18)

Here is no mystical or allegorical language but an unambiguous statement in plain words: "The woman ... is that great city." There is no justification for seeking some other hidden meaning. The woman is a *city*.

Furthermore, she is a city built on *seven hills*. That specification eliminates ancient Babylon. Only one city has for more than 2000 years been known as the city on seven hills. That city is Rome. The *Catholic Encyclopedia* states: "It is within the city of Rome, called the city of seven hills, that the entire area of Vatican State proper is now confined."[93]

There are, of course, other cities, such as Rio de Janeiro, that were also built on seven hills. Therefore, John provides at least seven more characteristics to limit the identification to Rome alone. There is only *one* city on the earth which, in both historical and contemporary perspectives, passes every test John gives, including its identification as Mystery Babylon. That city is Rome, and more specifically, Vatican City.

Even Catholic apologist Karl Keating admits that Rome has long been known as Babylon. Keating claims that Peter's statement "The church here in Babylon ... sends you her greeting" (from I Peter 5:13) proves that Peter was writing from Rome. He explains further:

"Babylon is a code word for Rome. It is used that way six times in the last book of the Bible [four of the six are in chapters 17 and 18 and in extra-Biblical works such as *Sibylling Oracles* (5, 159f.), the *Apocalypse of Baruch* (ii, 1), and 4 *Esdras* (3:1)].

Eusebius Pamphilius, writing about 303, noted that "it is said that Peter's first epistle... was composed at Rome itself; and that he himself indicates this, referring to the city figuratively as Babylon."[94]

As for "Mystery," that name imprinted on the woman's forehead is the perfect designation for Vatican City. Mystery is at the very heart of Roman Catholicism, from the words "*Mysterium fide*" pronounced at the alleged transformation of the bread and wine into the literal body and blood of Christ to the mysterious power which the faithful must believe the priests and Church wield.

Who Is the Whore?

The first thing we are told about the woman is that she is a "whore" (Revelation 17:1), that earthly kings "have committed fornication" with her (verse 2), and that "all the inhabitants of the earth have been made drunk with the wine of her fornication" (verse 3). Why would a city be called a whore and be accused of having committed *fornication* with *kings*? Such an indictment would never be made of London or Moscow or Paris—or any other ordinary city. It wouldn't make sense.

Fornication and adultery are used in the Bible in both the physical and the spiritual sense. Of Jerusalem God said, "How is the faithful city become a harlot!" (Isaiah 1:21). Israel, whom God had set apart from all other peoples to be holy for His purposes, had entered into unholy, adulterous alliances with the idol-worshiping nations about her. She had "committed adultery with stones and with stocks [idols]" (Jeremiah 3:9); "and with their idols have they committed adultery" (Ezekiel 23:37). The entire chapter of Ezekiel 16 explains Israel's spiritual adultery in detail, both with heathen nations and with their false gods, as do many other passages.

There is no way that a *city* could engage in literal, fleshly fornication. Thus we can only conclude that John, like the prophets in the Old Testament, is using the term in its spiritual sense. The city, therefore, must claim a spiritual relationship with God. Otherwise such an allegation would be meaningless.

Only one *city* in history could a charge of fornication be leveled against. That city is Rome, and more specifically *Vatican City*. She claims to have been the worldwide headquarters of Christianity since its beginning and maintains that claim to this day. Her pope enthroned in Rome claims to be the exclusive representative of God, the vicar of Christ.

The incredible wealth of this woman caught John's attention next. She was dressed "in purple and scarlet color, and decked with gold and precious stones and pearls, having a golden cup in her hand full of abominations and filthiness of her fornication" (Revelation 17:4). The colors of purple and scarlet once again identify the woman with both pagan and Christian Rome. These were the colors of the Roman Caesars, and with which the soldiers mockingly robed Christ as "King" (see Matthew 27:28 and John 19:2:5), which the Vatican took to itself. The woman's colors are literally still the colors of the Catholic clergy.

The "golden cup [chalice] in her hand" again identifies the woman with the Roman Catholic Church. Broderick's edition of *The Catholic Encyclopedia* declares of the chalice: "[It is] the most important of the sacred vessels.... [It] may be of gold or silver, and if the latter, then the inside must be surfaced with gold."[95]

John next notices, that the woman is drunk — and not with an alcoholic beverage. She is drunk with "the blood of the saints, and with the blood of the martyrs of Jesus..." (Revelation 17:6). The picture is a horrible one. It is not merely her *hands* that are red with this blood, but she is *drunk* with it! The slaughter of innocents who, for conscience' sake, would not yield to her totalitarian demands has so refreshed and exhilarated her that she reels in ecstasy.

One thinks immediately of the Inquisitions (Roman, Medieval, and Spanish) which for centuries held Europe in their terrible grip. In his *History of the Inquisition*, Canon Llorente, who was the Secretary to the Inquisition in Madrid from 1790-92 and had access to the archives of all the tribunals, estimated that in Spain alone the number of condemned exceeded 3 million, with about 300,000 burned at the stake.[96] Finally, the angel reveals to John that the woman "is that great city which reigneth over the kings of the earth" (Revelation 17:18). Is there such a city? Yes, and again only one: Vatican City. Popes crowned and deposed kings and emperors, exacting obedience by threatening them with excommunication.

One eighteenth-century historian counted 95 popes who claimed to have divine power to depose kings and emperors. Historian Walter James wrote that Pope Innocent III (1198-1216) "held all Europe in his net."[97]

Gregory IX (1227-41) thundered that the pope was lord and master of everyone and everything. Historian R.W. Southern declared: "During the whole medieval period there was in Rome a single spiritual and temporal authority [the papacy] exercising powers which in the end exceeded those that had ever lain within the grasp of a Roman emperor."[98]

That the popes reigned over kings is an undisputed fact of history. That in so doing horrible abominations were committed, as John foresaw, is also indisputable. Pope Nicholas I (858-67) declared: "We [popes] alone have the power to bind and to loose, to absolve Nero and to condemn him; and Christians cannot, under penalty of excommunication, execute other judgment than ours, which alone is infallible." In commanding one king to destroy another, Nicholas wrote:

We order you, in the name of religion, to invade his states, burn his cities, and massacre his people...[99]

The qualifying information which John gives us under the inspiration of the Holy Spirit for identifying this woman, who is a *city*, is specific, conclusive, and irrefutable. There is no *city* upon earth, past or present, which meets all of these criteria except Catholic Rome and now Vatican City.

What are the Mark and Number of the Beast?

Give glory to the LORD your God, before he cause darkness, and before your feet stumble upon the dark mountains, and, while ye look for light, he turn it into the shadow of death, and make it gross darkness.[100]

No one likes to stumble, trip or fall, especially if you are walking in the mountains. *Before your feet stumble upon the dark mountains* – literally the mountains of or at twilight – this phrase is meant to convey the arrival of bitter cold night air, the gathering gloom of the evening and the deepening, enveloping darkness.

Darkness, gross darkness. Stumbling in darkness. Tripping, falling, plunging headlong over a cliff or precipice…

Exodus 10:21; *"And the Lord said to Moses, 'Stretch out your hand toward heaven, that there may be darkness over the land of Egypt, even darkness which may be felt."* How creepy, frightening and depressing – a darkness that could be "felt." Cold, clammy, vile, damning; death like "mists of darkness."[101]

Additionally, in both Lot (Sodom and Gomorrah) and Noah's time, the period preceding destruction was characterized as very wicked, evil and spiritually "dark." It was a time filled with violence, partying, sexual immorality and dishonesty, much as it is today.

Darkness and the plagues of Egypt were real – and they were also meant to serve as an example and a dire warning for a future generation. Watch a similar scene unfold at the *End of Times*, viewed from the perspective of symbols in Chapter 16 of the Book of Revelation; (vs. 8) *"and the forth angel poured out his vial upon the sun…"* (vs.10) *"and the fifth angel poured out his vile upon the seat of the beast; and his kingdom* (the earth at this time – ed.) *was full of darkness…"* (vs. 13) *"unclean spirits like frogs came out of the mouth of the dragon…"* (vs. 14) *"they are the spirits of devils…"* These times describe an awful period where the sun is blotted out from the sky, the Earth is plunged into natural and spiritual darkness and a vast host of demons are loosed upon mankind.

The Book of Revelation is a book of prophecy, it was intended to forewarn about coming apostasy and eventual world and spiritual domination of and by the Devil and his hordes of Hell. This is a well established pattern of God – first He warns, then He brings judgment. Those that have read the Book of Revelation have difficulty comprehending its symbols and metaphors. Since much of the prophecies of Revelation are obscure and require interpretation, in the *Last Days* God promised He would "make plain the vision"[102] and reveal the mysteries that had been hidden.[103]

By God revealing the meaning of prophecy, He exposes darkness – in essence He turns on the light switch. One such hidden prophecy is the Who/What/Where/When about the coming Antichrist and *"the mystery of iniquity."*[104]

In Revelation Chapter 17, John's vision includes symbolic images of the Beast, the Great Whore, the Seven Hills and Mystery Babylon, which we have already seen is undoubtedly the Church of Rome. Revelation Chapter 13 gives us further symbols and an encrypted message, that once decoded will serve as a final warning; (vs. 13)

"Here is wisdom. Let him that hath understanding count the number of the beast: for it is the number of a man; and his number is Six hundred threescore and six."

Many people think that the seal of the Antichrist will be something like a stamp or brand, or an electronic chip implanted under the skin. Others believe that the 666 is the "root" owner or super-user in a multi-user computer system – and that this person having the power to set 666 file permissions is the most powerful user. Thus, on a worldwide system, the antichrist will control and have the absolute power to do anything to all of your computer files. He will change your bank files preventing you from withdrawing any money by changing the file permissions, etc. The basis for such thinking lies in the fantastically rapid development of science and technology in this direction. Most likely, however, this scientific development is designed to distract mankind's attention from the real ***spiritual*** mark of Antichrist, which may in actuality have its corporal counterpart with the advances of science, technology or medicine – as an outward indicator of an inner phenomenon.

At a time when people's suspicions and anxieties are fixed upon some innovation of progress – the implantation of computer chips in humans, for example – the real seal of Antichrist will be imprinted quietly, without any particular commotion. As individuals reject the dominion and authority of Jesus Christ and the commands and edicts of Bible, they will in turn receive the invisible mark of their denial.

In a spiritual sense, this satanic mystery – the imprinting of the mark of Antichrist – will be the antithesis of the both the Orthodox Hebrew tradition of wearing their "faith" upon their hand and forehead; and the Greek Orthodox Mystery of Chrismation, the symbolic reception of the seal of the Holy Spirit. In the Mystery of Chrismation, the priest anoints the newly dedicated on the forehead and hands. The forehead is anointed for the sanctification of the mind, and the hands for the sanctification of actions and the entire conduct.

In the Old Testament, the Jews were told that they were to keep the commandments and to worship the one true God with all their heart, soul and might.[105] Their worship, devotion, love and obedience were outwardly symbolized by wearing on their hand and between their eyes (on the forehead), strips of parchment on which were written four passages of scriptures[106] attached to bands of leather. Deuteronomy 6:8;

"And you shall bind them for a sign on your hand, and they shall be as frontlets between your eyes."

As the ***Anti*** implies, the devil replicates much of what God does, but on his own terms - Satan and his practices are the counterfeit to God's original and genuine.

What therefore is the number of the beast, the number of a man – 666?

Near Rome, in Vatican City, sits the famous Saint Peter's Basilica. Above the throne is a cupola or dome. The dome was first designed by Michelangelo, and completed by Giacomo della Porta and Domenico Fontana in 1589-1593.

On the inside, at the bottom of the dome are written the words Christ spoke to Peter: TV ES PETRVS ET SVPER HANC PETRAM AEDIFICABO ECCLESIAM MEAM. TIBI DABO CLAVES REGNI CAELORVM ("...you are Peter, and on this rock I will build my church. ... I will give you the keys of the kingdom of heaven...." Latin Vulgate, Matthew 16:18-19.)

Vicarivs Filii Dei

During the Papal Coronation of Pope Pius XII in 1939, he is told in Latin to "receive the tiara adorned with three crowns and know that thou art Father of Princes and Kings, Ruler of the World, and Vicar of Our Savior, to Him be the honor and glory forever and ever." From the days of Constantine, Peter's supposed successor has been given the title of Vicar. During this coronation the variation Vicarium Salvatoris is used. [See: The Coronation of Pope Pius XII[107]]

Though many theologians and church historians have identified the man of sin as a papal representative, and have even speculated on both the name and number of his name, Vicarivs Filii Dei as 666 is first thought to have appeared in print originally in a 1915 article in *Our Sunday Visitor*[108] [109] (the largest Catholic weekly in America). This article stated the Pope's tiara had the title Vicarius Filii Dei on it and sought to address the circulating theory that this particular title was the one that equaled 666. Despite attempts to downplay or dismiss this detail, Catholic apologists admit that Vicarius Filii Dei is "theologically accurate", but at the same time they deny that it is an "official" title.

In the mid 1940's Jesuit Monsignor Lardoni, former editor of the Vatican newspaper and a notable Rector at Catholic University in Washington, D.C. appraised documents relating to the authenticity of the Papal title Vicarius Filii Dei.

He commented first on the Moroni[C] document[110], saying he had used it in his classes and was unaware that it mentioned the Pope's title, Vicarius Filii Dei. He translated this Italian document and said its reference to the Pope's title was vague, though the title plainly appears in Volume 99, page 21, in the entry for VICARIO DI GESU' CRISTO [Vicar of Jesus Christ], where it states very briefly that the title Vicarius Filii Dei is to be found in an inscription at the Vatican.[111]

[C] The author of the well-known "Dizionario di erudizione storico-ecclesiastica" (1802-1883). When Mauro Cappellari became a cardinal, he made Moroni his *cameriere*: and when he became pope as Gregory XVI, he took Moroni for *primo aiutante di camera*, employing him also as private secretary, in which capacity Moroni wrote over 100,000 letters. Moroni also served Pius IX as *aiutante di camera*.

For 1600 years the title Vicar of Christ has been used almost exclusively of the Bishop of Rome as successor of Peter and, therefore, the one in the Church who particularly takes the place of Christ. "The title further denotes they exercise their authority in the Church not by delegation from any other person, but from Christ Himself."[112]

In reference to the Gratian document[113] [114], phrase 228-230 reads "in terris *Uicarius Filii De* esse uidetur constitutes, ita et Pontifices, qui ipsius principis apostolorum…," which roughly translates to be "on Earth the Pontiff is the Vicar of the Son of God, and the Chief Apostle." Lardoni said this document was the best source of authentication, yet he referred to Dr. Johannes Quasten [1900-1987] their greatest authority in this field [he was a renowned patristic scholar] for the final verdict.

Dr. Quasten is known to have acknowledged both verbally and in writing, that, "The Pope has many titles. Although Vicarius Filii Dei is not as common, it is, however, an ancient title and should be accepted by any good Catholic scholar." In 1943 he wrote on official Catholic University stationary the following: "The title Vicarius Christi, as well as the title Vicarius Filii Dei is very common as the title of the Pope." [The Quasten document[115]]

Additional evidence of this Title's use is found on Page 343 of a recently digitized Vatican document *"Deusdedit cardinalis ... collectio canonum."*[116] This publication clearly articulates the title Vicarius Filii Dei is valid. A Pio Martinucci doesn't refute this fact, though he does attempt to explain why it is a trivial matter that it equals 666.

In 1865, Archbishop of Westminster stated that the concept of the Catholic Church leaders being Vicars of Christ, and the Pope being the "Vicar of the Son of God" was one of the Church's great dogmas and "a theological certainty."[117]

Finally, contemporary Roman Catholic Theologian and Author Malachi Martin uses this exact same title for the Pope on pages 114 and 122 of his book, *"The Keys of this Blood."*[118]

The Latin Papal title Vicarivs Filii Dei means: *in place of, instead of,* or as a *valid substitution for the Son of God. "Here is wisdom. Let him that hath understanding count the number of the beast: for it is the number of a man; and his number is six hundred threescore and six."*

Most attempts at interpreting the number 666 begin with the fact that in ancient times letters were commonly used to stand for numbers. This meant every name was also a numerical sum obtained by totaling its entire letters (gematria). A piece of graffiti from Pompeii is often used as an example of how letters stood for numbers. This one reads, "I love the girl whose name is phi mu epsilon."[119] If you take the letters in the title Vicarivs Filii Dei, which represent Latin numerals and add them together they come to 666.

V	I	C	A	R	I	V	S	F	I	L	I	I	D	E	I
5	1	100			1	5			1	50	1	1	500		1

This explanation for the number cannot be any clearer. Yet for centuries Christians have speculated about the meaning of the "mark of the beast" and the number 666, both of which are discussed in Revelation, chapter 13. We are told that a symbolic beast with two horns, and who spoke like a dragon "forced everyone, small and great, rich and poor, free and slave, to receive a mark on his right hand or on his forehead" (13:16). Now that we know the "number", what is this strange "mark"?

The Beast's "Mark"

The Greek word used for "mark" is *charagma.* It was the technical term for the Roman imperial stamp that appeared on various documents. The *charagma* was a seal stamped with the name and date of the emperor and attached to commercial documents. Apparently, it also stood for the emperor's head stamped on coins. Thus, the *charagma* represented the likeness or name of the emperor.

The *charagma* was also a type of brand. In Roman times, disobedient slaves were often branded with marks of ownership, much like cattle are today. Religious tattooing was also widespread. Soldiers had a custom of branding themselves with the name of a favorite general. Devotees of a god labeled themselves with tattoos to designate their loyal devotion.

What point was John trying to get across, then, when he was speaking of a "mark"? The mark is probably not meant to be something visible to the eye, as was the Nazi practice of tattooing numbers on concentration camp inmates. Nor should we assume it to be an computer program or system, identity card of some kind, like a Social Security or a credit card.

More likely, the mark is to be taken as a symbol. It is that which identifies who belongs to the beast – or to God. There is an Old Testament parallel in Ezekiel on which Revelation draws. John's readers would have readily understood the point he was making. In vision, Ezekiel saw a man with a writing kit at his side. He heard the Lord say to the man, " *Go through the middle of the city, through the middle of Jerusalem, and set a mark on the foreheads of the men that sigh and that cry for all the abominations that be done in the middle thereof.*" (Ezekiel 9:4). Here are people who are "marked" for protection.

In like manner, Israel was "marked" by blood smeared on the doorpost. On the eve of the Exodus, the death angel swept through Egypt, killing the firstborn. He passed over any door marked with blood (Exodus 12:21-23). This mark, of course, was merely a symbol, as the angel would have been quite able to distinguish between an Israelite and Egyptian.

Earlier in Revelation we read of the 144,000 servants of God who were sealed on their foreheads with "the seal [*sphragis*] of the living God" (7:2). They were also to be protected from the trumpet plagues that would devastate the earth (7:3). Those not having the seal were afforded no protection (9:4).

The "mark of the beast," then, is a parody of the sealing of the faithful people of God. The beast will attempt to identify and protect his own (and destroy his enemies) even as God knows and protects those who are his people.

The Beginning of the Con – The Council of Nicaea

More than Buddha, Mohammed or the Dalai Lama, Jesus Christ was a historical figure of staggering influence, perhaps the most enigmatic and inspirational leader the world has ever seen. As the prophesied Messiah Jesus toppled kings, inspired millions, and established novel and enduring philosophies. As a descendant of the lines of King Solomon and King David, Jesus possessed a rightful claim to the Jewish throne and the title of *the* King. Understandably, His life was recorded by thousands of followers and over several millennia.

Being that Jesus Christ was such an important figure, with an equally important message, it should be no surprise that His enemies would seek to thwart His purpose by corrupting His message. His gospel and the example life He lived were not only under attack during His earthly existence, but even more so after His death, burial and resurrection. Within thirty years of Christ's death, His apostles had to begin to warn Christian believers *"to earnestly contend for the faith once delivered to the saints."* (Jude 3) St. Paul "marveled" that Christ's followers could be both shaken and removed from the original gospel interpretations so soon after having learned them. (Galatians 1:6) This attack on both the church's written gospel and its traditions continued unabated for decades, culminating in the *Great Con of Man* – the First Council of Nicaea in 325 AD.

After Jesus' resurrection and subsequent pouring out of His spirit, the early disciple travelled throughout the immediate countries, spreading the Gospel. Despite the early church leader's best efforts, minor, major and heretical doctrinal differences arose. Attempts to blend traditional religious belief and custom, with Christianity were constant, and often divisive. What often began as local disputes, at times became large enough to even threaten to tear apart the fabric of Christian unity as a whole.

Such was the great clash between the pre-Nicaean Christianity of what was referred to as the Jerusalem Christianity and that of the Romans. The Roman Christians began to blend the pagan beliefs and traditions of their forefathers, with the original Christianity taught to them by St.

Paul and other early leaders. A few such notable examples were; the day of worship, the date of Jesus birthday, the date of His resurrection and worship of pluralistic deities. The pagan gods Osiris, Adonis, Dionysus and Mithras [called the *Son of God* and the *Light of the World*] birthdays were celebrated on December 25.

Christianity's weekly holy day was also taken from the pagans. Originally, Christianity honored the Jewish Sabbath on Saturday, some believers sought to distance themselves from the Jews and their customs by holding their services on Sunday, supposedly to honor the resurrection which had occurred on a Sunday. Couched in this excuse, the Romans shifted it to coincide with the pagan's veneration day of the sun. To this day, most churchgoers attend services on Sunday morning with no idea that they are there on account of the pagan sun god's weekly tribute - Sunday.

It was during this tumultuous time, with the Christian Church in a divisive doctrinal and traditional battle that threatened to tear apart the fabric of societal order, Constantine held a famous ecumenical gathering known as the Council of Nicaea. As earlier mentioned, at this gathering many aspects of Christianity were debated and voted upon - the date of Easter, the date of the Resurrection, the role of the bishops, the administration of sacraments, and, even the divinity of Jesus. Once a vote was made, the civil power and might of Constantine enforced the doctrinal views and traditions of the Roman version of Christianity. From that time, the true believers became a persecuted minority.

As this momentous council was about to begin, neither Constantine nor the Roman Church made any attempt to camouflage their blatant paganistic roots or their disdain for the Scriptural warnings of Timothy[120] and Saint John the Beloved:

"1 And there came one of the seven angels which had the seven vials, and talked with me, saying unto me, Come hither; I will shew unto thee the judgment of the great whore that sitteth upon many waters: 2 With whom the kings of the earth have committed fornication, and the inhabitants of the earth have been made drunk with the wine of her fornication. 3 So he carried me away in the spirit into the wilderness:

and I saw a woman sit upon a scarlet coloured beast, full of names of blasphemy, having seven heads and ten horns. 4 And the woman was arrayed in purple and scarlet colour, and decked with gold and precious stones and pearls, having a golden cup in her hand full of abominations and filthiness of her fornication: 5 And upon her forehead was a name written, MYSTERY, BABYLON THE GREAT, THE MOTHER OF HARLOTS AND ABOMINATIONS OF THE EARTH. 6 And I saw the woman drunken with the blood of the saints, and with the blood of the martyrs of Jesus: and when I saw her, I wondered with great admiration."(Revelation 17:1-6)

"Resplendent in purple and gold, Constantine made a ceremonial entrance at the opening of the council, probably in early June, but respectfully seated the bishops ahead of himself."[121] As Eusebius described, Constantine "himself proceeded through the midst of the assembly, like some heavenly messenger of God, clothed in raiment which glittered as it were with rays of light, reflecting the glowing radiance of a purple robe, and adorned with the brilliant splendor of gold and precious stones."[122] He was present as an observer, but he did not vote. Constantine organized the Council along the lines of the Roman Senate. "Ossius [Hosius] presided over its deliberations; he probably, and the two priests of Rome certainly, came as representatives of the Pope. Eusebius of Nicomedia probably gave the welcoming address."[123]

In the summer of 325, the bishops of all provinces were summoned to Nicaea (now known as İznik, in modern-day Turkey), a place easily accessible to the majority of them, particularly those of Asia Minor, Syria, Palestine, Egypt, Greece, and Thrace.

Approximately 250 to 318 bishops attended, from every region of the Empire except Britain. Of the bishops whose successors would much later be termed Patriarchs, Alexander of Alexandria, Eustathius of Antioch, and Macarius of Jerusalem attended, and Sylvester I, Bishop of Rome, sent legates. Another participant was the first church historian, Eusebius of Caesarea.

The First Council of Nicaea was convened by Constantine I upon the recommendations of a synod led by Hosius of Cordoba in the Eastertide of 325. This synod had been charged with investigation of the trouble brought about by the Arian controversy in the Greek-speaking east. To most bishops, the teachings of Arius were heretical and dangerous to the salvation of souls. Primarily there was one basic issue at the center of the Arius debate: What is the relation of the divine in Christ to the divine in the Father? Or put another way, how does the church integrate and then express their beliefs about the doctrine of one God, Father and Creator (inherited from the Old Testament and Judaism), with the revelation that this same God had disclosed himself uniquely in Jesus?

For the Jewish converts to Christianity, this mystery of God's indwelling in human form (theophany) was understood by several scriptures and Old Testament stories, as well as Pauline writings (1 Timothy 3:16):

"And without controversy great is the mystery of godliness: God was manifest in the flesh, justified in the Spirit, seen of angels, preached unto the Gentiles, believed on in the world, received up into glory."

A theophany is an explicit appearance of God to a person, which is tangible to the human senses. Theophanies are relatively rare in the Bible, perhaps because it is very dangerous to be visited by the presence of God – we know from Exodus 33:20 that it is normally fatal to experience a theophany. In a sense the story of Jesus on Earth is one long theophany (John 14:9) but the term is generally reserved for dramatic, short-lived, super-natural experiences of God.

God Walking in the Garden of Eden
And they [Adam and Eve] heard the voice of the LORD God walking in the midst of the garden in the cool of the day. (Genesis 3:8)

Abram at Moreh in Shechem
...the Lord appeared to Abram and said "To your offspring I will give this land" (Genesis 12:7-9)

Abraham at the Plains of Mamre [Pre-destruction of Sodom & Gomorrah]
The Lord appeared to Abraham near the plains of Mamre... (Genesis 18:1-33)

Jacob at Peniel
"... I saw God face to face, and yet my life was spared." (Genesis 32:22-30)

Moses on Mount Sinai
Then the Lord descended in the cloud, and stood with him [Moses] there, and proclaimed the name of the Lord. And the Lord passed by before him, and proclaimed, "The Lord, the Lord God, merciful and gracious..." (Exodus 34:1-7)

For God to create a body (temporary or otherwise) was no difficult matter, for Him to choose to "temporarily" dwell in that body was established by precedent. In theory, Jesus being a body or THE body God chose to inhabit and live in was not problematic to Jewish thought, though it was troubling in its reality. God inhabiting creation is a central theme throughout the Old Testament. Whether it was the *Tabernacle in the Wilderness*, the *Temple at Jerusalem* or the Christ body, God's presence or Shekinah glory filled up chosen creations. In the above examples, every theophany wherein God took on human form foreshadowed the incarnation, where God took the form of a man to live among us as Emmanuel, "God with us" (Matthew 1:23).

So, the one God changing forms was not a mystery to the Jew. Yet on the other hand, non-Jewish believers came from a pluralistic (several gods) religious world view, and the non-Jewish sects of Christianity constantly leaned in this divine pluralistic direction, seeking to transfigure the monotheistic into anything other than a one-God religion. Despite the fact that there is absolutely no doctrine of the Trinity, in the Nicene sense, present in the Old or New Testaments, non-Jewish sects of Christianity looked for any scriptural pattern to legitimize their earlier pagan beliefs and practices. This is why the top two issues in question at the Council of Nicaea were the explanation of Jesus divinity (all God or part God), and the selection of the date for Christ's resurrection. One belief was that the resurrection followed the Jewish tradition of the Passover sequence of time and dates, the other belief was not based on scripture, and rather it was solely based on human thought and emotion.

By the year 300, some churches had adopted a divergent style of celebrating the festival, placing the emphasis on the resurrection which they believed occurred on Sunday. Others however celebrated the festival on the 14th of the Jewish month Nisan, the date of the crucifixion according to the Bible's Hebrew calendar (Leviticus 23:5, John 19:14). Hence this group was called Quartodecimans, which is derived from the Latin for 14. The Eastern Churches of Syria, Cilicia, and Mesopotamia determined the date of Christian Passover in relation to the 14th day of Nisan, in the Bible's Hebrew calendar. Alexandria and Rome, however, followed a different calculation, attributed to Pope Soter, so that Christian Passover would never coincide with the Jewish observance and decided in favor of celebrating on the first Sunday after the first full moon following the vernal equinox, independently of the Bible's Hebrew calendar.

Although it is called the "Christian celebration of Easter" the Bible never specified that the date of the Passover should be changed or abolished; in fact even Jesus Christ kept the feast of Unleavened Bread which began with the day of Passover (Matthew 26:17, Luke 22:7). Easter, as a note, should be regarded as a separate teaching officially sanctioned by Emperor Constantine and the Roman Catholic Church, not a teaching from the Bible. Many early Christians had become martyrs due to the fact that this law was implemented shortly after the 325AD Council of Nicaea; those found keeping the early Christian feasts based upon the Bible [Jewish tradition and calendar] were exiled and/or put to death.

This *Great Con of Man* perpetrated by the Priory of Sion therefore was not a hidden Royal bloodline traced back to Jesus and Mary Magdalene; the *Greatest Con of Mankind* is the perverted Gospel of Jesus Christ promulgated by the Roman Catholic Church, post-Nicene Council. The spirit behind changing God's Word is the anti-Christ spirit. The progression towards the devil incarnate goes like this: first come false doctrine, then the accompanying deed and finally the incarnation of a man (The Anti-Christ) by the devil.

The rise of and subsequent dominion by the Roman Catholic Church is the fulfillment of many prophecies:

"And I saw one of his heads as it were wounded to death; and his deadly wound was healed: and all the world wondered [followed] after the beast." (Revelation 13:3)

Since its rise to power and subsequent attempt at world dominion, The Roman Church has had two thousand years of experience pressuring those who threaten to unveil its lies. Since the days of Constantine, the Church has successfully hidden the truth about the pagan origins of December 25th, Easter and even the Trinity. For years, either through force or deception, they have found a way to keep the world in the dark. As Dan Brown's *Leah Teabing* character would say, *"The Church may no longer employ crusaders to slaughter nonbelievers, but their influence is no less persuasive."*[124]

3

If God Was a Gambler

If God Was a Gambler

Life is a gamble. Every day we are forced to make decisions based on imperfect knowledge, unsure of the outcomes of our choices. We do the best we can with what we have available, developing strategies based on experience, accumulated information, and calculations of probabilities. Traveling to Seattle in April? We pack an umbrella since it's likely to rain. Meeting a co-worker for lunch? No reason to rush since she is never on time.

Almost every rational decision we make in life is a based on what we assume to be the expected outcome. We make our choices in order to maximize our gains and minimize our losses, attempting all the while to boost our expected value of every specific outcome.

Life is a gamble. Every day we are forced to make decisions based on imperfect knowledge.

Why do people say they gamble? In a survey in Washington, those sampled reported that they gambled for fun, to win money, or they were looking for excitement and a challenge.[125] [D]

[D] Average or typical "gambling" must be distinguished from pathological or problem gambling, of which the latter I do NOT at all suggest about God.

Let's be clear, gambling is a big-time activity in the United States. Ten times bigger than all spectator sports combined - ten times... Think about that last $25-300 Red Sox, Yankee or Dodger ticket you shelled out for. How about the $100-300 Patriot or Cowboy's ticket that you last put on your Visa or Mastercard? According to International Gaming and Wagering Business, in 1995 $44.4 billion dollars were spent gambling; for every one dollar spent on a ticket to a spectator sport, ten were spent gambling. That figure rose an astounding 204%, for combined gambling revenue of over $90 billion in 2006.[126] Is one billion a lot? A billion seconds ago it was 1959.

A billion minutes ago Jesus was alive. So is $90 billion a lot? Well, $90 billion is *more* than the individual Gross National Income of 140 of the wealthiest 172 countries (81 percent). Anyway, I digress…

People gamble – a lot and often. What advantage could possibly be conferred by ignoring probabilistic laws? Some say the basis for gambling behavior is confidence, and that risk-taking behavior is favored in most winner-take-all games that establish the reigning "king-of-the-hill." [127] In other words, I'm *the* man and you aren't.

The Great White Lie

"Christmas Day. Jesus' birthday." Also a $200 billion dollar a year lie. Originally Yule was a celebration of the winter solstice, marked by pagan traditions such as hanging mistletoe, holly, and wreaths. It's interesting that Christians don't question the holiday. The ancient prophet Jeremiah even wrote about the tradition of decorating trees, and rebuked those who practiced such blatant paganism. (Jeremiah 10:1-5) Bery, bery inter-resting-ah.

"And while we're on the subject, take a look at the Son of God's name. Yeshua. "Yehovah Saves." wait… Yeshua, Yehovah? Where's the "J"? "Actually there never was a 'J' sound in the name. In fact, there is no 'j' sound in the entire Hebrew language. Why was the letter used in translating Yehovah? Well, the Old English 'j' was actually pronounced like the 'y' in 'yes.' Thus, when the first Hebrew Scriptures were translated into English, 'y' became 'j' (think 'Hallelujah').

And thus, Yoseph, Yoshua, Yoel, and Yehovah became Joseph, Joshua, Joel, and Jehovah. We just pronounce them wrong.

And the "s" in Jesus, versus the "sh" in Yeshua? Greek, like many other languages, has no "sh" sound. Translators of English versions of the New Testament transliterated the Greek transcription of a Hebrew name. This was doubly unfortunate, first because the "sh" sound exists in English, and second because in English the "s" sound can shift to the "z" sound. The fourth sound one hears in the name Yeshua is the "u" sound, as in the word "true". Like the first three sounds, this also has come to be mispronounced but in this case it is not the fault of the translators. They transcribed this sound accurately, but English is not a phonetic language and "u" can be pronounced in more than one way. At some point the "u" in "Jesus" came to be pronounced as in "cut," and so we say "Jee-zuhs." On and on it goes, to the painful end of the badly mangled transliteration.

And Yeshua? In Hebrew, "Yehovah Saves." Matthew 1:21 "And you shall call his name Yeshua. For He shall save His people from their sins." Not Jesus. Yeshua. There's misinterpretation for you... Yet, I still love *Jesus*!

Mirrors

Walk into a Gold's Gym. A wall full of mirrors. I believe that wall of mirrors is Gold's single best marketing tool. Hope. An interesting concept. Not want, not need, not have, not being. Not know. Hope, an optimist's unknown. It could lead a man to give his fortune, his life. It could lead a man to sin, or to stop sinning.

Vegas is America's mirror to its soul. Las Vegas. The lights, the colors… the women. Porn lining the streets. The card pushers and magicians and fake looking fake buildings inside fake looking real buildings. Monstrous screens projecting fake looking people with big, fake smiles. I remember envisioning a city and gaming palace flyover, and thinking "…all those poor, lost people." That's what I learned in Sunday School. I remember wondering how any sane person could sit at a machine, shoving quarter after quarter, dollar after dollar, just dropping them into a faceless hole. "How could people be so stupid?" I thought. I always figured I'd never know. I only thought of the gambler as a faithless sinner, hungry for profit and starving for faith.

Apart from traditional, prescribed religious disdain, there is furthermore of course the pragmatic issue that gambling is habit-forming, even with people who have some degree of self-discipline. It can very easily, and very quickly become an addiction, especially if one, early on has the 'thrill' of actually getting an inordinate reward for a tiny investment.

Lately when I think of all those lost people, I began to realize I no longer feel sorry for them. I am no longer wishing they were better. In fact, I no longer feel superior to them.

Years ago, I said. "Look at all those lost people." And now? "Look at all these people searching. Look at all these people hoping. Look at all these people trying."

And your life is about to change.

Watch: A poker game. Four men at a table. The Cross. Soldiers drawing lots, straws. Pick a card. Roll the dice. Flip a coin."Steve. 30 years old. Stuck in a boring job. Pretty wife, good friends, no life. Bored, and desperate for some kind of challenge, some kind of risk, some kind of excitement. Enter, the lottery. A three dollar gamble. A cheap chance. An easy hope.

Just enough excitement to keep his mind off the fact that his life needs change. Just enough risk to satisfy that incessant desire deep within his soul to be free. To be human and to feel alive.

Is God a Gambler?

As I think about Albert Einstein's famous comment, "God does not play dice with the universe,"[128] God may not shoot craps, but it's possible He may be willing to wager a bet now and then. For most

Christians, gambling is a no-no, and to suggest that God may gamble is heretical. But let's look at the facts.

To gamble. To accept a challenge. To throw down or to pick up the gauntlet after it's been thrown down. To give your best, and hope it's good enough. To face fear. To risk, because you believe. To have faith. Gamblers have faith in their ability to win. They risk their money and pride because of that belief.

Peter had faith in his ability to follow God, and God's ability to hold him up.

Peter took a gamble and a walk on the wild the side - Peter walked on water.

Any discussion of the motivation of gambling usually starts with the natural comparison to life. Life is a gamble. Every day, people are faced with situations which involve risk and chance.

Gambling activities are extensions of the risk and chance in life. The activity of gambling becomes play, it becomes a game. Gambling allows the person the choice of engaging in the activity, the amount of risk and, in many cases, the stakes. The stakes are a necessary element for many people. It turns the bet into not just an opinion but a commitment. Put up or shut up…

God has faith – in Himself and in humanity. He risked Yeshua and His love because of that belief. Peter had faith in his ability to follow God, and God's ability to hold him up. Peter took a gamble and a walk on the wild the side - Peter walked on water. David had faith in God's strength. He killed the giant. How do you kill a giant? How do you walk on water? How do you tackle your insecurities? How do you move mountains? You make a reasoned risk, you take a gamble.

God is a perpetual gambler. Take Job, for instance. Satan just went to see what's up, to challenge God, and God's like "Have you seen my servant Job?" Was God looking for a challenge or just willing to accept. Satan called, the bet was on. Another time God was the initiator of the dance, saying to Adam "Eat anything you want, except that fruit riiight there."

And finally, God's greatest risk, in a world of good and bad, in a world with choice - free moral agency is His greatest gamble of all.

Should I buy the Cadillac or the Chevy? I may need to marry the Chevy, but my heart is in bed with the Caddy. Flat matte pictures may be more practical, but I desire the high gloss that if held at just the right angle and in the perfect light will leave you panting – messy fingerprints and all.

Addicts are gamblers, they love high gloss & Cadillacs. They always want more and they always want it now. They will cut a hole in God's roof to avoid the cue and bypass the long line waiting to enter His presence. To gamble. To risk. That balance of fear and hope. Drama. Excitement.

Jesus said "Seek, and you will find. Ask, and it shall be given to you. Knock, and it shall be opened." Take a step of faith.
Take a gamble.

Stop Reading This Book Right Now.

Most people get to this point of a book, make a mental assessment of the story thus far, and decide - maybe subconsciously - what the ending will be. It's called assuming, and it happens even without their acknowledgement. It is your mind trying to assert control on at least a partial level.
But here, there is no definite story. There are no definite characters. In fact, there may even be no purpose at all. If you were smart, you would realize this, and stop reading.

I'll just tell you right now. There is no purpose at all to this book.

Of course, I might be lying…And that, right there, is curiosity.
You don't know the future, and you want to, so you are still reading.

You're not risking much, but you are gambling.

There. Feel that? You're changing. By tomorrow you'll be questioning your pastor and starting revolutions.

Read on.

Almighty God gambled His only Son away, so that you might believe. You. You filthy, heathen dog.

We are the dogs under the master's table. If you will - the underdogs. We are David, facing Goliath. We are gamblers.

We go to the Master's table to ask for mercy, even when we know it belongs to the Jews.

That's why when the Samaritan woman embraced Yeshua's put-down and replied "True, Lord. So, the dogs delight to eat the crumbs that fall from their master's table," Yeshua said "Woman, you have extraordinary faith. I will do what you ask."

The Need for Fresh Inspiration

I have a question: when did God say He quit inspiring people or providing insight and revelation? Many people point to Revelation 22:18, where John writes "If anyone adds anything to these words, God will add to that person the disasters written about in this book." It seems to make sense, because it's close to the end of our little assembly of old writings, and seems like a good closing command. The problem, of course, is the fact that this was written three hundred years before anyone had the notion that the Law, Prophets, Psalms and Proverbs, Gospels, Letters, and other writings needed to be put together into a Holy Bible – the inerrant Word of God.

Obviously, John wasn't talking about everyone else's writings, or even his own previous writings. He was talking about another book, The Book of Revelation.

That's it. So, if John didn't command God to stop inspiring people, or providing insight and revelation, then who did?

I'll tell you. You did. You still do...

When you raise your Bible in the air and chant "This is my Bible. The only inspired and written Word of God. I will believe what it says, and follow what it teaches. This is my guide. It will lead me closer to God. I will keep it close to my heart and meditate on its every word."

In neuro-linguistic programming[129] lingo, this is called "anchoring." You use words to induce a feeling or emotion, while allowing your subconscious mind to associate that feeling with the awareness of an object (the anchor) - in this case a book. Thus, whenever the object - or the anchor - is brought into your awareness, those same feelings will seem natural.

So, when I say 'In Hebrews 1:11,' you automatically open yourself up to whatever is going to be said next.

You have willingly programmed yourself to be a mindless drone. In neuro-linguistic programming lingo, you're in big trouble. Over and over you've told God "No, I won't let You inspire people or bring fresh revelation. Even if You do, I won't believe it!" Over and over you've told God "I will decide who You are, what You say, and how You say it, and if You go against my beliefs or my church's traditions I won't believe it's You." Over and over and over, one shovel full at a time, you have dug your own grave.

If God ever wanted to open Himself up to a Gentile, it would not be you.

It could not be you.

And that is why you are here.

Why else pick up a book about prophecy, odds and God as a Gambler?

Here is what you are going to do: Tell God you're sorry. Tell Him "I'm sorry I've limited who You could be in my life - how You could speak to me. I'm sorry I closed my heart and my mind off to Your Holy Communication. God, I now ask that You will forgive me, because I didn't know I was doing it.

I ask that You Yourself show me Who You are, and how You want to speak to me. Even if You decide to be an eggplant, and bring Your revelations through my best friend Billy Bob, I will follow You, God, and I will believe. Thank You."

How does it feel? Scary? It should be a little scary, because if God really does turn out to be an eggplant and speak through your best friend Billy Bob, you're going to feel pretty silly.

A Case for God as a Gambler

Many historians say that the Book of Job is the oldest of the sacred texts. If this is so, God chose to showcase a part of His personality, and give some interesting insight into the dynamics of the divine-human relationship.

In the opening two chapters of the Book of Job, we're informed that God and the angelic folk that roam the visible and unseen dimensions were known to conduct Board meetings now and again.

During one such meeting, the Lord said to Satan, "Where have you come from?" Being that Satan understood the pecking order of the dominion in which he belonged to, he answered without sarcasm, "From roaming through the earth and going back and forth in it." It appears that the Bible uses this angel's name *Satan*, knowing the average person back then would understand that it meant "adversary." That's what the former archangel did after his banishment, he hunted humans and did whatever he could to trick, trap, entice and otherwise just plain spoil their souls.

Anyway, The Lord (the Lord, again, specifically chosen over other God-type names – this appellation meaning Adonai or "Lord over all other lords") asks His adversary how the hunt was going – how many souls had he harvested that day? What kind of mischief had he been getting into, was he living up to his name?

I don't know, maybe Satan wasn't doing well, or knowing the frailty of humankind, possible too well. Anyway, from the dialogue, The Lord throws down a challenge, a wager if you will – He says "Have you considered my servant Job?" Kind of like the movie *Casino Royale* when the British MI6 nominates 007 to compete in a high stakes poker match for their pleasure and ultimate end-purpose. God goes a-gambling. High stakes gambling with Job's life, his family and quite possible his soul. Whew. The wager? Will Job curse God.

> Job was ignorant to the *Divine Wager* that was going on in the empyreal realms.

I can hear some people moaning right now, "Aaargh! God didn't gamble, He KNEW the outcome." Did He? Does it say He knew? This whole Satan talking with God, giving monthly reports interaction steps out on some slippery theological ice. It reminds me of the Gene Wilder version of *Willy Wonka*[130], where the bad guy Otto Slugworth at the end of the movie is discovered to actually be working with/for the big guy. Strange plot twist…But this God-Satan interaction gets even more intense.

Poor Job. Poor, poor, upright, perfect Job. Toiling away on the earth, living the righteous life within the parameters God has set for him, and ignorant to the *Divine Wager* that is going on in the empyreal realms. Job is thinking, "I offer the right sacrifices for me and my family, I even hedge my bets and sacrifice for the sins I MAY have committed unintentionally or accidentally; yet I'm knee deep in trouble." He hasn't got a clue that the spiritual power brokers are anteing up at the

Casino Royale on Cloud Nine over his ability to withstand demonic slings and arrows of outrageous fortune. If he doesn't know where the arrows are coming from, how can he possibly take arms against his sea of troubles?

Eventually God completely turns Satan loose on Job (except to take his life); Jobs children are dead, his wife has lost faith, his body is diseased, his friends have turned on him and he has become the bi-lines for all the news jockies and late night TV comedy hosts. At this point, Job at least gets one part of Shakespeare's sonnet right – "To die: to sleep; No more; and by sleep to say we end the heartache and the thousand natural shocks that flesh is heir to." (Hamlet, Act III Scene i) Well he doesn't say it quite so eloquently, but he does say, "My soul chooses strangling and death." (Job 7:15)

Oh yeah, why am I talking about this. The life and times of Mr. Job is in the Bible, this said life and times, as well as Sacred Text are meant to teach us both moral lessons and something about the nature and personality of God. Now you may read this text and have a completely different interpretation about the *Divine Wager* subtext, but the average, unbiased, logical, "if it looks, walks and quacks like a duck – it is a duck" type of person reads the Book of Job, his/her conclusion will be that there is some serious wagering going on.

4 The Divine Wager – The Divine Mirror

The Divine Wager – The Divine Mirror

Wow, man against archangel, mortal versus immortal, terrestrial versus celestial, Rocky against Apollo Creed – simple faith against all the powers of heaven & earth. Is it about God's need for intensity? To walk on the wilder side? To live *la vida loca*? Is God just toying with Satan and/or Job? Or has God truly given mankind free moral agency, and based upon Job's past behavior, character and lifelong patterns of faithful actions, God takes a very well-calculated risk and places his bets on Job withstanding Satan?

The story is there for a reason. Theologians tell us that Sacred Canon was meant to instruct, educate and inspire us in our daily living tasks; as well as inform us about God and His nature and behavior that we might learn via emulation to live and act as He does. God commands us to comply with His directives, He issues these directives with an expectation that we will obey. How can He expect this response? Each directive or commandment is predicated upon the idea that He has given enough prior information and/or has established a trusting enough relationship to make a reasoned and informed decision. There are few, if any examples of "blind" faith.

Even the Biblical examples that you are running through right now in your head are not truly "leaps of faith" – they are more like baby-steps of faith or reasonable gambles. Take a breath, Mister or Miss conventional religious person! I know about Abraham being asked to sacrifice his only son Isaac; I know about stuttering, stammering, persona-non-grata Moses being asked to stand alone against Pharaoh, the ruler of the known world; I remember after Moses was asked to deliver Israel and bring them to the promised land, he is sandwiched by the Red Sea and Egypt's army; I can call to mind my childhood Sunday School stories and the Battle of Jericho or the face-off between David and the ten foot giant Goliath; I can call to mind Noah being asked to build the largest boat in history, in which to save the human race from a rainstorm and ensuing flood neither of which had ever occurred before (that's correct, the Bible states clearly that up until the time of the rains by which the heavens are opened, the Earth had been watered by thick mist – envision a terrarium). All these appear to be monumental leaps of faith – but they are not.

Each of the above examples are used to portray great or blind faith, but are actually the culmination of either years of small(er) tests and trials or the fruition of prior faith-infused exploits. David foregoes King Saul's armor in lieu of his own sling, why? His sling had been tested before. Not against a man, and certainly not against the champion of the Nephilim, a race of giants – his skills came against both lion and bear. He had played a hand or two of sling poker and both he and God knew what the reasoned gamble would be. Each Biblical *hero* in actuality is similar to you and I – and by extension, God.

Though imagining God taking baby steps, is difficult, if not impossible for some people to do. God in a laboratory, blowing things up, just isn't a portrait most religious people are painting in their minds. Now, Gary Larson of The Far Side could imagine it, but the concept of God growing and experimenting and taking reasoned risks (gambling?) is a theological hurdle too tall or maybe too novel. But wait, isn't there Sacred Text somewhere that said God was born a babe, and then "grew in wisdom and stature, and in favor with God and men…"? I must be wrong, Luke 2:52, nor Isaiah 7:14 exist. Sorry.

God being born. God, a helpless baby wrapped in a rough horse blanket. God in a human form and with a tabula rasa – a blank slate. God having to learn and grow, and accumulate knowledge by learning and thru experience. God being held, then crawling, then toddling, then baby steps, then running… God taking measured risk. God gambling.

Such utter nonsense! Who would believe such a thing – God a helpless infant or learning sentient being. Hahaha. LOL – laugh out loud.

A dying seed, a dying star – but a dying God?

Sure. Because the seed doesn't die, it is transformed into a tree. Our sun that is currently burning up its hydrogen won't die, it will one day become a red giant. Likewise the red giant will someday be transformed by supernova into a blue star. And the dying God? He too had to die that life could come to many. Upon His death he became a savior, and after His resurrection he was transformed from a man into an immortal and a conqueror of death, hell and the grave – the King of Kings and Lord of Lords.

What a story. What an unbelievable fairy-tale. Or is it?

5
Prologue to Genesis – God Evolves (and the Earth between Genesis 1 & 2)

Prologue to Genesis – God Evolves (and the Earth between Genesis 1 & 2)

God.

Evolution.

Are the two mutually exclusive or can they be compatible?

How can God evolve? The religious person believes that God is alive; therefore, as a living entity, can he change like other organisms have and continue to do? Whether those changes in God are growth to a determined end-point, or a growth that is evolutionary, from one form/substance to another – does God change?

We are told that God doesn't change, that there is no variableness or turning (from one set being or personality to another), but does that makes sense from a Scriptural or logical point of view? Is it the change like that described by evolutionists, from an amoeba, to a single cell organism, and on and on from higher form to higher form of living species – eventually arriving to primates and "man." Is it the change the Bible describes whereby a human being that is saved by Jesus Christ can be transformed, and upon his/her death their mortal being is swallowed up in immortality and terrestrial takes on the garments of celestial power and glory thus achieving godhood? Can God and does God change, evolving over some known or unknown span of time or inter-dimensionality?

Is God alone, singular in His race, class, species etc.? Reviewing Scriptures we deduce that he may be sovereign (Psalm 24:7-10; Job 2; Romans 14:11; Revelation 19:11-16), but he is not the only ruler of this earth, let alone of the cosmos or dimensions (Ephesians 1:20-21; 6:11-12; Romans 8:38; Colossians 1:16).

In order to do justice to this subject matter, it is appropriate to go into the book of beginnings; the book of origin where all things began, called the book of Genesis. There in chapter 1:26-28, we see that God specially made and created "man" in His own image and gave him not only a royal position but a royal mandate, a mandate of dominion and mandate of sovereign rule. Man was created to rule the earth as God's representative possessing delegated power and authority, possessing delegated sovereignty.

We also can infer from Biblical examples that he delegates and grants earthly (Adam) and heavenly/spiritual (Michael, Gabriel, Lucifer, Lot's angels etc) authority. There are several types of dominion that come to mind – earthly/natural vs. earthly/natural, celestial/supernatural vs. celestial/supernatural (Daniel Chapter 10), and earthly/natural vs. celestial/supernatural. Men fighting with men and ruling over each other we know about; angelic warfare we have heard about; and lastly, the invisible battle between man and angel/spirit. A recitation of Saint Paul's description from Ephesians 6:11-12 is appropriate here;

"Put on the whole armour of God, that ye may be able to stand against the wiles of the devil. For we wrestle not against flesh and blood, but against principalities, against powers, against the rulers of the darkness of this world, against spiritual wickedness in high places."

The concept of principalities is understood by the Greek word *arche* meaning chief or ruler. These principalities are ruling entities possessing executive authority or governmental rule in the world. This ruling power usually involves a particular nation, people, race or dimension. There are contrary agents (aka evil spirits) ruling the kingdoms of the world that oppose God, and of which Satan is the chief prince or ruler, of both the world system and its organization of demons (Luke 4:5-7).

I Corinthians 15:22-28 declares that all antagonistic and derivative authority will at some point be subdued and placed [back – ed.] under one authority – Almighty God's;

For as in Adam all die, even so in Christ shall all be made alive. But every man in his own order: Christ the firstfruits; afterward they that are Christ's at his coming. Then cometh the end, when he shall have delivered up the kingdom to God, even the Father; when he shall have put down all rule and all authority and power. For he must reign, till he hath put all enemies under his feet. The last enemy that shall be destroyed is death. For he hath put all things under his feet. But when he saith all things are put under him, it is manifest that he is excepted, which did put all things under him. And when all things shall be subdued unto him, then shall the Son also himself be subject unto him that put all things under him, that God may be all in all.

Finally, in type and by nature we can see a historical pattern clearly established that suggests ruler/subject relationships – both among men and within nature. Communism may have been a noble concept, but in reality an abject failure. For millennia, men and women have rose up and become lords, leaders, rulers or powerbrokers in nearly every culture and civilization.

Will the need, necessity or urge to rule ever cease from within mankind? The Bible does speak of an age, or an era at the end of time where men, beasts and angels live at peace – yet still governed by rulers (Isaiah 2:2-4; 11:6-9; 65:20; Zechariah 14:9; Revelation 20:1-7). According to eschatology (the study of events related to the "Last Days"), at some point in the near future, an angel – the seventh angel – will come to the earth preparing faithful followers of Jesus Christ for their resurrection. Once this preparation is accomplished, a signal is given that the angel's work is done and the temporary reign of minor deities is over; **Rev 11:15 *"And the seventh angel sounded; and there were great voices in heaven, saying, The kingdoms of this world are become the kingdoms of our Lord, and of his Christ; and he shall reign forever and ever."***

As a matter of fact, to a select, elect few, it is promised that they will rule and reign with God during this period called "forever and ever", which is not eternity, rather it is a time span of one thousand years known as the Millennium. (Luke 19:17-19; 2 Timothy 2:11-13; Revelation 20:7).

On the day God came into being, was he as "good as it gets" from that point onward, never to change or improve or grow in any way, forever and ever, amen? Hmmm.

Maybe, maybe not. As mortal beings we really can only speculate and make assumptions based upon a few things; 1) our reasoning alone (faulty and limited at best), 2) our inferences based observation of things created (often described as God's first Bible), and for those Christian-Judeo adherents, we can additionally use 3) accepted Sacred text – generally "the Bible."

We mortals may gain understanding and insight as we study and meditate upon the notion of an evolving God, but most likely the absolute and definitive answer will elude us. Even if a life after death opens our eyes to this and other mysteries, and elevate us to untold heights and realms, God may yet go higher still – staying one step ahead of us. Much like a child that grows to adulthood to only discover that his knowledge base remains behind that of his parents and that his new life holds additional mysteries that only middle age will bring.

So when (and if) we arrive in heaven, the heaven above and beyond our heavens, will God go higher yet or remain behind with equals or with beings less advanced than he? And if less advanced, will we even be able to understand Him, or will he once again serve as a guide and elder brother? So many questions, such a dark mirror that we attempt to look through.

Evolution. To a conservative, traditional, Bible "believing" person, that term sounds so dirty, gritty, primordially soupy and speculative. Evolution to us appears to be uncertain, shaky, and iffy – like the prevarication told by an errant child, found out after raiding the cookie jar. Jar lid askew, crumbs on the counter and on his shirt front, chocolate smears on his hands and face, yet proclaiming with faux confidence the culprit isn't he.

I don't believe in the "creation." I don't believe in a Creator. I believe in a Big Bang that just happened and an ensuing cosmic rearrangement and by happenstance the appearance of life amidst a primordial soup. And from that soup a remarkable and almost impossible order occurs on a particular rock three planetary parking places away from an inconsequential dying star in a galaxy amidst billions of others. "No, mother, I did not take the cookie, really, honestly, I promise!" Uhuh. Alright, let's try and comprehend this theory (or experience if you prefer) through the lens of natural creation, our Earth and its fairly immediate cosmos.

Nature, God's First Bible

When Einstein said, "I am not interested in this phenomenon or that phenomenon, I want to know God thoughts,"[131] he did not open the Bible. He studied the stars and the physical laws that govern earth and the universe. As Albert Einstein lay on his deathbed, he asked only for his glasses, his writing implements and his latest equations. He knew he was dying, yet he continued his work. In those final hours of his life, while fading in and out of consciousness, he was working on what he hoped would be his greatest work of all. It was a project of monumental complexity. It was a project that he hoped would unlock the mind of God.

When he said he did not believe in God, he later confessed to believe in a God, just not the God of organized religion, which he felt was chaotic. He rightly believed that if God existed, he was orderly and logical, and could most likely be seen and understood by examining nature.

The heavens declare the glory of God, and the firmament displays his handiwork. Day to day utters speech, and night to night shows knowledge. There is no speech or language where their voice is not heard. Their line has gone out to all the earth and their words to the end of the world. (Psalms 19:1-4)

Early Christians believed that God speaks through nature. It was common for the earliest Christians to argue that the death of trees each winter and their rebirth to life in the spring was a testimony from God himself that there is a resurrection. Clement of Rome, appointed as an elder by the apostles and probably the earliest Christian writer outside of the New Testament writers, argues from the process of a fruit maturing that Christ will surely return. He describes the steps from losing its leaves through the bud and flower to the ripe fruit, and then uses it as proof of Christ's return just as though he were quoting a Scripture.[132] [133]

This is Scriptural. David, the Psalmist, tells us that both day and night testify to all the world. Saint Paul, after quoting David, tells us that "the invisible things of him from the creation of the world are clearly seen, being understood by the things that are made" (Romans 1:20). Followers of Jewish, Muslim and Christian faiths are required to learn from nature. Those who reject what nature says about God are "without excuse" in regards to understanding God's plans and gaining insight into His mind (Romans 1:20).

Naturally and spiritually, we know that things evolve. We are not born or born again into complete maturity. We have to grow. That growth comes the same way that life evolves in nature. It comes by suffering and adapting and even by death. We have clearly been given eyes, ears and senses to contact and communicate with the world in which we find ourselves living in.

Einstein was asked if he believed in God. His reply was to state; *"I'm not an atheist. I don't think I can call myself a pantheist. The problem involved is too vast for our limited minds. We are in the position of a little child entering a huge library filled with books in many languages. The child knows someone must have written those books. It does not know how. It does not understand the languages in which they are written. The child dimly suspects a mysterious order in the arrangement of the books but doesn't know what it is. That, it seems to me, is the attitude of even the most intelligent human being toward God. We see the universe marvelously arranged and obeying certain laws but only dimly understand these laws."*[134]

"Try and penetrate with our limited means the secrets of nature and you will find that, behind all the discernible laws and connections, there remains something subtle, intangible and inexplicable. Veneration for this force beyond anything that we can comprehend is my religion. To that extent I am, in fact, religious."[135]

The Bible says that God created the heavens and the Earth. Period. It does not actually say how long it took God, or how long God took to do this – it may indeed have been hundreds of millions of years or more. Regardless of the length of time for the heavens and the Earth to come into existence and then to become stable, during this time celestial, terrestrial, light, dark, angel, devil, man, beast, talking serpents[E], fish, fowl and creeping things all appeared and settled into their spiritual and cosmological order.

There is no *actual* conflict between the realities of scripture and nature, but sometimes there is a perceived conflict when we compare our interpretations of scripture and nature.

God created the heavens and the earth – and it was perfectly perfect. Or did he experiment and create progressively more complex living things, environments and eras, even visiting the pre-Adamic earth with totally cataclysmic destruction on at least one occasion?[136] [137] [138] Though the current earth and its inhabitants may be only six to ten thousand years old, the universe may be 10-15 billion years old and the earth itself is estimated to be 4.5 billion years old.[139]

Studying Scriptures leads us to understand that there were at least two floods and resulting cataclysm. One was pre-Adamic (ante-chaotic age – also called Lucifer's Flood) and the other was during the time of Noah (antediluvian age). Psalms 47:7-8 eloquently speaks of the time

---

[E] The serpent is believed to possibly be the missing link between man and primate. In Hebrew serpent is called *nachash*, which means "one that casts a spell using words." This serpent talked and was an upright creature that walked before it was cursed, it was also described as beautiful and very cunning. Early Jewish and Christian scholars believed the serpent to be close enough in physical and genetic composition to mingle its seed with Eve, and thus to produce offspring – Cain.

that God bested Lucifer and the other lords of the earth and empyreal realms:

The LORD sat as King at the flood; Yes, the LORD sits as King forever.[140]

The term "Lucifer's flood" is a theological way of talking about the fall of Satan and the cataclysm that came upon the earth and its inhabitants millions of years ago, most likely during the Earth's Tertiary Period. "Lucifer's flood", is the term used quite frequently by Dake who wrote *God's Plan for Man.*[141]

Please let me explain. In the beginning God created the heavens and the earth. Then, in Genesis verse 2, it said the earth was without form and void. In other words, in verse 1, God created the heavens and everything in them, including the sun, moon, and stars; then sometime between verses 1 and 2, Satan was cast out of heaven and fell to the earth. The Earth's inhabitations by Satan, combined with God's decision to reset/refresh the earth are some of the causative factors on it becoming void.

The Apostle Peter said that the earth that then was, before Adam was created, was overthrown by a flood; then God created a new heaven and earth because the first ones became void. Then He created Adam and told him to replenish the earth. *Replenish* – to populate again, to make plentiful again.

The following verses talk about the fall of Satan, and the earth becoming void. Remember that when these scriptures talk about the earth becoming void, it is talking about the earth's social system and animal life that then was, which was destroyed; not plant or botany life, nor planet earth itself. (2 Peter 3; Revelation 12; Genesis 1:1-2; Isaiah 14:12-14; Jeremiah 4:23-26; Ezekiel 28:11-17; Luke 10:18).

In the Scofield Reference Bible (Genesis 1:11), this explanation is found:

It is by no means necessary to suppose that the life-germ of seeds perished in the catastrophic judgment which overthrew the primitive order. With the restoration of dry land and light the earth would "bring forth" as described. It was "animal" life which perished, the traces of which remain as fossils. Relegate fossils to the primitive creation, and no conflict of science with the Genesis cosmogony remains.

It is not a novel belief that the creation account in Genesis Chapter Two is different and separate from the creation account in Genesis Chapter One, and that there was a gap of time in the Biblical account that lasted an unknown number of years. Christian theologians such as Cyrus C.I. Scofield, G.H. Pember, and Clarence Larkin firmly believed this theory, and wrote extensively about it. Scofield[142] even compiled a study Bible that was widely popular and revered among many Protestants. Canadian physiologist Arthur Custance has argued that the belief can be traced back to biblical times, citing the Targum of Onkelos (2nd c. BC), Akiba ben Joseph's *Sefer Hazzohar* (1st c. AD), Origen's *De Principiis* (3rd c. AD), and Caedmon (7th c. AD).

Why the old "world that then was" ended, and why God made a new world and modern Man, requires a study into the ancient origins of Satan and the Angels. The Earth has an ancient natural history that can be deciphered from the geologic record, but it also has an equally important ancient spiritual history that can only be deciphered from Rightly-Dividing the Holy Bible. Knowledge of both is required to correctly reconcile Geology and the Book of Genesis.

Suffice it to say, the answer to an age-old paradox explains why battles end: What happens when an irresistible force meets an immovable object? According to the Theory of Relativity, we live in a Universe where both cannot exist simultaneously. If there were an irresistible force (God), the same Universe could not contain an immovable, implacable object. Thus, there can only be one Lord of Lords and King of Kings. The Greeks called him Kouros, the Jews call him YHWH Tseva'ot – the Lord of ALL armies.

Filling in the Gap between Genesis One and Two

"In the beginning God created the heaven and the earth." (Genesis 1:1 KJV)

"And the earth was without form, and void; and darkness was upon the face of the deep.

And the Spirit of God moved upon the face of the waters." (Genesis 1:2 KJV)

Is there a time-gap between the first two verses of Genesis? A lesser known interpretation of the Genesis narrative exists, which does not contradict the scientific evidence for an Old Earth. Commonly called the "Gap Theory" or Ruin-Reconstruction interpretation, it is a theology much older than Darwin and the Theory of Evolution. It is based on the Scriptural fact that in the second verse of Genesis, the Bible simply and clearly states that the planet Earth was already here (but in a ruined state) before the creative process of the seven days even begins. To understanding this Biblical mystery, we begin with the precise wording of this New Testament cross-reference:

> *"For this they willingly are ignorant of, that by the word of God the heavens were of old, and the earth standing out of the water and in the water: Whereby the world that then was, being overflowed with water, perished: But the heavens and the earth, which are now, by the same word are kept in store, reserved unto fire against the day of judgment and perdition of ungodly men."* (2 Peter 3:5-7 KJV)

Contrary to popular interpretation, the above passage is NOT a reference to Noah's flood. And the only other place in the Bible where the Earth was covered in waters is Genesis 1:2. The ramifications are obvious: The literal wording suggests that the "heavens and the earth, which are now" (made during the seven days) was not the first-time creation of all things as is traditionally assumed. The Scriptures appear to be telling the reader there was a previous populated world on the face of this old Earth before God formed the present world of modern Man.

The Bible itself provides insight into a great mystery in Earth's natural history at what is known as the Pleistocene - Holocene boundary. Science remains at a loss to definitively explain the Ice Age and the anomaly of the mysterious mega fauna extinctions across the face of the Earth about 12,000 to 10,000 Radio Carbon years ago. Geologic evidence from that period indicates extraordinary global massive volcanism, gigantic tidal waves, seismic activity on a vast scale, and extreme climate swings on the Earth over a geologically brief period of time. It is no coincidence that the Bible at Genesis 1:2 describes the Earth as flooded, desolate, and in darkness in the timeframe closely corresponding to these catastrophic events in the Earth's natural history. Many believe these two mysteries are linked.

Semantics: Sometimes Splitting Hairs Does Matter

The generally accepted belief among Christians regarding the first chapter of Genesis is that the very first verse is a basic introduction or premise, and that the following works which are done in the six days explain it. The writer having mentioned when God created the heavens and the earth, then continues by telling what condition the earth is in and how God day after day creates light, air, earth, plants, animals, and so forth. Such is the popular view as to how Genesis 1 narrates the creation story and how the universe was created out of waste and void. Yet those who carefully study the first chapter of Scripture hold this interpretation to be inaccurate. Due to this incorrect interpretation and not due to the Bible's narration itself, great controversy has arisen between the church and the world.

In the original Hebrew, this initial verse of the first chapter of Genesis contains seven words which carry within themselves a sense of independence. These words do not say that in the beginning God "formed" or "made" the world out of certain raw materials. No, the heavens and the earth were *created*. This word "created" is "bara" in the original.

So that in the beginning God *bara* the heavens and the earth. This word "bara" is used three more times in Genesis 1 and 2: (1st) "And God created [bara] the great sea-monsters, and every living creature that moveth, wherewith the waters swarmed, after their kind, and every winged bird after its kind" (1:21); (2nd) "And God created [bara] man in his own image, in the image of God created he him; male and female created he them" (1:27); and (3rd) "And God blessed the seventh day, and hallowed it; because that in it he rested from all his work which God had created [bara] and made" (2:3). To "create" is to "call the things that are not, as though they were" (Romans 4:17). These sea-monsters and living things not only had physical bodies but also had an animated life within them. They therefore required a direct creative act of God. In similar manner, though man's body was formed out of the dust of the ground, his soul and spirit could not be made out of any physical material, and hence the Bible declared that "God created man in his own image."

In the first two chapters of Genesis three different words are used for the act of creation: (1) "bara"—calling into being without the aid of pre-existing material. This we have already touched upon; (2) "asah"—which is quite different from "bara," since the latter denotes the idea of creating without any material whereas "asah" signifies the making, fashioning, or preparing out of existing material. For instance, a carpenter can *make* a chair, but he cannot *create* one. The works of the Six Days in Genesis are mainly of the order of "asah"; (3) "yatsar"—which means to shape or mold as a potter does with clay. This word is used in Genesis 2:7 as follows: "And Jehovah God formed man of the dust of the ground."

The words "In the beginning" reinforce the thought of God creating the heavens and the earth out of nothing. This heaven is not the firmament immediately surrounding the earth; rather, it points to the heaven where the stars are. What significant changes the heavens have incurred since they were created are speculative, but the earth is no longer the same.

To understand the first chapter of Genesis, it is of utmost importance that we distinguish the "earth" mentioned in verse 1 from the "earth" spoken of in verse 2. For the condition of the earth referred to in verse 2 is not what God had created originally. Now we know that "God is not a God of confusion" (1 Corinthians 14:33). And hence when it states that in the beginning God created the earth, what He created was therefore perfect. So that the waste and void of the earth spoken of in verse 2 was not the original condition of the earth as God first created it. Would God ever create an earth whose primeval condition would be waste and void? A true understanding of this verse will solve the apparent problem.

"Thus saith Jehovah that created the heavens, the God that formed the earth and made it, that established it and created it not a waste, that formed it to be inhabited: I am Jehovah; and there is none else" (Is. 45:18). How clear God's word is. The word "waste" here is "tohu" in Hebrew, which signifies "desolation" or "that which is desolate." It says here that the earth which God created was not a waste. Why then does Genesis 1:2 state that "the earth was waste"? This may be easily resolved. In the beginning God created the heavens and the earth (Genesis 1:1). At that time, the earth which God had created was *not* a waste; but *later on*, in passing through a great catastrophe, the earth *did* become waste and void. So that all which is mentioned from verse 3 onward does not refer to the original creation but to the *restoration of the earth.* God created the heavens and the earth in the beginning; but He subsequently used the Six Days to remake the earth habitable. Genesis 1:1 was the original world; Genesis 1:3 onward is our present world; while Genesis 1:2 describes the desolate condition which was the Earth's during the transitional period following its original creation and before our present world. Such an interpretation cannot only be arrived at on the basis of Isaiah 45:18, but other evidences as well. [143] [F]

This notion of falling from an original pristine condition, to a fallen one and then on to restoration appears to be *the* central theme of the

[F] God is a thoughtful architect and everything he does is sound, so a newly created earth from the hand of God shouldn't have been without form and void and shrouded in darkness. Deuteronomy 32:4, Isaiah 45:18 1 John 1:5; The Holy Spirit was "renewing" the face of the earth as he hovered over the face of the waters. Psalms 104:30; Angels already existed in a state of grace when God "laid the foundations of the Earth", so there had been at least one creative act of God before the six days of Genesis. Job 38:4-7; Satan had fallen from grace "in the beginning" which, since the serpent tempted Adam and Eve and subsequently seduced Eve, had to have occurred before the fall of man. Isaiah 14:12-15, Ezekiel 28:11-19, John 8:44

Bible and of God's "Plan of Salvation." Jesus says in Luke 19:10; "The Son of Man is come to seek and to save that which was lost." In the Greek, "lost" means "marred" – damaged, disfigured, in ruins. It appears to me that after Genesis 1:1, God's business, if we could use such a term, would be that of shaping, forming, molding and ultimately of restoring – not of creating.

The more we study Genesis 1, the more convincing the above argument is true. In the first day, God commanded light to shine forth. Before this first day, the earth had already been existing, but it was now buried in water, dwelt in darkness, and was waste and void. On the third day, God did not create the earth. He merely commanded it to come out of water. On the first day, God did not *create* light, He instead commanded light to shine out of darkness. The light was already there. Neither did God create heaven on the second day. The heaven here is not the starry heaven but the atmospheric heaven, that which surrounds the earth. There was no need to create but simply to remake.

"In the beginning God created the heavens and the earth." Note that there is no detailed description here. We therefore do not know whether the original heaven and earth were created instantaneously or through many ages. Was it done in thousands of years or in millions of years? What were the earth's original rotation lines? Did the earth shift off its first axis, begin to wobble and reel to-and-fro like a drunk man?[144] Were the continents connected together, and then drifted over time due to natural and catastrophic forces?

We only know that God created the heavens and the earth in the beginning. Neither do we know how many years elapsed between the time of the first verse and that of the second verse of Genesis 1. We do not know when God created the heavens and the earth, nor do we know how long was the period after the original creation that the desolation described in verse 2 occurred. But we do believe that the original, perfect creation must have passed through many many years before it became waste and void. Such a long period would be enough to cover the so-called pre-historic age. All the years which geology demands and all the so-called geologic periods which it distributes among those years can fall into this time frame. We do not know how long the earth underwent change nor how many changes there were before it became waste and void because the Scriptures do not tell us these things. Yet we *can* affirm that the Bible never states that the *age of the earth* is but six thousand years in length. It merely shows that the *history of man* is approximately six thousand years old.

So, accepting that certain facts about the past and the age of the Earth have been omitted from the Genesis account; specifically that there was a gap of time in the Biblical account that lasted an unknown number of years between a first creation in Genesis 1:1 and a second creation in Genesis 1:2-31. By positing such an event, various observations in a wide range of fields, including the age of the Earth, the age of the universe, dinosaurs, pre-historic humanoids, fossils, ice cores, ice ages, and geological formations are allowed to have occurred as outlined by science without contradicting a belief in the Scriptures' divine inspiration.

Not Yo Momma's God

If we look at creation, the known and even speculated upon universe, a different portrayal of God is presented. He is not the neatly packaged One told to us by the silver-haired ladies in Bible School 101. What unfolds is a God with personal complexity, depth and variability, not a one-dimensional caricature deity. Rather, God is seen as speculative, passionate, remorseful, resentful, daring and multi-dimensional. Truly mankind's Papa – Papa God.

Wait. Back up. I just said variability. The dogmatic say that God never changes, nor is there any variability in or with Him. Scriptural references[145] are given for their position, but a scripture taken at face value (Gk: rhema - words) isn't the same as a scripture used with the understanding that comes with insightful revelation (Gk: logos – words with meaning). For example, if I asked my son to "fill my car up." He may take my request at face value and place books, bags, pots & pans and other items inside the vehicle until it is "full." He has taken my words, the rhema of my dialogue, and attempted to satisfy my request. On the other hand, if he knows me well, and has been exposed to personal and cultural details of my life, he will comply with the intent or logos of my words and put gasoline in my car's tank.

The earth, let alone the universe is complex, its development and formation show great change, variation and upward progression of complex life development (dare I say evolution?). It is this same earth that is described as the mirror in which to behold and understand God, a God not completely unlike us.

In caricature form, the great and mighty God above and beyond the mortal pale may inspire fear and obedience. He may inspire the lesser life forms, created beings to build and dedicate temple, obelisk and other monuments to His grandeur – but the personality of a distant, incomprehensible, emotionally disconnected higher power isn't conducive to an intimate personal relationship.

We want, no, we need a personal God to satisfy the really deep longing at the very recess of our being. Nothing else will do, we need love. The group *Sixpence None the Richer* articulated this need so well in their song "I Need Love;"

I need love
not some sentimental prison
I need God
not the political church
I need fire
to melt this frozen sea inside me
I need love

We need love – does God?

6 The Greatest Gamble of All – Free Will

The Greatest Gamble of All – Free Will

Choice. Choice is the power, right or freedom to choose what to do, what to think and what to believe. Even when it appears all choices have been removed from us, in truth, choice remains. Choice appears to be such an intrinsic part of the human fabric that if all else was lost or taken away, choice would remain. It is the last and ultimate of human freedoms. Viktor Frankl penned this powerful sentiment in his classic semi-autobiography, *Man's Search for Meaning*[146]:

> *We who lived in concentration camps can remember the men who walked through the huts comforting others, giving away their last piece of bread. They may have been few in number, but they offer sufficient proof that everything can be taken from a man but one thing: the last of the human freedoms -- to choose one's attitude in any given set of circumstances, to choose one's own way.*

At every stage of creation, God, as an artist made choices that resulted in limitations. Similar to Michelangelo choosing to paint the Sistine Chapel, rather than doing reliefs or sculptures – limiting him to what he could and could not reveal of the images in his mind's eye.

In Genesis, God makes his final choices – on the sixth day man and woman came into being. They were different than other entities; they were made in the likeness of God and designed to reflect characteristics and attributes that were in Him. They were to be like a mirror, expressing a spiritual being to an earthly world. Alone of all the other creatures motivated by instinct, humans were given a moral capacity to make choices – they could choose a path or course of action for themselves that was counterproductive to their well-being and survival. All other species followed innate drives; the geese would fly south in winter, the salmon would return to its birthplace to spawn, the female penguins would perform their long, long trek while the males kept watch over their egg – in a word, they would do what they were programmed to do. No rebellion. No second-guessing. No identity crisis.

Only man had a free moral capacity to rebel against his creator. The painting could push away the painter's hand; the actors could rewrite the script – man was free. And man's freedom was a huge risk. Man was God's risk. As Soren Kierkegaard said, "God has, so to speak, imprisoned himself in his resolve."

Imagine if we could have heard the inner dialogue that ran through God's mind during this thrilling and wonderful time, it may have sounded something like this:

"If I create a perfect world, I know how it will turn out. In its absolute perfection, it will revolve like a perfect machine, never deviating from my absolute will. But what if I create a universe that is free, free even of me? What if I veil my divinity so that the creatures are free to pursue their individual lives without being overwhelmed by my overpowering presence? Will creatures love me? Can I be loved by creatures whom I have not programmed...? Can love arise out of freedom?"

"But if I introduce freedom into this universe, I take the risk of introducing evil into it as well, for if they are free, then they are free to deviate from my will. Hmmm. But what if I continue to interact with this dynamic universe, what if I and the creatures become creators together of a great cosmic play? What if I join with them in the world of limitation and form, the world of suffering and evil? Ahh, in a truly free universe, even I do not know how it will turn out. Do even I dare to take that risk for love?"[147]

Scientia media, or middle knowledge,[148] presents a picture of divine omniscience which includes not only knowledge of the past, present and future, but also knowledge of conditional future contingents (propositions which refer to how free creatures will choose in various circumstances), counterfactuals (propositions which refer to how things would actually be if circumstances were different than they are or will be), and counterfactuals of creaturely freedom (propositions which refer to what a free creature would have chosen (freely) to do if things had been different). This knowledge, together with natural knowledge, informs God's decision about what He will do with reference to creation.

Middle knowledge affords God comprehensive knowledge of the future (when taken with both His natural and free knowledge), and of how creatures will exercise their freedom when faced with decisions, and since that knowledge is used by God in determining how He will providentially guide the world; though God may initially be surprised, He specifically can plan for everything that will occur. With the concept of middle knowledge, creaturely freedom requires risk on the part of God.

Not only does God know exactly how the world really is, He also knows the way the world would be if events were different. A great example of this is in Acts 27:21-32 where Paul is aboard a ship in a great storm. He there delivers a prophecy given by God saying "there will be no loss of life among you, but only of the ship." However, some of the sailors sought to escape. Paul then warns them that "unless these men stay in the ship, you cannot be saved." Paul knew that all aboard would be saved. But if events were different, he knew that the outcome would be different and the prophecy would be false.

Consider a concrete case within Christianity. Jesus said to Peter: "Truly, I say to you, this very night, before the cock crows, you will deny me three times" (Matthew 26:34, RSV). Let us assume that the denial and obedience are essentially free acts.[149] Can we not account for this by simple foreknowledge? Jesus foreknows that Peter will deny him three times. And so he says this to Peter. This seems simple and unproblematic, assuming foreknowledge is unproblematic.

God needs, I will assume, complete certainty when issuing prophecies. Scripture is clear on the complete reliability of God. I will assume that it also will not do to suppose that God is 99% sure that Peter will freely deny him, and in the unlikely 1% case, God is committed to *forcing* Peter (or allowing a non-free devil to force him) to non-freely deny God. Thus, God's belief that Peter will deny him must be responsive to Peter's choice.

Observe that in the Biblical account after the cock crowed, "Peter remembered the saying of Jesus, 'Before the cock crows, you will deny me three times.' And he went out and wept bitterly" (Matthew 26:75, RSV). This implies that Peter had *forgotten* the saying of Jesus when he denied Jesus. Thus Peter was making his decision whether to deny Jesus as if the prophecy had not even been made. Then why make the argument at all you might ask?

It may be that as the moment drew nearer for him to leave his limited body of earthly matter, as well as time and space to reenter a spiritual, heavenly realm he lost human limitations and knew all things as only God could know.

Some forget that there is a vertical dimension to Christian spirituality – the urge to leave this bag of bones, the self we normally think of as ourselves and realize a unity with the Sacred Dimension of Timelessness.

The symbolism of the cross reflects an ultimate truth – that we all are suspended between these two dimensions, the horizontal and vertical, the temporal and the eternal. In this realm of time and space we are born, we evolve in consciousness, we suffer the agony and ecstasy of life, give our lives to serving the purposes of the universe and then when our physical bodies die – we "shuffle off this mortal coil" to quote Shakespeare.

In this realm physical death is real. Jesus was crucified and died as the ancient Creed puts it. But in the vertical dimension of timelessness death has no reality – there is only the timelessness of Eternal life.

Another reason for the contemporary and imminent prophecies given may be that Jesus wanted to give Peter a memory which would help guide him back to faith – a memory where Jesus knows he will be betrayed, yet speaks this prophecy to him in gentleness and without recrimination?

Finally, it may have simply been another opportunity to predict an outcome based upon his *Scientia media* (middle knowledge), and gamble yet again.

But this begs the question, why gamble so recklessly with a creation that may have taken 15 billion years to come to fruition? Why dare to take that risk – for love or otherwise? Because God was a gambler.

> *"Perhaps we do not realize the problem, so to call it, of enabling finite free wills to co-exist with Omnipotence. It seems to involve at every moment almost a sort of "divine abdication."* – C.S. Lewis

In the 1990's D. Brian Shafer wrote a series called "Chronicles of The Host."[150] The four books are a fictionalized re-telling of the Old Testament and the Gospels from the point of view of the angels. The first book's subject, its title is "Exile of Lucifer" Reading an account of Lucifer's story is sort of like watching "Titanic", we all know what will happen, but we want to see it happen. Shafer creates a vivid, colorful Heaven full of angels. They live and do the work of The Lord in various ways and even have an Academy, a place to be educated and discuss the ways and will of The Almighty.

The reader is introduced to Lucifer, worship leader and songwriter for the Host, and his aide Serus. The Lord is appointing a new class of angel, the archangel. Michael has been given his new rank and Lucifer is busy writing music for Gabriel's ceremony.

Lucifer is a gifted worship leader, beautiful and awe-inspiring. "God had so created Lucifer that holy praise manifested from his very being, and one could not spend a length of time with him and not feel compelled to worship The Almighty." (p. 13) Lucifer heads up an angelic

Council, one that discusses and resolves issues brought up in the body of the Host. The major issue of late has been the upcoming Creation. God was going to produce a new world, and would appoint some creature to represent Him. The natural choice would be an angel, right? Lucifer is highly favored by a full third of the Host to be God's representative on this new world.

At the Academy, changes have been taking place and a division has been growing among the wisdom angels. The topic of God's sovereignty and His gift of free will have been widely and hotly discussed. Are angels bound to follow a narrow definition of God's will or does the freedom to choose indicate that God wants angels to follow their own will?

Free will and its practice, is a long-argued and hotly debated topic among those who would want to understand God. God gives us the power to obey Him or go our own way, to love Him, be indifferent, or outright hostile to Him. Other than man, the whole universe in all its immensity is exactly the way God commands it to be. In the entire universe, only man can choose to stand opposed to the will of God.

At some point in the long workings of time, the creature called man emerges, flesh, blood, bone, into whom his Creator breathes a soul, and the essence of this soul is the endowment of freedom of choice, the pledge of His love... Indeed we may say, that evil is a necessity, since if there were only good there would be only good to choose, and that would actually be no choice.

So we highly evolved spiritual beings always make the correct choices, right? Don't we wish – wish we could take back the many awful decisions we have made over the course of our lifetime. We wish we didn't sin, or confuse the truly or divinely good with what the fallen Son of the Morning represents as a higher good. Of course, there is no higher good than God's good, but, in our blindness, in the fleshly net that exalts mere appetite, in the credulity of our fallen state -- we may all too often succumb to the diabolic skill and cunning, accepting the ugly as beautiful, the false as true, and the evil as good. But that's the point isn't it? We have this great and divine gift of freedom and choice to chase demon's pleasure or to perceive the truly and beautifully good and to pursue the struggle.

Man was made by God in His own image. God made man without flaw, but also free to become flawed. Yet the flaws are reversible, the return to perfection is possible. If we call ourselves, sometimes with great justice, "miserable sinners," we must remember that we have willed ourselves to be so, that this is not the state that the Divine Creator has imposed upon us; that this fallen, scarred, wounded, sinful estate is the working of free will. But that free will which enables us to sin is the most glorious gift of the Heavenly Father. This is, in a word, the meaning of our human life - if we can but learn to accept His free gift of grace and then join our free will to His, and not to that of the Adversary.

But, we often ask (usually in frustration), "what does God want from us?"

When we talk of a man doing anything for God or giving anything to God, I will tell you what it is really like. It is like a small child going to his father and saying, "Daddy, give me sixpence to buy you a birthday present." Of course, the father does, and he is pleased with the child's present. It is all very nice and proper, but only an idiot would think that the father is sixpence to the good on the transaction. – C.S. Lewis, Mere Christianity

I don't think God needs much – Hmmm, can we build Him a home?[151] The entire universe is God's. We exist in His home. There is no object we can give or make for God that He could use. There is no material in the universe that did not come from God in the first place. Maybe we could bake Him a cake? Nah. Giving God something He has created, made or fashioned doesn't make much sense, unless…

Unless, the giving involves something more than the gift itself…

There is only one thing that we can give to God, love. A non-coerced, from the heart, free-will, unconditional love. "I love you Lord because I want to – even if you walked away from me, took away salvation, left me crippled and hurting inside and ultimately sent me to Hell. I love you."

Putting aside the multi-millennia debate over determinism[G], I say, giving man the gift of free will for the sake of love was God's greatest risk. Vive grâce! Vive l'amour!

So is God a gambler? Other than risking His Kingdom for love ("It is the Father's good pleasure to give you the Kingdom..." Luke 12:32), there is that small issue of prophecy.

[G] Augustine (*De Libero Arbitrio – On Free Choice of the Will*) holds that though men have the freedom to choose between good and evil, and so are responsible for their good deeds and wicked actions; so that their actions deserve praise and blame, reward and punishment, nevertheless they cannot consistently do right and follow the goodness without grace. Free will *and* grace – Arminianism *and* Calvinism – both.

7 The Watchmaker Analogy – The Probability of Life on Earth

The Probability of Life on Earth

Could life on earth be the product of a watchmaker? Or could it be strictly the result of blind chance?

Some scientists have concluded that earth may be the only planet in the universe that harbors life because the conditions necessary for life are so exacting that the possibility of life on other planets is infinitesimal.

Extraterrestrial life has been one of the major topics of science fiction since the advent of the genre. Since the dawn of time humans have looked to the stars and wondered if there is life beyond our own Earth.

Earth is unique in the Solar System as being the only planet which is able to support life in all its forms: from basic living micro-organisms to highly sophisticated and intelligent human beings. There are many reasons why this happens. To exist, life has three main requirements: a medium that allows for chemical reactions to occur, chemical elements (such as carbon, hydrogen, nitrogen, oxygen, sulfur, and phosphorus), and a source of energy (the Sun) and relative position. The last two requirements are readily available throughout the universe. On Earth, liquid water is the essential medium for the types of chemical reactions needed to create and sustain life as we know it.

Scientists today are using what we know about life on Earth to determine what requirements and criteria are necessary for life to exist on other planets in the universe. Regions that scientists believe to be the most likely sites for the evolution of life on planets are known as habitable zones. There are two habitable zones that are often considered. These are the circumstellar and the galactic habitable zones.

The circumstellar habitable zone is a donut-shaped region around a star where the warmth from the star is conducive to the existence of liquid water. Too close, and liquid water would evaporate from the planet. Too far, and water freezes and cannot participate in the chemical reactions that spark life. But in this our circumstellar habitable zone, the temperature is just right. Liquid water is believed to be the first requirement for life as we know it.

However, not all planets that reside in the habitable zone will necessarily harbor life. If a planet is very massive, like Jupiter, it will be a gas giant planet without a solid surface for oceans. If a planet is too small, it will not have enough gravity and its inventory of water will evaporate away. A good example is our Moon, which is certainly located in the habitable zone of the Sun, but could not retain an atmosphere or liquid water. So, evolution of life as we know it requires a planet that ranges from the size of Mars to a couple times the size of the Earth and orbits at a distance from its host star where liquid water could exist.

Life-sustaining Water

So many of earth's forms of life are dependent on an environment in which liquid water is stable. This means that earth must not be too close or too far from the sun. Astronomers estimate that, if the distance from earth to the sun changed by as little as 2-5 percent, all life would be extinguished as water either froze or evaporated.[152]

Another factor making life on earth possible is frozen water's set of unusual characteristics. Ice is such a common substance that most of us do not stop to consider that the balance of life depends on the simple chemical properties of ice.

Ice is one of the few substances that expands when frozen. Most substances when frozen become more dense and sink when placed in a container of the same substance in liquid form. But not ice. Since water expands by one tenth its volume when frozen, frozen water has the unusual characteristic of floating on top of liquid water. When rivers and lakes freeze in the winter, they freeze from the top down. If ice acted like almost all other compounds, it would sink, and rivers and lakes would freeze from the bottom up. All bodies of water would eventually become solid bodies of ice, eliminating most life as we know it.

Astronomer Hugh Ross points out some of the other ways earth is perfectly balanced for life to exist: "As biochemists now concede, for life molecules to operate so that organisms can live requires an environment where liquid water is stable. This means that a planet cannot be too close to its star or too far away. In the case of planet Earth, a change in the distance from the sun as small as 2 percent would rid the planet of all life.[153]

"The rotation period of a life-supporting planet cannot be changed by more than a few percent. If the planet takes too long to rotate, temperature differences between day and night will be too great. On the other hand, if the planet rotates too rapidly, wind velocities will rise to catastrophic levels. A quiet day on Jupiter (rotation period of ten hours), for example, generates thousand mph winds . . ."[154]

In contrast to Jupiter's 10-hour rotation, our neighboring planet Venus rotates once every 243 days. If earth's rotation took as long, plant life would be impossible because of the extended darkness and extremes of heat and cold from such long days and nights.

Earth's Atmosphere - Oxygen

Earth's atmosphere is one way our planet is finely tuned for life. No other planet in our solar system has anything remotely like it. High in the atmosphere, ozone blocks cancer-causing radiation emanating from the sun. The atmosphere shields us from meteors, burning up the overwhelming majority long before they reach earth. Otherwise they would cause great damage and loss of life.

Our atmosphere contains a mixture of gases in perfect proportions to sustain life. Oxygen makes up 21 percent of our air. Without oxygen, all animate life - including humans - would die in minutes. But too much oxygen is toxic and makes combustible materials more flammable. If the proportion of oxygen in the air increased to only 24 percent, destructive fires would frequently break out and be much harder to bring under control. Objects around us could literally burst into flame.

Nitrogen, making up 78 percent of earth's atmosphere, dilutes the oxygen and serves a vital function as a fertilizer for plants. During thunderstorms millions of lightning bolts around the earth each day combine some nitrogen with oxygen, creating compounds that are then washed to earth by rain, where they can be utilized by plants.

Moderate amounts of carbon dioxide make up much of the rest of our atmosphere. Without it plant life would be impossible. Plants require carbon dioxide, which they take in while giving off oxygen. Animals and humans are the opposite, breathing in oxygen and exhaling carbon dioxide. Plant life sustains human and animal life and vice versa in a magnificent, precise, self-sustaining cycle.

Even the thickness of the earth's crust plays a part in regulating our atmosphere. If earth's crust were much thicker, it would hoard oxygen below the surface as oxides. But a thinner crust would leave us susceptible to frequent earthquakes and devastating volcanoes that would permeate our atmosphere with volcanic ash.

How important is the precise balance in our atmosphere? Our neighboring planet Venus suffers from what is thought to be a runaway greenhouse effect in which heat is trapped and cannot escape. One NASA astronomer noted that our sterile, lifeless moon "is a friendly place compared to Venus, where, from skies forty kilometers high a rain of concentrated sulfuric acid falls toward a surface that is as hot as boiling lead".[155]

Earth's Size, Position and Elemental Composition

Another condition that makes the earth hospitable for life is its size, which determines its gravity and in turn affects its atmosphere. If earth were only a little larger, making its gravity slightly stronger, hydrogen, a light gas, would be unable to escape earth's gravity and would collect in our atmosphere, making it inhospitable to life. Yet, if earth were only slightly smaller, oxygen—necessary for life—would escape, and water would evaporate. Thus, if earth were slightly larger or smaller, human life could not have existed on earth.

The earth travels through space at 66,600 miles an hour as it orbits the sun. That speed perfectly offsets the sun's gravitational pull and keeps earth's orbit the proper distance from the sun. If earth's speed were less, it would be gradually pulled toward the sun, eventually scorching and extinguishing life. Mercury, the planet closest to the sun, has a daytime temperature of about 600 degrees Fahrenheit.

On the other hand, if earth's speed were greater, it would in time move farther away from the sun to become a frozen wasteland like Pluto, with a temperature of about minus -300 degrees, also eliminating all life.

As earth rotates in its orbit, it is tilted at a 23.5-degree angle relative to the sun. Although not a direct factor in whether life is possible, the angle creates the change of seasons we are able to enjoy. Were the earth not tilted, our climate would always be the same, with no change of seasons. If the tilt were greater, summers would be hotter and winters much colder, wreaking havoc on plant cycles and agriculture.

If Earth were only a half of a percent closer to the sun, we would experience a run-away greenhouse effect. If as little as four percent closer to the sun, oceans never would have condensed and Earth's climate would have moved toward the inhospitable hothouse of Venus. If it were only one percent farther from the sun, Earth would become a frozen ice planet like Mars and the outer planets, and atmospheric greenhouse gases would become denser. Lungs could not function under higher air pressures than those found at Earth's surface.[156]

Our Amazing Solar System

Dr. Hugh Ross, Founder of *Reasons to Believe* describes how other planets in our solar system play a vital role in preserving life on earth: "Late in 1993, planetary scientists George Wetherell, of the Carnegie Institution of Washington, D.C., made an exciting discovery about our solar system. In observing computer simulations of our solar system, he found that without a Jupiter-sized planet positioned just where it is, Earth would be struck about a thousand times more frequently than it is already by comets and debris. Without Jupiter, impacts such as the one that may have wiped out the dinosaurs would be common.

Here is how the protection system works. Jupiter is two and a half times more massive than all the other planets combined. Because of its huge mass, thus huge gravity, and its location between the earth and the cloud of comets surrounding the solar system, Jupiter either draws comets (by gravity) to collide with itself, as it did in July 1994, or, more commonly, it deflects comets (again by gravity) right out of the solar system. In Wetherell's words, if it were not for Jupiter, 'we wouldn't be around to study the origin of the solar system.'

Neither would we be around if it were not for the very high regularity in the orbits of both Jupiter and Saturn. French astrophysicist Jacques Laskar determined that if the outer planets were less [orbitally] regular, then the inner planets' motions would be chaotic, and Earth would suffer orbital changes so extreme as to disrupt its climatic stability. In other words, Earth's climate would be unsuitable for life . . . Thus even the characteristics of Jupiter and Saturn's orbits must fit within certain narrowly defined ranges for life on Earth to be possible.

Our Sun deviates little from its circular orbit around the center of the Milky Way or from the plane of our galaxy's disk.[157] The other stars in our galaxy exhibit large deviations from their orbital paths in up and down, back and forth, and side to side random motions. The Sun's slight orbital deviations of just 13.4 kilometers per second keep our solar system from getting too close to the spiral arms[158 159] and protect us from the deadly radiation from our galaxy's nucleus and cataclysmic deaths of nearby stars. Our Sun appears to be an average star.

However, to be capable of having a planet suited to life as we know it, scientists currently believe that the sun could be no more than 17% smaller or 10% larger.

The moon plays a critical role for life as well. Our moon is unique among solar system bodies in that it is so large relative to its planet. As a result, our moon exerts a significant gravitational pull on Earth.[160] Thanks to this pull, coastal sea waters are cleansed and their nutrients replenished, also the obliquity (tilt of the rotation axis relative to the orbital plane) of Earth is stabilized (a critical factor for avoiding climatic extremes) . . . So we see that Earth is prepared for life through a variety of finely tuned characteristics of our galaxy, star, planet, and moon.

"This discussion by no means exhausts the list of characteristics that must be fine tuned for life to exist. The astronomical literature now includes discussions on more than forty different characteristics that must take on narrowly defined values. And this list grows longer with every new year of research".[161]

No wonder the Genesis creation account concludes with this summary of God's handiwork: "Then God saw everything that He had made, and behold it was very good" (Genesis 1:31).

The miraculous parameters for life on earth are fine-tuned into the laws that govern not only our solar system, but also the universe. Not long ago astrophysicist Carl Sagan estimated there were millions of planets in our galaxy capable of sustaining life. But the many parameters for life on earth render Sagan's estimates sheer speculation. Thus, Professor Ben Zuckerman, an evolutionist at UCLA, countered that Earth is unique in our entire galaxy.[162] In calculating the probability of the existence of a planet like Earth, the probability is 1 chance in 10^{99} for just seventy-five parameters to occur simultaneously by chance.[163]

In 1974 Brandon Carter a British mathematician, coined the term "Anthropic Principle." The Anthropic Principle says that the universe appears "designed" for the sake of human life. *Unbiased* cosmology appears to be pointing in this direction.[164]

The Watchmaker Analogy

The watchmaker analogy, or watchmaker argument, is a teleological argument for the existence of God. By way of an analogy, the argument states that design implies a designer. In the 17th and 18th centuries, the analogy was used (by Descartes and Boyle, for instance) as a device for explaining the structure of the universe and God's relationship to it. Later, the analogy played a prominent role in natural theology and the "argument from design," where it was used to support arguments for the existence of God and for the intelligent design of the universe.

The most famous statement of the teleological argument using the watchmaker analogy was given by William Paley in 1802. Paley's argument was seriously challenged by Charles Darwin's formulation of the theory of natural selection, and how it combines with mutation to improve survivability of a species, even a new species. In the United States, starting in the 1980s, the concepts of evolution and natural selection (usually referred to by opponents as "Darwinism") became the subject of a concerted attack by Christian creationists. This attack included a renewed interest in, and defense of, the watchmaker argument by the intelligent design movement.

The watchmaker analogy consists of the comparison of some natural phenomenon to a watch. Typically, the analogy is presented as a prelude to the teleological argument and is generally presented as:

1. The complex inner workings of a watch necessitate an intelligent designer.
2. As with a watch, the complexity of X (a particular organ or organism, the structure of the solar system, life, the entire universe) necessitates a designer.

In this presentation, the watch analogy (step 1) does not function as a premise to an argument — rather it functions as a rhetorical device and a preamble. Its purpose is to establish the plausibility of the general premise: *you can tell, simply by looking at something, whether or not it was the product of intelligent design.*

In most formulations of the argument, the characteristic that indicates intelligent design is left implicit. In some formulations, the characteristic is *orderliness* or *complexity* (which is a form of order). In other cases it is *clearly being designed for a purpose,* where *clearly* is usually left undefined.

Arguments that emphasize the appearance of *purpose* (as in Voltaire, see below), often appeal to biological phenomena. It seems natural to say that the *purpose* of an eye is to enable an organism to gather information about its environment, the purpose of legs is to enable an organism to move about in its environment, and so on. Even for nonbiological phenomena, scientific explanations in terms of *purpose* were accepted well into the 19th century. Natural phenomena were explained in terms of how they were designed for the benefit of humanity. It was held for instance, that the highest mountains on earth are located in the hottest climates *by design* — so that the mountains might condense the rain and provide cool breezes where mankind needed them the most. In arguments that emphasize on *orderliness* or *complexity*, the argument is often supplemented by a second argument that proceeds this way: Phenomenon X (the structure of the solar system, DNA, etc.) must be the result of:

1. random chance, blind fate, etc.
2. natural causes, natural law
3. intelligent design

In the case of the watch for example, neither (1) nor (2) is held to be plausible. The complexity of a watch is taken to mean that it could never have come about through random chance or through any natural process; it must have been designed by an intelligent watchmaker. Similarly (the argument continues), the complexity of X means that it could never have come about through random chance or through any natural process; it must have been designed by an intelligent designer.

This argument is basically a process of elimination: three possible explanations are offered. If the first two (random chance, natural causes) can be ruled out, intelligent design is left standing as the only plausible explanation.

History of an Analogy

Cicero (106 BC – 43 BC) anticipated the watchmaker analogy in *De natura deorum*, (About the nature of the gods)*, ii. 34*

"When you see a sundial or a water-clock, you see that it tells the time by design and not by chance. How then can you imagine that the universe as a whole is devoid of purpose and intelligence, when it embraces everything, including these artifacts themselves and their artificers?"[165]

One of the earliest expressions of the idea that human and animal bodies are clockworks made by God can be found in the work of René Descartes. Descartes developed the concept of Cartesian dualism, which held that human beings are composed of two distinct substances: matter and spirit. According to this theory, humans have both material bodies and non-material souls, whereas animals have only material bodies but no souls.

The Description of the Human Body (*La description du corps humain*) is an unfinished treatise written in the 1640s by René Descartes. Descartes felt knowing oneself was particularly useful. This for him included medical knowledge. He hoped to cure and prevent disease, even to slow down aging.

René Descartes believed the soul caused conscious thought. The body caused automatic functions like the beating of the heart and digestion he felt. The body was necessary for voluntary movement as well as the will. However, he believed the power to move the body was wrongly imagined to come from the soul. A sick or injured body does not do what we want or moves in ways we do not want. He believed the death of the body stopped it from being fit to bring about movement. This did not necessarily happen because the soul left the body.

René Descartes believed the body could exist through mechanical means alone. This included digestion, blood circulation, muscle movement and some brain function. He felt we all know what the human body is like because animals have similar bodies and we have all seen them opened up. He saw the body as a machine,

"Nor will this appear at all strange to those who are acquainted with the variety of movements performed by the different automata, or moving machines fabricated by human industry, and that with help of but few pieces compared with the great multitude of bones, muscles, nerves, arteries, veins, and other parts that are found in the body of each animal. Such persons will look upon this body as a machine made by the hands of God, which is incomparably better arranged, and adequate to movements more admirable, than is any machine of human invention."

The "Evolution" Towards Synthesis

"Science without religion is crippled, religion without science is blind." – Albert Einstein[166]

Voltaire (1694–1778) was fond of the argument from design, but also seemed aware of its limitations and treated it gingerly. In his unpublished *A Treatise on Metaphysics* (1736) Voltaire considered the watchmaker analogy and concluded that it probably indicated the existence of a powerful intelligent designer, but that it did not prove that the designer must be God.

"[One way] of acquiring the notion of a being who directs the universe...is by considering ... the end to which each thing appears to be directed... [W]hen I see a watch with a hand marking the hours, I conclude that an intelligent being has designed the springs of this mechanism, so that the hand would mark the hours. So, when I see the springs of the human body, I conclude that an intelligent being has designed these organs to be received and nourished within the womb for nine months; for eyes to be given for seeing; hands for grasping, and so on. But from this one argument, I cannot conclude anything more, except that it is probable that an intelligent and superior being has prepared and shaped matter with dexterity; I cannot conclude from this argument alone that this being has made the matter out of nothing or that he is infinite in any sense. However deeply I search my mind for the connection between the following ideas — *it is probable that I am the work of a being more powerful than myself, therefore this being has existed from all eternity, therefore he has created everything, therefore he is infinite, and so on.* — I cannot see the chain which leads directly to that conclusion. I can see only that there is something more powerful than myself and nothing more."[167] - Voltaire

When Charles Darwin (1809–1882) completed his studies of theology at Christ's College, Cambridge in 1831, he read Paley's *Natural Theology* and believed that the work gave rational proof of the existence of God. This was because living beings showed complexity and were exquisitely fitted to their places in a happy world.

Subsequently, on the voyage of the *Beagle*, Darwin found that nature was not so beneficent, and the distribution of species did not entirely support the strict ideas of divine creation as posed by most organized religions. In 1838, shortly after his return, Darwin conceived his theory that natural selection, rather than an exclusively divine design, was the best explanation for gradual change in populations over many generations.

Darwin sought to provide a general and simplistic explanation of the voids left in religious creationism. Natural selection described the lawful and intelligent actions of both the cosmos and living beings, inferring the voids "caused by the action of His laws."[168]

The idea that nature was governed by laws was already common, and in 1833 William Whewell as a proponent of the natural theology that Paley had inspired had written that "with regard to the material world, we can at least go so far as this—we can perceive that events are brought about not by insulated interpositions of Divine power, exerted in each particular case, but by the establishment of general laws." [169] By the time Darwin published his theory, liberal theologians were already supporting such ideas. In science, evolution theory incorporating Darwin's natural selection became completely accepted. This synthesis became widely accepted within liberal theological circle, as well as providing a rational explanation for the "voids" that science sought to fill in the theological story.

Some Limitations of Intelligent Design

Cultural anthropologists challenge the watchmaker argument both as a 1) faulty analogy and also as a 2) mistaken idea about the matching of people, animals, and plants to their natural settings. That is, a man's mother and father make the man, not a god. And people, animals, and plants have many biological mistakes in their design.[170]

Furthermore, anthropologists Richerson and Boyd (see below) note that, though one man or woman may make a watch, the know-how that the watchmaker uses consists of the accumulated learning of many generations of technology workers that managed to make minor improvements on the traditions of prior generations. That is, the cultural evolution in watch-making from generation to generation demonstrates the very Darwinian accumulation of variations between generations in a population that creationists try to use the watchmaker analogy to disprove. It is not even a case of the watchmaker standing on the shoulders of giants. Developing the art of watch-making is a case of "midgets standing on the shoulders of a vast pyramid of other midgets."[171]

For example, when John Harrison in 1759 created the most accurate watch that had ever been made for use on sailing ships, he used techniques from many generations of traditions in watch-making and added in "a number of clever tricks borrowed from other technologies of the time". The fact that so many hundreds of generations of innovations go into making any good watch leads to claims that William Paley's famous Argument from Design would better support a developing God than a perfect Christian Creator.[172]

If I define perfect as nothing less than correct each and every time, and never needing to change or grow or ever develop; then the notion that God may be less than perfect is for many utter heresy. I do realize this. Honestly I do - Scout's honor.

On some childish level, even I would like to believe this notion of God as "perfect." But, if this were true, then the creation He provided as a mirror of His nature and personality is flawed. Flawed, meaning that I see in the entire creation story, the entire redemption story, and the lifecycle of man & nature a pattern of growth – dynamic change. Not stasis… For me I find it easier to believe that God's "perfection" is likened unto Wolfgang Amadeus Mozart's musical "perfection." It is said that Mozart did not commit to any musical endeavor until he composed the entire symphony in his head, hearing the part for every instrument before he set the first note on paper. Mozart typically composed with a facility and speed that Viennese court composer Salieri reportedly described as "taking dictation from God."[173]

Yet Ludwig von Beethoven (equally a musical genius) was also a fascinating composer for many reasons; among them the method with which he composed. He too may be thought of as an example of a less perfect, evolving God the creator. Unlike Mozart, he did not write completed works in his head - he slaved over each composition, filling innumerable sketch books with his struggles to produce perfection.

At times, Beethoven composed quickly and with little apparent struggle. But more often he filled sketchbooks with musical fragments, doggedly reworking and refining them like a miner scratching for diamonds in a black-walled shaft. With his wild hair, scowling gaze, deafness — a particularly cruel infirmity for a musician — and volcanic temper, he is the very model of God working towards perfection. The operative word being, *working*.

Interestingly, like the transition from Genesis 1:1 to Genesis 1:2, Beethoven in 1800 is reported to have turned to his friend Krumpholz and said, "I am not very well satisfied with the work I have thus far done. From this day on I shall take a new way."[174] And basically, he did. Beethoven abandoned the classical forms of the previous century and set out for a more expressive (Romantic) musical voice. His musical imagination began to grow beyond that of the piano. This period, which later became known as the Heroic Period because of his productivity, the larger than life nature that his compositions took on, and the creation of countless masterpieces [the *Tempest* Sonata, Op. 31 (1801-2), the 3rd Symphony (*Eroica*), Op. 55 (1803), his only opera, *Fidelio*, Op. 72 (1803-5), and the 5th Piano Concerto (*Emperor*), Op. 73 (1809)].

I love the finished compositions of both artists. I envy the ease with which Mozart's genius flowed from him, and I admire the gritty perseverance of Beethoven. I cannot say I *know* which composer is better. I also cannot say that I *know* that the Watchmaker Argument is the most accurate way to describe creation, or for that matter, that it is even true. I have simply happened upon a watch as I made my way through a field, and based upon the historical, cultural, textual and spiritual information available to me, I *believe…*

8

What is Prophecy – the Science of Probability

What is Prophecy – the Science of Probability

When we think of prophecy, we often think of improbable declarations of what may or what will come to pass. Probabilities – Odds...

The reason why prophecy is an indication of the divine authorship of the Scriptures, and hence a testimony to the trustworthiness of the message of the Scriptures, is because of the minute probability of fulfillment. Anyone can make predictions, for that is simple. However, having prophecies fulfilled is vastly different. In fact, the more statements made about the future, and the more the detail, then the less likely the precise fulfillment will be.

For example, what is the likelihood of a person predicting today the exact city in which the birth of a future leader would take place, well into the 21st century? This is indeed what the prophet Micah did 700 years before the Messiah. Further, what is the likelihood of predicting the precise manner of death that a new, unknown religious leader would experience, a thousand years from now - a manner of death presently unknown, and to remain unknown for hundreds of years? Yet, this is indeed what David did in 1000 B.C.

For the purpose of this book I am defining *Prophecy* in a broad sense, as the prediction of future events or the speaking of divine words (divine Revelation) through chosen human messengers (prophets). The etymology of the word is Greek, from *pro-* "before" plus the root of *phanai* "speak"[175], i.e. "speaking before" or "foretelling" (proclamation). Prophecy is a general term for assertions presented as the revelation of divine will.

More than simple curiosity lies behind man's desire to know the future. There are practical reasons for knowing the future; predicting the weather, estimating the yield of a crop or knowing the migration patterns of fish or beasts for survival. Forecasts underlie all decisions, whether for market planning, staffing or economic feasibility. Leaders and executives must anticipate problems.

National security depends on threat assessments—strategic or tactical. Empires and whole civilizations have risen, or been destroyed, on the basis of predictions or forecasts about weather, resources needed, terrain and other logistical details. Our personal decisions about careers, marriage, raising a family and buying a new car all rely on our educated guesses—our predictions—about the future.

As early as 1390 the nursery rhyme *For Want of a Nail*[176] has been used to teach and encourage children to apply logical progression to the consequences of their actions - in other words, to predict the future.

> For want of a nail the shoe was lost.
> For want of a shoe the horse was lost.
> For want of a horse the rider was lost.
> For want of a rider the battle was lost.
> For want of a battle the kingdom was lost.
> And all for the want of a horseshoe nail.

Sound management, whether of our personal lives or of the universe, requires a broad, long-term perspective. Trusted leaders develop proven track records for navigating difficulties by foreseeing danger or peril in nature and humans. The prophet Isaiah recognizes the utility of this leadership trait and states that God "*makes known the end from the beginning*" (Isaiah 46:10)

God provided us with the Bible, as a sort of map - a way to navigate time and circumstance. The Bible has anticipated our most advanced discoveries on the very frontiers of science. It is astonishing to many to discover the *technological* perspectives of the Bible.

There are many technological and scientific statements in the Bible that the average reader takes for granted: the idea that the earth is round (Isaiah 40:22), the fact that the solar system migrates throughout the galaxy (Psalms 19:1-6), and the fact that something outside of space-time can transcend our three-dimensional comprehension of reality.[177]

Sound management, whether of our personal lives or of the universe, requires a broad, long-term perspective...

Divinely inspired prophecy is more than a glimpse into the future; it is evidence that there is a *plan. THE* plan of God.

Furthermore, Jesus warned of a time in history which "*unless those days be shortened, no flesh would be saved.*"[178] A statement like that would seem exaggerated and fanciful if studied over a century ago. In the 1800's, we could not have imagined the world completely destroying itself with bows and arrows or even muskets and bayonets. But today the nuclear cloud hangs over every geopolitical decision on earth.

Ezekiel speaks of a battle that will be resolved by hailstones of fire, and in which the leftover weapons provide all the energy needs of the nation of Israel for seven years (Ezekiel chapters 38-39). Ezekiel also mentions that professionals will spend months clearing out the remains, burying them downwind. He even indicates that while passing through the war zone, if a traveler finds something that the professionals have missed – should not touch it. Rather, he is to mark the location and leave it for the professionals to handle. This is a surprisingly contemporary procedure of nuclear-biological-chemical warfare.

Zechariah describes the unique effects of the neutron bomb (Zechariah 14:12). Jeremiah speaks of smart weapons: the intelligence and perception is in the arrow rather than the shooter – arrows that cannot miss (Jeremiah 50:9).

Divinely inspired prophecy is more than a glimpse into the future; it is evidence that there is a *plan*. *THE* plan of God.

A difficulty with accepting prophecy is that it challenges our concept of reality. To accept prophecy we must accept that there is more than our perception or comprehension of the space-time continuum. Knowledge must come from outside our dimension. Prophecy challenges our presumptions about reality.

Until recently, our knowledge of the world was limited to our sensate being – sight, sound, smell, taste and touch. Nothing existed beyond these five senses.

We now know of course that there are many dimensions and literally innumerable and immeasurable layers to our world that go well beyond our senses and ability to perceive. We know that we see less than ten percent of what can be seen (if the proper mechanism is employed). For example there are three types of waves below the visible spectrum, and four above it. The entire electromagnetic spectrum is thus: Gamma ray – X-ray – Ultraviolet – Visible – Infrared – Terahertz radiation – Microwave – Radio wave. Within these spectra are subcategories that are broken up yet further, all (except visible) beyond our innate ability to perceive them unaided. *Yet they exist.*

We do not see the radio or television waves that are sent through the air, yet with the correct device or equipment, we see and hear the exact thing on the receiving end that has been sent from the originating end. Until recently we could only see the effects of viruses and bacteria, unaided we could not see the actual virus or bacterium.

Despite this recent ability to discover the micro and macroscopic levels, even new quantum physics (the study of visible units, or *quanta*) has revealed that at some point the length of something cannot be divided or multiplied any more – this is a discovery in "finiteness." This phenomenon is called the *Planck length*.[179] The philosophical implications of quantum theory are disturbing to some scientists. They imply that man and the universe had a beginning and will have an end – they imply *creation.* Science therefore brings us back around to our own finiteness, and the reality that prophecy or a message must come from outside our closed world, from a being or entity that transcends our world – a higher power – God.

From *A Brief History of Time*, physicist Stephen Hawking concedes; "However, if we discover a complete theory, it should in time be understandable by everyone, not just by a few scientists. Then we shall all, philosophers, scientists and just ordinary people, be able to take part in the discussion of the question of why it is that we and the universe exist. If we find the answer to that, it would be the ultimate triumph of human reason -- for then we should know the mind of God." [180]

In many religions, gods or other supernatural agents, are thought to sometimes provide prophecies to certain individuals, sometimes known as prophets, by dreams or visions. The Old Testament contains prophecies from various Hebrew prophets who spoke judgment upon the Israelites, foretold of their impending trials, tribulations, and then promised divine blessings if the Hebrews repented from their evil ways.

In the Bible, prophecy is often referred to as one of the fivefold ministries or spiritual gifts that accompany the indwelling of the Holy Spirit. The five ministries are: Apostles; Prophets; Evangelists; Teachers and Pastors. (Ephesians 4:11) The focus of prophecy is not just future events though; this is only part of the prophetic gifting. Prophets often brought words of comfort, exhortation or general help to the Church.

Evidence of Prophecy

Prophecy usually involves some kind of communication regarding the future or with different realms of existence, which are sometimes not identifiable through history, discernible by or in harmony with empirical science. Therefore, some skeptics consider prophecy to be false. Believers, however, claim that prophecy is possible through supernatural means, which bypass the natural laws and is witnessed historically. Scientists tend to reject phenomena regarded as supernatural because they do not believe there is a way to bypass the physical laws of this universe.

Biblical Prophecy: Divine Inspiration?

Biblical Prophecy is evidence Christians hold to validate the Bible's claims of Divine inspiration. Is this authentic evidence or an illegitimate claim to bolster Christianity? Another way to define prophecy is a Divine declaration of events yet to pass. As natural man is unable to foresee future events, prophecy would be an acceptable evidence of Divine inspiration. The Authorized Version of the Bible, written by at least 40 authors over a period of at least 1,500 years, comprises 66 books. These 66 books contain over 1,000 divinely inspired prophecies. We will examine a few...

If one were to conceive 50 specific prophecies about a person in the future, who one would never meet, just what is the likelihood that this person will fulfill all 50 of the predictions? How much less would this likelihood be if 25 of these predictions were about what other people would do to him, and were completely beyond his control?

For example, how does someone "arrange" to be born in a specific family? How does one "arrange" to be born in a specified city, in which their parents do not actually live? How does one "arrange" their own death - and specifically by crucifixion, with two others, and then "arrange" to have their executioners gamble for their clothing? How does one "arrange" to be betrayed in advance? How does one "arrange" to have the executioners carry out the regular practice of breaking the legs of the two victims on either side, but not their own? Finally, how does one "arrange" to be God? How does one escape from a grave and appear to people after having been killed?

The science of probability attempts to determine the chance that a given event will occur. The value and accuracy of the science of probability has been well established beyond doubt - for example, insurance rates are fixed according to statistical probabilities. Professor

Emeritus of Science at Westmont College, Peter Stoner, has calculated the probability of one man fulfilling the major prophecies made concerning the Messiah. The estimates were worked out by twelve different classes, representing some 600 college students. The students carefully weighed all the factors, discussed each prophecy at length, and examined the various circumstances necessary to fulfill a particular prophecy.

Later, he submitted his figures for review to a Committee of the American Scientific Affiliation. Upon examination, they verified that his calculations were dependable and accurate in regard to the scientific material presented.[181] For example, concerning Micah 5:2, where it states the Messiah would be born in Bethlehem Ephrathah: Stoner and his students determined the average population of Bethlehem from the time of Micah to the present; then they divided it by the average population of the earth during the same period. They concluded that the chance of one man being born in Bethlehem was one in 2.8×10^5 - or rounded, one in 300,000.

After examining only eight different prophecies (Idem, 106), they conservatively estimated that the chance of one man fulfilling all eight prophecies was one in 10^{17}. To illustrate how large the number 10^{17} is (a figure with 17 zeros), Stoner gave this illustration : If you mark one of ten tickets, and place all the tickets in a hat, and thoroughly stir them, and then ask a blindfolded man to draw one, his chance of getting the right ticket is one in ten. Suppose that we take 10^{17} silver dollars and lay them on the face of Texas. They will cover all of the state two feet deep. Now mark one of these silver dollars and stir the whole mass thoroughly, all over the state. Blindfold a man and tell him that he can travel as far as he wishes, but he must pick up one silver dollar and say that this is the right one. What chance would he have of getting the right one? Just the same chance that the prophets would have had of writing these eight prophecies and having them all come true in any one man.

Whether we are aware of it or not, many of our routine expectations are based on probabilistic calculations. Every day our physical safety is affected by the probability of failures associated with machines that we use. Designers of machines for use with the public follow probabilistic approaches in determining whether a machine is safe to use.

If we use these analytical tools to evaluate life and death issues in the secular world, it would be hypocritical or prejudiced to discredit or fail to use the same tools in the investigation of theology. If we accept this as a rational approach to self-preservation (and we do), then it seems reasonable to apply the same probabilistic criteria to the analysis of the Bible

In most cases, the average person has a misunderstanding of the basic nature of gambling: what odds are. Although most people believe they understand odds and the risks involved in gambling, in fact they do not. And their confusion about risks, along with other misunderstandings and biases, makes it difficult to act wisely regarding probability events. Gambling is one thing, wanting to lose is another thing all together. If we or God are gonna toss the dice, we want decent odds.

Odds become clearer when we think of simple examples, like the silver dollar one mentioned earlier. Or the one below of Daniel 9:25, which has a probability of chance fulfillment = 1 in 10^5 (one in 100,000). By the way, what would 1 in 10^5 look like? There are approximately 100,000 hairs on the average head…pick one.

Biblical Prophecy: Daniel 9:25

One compelling Biblical prophecy supporting divine inspiration is found in Daniel, chapter 9, verse 25. Written 500 years before the birth of Jesus Christ (the oldest preserved copy dating 200 years before the birth of Christ),[182] it foretells the very day Christ would enter Jerusalem. The prophecy states: 69 weeks of years (69 x 7 = 483 years) would pass from the decree to rebuild Jerusalem, until the coming of the Messiah. This is according to the Babylonian 360-day calendar, since Daniel was written in Babylon during the Jewish captivity after the fall of Jerusalem. Thus, 483 years x 360 days = 173,880 days. According to records found by Sir Henry Creswicke Rawlinson in the Shushan (Susa) Palace, and confirmed in Nehemiah 2:1, this decree was made on March 14th, 445 BC, by Artaxerxes Longimanus[183]. Exactly 173,880 days later, on April 6th, 32 AD, Jesus Christ rode into Jerusalem upon a colt (fulfilling the prophecy in Zechariah 9:9). The Christian world celebrates this day as Palm Sunday. Four days later, Christ was murdered upon the cross. Actually, the form of His execution and even His last words were foretold in Psalm 22. Three days later, Jesus rose from the dead on Easter Sunday, fulfilling numerous other prophecies of our Messiah.[184]

Dreams and visions can be a part of the body of Christ in this day and time if we will open our Spiritual eyes and ears and listen to His voice. When the Spirit was poured out on the day of Pentecost as described in Acts 2, Peter quoted Joel (Chapter 2:17-18) in saying, "*And it shall come to pass in the last days, says God, That I will pour out my Spirit on all flesh, Your sons and daughters shall prophesy, Your young men shall see visions, Your old men shall dream dreams, And on My men servants and My maidservants.*" Peter was speaking of the days before the return of the Lord. No one knows the day or hour that He will return, but He did tell us to discern the times. The signs we see today of the imminent return of the Lord are very clear. The light of the Lord is getting brighter, while the darkness is getting darker. Though the devil is busy blinding the eyes of the world, the Lord is pouring out His latter rain[185] - A strong occurrence of the prophetic has been taking place since the turn of the century and the Azusa Street Revivals in California starting in 1906.[186] [187]

There is certainly a lot in the Word of God about dreams and visions. A general search will reveal that dreams are mentioned 74 times in the entire Bible. Trance is mentioned 5 times. Visions are mentioned 107 times, prophecy 44 times and "thus saith the Lord" is used over 500 times. The term seer is mentioned 33 times and prophet 322 times.[188]

During the period of time that Abraham, Isaac, and Jacob were on the earth, the Lord communicated a great deal through dreams and visions. (Genesis 12 through 49) Many of the Prophets of old saw visions and had dreams from the Lord. Ezekiel saw the throne of God (Ezekiel 1), Daniel dreamed dreams that deeply disturbed him and were prophetic (Daniel 8: 27, Daniel 10), Isaiah saw the seraphim worshiping God (Isaiah 6).

The Lord is specifically pointing out that he speaks to us in different ways. The Lord chose to speak to Moses face to face on Mount Sinai.[189] But the scriptures indicate that he speaks to everyone else (including His prophets) by his written Word and in dark sayings, dreams and visions.[190]

What is a Prophet?

The secular and commonly held beliefs about prophets are that they are people who are able to "see" the future and make it known to someone, thus they are sometimes referred to as "seers." The term seer was used because God most often would reveal Himself to individuals through or by visions - 1 Samuel 9:9 says that a prophet was originally called a "Seer."How these "prophets" are chosen is an important matter and is often misunderstood so let us look at this next.

What is a prophet? Who are prophets? What do they have to say? These are important questions of our day. Everyone seems to have a different answer to these questions. Some will make mention of accuracy in prediction. Others will say they were reformers of culture. Some will say that they only spoke what they heard. Others will make them out to be men who are great Bible expositors. None of these assessments are entirely wrong, yet none of them encompass all the truth either.

Historically and Presently, What is a Prophet?

What rises in your own thought and in your own heart when the word "prophet" is invoked? What image, what sense of things comes to your own understanding? We need to remember that the false prophets were those who wore rough garments to deceive. One reason they could succeed was because the people whom they deceived had a stereotypical view of a prophet, which was a false depiction.

Does a prophet have to be some long-haired wilderness guy in a rough garment, who acts strange and peculiar, and who looks with great intensity in his eyes? How would you define what a prophet is? How is he different from an apostle, or a teacher, or an evangelist? Are prophets still in existence or are they strictly an Old Testament phenomenon? Is there such a thing as a New Testament prophet, is this something very different from the Old Testament prophet?

The true prophet is rubbing salt into wounds. He deepens the dilemma and makes clearer the painful contradictions of the age, and he says, "There is no peace." He is bringing the dilemma into yet a deeper focus and saying, "You are not going to find peace until there is a judgment for this." He brings an unwelcome message that the flesh wants to shrink from, and the most common way to nullify the message is to kill or render null and void the man who brings it.

That is why we are probing what the classic, timeless elements are that have constituted prophets and prophecy in every generation, whether or not it is Elijah, Isaiah, or Jeremiah. What, in fact, is the difference between Isaiah and Jeremiah, or Samuel, or any of the minor prophets? However diverse these men are, is there anything central that runs through them all, which is intrinsic to being prophetic? Whatever the differences, what are the things that are the same? What is the heart, the quintessence of that which is prophetic?

If we were to examine the callings of all of the prophets and their responses, we would see how often these men cry out, "But I am a child and cannot speak."[191] After all of our examining we would have a portrait, and it would be a composite portrait of the prophetic genius. However much these men differ in their calling and personalities, there is some central thing that runs through them all that is designated "prophetic."

We cannot even conceive of Christ's church[192] independent of the restoration of prophets. In the last decade this subject has become more prevalent than in any other generation and men seem to be running everywhere to hear prophets. This is, therefore, a phenomenon that we need to examine to see how legitimate it is, and whether indeed it is the Lord or some kind of counterfeit.

It is important to know and understand that whenever the authentic thing is about to come, it is often preceded and followed by something fictitious or counterfeit. I want to say that I am watching this present prophetic phenomenon very carefully and have an extreme sense of caution in my own spirit. There must be an *original* for there to be a *counterfeit* – what we want is to discover the original and then sit at his feet and listen to "thus saith the Lord."

> There must be an *original* for there to be a *Counterfeit*

In the study of prophecy and the prophets I discovered that there is an evaluative test for both prophecy and the prophet. It defines the parameters and the veracity of every prophecy and every prophet. The test is basically twofold.

The first test is "are the prophecies and the messages of the prophet true?" Does what they predict actually happen? There is no wrangling out of this test. If the dreams, visions or prophetic messages do not align with the scriptural pattern it is time to quit listening to that individual. In Hal Lindsey's popular book *The Late Great Planet Earth*, Mr. Lindsey points out that the Old Testament prophets were subject to stoning if their prophecies were wrong.[193] He was right about that but today most people do not care if a prophet is occasionally wrong or if his messages are veiled or obscured like those of Nostradamus. Maybe we will not stone such prophets today but by all means we should not listen to them. There is no room for even small error in prophecy.

On the other hand a far more pervasive and deadly problem is getting anyone to keep from speaking evil of, maligning or just generally ignoring a true prophet. The religious leaders first ignored Jesus, then they sought to destroy him (Luke 7:36-50; John 7:25-30; John 8:37-40; John 10:39). What might happen if Jesus were conducting his ministry in today's self assured world of science, secularism and self? CS Lewis said that if Christ were ministering today they may not crucify him but rather would invite him to dinner, hear him and then make fun of him.[194]

The second test for all prophecies has to do with "prior revelation." Simply said, any revelation or prophetic utterance given today must agree with any and all the words and messages of the ancient Biblical prophets, Christ and his Apostles. God never contradicts himself. Scripture or the "prior revelation" is foundational and indispensable to all revelation now or at any time to come. Because this is true, I am always reminded that even of the few world events that I have been privileged to see they are only meant to be supplemental in nature and are never meant to "supplant" any part of the Biblical revelation.

There are serious and grave penalties for adding anything to scripture that comes down as "extra-biblical" in nature.[195] A true prophet's prophecies will ALL come to pass 100% of the time [excepting those that are made conditional by God] and his teachings can ALL be traced back to the Biblical writings contained in the Old and New Testaments.

Some things may be "hard to understand." (2 Peter 2:15-16) Or the teachings may be absent from the compromised, tickle-your-ears, feel-good sermons preached in modern churches; but it will be scriptural – that is, if one is willing to "search the scriptures." (2 Timothy 4:3; John 5:38-39)

9
Preparing the Way for an American Dictator

Preparing the Way for an American Dictator

[Sacrificing to the god of Status Quo – Establishing Martial Law and a Virtual Dictatorship in the United States of America]

In its simplest form, the basis for any government of mankind, be it benign or dictatorial, is the rejection of God. According to Judaic tradition, God once directly governed the affairs of man.[196] But, at some critical juncture in time, the Jews rejected God and called for one of their own to rule over them; God acquiesced and granted them a king, albeit with warning attached:

11 And he said, This will be the manner of the king that shall reign over you: He will take your sons, and appoint them for himself, for his chariots, and to be his horsemen; and some shall run before his chariots. 12 And he will appoint him captains over thousands, and captains over fifties; and will set them to ear his ground, and to reap his harvest, and to make his instruments of war, and instruments of his chariots. 13 And he will take your daughters to be confectionaries, and to be cooks, and to be bakers. 14 And he will take your fields, and your vineyards, and your oliveyards, even the best of them, and give them to his servants. 15 And he will take the tenth of your seed, and of your vineyards, and give to his officers, and to his servants. 16 And he will take your menservants, and your maidservants, and your goodliest young men, and your asses, and put them to his work. 17 He will take the tenth of your sheep: and ye shall be his servants. 18 And ye shall cry out in that day because of your king which ye shall have chosen you; and the LORD will not hear you in that day. -- 1 Samuel 8:5-19

The search for political "truth" is not new to our generation. In a speech to the Federal Convention in 1787, Benjamin Franklin differentiates between a political system with and without God's guidance: *"In the beginning of the contest with Britain, when we were sensible of danger, we had daily prayers in this room for Divine Protection. Our prayers, Sir, were heard -- and they were graciously answered. All of us who were engaged in the struggle must have observed frequent instances of a superintending Providence in our favor. . . . And have we now forgotten that powerful Friend? Or do we imagine we no longer need its assistance? I've lived, Sir, a long time, and the longer I live, the more convincing Proofs I see of this Truth — That God governs in the Affairs of Men. And if a sparrow cannot fall to the ground without his Notice, is it probable that an Empire can rise without his Aid? We have been assured, Sir, in the Sacred Writings, that except the Lord build the House they labor in vain who build it. I firmly believe this, — and I also believe that without his concurring Aid, we shall succeed in this political Building no better than the Builders of Babel: We shall be divided by our little partial local interests; our Projects will be confounded, and we ourselves shall become a Reproach and Bye word down to future Ages."*[197] [198]

In addition to Franklin, many other early founders of our country's form of government also believed that America's form of Democracy was not intended to be apolitical or a-religious. It was designed with both the Christian sacred text and the Christian practitioner in mind. Our first president said that it was *"impossible to rightly govern the world without God and the Bible."*[199]

The three major foundational documents of the United States of America are the Declaration of Independence (July 1776), the Articles of Confederation (drafted 1777, ratified 1781) and the Constitution of the United States of America (1789). If one combines the total number of signatures on the Declaration, the Articles of Confederation and the Constitution with the non-signing Constitutional Convention delegates, and then adds to that sum the number of congressmen in the First Federal Congress, one obtains a total of 238 "slots" or "positions" in these groups which one can classify as "Founding Fathers" of the United States.

It was majority opinion of America's founding fathers, as it is mine, that to ensure a continuity of both Divine blessing and protection, our country was intended to be run by Christians under the guidance, leadership, inspiration and moral underpinnings of the Bible. Though a few founding fathers, such as Thomas Jefferson, may be portrayed as non-Christian, the overwhelming majority of these men were identified as Christians.[200] [201] [202]

In a letter written to Thomas Jefferson, John Adams seems to state that with our type of government, the potential for dictatorial abuse was imminent without morally religious individuals in positions of leadership..."*We have no government armed with power capable of contending with human passions unbridled by morality and religion. Avarice, ambition, revenge, or gallantry, would break the strongest cords of our Constitution as a whale goes through a net.* ***Our Constitution was made only for a moral and religious people. It is wholly inadequate to the government of any other.***"[203]

Without the type of leader envisioned by John Adams, George Washington and Patrick Henry, a dictator could arise. According to Encarta, *demagogue* means "emotive dictator: a political leader who gains power by appealing to people's emotions, instincts, and prejudices in a way that is considered manipulative and dangerous." The movement towards dictatorship or demagoguery in America has been gradual. For example, an individual, who is ruled by a fear of the loss of status quo, will make small sacrifices for the sake of keeping said status quo intact. Short-term conflict is avoided, and the status quo is maintained. In the long run, though, there is a price to be paid: the many small sacrifices become the proverbial "death by 1000 cuts"[204] and the result is the loss of individual freedom and an establishment of a virtual dictatorship.

In any relationship, if one partner defers to the other and is willing to sacrifice himself more completely, then the other partner has more power and control over the relationship. When the balance of power is unequal, the relationship becomes unsatisfying; almost inevitably, the bi-lateral relationship ends and for all intent purposes, a quasi-dictatorship begins.

In a letter written by John F. Kennedy in 1942, the demise of the British Empire was referred to as a needed "obituary." Speaking about the fall of the Roman Empire [and any other empire], he says, *"When a nation finally reaches the point that its primary aim is to preserve the status quo, it's approaching old age. When it reaches the point where it is willing to sacrifice part of that status quo to keep the rest, it's gone beyond old, it's dying."*[205]

Ben Franklin once said, *"They that can give up essential liberty to obtain a little temporary safety deserve neither liberty nor safety."*[206]

The majority of people love the peace and tranquility of their daily existence. They are comforted and mildly sedated by the well-worn paths they trod each and every day. Mankind is emotionally driven to find and maintain stasis, and in the see-saw of choices faced to pursue equilibrium – some or many sacrifices are willing to be made – even sacrifices of practicing religious conviction or personal freedoms.

With his typical insight into both human and political nature, former Secretary of State Henry Kissinger made this observation, *"Today, America would be outraged if U.N. troops entered Los Angeles to restore order [referring to the 1991 LA Riot]. Tomorrow they will be grateful! This is especially true if they were told that there were an outside threat from beyond, whether real or promulgated, that threatened our very existence. It is then that all peoples of the world will plead to deliver them from this evil. The one thing every man fears is the unknown. When presented with this scenario, individual rights will be willingly relinquished for the guarantee of their well-being granted to them by the World Government."*[207]

In writing the *Constitution for the United States of America*, James Madison said that States in order to enhance their power, often resorted to "the old trick of turning every contingency into a resource for accumulating force in the government."[208] The idea is to foster an emergency, and then step in to "save the people" by drastically increasing state power. This is precisely the scenario since the Great Depression in the United States, but includes as well the response to droughts, floods, depressions, illicit drugs, acts of war, and so forth.

There is virtually no natural or man-made disaster which cannot be used to garner greater power into the hands of an increasingly greedy-for-power government or a sitting President.

Deepening the controls of the government, the United States, on October 6, 1917, passed the Trading with the Enemy Act (H.R. 4960, Public Law 91) - ostensibly in connection with World War I. This extraordinary act gave the President immense, unconstitutional authority (particularly over any private ownership of gold and silver), *but* included within the term, "enemy", individuals "other than citizens of the United States." The Emergency War Powers had been greatly extended, but thus far had not been directed against *the people* of the United States. This was not to be the end of the matter, however.

On March 9, 1933 The Amendatory Act (Presidential Executive Order 6102) was passed, which *included* the people of the United States under the definition of "enemy". Essentially, "any person within the United States of any place subject to the jurisdiction thereof..."[209] This is the infamous Emergency *War Powers Act* that is credited to Franklin D. Roosevelt.[210]

This reprehensible act was passed just after Franklin Roosevelt's inauguration as President of the United States, and significantly at a time when the United States was *not* in a shooting war with any foreign foe. Emergency war powers in time of peace may seem to be a contradiction in terms, but not in government.

The Amendatory Act also made the President a monarch and/or king in everything but name (which might have been okay with Roosevelt – William Branham actually said that Roosevelt conducted a "preliminary dictatorship" and "we haven't got no more Constitution. She's broke to pieces."[211]).

It gave the Secretary of the Treasury commensurate powers (with that office - no longer being a "United States Treasury" - but reporting directly to the creditors of the bankruptcy). Finally, the Amendatory Act placed the American people under commercial law (which has been formalized as the Uniform Commercial Code). The latter action effectively made all citizens "merchants", entities whose records and affairs were totally subject to inspection and harsh penalties imposed for any violations of Mercantile Law. Thus the citizens were not only designated as the "enemy", they were also merchants and subject to invasive inspection of all their activities.

The "Bank Holiday" of March 6, 1933 was part and parcel of the Emergency War Powers Act and the actions which followed, and was primarily intended to prevent the continuing and increasing withdrawal of currency and gold from the banks. This, in effect, was the true national emergency of 1933 (but more an emergency for the bankers than the nation). Subsequently, every President of the United States since Franklin Roosevelt has reaffirmed the "national emergency" and issued Executive Orders under 12 USC 95(a).[212]

With our foundation laid, let us begin to examine *the Making of an American Dictator.* Beginning in 1983, a series of Executive orders were written by President Reagan. The orders were written during the height of the Cold War, when tension between the two nuclear-weapon capable nations of America and the Soviet Union were greatest. They ostensibly were written to expedite the progress of the war machine if needed.

Executive Order 12407[213] [214], signed by President Reagan on Feb. 22, 1983, provides the regional and local mechanisms and manpower for carrying out the provisions to set up ten Federal Regional Councils to govern ten Federal Regions made up of the fifty States.

Originally these regions were established by President Nixon, on March 27, 1969, through the Government Reorganization Act which divided the United States into eight (subsequently ten) Regions. To further implement this Regional Governance over the United States, President Nixon signed *Executive Order 11647*[215] and entered it in the *Federal Register February 12, 1972. (Vol.37, No.30)* Supplementing these ten regions, each of the States is to be divided into sub-regions, so that Federal Executive control is provided over every community.

The 10 Federal Regions

- REGION I: Connecticut, Massachusetts, New Hampshire, Rhode Island, Vermont. Regional Capitol: Boston
- REGION II: New York, New Jersey, Puerto Rico, the Virgin Islands. Regional Capitol: New York City
- REGION III: Delaware, Maryland, Pennsylvania, Virginia, West Virginia, District of Columbia. Regional Capitol: Philadelphia
- REGION IV: Alabama, Florida, Georgia, Kentucky, Mississippi, North Carolina, Tennessee. Regional Capitol: Atlanta
- REGION V: Illinois, Indiana, Michigan, Minnesota, Ohio, Wisconsin. Regional Capitol: Chicago
- REGION VI: Arkansas, Louisiana, New Mexico, Oklahoma, Texas. Regional Capitol: Dallas-Fort Worth
- REGION VII: Iowa, Kansas, Missouri, Nebraska. Regional Capitol: Kansas City
- REGION VIII: Colorado, Montana, North Dakota, South Dakota, Utah, Wyoming. Regional Capitol: Denver
- REGION IX: Arizona, California, Hawaii, Nevada. Regional Capitol: San Francisco
- REGION X: Alaska, Oregon, Washington, Idaho. Regional Capitol: Seattle

What is an Executive Order?

What is an Executive Order? Where does the President get the authority to issue them?

Executive Orders (EOs) are legally binding orders given by the President, acting as the head of the Executive Branch, to Federal Administrative Agencies. Executive Orders are generally used to direct federal agencies and officials in their execution of congressionally established laws or policies.[216] However, in many instances they have been used to guide agencies in directions contrary to congressional intent.

Not all EOs are created equal. Proclamations, for example, are a special type of Executive Order that is generally ceremonial or symbolic, such as when the President declares *National Take Your Child to Work Day*. Another subset of Executive Orders is concerned with national security or defense issues. These have generally been known as National Security Directives. Under the Clinton Administration, they were termed "Presidential Decision Directives."[217] [218]

Executive Orders do not require Congressional approval to take effect but they have the same legal weight as laws passed by Congress. The President's source of authority to issue Executive Orders can be found in Article II, Section 1 of the Constitution which grants to the President the "executive power." Section 3 of Article II further directs the President to "take Care that the Laws be faithfully executed."[219] To implement or execute the laws of the land, Presidents give direction and guidance to Executive Branch agencies and departments, often in the form of Executive Orders.

A Brief History and Examples

Executive Orders have been used by every chief executive since the time of George Washington. Most of these directives were unpublished and were only seen by the agencies involved. In the early 1900s, the State Department began numbering them; there are now over 13,000 numbered orders. Orders were retroactively numbered going back to 1862 when President Lincoln suspended the writ of habeas corpus and issued the Emancipation Proclamation by Executive Order. All new Executive Orders are easily accessible in multiple locations, at both independent and government sponsored sites.[220]

President Clinton came under fire for using the EO as a way to make policy without consulting the then Republican Congress (see the following quotes). Clinton signed hundreds of EOs in only a few years of his presidency. In one case, he designated 1.7 million acres of Southern Utah as the Grant Staircase - Escalante National Monument. He also designated a system of American Heritage Rivers and even fought a war with Yugoslavia under Executive Order 12846 in 1993.[221]

"Stroke of the pen. Law of the Land. Kinda cool."
Paul Begala, former Clinton advisor, The New York Times, July 5, 1998[222]

"We've switched the rules of the game. We're not trying to do anything legislatively."
Interior Secretary Bruce Babbitt, The Washington Times, June 14, 1999[223] [224]

Controversy

Executive Orders are controversial because they allow the President to make major decisions, even law, without the consent of Congress. This, of course, runs against the general logic of the Constitution -- that no one should have power to act unilaterally. Nevertheless, Congress often gives the President considerable leeway in implementing and administering federal law and programs. Sometimes, Congress cannot agree exactly how to implement a law or program. In effect, this leaves the decision to the federal agencies involved and the President that stands at their head. When Congress fails to spell out in detail how a law is to be executed, it leaves the door open for the President to provide those details in the form of Executive Orders.

Executive Orders Could Result in Virtual Dictatorship

If Congress does not like what the executive branch is doing, it has two main options. First, it may rewrite or amend a previous law, or spell it out in greater detail how the Executive Branch must act. Of course, the President has the right to veto the bill if he disagrees with it, so, in practice, a 2/3 majority is often required to override an Executive Order.

The ultimate criticism of Executive Orders is that the runaway use of EOs could result in a President becoming a virtual dictator, capable of making major policy decisions without any congressional or judicial input.

The following Executive Orders, now recorded in the Federal Register[225], can be put into effect at any time an emergency is declared:

- 10995 - Seizure of all communications media.
- 10997 - Seizure of all electrical power and fossil fuels.
- 10998 - Seizure of all food resources, farms and farm equipment.
- 10999 - Seizure of all transportation and control of all highways and seaports.
- 11000 - Seizure of all civilians for work under Federal supervision.
- 11001 - Federal takeover of all health, education and welfare.
- 11002 - Authorizes FEMA to order Postmaster General to register every man, woman and child in the United States.
- 11003 - Seizure of all aircraft and airports.
- 11004 - Housing and Finance given authority for population relocation.
- 11005 - Seizure of railroads, inland waterways, and storage facilities.
- 11051 - The Director of the Office of Emergency Planning authorized to put Executive Orders into effect in "times of increased international tension or financial crisis". Is also to perform such additional functions as the President may direct.

These Executive Orders are in gross violation of Article 4 Section 4 of the United States Constitution. "*The United States shall guarantee to every State in this Union a Republican form of government, and shall protect each of them against invasion; and, on application of the Legislature, or of the Executive (when the Legislative cannot be convened), against domestic violence.*"[226]

When the government can no longer be controlled by the people, there are two ways the government keeps the people in line: police power and the controlling of necessities. Stated simply, the dictatorial power of the Executive rests primarily on two Executive Orders - Executive Order 12919 and Executive Order 12407.

EO 12919[227] was signed into law by President Clinton June 3, 1994. This EO gathers together into one document the authority of the previously mentioned 11 Executive Orders. This means that FEMA would take over 28 Executive Departments and Agencies whenever the President of the United States declares a national emergency. In large part this was all made possible by the 1933 War Emergency Powers Act, which authorizes the President to suspend the Constitution. There is no known Executive Order outlining the restoration of the Constitution after the national emergency has ended.

Executive Order 12407 provides the regional and local mechanisms and manpower for carrying out the provisions of EO 12919. Signed by President Reagan on Feb. 22, 1983, Executive Order 12407 set up ten Federal Regional Councils to govern ten Federal Regions made up of the fifty States.

The President need not wait for some emergency to occur, however. He can declare a National Emergency at any time, and freeze everything. Congress and the individual States are powerless to prevent such an Executive Dictatorship, as long as the President advises Congress in a timely matter.

By proclaiming and putting into effect Executive Order No. 12919, the President would put the United States under total Martial Law and Military Dictatorship.

Lamentably, with the attacks of September 11, 2001, many American's decided that to maintain the status quo of what they perceived to be "freedom," sacrifices had to be made. Beginning with The Patriot Act, recent Presidential Executive Orders affecting personal liberties and civil liberties have become numerous and to properly describe them all would be tedious. Originally, the stated purpose of USA Patriot Act (USAPA) PUBLIC LAW 107-56 (H.R. 3162) passed by Congress on October 25, 2001, was the Uniting and Strengthening [of] America by **P**roviding **A**ppropriate **T**ools **R**equired to **I**ntercept and **O**bstruct **T**errorism Act. Additionally, the Act was intended to "deter and punish terrorist acts in the United States and around the world, to enhance law enforcement investigatory tools, and for other purposes."[228]

So broad is the scope of the Patriot Act, and so pervasive is its influence in America, that much of its language has become a part of our everyday life and experience. Its words and phrases read like a contemporary anti-terrorism movie or spy novel. The following is a short list of terms found in Patriot Act I: biometrics, civil liability, cyber security, critical infrastructure, domestic preparedness, domestic terrorism, illegal activity, long-arm jurisdiction, material support, national security, roving surveillance, and suspicious activity.

On the heels of the first Patriot Act, Patriot Act II, known by the formal name Justice Enhancement Domestic Security Act of 2003 was signed in 2003.[229] Commonly referred to as "The Act," President George W. Bush signed this act with little public scrutiny due to the media frenzy of a simultaneous event – the capture of Saddam Hussein. This Act, for all intents and purposes is still secret.

With what we now know about the spate of recent Presidential executive orders, the National Security Presidential Directive 51 / Homeland Security Directive 20[230] is ominous - the provisions contained within it outline preparations for the implementation of open martial law in the event of a declared national emergency.

This new legislation signed on May 9, 2007, declares that in the event of a "catastrophic event", the President can take total control over the government and the country, bypassing all other levels of government at the state, federal, local, territorial and tribal levels, and thus ensuring total unprecedented dictatorial power.

The National Security and Homeland Security Presidential Directive, which also places the Secretary of Homeland Security in charge of domestic "security", was signed May 2007 without the approval or oversight of Congress and seemingly supersedes the National Emergency Act which allows the president to declare a national emergency but also requires that Congress have the authority to "modify, rescind, or render dormant" such emergency authority if it believes the president has acted inappropriately.

Apart from potential presidential abuse of power, the Homeland Security Act provides its own Secretary with inordinate power to circumvent and/or override other established balances of power. On the heels of Iraq War Supplemental being passed, the Senate also gave the Secretary of Homeland Security the power to waive any and all law in the course of building roads and barriers along the U.S. borders - without limit and with no checks and balances. The measure is part of the "REAL ID Act of 2005," the controversial immigration bill attached by the House as a rider to the Iraq war supplemental.

With his newly minted power, Bush's Homeland Security Secretary Michael Chertoff announced he was waiving all environmental rules in order to clear the way to complete the last 670 miles of border fence. The result of his action circumvents the Endangered Species Act, the Federal Water Pollution Control Act and the National Environmental Policy Act, to name a few. One attorney, Brian Segee, described this act as both dangerous and arrogant.

The consequence of this decision is that Congress has given one man a license to waive any law, for any reason or for no reason at all. Any sitting Secretary of Homeland Security, now has the power to simply waive away laws that protect the environment, safeguard public health, ensure consumer and workplace safety, prevent unfair business practices, etc. -- at his or her sole and unreviewable discretion.

All this power in only a few hands – the Secretary of Homeland Security and obviously, the President. Can anyone hear William Branham's prophecy, "There'll be a great powerful woman raise up, either be President, or dictator, or some great powerful woman in this United States," ringing in their ears? Do you know what? On Monday morning December 1st, 2008, President-elect Obama named Arizona Governor Janet Napolitano as Secretary of the Department of Homeland Security. If confirmed, Napolitano would be the first woman to serve as DHS Secretary.

Hmmm. Women with unimaginable power and the potential for dictatorial power: Hillary Clinton as Secretary of State, and Janet Napolitano as Secretary of the Department of Homeland Security.

Though anathema to any notion of liberty or freedom, this legislation has not come out of the blue, it is merely an open declaration of the infrastructure of martial law that the federal government has been building since the turn of the last century, which was first publicly codified in the 1933 War Powers Act under Franklin D. Roosevelt.

The exercise of emergency powers had long been a concern of the classical political theorists, including the eighteenth-century English philosopher John Locke, who had a strong influence upon the Founding Fathers in the United States. A preeminent exponent of a government of laws and not of men, Locke argued that occasions may arise when the executive must exert a broad discretion in meeting special "emergencies" for which the legislative power provided no relief or existing law granted no necessary remedy. He did not regard this prerogative as limited to wartime, or even to situations of great urgency. It was sufficient if the "public good" might be advanced by its exercise.[231]

Hillary Clinton as Secretary of State, and Janet Napolitano as Secretary of the Department of Homeland Security...

Can anyone hear William Branham's prophecy, "There'll be a great powerful woman raise up, either be President, or dictator, or some great powerful woman in this United States," ringing in their ears?

Senate Report 93-549[232], which was presented at the first session of the 93rd Congress, outlines just a handful of the declared national emergencies or martial law declarations that preceded the latest one. Below is a direct quote from Senate Report 93-549's preface:

"Since March 9, 1933, the United States has been in a state of declared national emergency. In fact, there are now in effect four presidentially-proclaimed states of national emergency: In addition to

the national emergency declared by President Franklin D. Roosevelt in 1933, there are also the national emergency proclaimed by President Harry S. Truman on December 16, 1950, during the Korean conflict, and the states of national emergency declared by President Richard M. Nixon on March 23, 1970, and August 15, 1971."

In alliance with these open declarations of martial law and the 1947 National Security Act, bills such as the Patriot Act, the John Warner Defense Authorization Act and the Military Commissions Act have all put the final jigsaw pieces in place to complete an infrastructure of dictatorship since 9/11. [233]

We're already living under an infrastructure of martial law and have been since 1933 – we're one catastrophe away from implementation.

We're already living under an infrastructure of martial law and have been since 1933, all that remains for it to be fully implemented is a big enough natural disaster, mass terror attack or other catastrophe that will cause the necessary carnage and panic that affords the federal government enough leeway to implement open dictatorship with the least possible resistance.

When the Constitution of the United States was framed it placed the exclusive legislative authority in the hands of Congress and with the President. Article I, Section 1 of the United States Constitution is concise in its language, "All legislative powers herein granted shall be vested in a Congress of the United States, which shall consist of a Senate and House of Representatives." That is no longer true. The Bill of Rights protected Americans against loss of freedoms. That is no longer true. The Constitution provided for a balanced separation of powers. That is no longer applicable. One authority has summed up the situation in the following words:

"Emergency powers are not solely derived from legal sources. The extent of their invocation and use is also contingent upon the personal

conception which the incumbent of the Presidential office has of the Presidency and the premises upon which he interprets his legal powers. In the last analysis, the authority of a President is largely determined by the President himself."[234]

Perhaps the concept of an American dictator can be summed up succinctly in the words of Howard J. Ruff, conservative activist and publisher of The Ruff Times,

"Since the enactment of Executive Order 11490 (assigning emergency preparedness functions to Federal departments and agencies), the only thing standing between us and dictatorship is the good character of the President, and the lack of a crisis severe enough that the public would stand still for it."[235]

10 America You Will be Destroyed! – Thus Saith the Lord

America You Will be Destroyed! – Thus Saith the Lord

At the Constitutional Convention on August 22, 1787 George Mason declared "As nations cannot be rewarded or punished in the next world, so they must be in this. By inevitable chain of causes and effects, Providence punishes national sins with national calamities."[236]

Let me first say that I love America, the country of my birth - The country where I, and many of my ancestors before me, have served patriotically in our Armed Forces. The country where my very son is an Army Scout and combat veteran, decorated twice with the Army Achievement Medal.

As a younger man I travelled to over thirty countries as a missionary and relief worker. I have seen many beautiful places, met many wonderful people, and I have also known much meanness and the despair that comes with non-democratic governments. While in these countries, I have experienced the loss of rights and privileges that most of us would consider inalienable. I have even been denied my own personal freedom in a country that was considered to be our friend and ally at the time.

I do not want to see my country destroyed – from within or from without. I would love for her to once again be a shining example of goodness and decency. But I am afraid, like all great nations before her, we have reached the autumn or maybe even the winter of existence and America's time is over.

Here is a brief overview of why America will be destroyed... A land of destiny; established by and for religious, Christian peoples; a land that has used its prosperity and inventiveness to spread evil (much like ancient Babel) and unite the world by immoral clothing, ungodly music and film, the perversions of family, marriage and heterosexual relationships; legalization of abortion; and the rejection of God and the Bible politically and legislatively.

In Murphy v. Ramsey, (1858) the Supreme Court defined the "basis of the family" as "One man and one woman" in a union for life[237]. Sodomy was yet a criminal offence in every State. As recent as the 1930's, America stood united on every front and in every sector of our Nation (see endnote #1 *The Motion Picture Code of 1930 a.k.a. The Hays Code,* as an example) – the institution of marriage, the sanctity of family, reverence and belief in an Almighty God – Americans still lived by a clear moral compass based upon the Bible.

Historically and cross-culturally, the basis of most societies has centered on the man-woman-children unit. Male and female homosexuality stress resistance to, or subversion of, normative models of sexuality, family and social organization and are not merely sexual practices which differ from the heterosexual norm or an ideological challenge.

Dominique Fernandez, for instance, emphasizes the symbolic rather than the sexual significance of the homosexual, positing him as an outcast ("un paria"), a dissident whose marginality involves a radical critique of normative values.[238]

Monique Wittig expresses a similar point of view in an article called *Paradigm*: "homosexuality is the desire for one's own sex. But it is also the desire for something else that is not connoted. This desire is resistance to the norm."[239]

At its heart, homosexuality is rebellion – rebellion against societal norms, rebellion against nature, and rebellion against God. Homosexuality is much like a cancer cell – a seemingly healthy cell that goes rogue and refuses to work harmoniously with the body; both are dissonant rebels and mutineers.

The concept of "the homosexual" as a specific type of human being, ontologically different from others, is relatively new. Foucault states: “As defined by the ancient civil or canonical codes, sodomy was a category of forbidden acts”. Foucault implies that a person committing sodomy was no more than a person engaging in illegal activity: his acts did not define him as a particular type.[240]

According to Westphal, “The sodomite had been a temporary aberration; the homosexual was now a species”.[241] Jonathan Dollimore too remarks on the historical shift in the conceptualizing of "homosexuality" from a behavior to an identity, stating: “In the nineteenth century a major and specifically "scientific" branch of this development comes to construct homosexuality as primarily a congenital abnormality rather than, as before, a sinful and evil practice”.[242]

In the United States, same-sex acts were considered both deviant and criminal in most states until the 1970’s when many state laws were repealed. As of 1998, there were still over twenty states with laws on their books prohibiting; “homosexuality”, “sodomy”, “buggery” and “crimes against nature”. Georgia’s anti-sodomy law was federally challenged as recent as 1986, but was upheld by the U.S. Supreme Court as constitutional [Bowers v. Hardwick, 478 U.S. 186 (1986)].

For over four thousand years, homosexual acts (and other non-procreative sexual behavior), apart from being considered morally and legally aberrant, were condemned as "unnatural" and held to be pathological.[243] Why unnatural? Homosexuality doesn't appear to benefit the cause of continuing the species, the driving force believed to underlie most behaviors and traits in living things – thus, the “against nature” argument.

The cry of last resort for homosexual "marriage" proponents is some variation of this: *I love so-and-so, therefore I should be allowed to marry him, just as heterosexuals are allowed to marry (and have children with) the ones they love.* An answer is forthcoming if we contest the terms of the debate. We are under no obligation to grant that the affection which a man may feel toward another man—that which he calls "love"—is synonymous with that which he is capable of manifesting toward a woman, or that it is even love. For one, many people say they love each other, but the reality is often at odds with the profession. Absolute conviction is not the same as absolute truth. Secondly (and in answer to those who argue from the notion of equal protection/opportunity under the law), a society is under no obligation to give legal recognition to what is essentially a recreational pursuit. The law regulates relations between a man and a woman because such unions, since they produce children, are tied to the good of the nation. Homosexual relationships, on the other hand, are sterile and, in this regard, there is no reason for the civil authorities to take an interest in protecting or preserving them.

Senator Rick Santorum (R-Penn.), for example, correctly stated:

...if you make the case that if you can do whatever you want to do, as long as it's in the privacy of your own home, this "right to privacy," then why be surprised that people are doing things that are deviant within their own home? If you say, there is no deviant as long as it's private, as long as it's consensual, then don't be surprised what you get. You're going to get a lot of things that you're sending signals that as long as you do it privately and consensually, we don't really care what you do. And that leads to a culture that is not one that is nurturing and necessarily healthy. I would make the argument in areas where you have that as an accepted lifestyle, don't be surprised that you get more of it. ...We have laws in states, like the one at the Supreme Court right now, that has sodomy laws and they were there for a purpose. Because, again, I would argue, they undermine the basic tenets of our society and the family. And if the Supreme Court says that you have the right to consensual sex within your home, then you have the right to bigamy, you have the right to polygamy, you have the right to incest, you have the right to adultery. You have the right to anything. Does that undermine the fabric of our society? I would argue yes, it does...this freedom actually intervenes and affects the family.[244]

On the medical front, in 1973 homosexuality per se was removed from the DSM-II classification of mental disorders and replaced by the category Sexual Orientation Disturbance. This represented a compromise between the view that preferential homosexuality is invariably a mental disorder and the view that it is a sexual variant that could result in significant mental and/or emotional issues. As Dr. Jon Meyer notes (see Comprehensive Textbook of Psychiatry, 4th ed., eds. Kaplan & Sadock), "...this change reflected the point of view that homosexuality was to be considered a mental disorder only if it was subjectively disturbing to the individual. The decision of the American Psychiatric Association (APA) Board was loosely based on weak biological inferences, but primarily based upon the current sociological pressures and in an atmosphere of confrontation. Beginning in 1970, various gay activist groups aggressively and violently demonstrated at APA meetings.

Gay Liberation Front sticker, 1970.

As mentioned earlier, in the 1930's Americans as a whole still lived by a clear moral compass based upon the Bible. Not so any more. If God destroyed Sodom and Gomorrah for similar behaviors, then, as the respected Evangelist Billy Graham is reported to have said; "If God doesn't judge America, He will have to apologize to Sodom and Gomorrah."[245] U.S. comedian and talk show host Jay Leno to some extent has "eyes to see" the truth, and at his wife's 60th birthday party in Jackson Hole, Wyoming echoed Mr. Graham's statement - "If God doesn't destroy Hollywood Boulevard, he owes Sodom and Gomorrah an apology"[246]

It astonishes the mind to realize how many professing Christians refuse to believe that acceptance of moral perversity leads to divine judgment. Such widespread misunderstanding of Holy Writ can only be attributed to a half century of impotent, shallow pulpits.

Unfortunately, the consequences of such willful ignorance can only mean we are doomed to repeat the mistakes of past nations that also ignored the warnings of Scripture.

If the Bible teaches anything, it teaches that God is sovereign in the affairs of men. America's Founding Fathers largely believed that. Our very form of government is predicated upon this principle. The writings of the Founding Fathers are replete with personal acknowledgments to this principle. Here are a few examples: "It is impossible to rightly govern the world without God and the Bible." – George Washington. "No truth is more evident to any mind than that the Christian religion must be the basis of any government intended to secure the rights and privileges of a free people." – Noah Webster. "The future and success of America is not in this Constitution, but in the laws of God upon which this Constitution is founded." – James Madison.

> Study the writings of America's Founders. *There is no mistaking it: this country made a Covenant with God.*

For Christians or Americans to now repudiate this principle is the height of arrogance and stupidity.

Since the destruction of the Canaanite empire, every nation throughout history that has repudiated the moral laws of God has fallen victim to the wrath of God [e.g. Greece, Rome, USSR]. There have been no exceptions.[247] Even more interesting is the fact that the vast majority of these nations fell at the zenith of their power and influence. The mightiest armies men can assemble are but toy soldiers when they march against God.

It is true that God made a special covenant with only one nation, Israel. However, it is equally true that only one nation, the United States of America, made a special covenant with God. From the earliest days of our nation, our forebears made it crystal clear that this country was founded for "the advancement of the Christian faith" and for "the glory of God."[248]

Reread the Mayflower Compact[249], The Fundamental Orders of 1639[250], and the First Charter of Virginia[251]. Study again the writings of America's Founders. There is no mistaking it: this country made a covenant with God. Furthermore, Holy Scripture is also clear that God charges every nation to honor His standard of righteousness. Scripture promises divine blessing to nations that elevate these principles and divine judgment upon those nations ignoring them. This has been accepted Christian dogma for 2,000 years! God has made another covenant with the nations of the world: bless Israel and be blessed; curse Israel and be cursed. (Genesis 12:1-3)

Another principle that God has determined will cause a nation to falter or prosper is the principle of leadership. Leaders without the fear of God will doubtless bring a nation into divine displeasure, while leaders who fear and honor God's laws will surely experience Heaven's favor.

For far too long, too many of these sacred principles have been violated in our country! Are we now shocked that God could be using pagan nations (as He repeatedly did with Old Testament Israel) to bring judgment to Christian America? Instead of ridiculing the brave men who attempt to call America back to God, we should be doing what God demands. That means the White House and the church house need to stop normalizing adultery, homosexuality, and other acts of moral & spiritual deviancy. We must begin holding our political leaders to the fundamental principles contained in our Declaration of Independence and Bill of Rights. Most of all, our pulpits must become, as DeTocqueville said, "ablaze with righteousness."[252]

Listening to many modern pundits, one would think they expect God to apologize to Sodom and Gomorrah; however, God owes no nation an apology. God is righteous in judgment as much as He is in blessing. The only apology owed is the one owed to God from disobedient people, this is called repentance, and it is time America did it.

This chapter outlines the principles behind the destruction of nations because of moral decay. Now we will examine the prophecy about America's destruction, as foreseen in 1932 and foretold by William Branham in July of 1933. Interestingly, the type and amount of destruction he describes was not even possible at the time. But, shortly after this prophecy is told to a small crowd of people at the old Masonic Hall on Meggs Avenue in Jeffersonville, Indiana, a relatively unknown Hungarian Physicist conceives the idea for the neutron chain reaction.[253]

Leo Szilard was the physicist that serendipitously conceived the idea on September 12, 1933, that presaged the atomic bomb. He had just finished reading an article in the London Times where Ernest Rutherford was quoted as saying "anyone who looked for a source of power in the transformation of the atoms was talking moonshine."[254] After reading this article Szilard was walking through the streets of central London, and as he waited for a streetlight at the corner of Southampton Row it occurred to him "In certain circumstances it might be possible to set up a nuclear chain reaction, liberate energy on an industrial scale, and construct atomic bombs."[255]

Below are a few of the different times that Wm. Branham repeated the prophecy of America being destroyed. [It is important to note that all of the direct quotations of William Branham are taken from spoken sermons, and thus reflect the grammar and locution of his 6th grade education. The structure of these quotes identifies William Branham as the speaker; the title of his sermon; the location; the year, month and day where the sermon was preached; and the paragraph as denoted by a letter and number.]

Picking up, the other day, an old book, up there, reading some of the things that the Lord had told, foretold, already come to pass - And all those things has hit--just the two things left - a great woman will rise up and be president, or something like that in the nation, and then there will come a total annihilation, the entire nation will be wiped out.
Wm Branham – *By Faith Moses* Jeffersonville, IN 1958-0720M ¶E-4

Listen. Here's to the church, here is in the Name of the Lord. (I am prophesying.) ...Hear it! That's in the Name of the Lord. America has seen its day; no more will it rise. It's on its downfall. I speak in the Name of the Lord.
Wm Branham – *From That Time.* Klamath Falls, OR 1960-0716 ¶E-133

And I said, "Then I seen some great powerful woman rise in the United States." ...And I seen a great woman rise up, beautiful to look at, but a cruel wicked heart.

Then I seen the end time when the United States looked like a big bunch of bursted up stones and things like that, just blowed out, smoldering everywhere. Five of them [1933 vision of seven major world events] has happened, two of them's on their road. That has been twenty-eight years ago (See?), when it was predicted. If five of them is perfectly hit, the other two's got too.

Oh, repent and flee from the wrath that is to come, church of the living God. Get back to the real Gospel, friend. You Methodists, you Baptists, you Pentecostals, the rest of you turn to God with all your heart, for your hours are short.
Wm Branham – *Faithful Abraham.* Richmond, VA 1961-0312 ¶E-77-78

Heavenly Father, O God, when day... Way down deep in my soul, I wonder, as I'm made to wonder, of seeing this great beautiful nation of America, and seeing those big bombs out there being laid up across the sea...
Wm Branham – *God Has a Provided Way* Louisville, KY 1954-0404 ¶173

Now, then after that, I turned and looked, and I saw this United States burning like a smolder; rocks had been blowed up. And it was burning like a--a heap of fire in logs or something that just set it afire; and looked as far as I could see and she'd been blown up.
Wm Branham – *Seventy Weeks of Daniel* Jeffersonville, IN 1961-0806 ¶212

The late Rev. Jerry Falwell has been mocked and ridiculed by several commentators for saying what is being said by many churches and individuals around the world.[256] He suggested that the terrorist attacks that America recently experienced may be a chastisement from God on this country because of our increasing wickedness.[257] I'm sure that many pastors across this nation also believe that the recent damage done by hurricane Katrina in 2005 was also a chastisement from God against not only those areas, but the nation as a whole. New Orleans, for instance, is arguably the sexual imagery and a decadence capital of the United States with its annual Marti Gras events.

This is not a popular message with many Americans who are in a state of rebellion towards God, but it very well may be the truth. There is also another aspect of this issue that many people often overlook. The suffering that God endures as a result of the wickedness of this nation is something we rarely think about because we're so focused on ourselves.

The reasons why God could be chastising our nation are many. If these terrorist attacks were the result of His judgment, I'm amazed that He did not hit us a lot harder than He did; given the way this nation has turned away from Him. Many feel our liberal news media, the entertainment industry,[258] [259] the public school system and the judicial system are leading our country in a headlong charge towards paganism, atheism and humanism. Many Christians are putting forth significant efforts to stop this tide of apostasy. But a far higher number of lukewarm Christians are deceived or are just sitting on the sidelines expecting someone else to do the hard work, make the sacrifices, and *actually live as Christians ought to.*

This is a list of just some of the many ways our nation offends God on a daily basis. (Note that both non-Christians and Christians are engaging in these sins in huge numbers.)

- **We are killing innocent babies by the millions in our** abortion clinics. Over 45 million abortions have been performed since Roe vs. Wade was passed in 1973.[260] We have passed laws that give protection to the murderers who engage in these savage acts of butchery. We try to sugar-coat the horror of these acts by referring to them as a "fetus" and with innocent sounding terminology like "pro-choice" and "a woman's right to choose". [For Barak Obama's contribution to the abortion industry, see Chapter 18.]

- **We kicked God out of the public school systems and** replaced Christianity with the false religion of evolutionism. A wall of protection has been built around this failed theory to shield it from nearly all criticism in the secular public arena (especially the public schools and the media). Many young people today are turning away from God because they erroneously believe evolutionism has proven the Bible wrong. In many states, their Boards of Education have contributed to this problem by adding blatant evolution as fact language to the science standards.[261] [262]

- **Through the "tolerance" movement, we embrace and even** elevate the false gods and false prophets of many religions while simultaneously mocking the true God of the Bible and persecuting His followers.[263] [264] Recent Senate [S 1105, (2007)] and Congressional [H.R. 1592, (2007)] laws now make speaking out against false religions, and immoral behavior "Hate Crimes."[265]

- **We indoctrinate our children in the public schools to believe** that homosexuality is a morally acceptable life-style. This is often done against the wishes of many parents. It is also in sharp conflict with God's Word.[266] Organizations like the Boy Scouts are attacked for their strong moral stand on the issue of homosexuality.[267]

- **Our society is so inundated by sexual imagery that most men** are caught up in the sin of lust in one way or another. From the scantily clad women in the newspaper and TV advertisements to the porn sites on the internet, we are bombarded with, or are tempted by many of these images every day.

Prior to the 1960's, women dressed far more conservatively than they do today. Today, women's clothing styles are often in direct conflict with God's command "*that women adorn themselves in modest apparel* (1Timothy 2:9)" and that their apparel should be uniquely feminine and different from that of men's. (Deuteronomy 22:5)

The advertising industry fans the flames with their increasing reliance on using sex to sell all kinds of products and services. The problem has gotten so bad that it has had a profound impact even on the church. A recent study indicated that about 55% of men who attend church admit to viewing pornography.[268] [269] Many women come to church dressed more like prostitutes than the Godly women they profess to be.

- **Premarital sex is rampant in our society, especially in our** secular high schools and colleges. It has almost completely lost the stigma it had several decades ago of being sinful.[270] Findings from the *National Center for Health Statistics* in 1995 showed that 50% of 15 to 19 year old young woman and 55% of young men have engaged in premarital sexual intercourse.

  According to federal data gathered into a report called *Trends in Premarital Sex in the United States, 1954-2003*, premarital sex is normal behavior for the vast majority of Americans, and has been for decades," says study author Lawrence Finer, director of domestic research at the Guttmacher Institute. Finer's analysis of this data states that 95% of respondents had premarital sex.[271]

- **Many children today are born out of wedlock. This is an** especially bad problem in the African-American community where 70% of all children born are to single mothers.[272] In many cases, single mothers have children with the up-front intention of not getting married to the father because they do not feel they need a husband to properly raise the child. Having a child out of wedlock has almost completely lost the stigma that it once had of being sinful.[273]

- **Stay-at-home mothers are mocked as being out-of-touch** with the way today's modern woman should be living her life.[274] [275] Recently Hillary Clinton denigrated stay-at-home mothers in a *Nightline* interview with Ted Koppel, jibing, "I suppose I could have stayed home and baked cookies and had teas, but what I decided to do was to fulfill my profession."[276]

- **Corporal punishment, which is strongly supported by God** in the Bible, is being increasingly attacked by the liberal secular psychology community[277] and liberal media as being cruel and abusive.[278] Because parents are more and more turning away from training their children the way God commands them to, children that are disrespectful towards their parents and other authority figures have become commonplace.

- **Divorce is a common practice and liberally accepted in** society[279] [280], as well as within most churches[281] despite God saying He hates divorce. (Malachi 2:16) The Americans for Divorce Reform estimate is that "probably, 40 or possibly even 50 percent of marriages will end in divorce if current trends continue." Other estimates range from 40% to 50% for first marriages, with higher than 60% for second marriages, and over 70% for third marriage. The rate of divorce varies between different age groups, the rate for women and men between ages 20 and 24 is 36.6% and 38.8%, respectively.[282]

- **Feminism and political correctness have poisoned the** church.[283] Women pastors, who are forbidden by God in the Bible to hold such an office, are being ordained in increasing numbers.[284]

God is loving and merciful. But He has made it clear in His Holy Word that like a father who disciplines his children out of love when they go astray, He will also out of love chastise those nations that turn their backs on Him. There is a long history of God using the enemies of His children to punish those He loves for their grievous acts against Him. That does not mean that He sides with our enemies, or that He hates us. It simply means He sometimes uses them as instruments of chastisement to get our attention to encourage us to repent of our wickedness.

The whole idea behind his chastisement is to get us to a point of turning our hearts back towards him, and away from whatever sinful behavior or thoughts were keeping us from a close relationship with him. Sometimes this is accomplished with only minor chastisement. In other cases, God has to bring individuals, cities and even nations to their knees with devastating chastisement before they will give up their stubborn refusal to honor and worship him.

Too many people today are caught up in a feel-good religion and are quite uninformed about, or are unwilling to accept what God's Word has to say on the matter of His character. These misguided people are fond of talking about God's mercy and love. However what they often overlook, I suspect intentionally, is His justice, wrath and chastisement. It is no secret that He has these characteristics as well. He tells us about them in several Bible verses so there is no excuse for not knowing about them if one claims to be a Christian, or claims to understand what the God of the Bible is like. (Hebrews 12:6; Revelation 3:19)

The whole idea behind God's chastisement is to get us to a point of turning our hearts back towards Him, and away from…behavior or thoughts that keep us from a close relationship with Him.

What are needed to restore our Nation to greatness are Godly living people, filling Godly churches – both advocating for and contributing to a Godly, Christ-centered nation. What we don't need are lukewarm Christians in "Cool Churches."

One can imagine how poorly a father would be viewed if he never disciplined his children. Can you further imagine how awful his children would grow up to be? It is the same with God, except on a much larger scale. What happened with these terrorist events, as bad as they were, are miniscule compared to what God has done in the past to other nations when they refused to turn from their wickedness. Remember the global flood in Noah's day? It is estimated that billions of people were killed during that event.[285] And like our secular media today, skeptics and unbelievers responded in Noah's day to God's warnings about His chastisement with indignation. Noah was mocked, but in the end Noah was right.

Shi'ite Messianic Beliefs and Russian Nuclear Weapons

Iranian President Mahmoud Ahmadinejad is devoted to a mystical religious figure, and an eschatological belief system that worries Western leaders. He speaks often about his strong belief in the second coming of the Shi'ite Muslims' "hidden" 12th Imam. "Our revolution's main mission is to pave the way for the reappearance of the 12th Imam, the Mahdi,"[286] he has said.

According to Shi'ite Muslim teaching, Abul-Qassem Mohammad, the 12th leader whom Shi'ites consider descended from the Prophet Mohammed, disappeared in 941[287] but will return at the end of time to lead an era of Islamic justice.

There is a possibility that Ahmadinejad's belief in the 12th Imam's return may be linked to the supposed growing influence of a secretive society devoted to the Mahdi which was banned in the early 1980s.[288]

Founded in 1953 and used by the Shah of Iran to try to eradicate followers of the Bahai faith, the Hojjatieh Society[289] is governed by the conviction that the 12th Imam's return will be hastened by the creation of chaos, war and bloodshed upon the earth – what Christians call the Apocalypse.

Ahmadinejad, who is only the second non-cleric to become president since the revolution, has made clear his immense respect for Ayatollah Mohammad Taghi Mesbah-Yazdi, a deeply conservative cleric with close ties to the Hojjatieh-founded Haqqani theological school in Qom.

An example of his messianic tendencies surfaced after 108 people were killed in an aircraft crash in Teheran. Mr. Ahmadinejad praised the victims, saying: "What is important is that they have shown the way to martyrdom which we must follow."[290]

For many of the hundreds of delegates who attended Mr. Ahmadinejad's speech to the UN in September 2007[291], his discourse on the merits of the 12th Imam finally brought home the reality of the danger his regime poses to world peace.

Rather than allaying concerns about Iran's nuclear ambitions, Mr. Ahmadinejad spoke at length about how a Muslim savior would relieve the world's suffering. [292]

The era of Western predominance was drawing to a close, he said, and would soon be replaced by a "bright future" ushered in by the 12th Imam's return. "Without any doubt, the Promised One, who is the ultimate Savior, will come. The pleasing aroma of justice will permeate the whole world."[293] It is believed that this one man will lead all nations and religions, and usher in an era of world peace.

Iranian President Mahmoud Ahmadinejad is described as aggressive, frightening and violent. Yet, he is frank and direct, stating openly the true intentions of the Iranian regime.[294] Foreign policy and national security analysts are attempting to discern the potential impact of his fundamentalist beliefs. Their conclusions so far are that from the information available, his beliefs points to a purist fundamentalism potentially even more radical and dangerous than that of al-Qaeda.

Ahmadinejad has made repeated statements (as have many Iranian officials) regarding Iran's "right" to a full nuclear fuel cycle.[295] The really alarming aspect is that – if the world's leading intelligence agencies are to be believed – he is seriously attempting to acquire a nuclear weapons arsenal.[296]

Ahmadinejad is dangerous, given his apparent disposition, as the president of the world's foremost state sponsor of terrorism. But as the president of a nuclear armed nation, the situation could be untenable.

Considering his aggressive radicalism in context with the potential convergence of nuclear opportunity, Mahmoud Ahmadinejad could be the most dangerous foreign leader we have faced. He must be seen and analyzed as more than just "potentially" irrational, as his religious beliefs must be clearly and thoroughly understood.

And he really does believe. The mahdaviat is central and preeminent in Mr. Ahmadinejad's outlook[297], in things both religious and political. Mahdaviat it is a technical religious term derived from mahdi, Arabic for "rightly-guided one," a major figure in Islamic eschatology. He is as the Encyclopaedia of Islam[298] explains, "the restorer of religion and justice who will rule before the end of the world."

DAILY NEWS

THE EVIL HAS LANDED

STORIES ON PAGES 4-7 EDITORIAL PAGE 22

Hate-spewing Iran prez speaks today at Columbia

Outrage grows as school defends HITLER 'invitation'

It is clear that he believes the United States (the Great Satan) and Israel (the Little Satan)[299] are impediments to his ideas of world peace, and that by destroying them he will pave the way through bloodshed, for his messiah. His openly stated desires to "wipe Israel off the map" and "pave the way for the reappearance of the 12th Imam"[300] open the possibility that, with the power of nuclear weaponry at hand, he could unthinkably forsake the well-being of his own nation in order to serve a "greater purpose".

Make no mistake, nuclear capability in the hands of Iran or Iraq will mean certain destruction of the United States. Ahmadinejad is capable of creating a situation so cataclysmic that it would usher in the 12th Imam, thereby, potentially in his mind, saving the world and restoring Islam. To do this though, according to his convoluted thinking, Israel and America must first be destroyed.

With the Iran-Russia nuclear deal signed, there is the accessibility of plutonium from spent nuclear fuel rods from his country's atomic plant in Bushehr, nuclear weapons must be considered a possibility.[301] Though William Branham in 1932 saw the decline of the Soviet Union and of Russia's hegemony, he continued to receive prophetic warnings about Russia's involvement in the destruction of America.

In a sermon titled *Water from the Rock*, he says "*The bomb that would probably burst every atom in the earth is hanging yonder in Russia tonight. It ought to a been fired a long time ago, but God's long-suffering, not willing that any should perish, past due.*"[302] In 1956 he said "*this old world's going to be blowed up, the Bible said so. Russia thinks so right now. She's got the bomb hanging right there, your name wrote on it.*"[303]

William Branham says God will use Russia and other heathen nations to chastise America, just as He has done in the past with Israel when she had backslid. "*But now the end of the Gentiles dispensation is here, and Russia has a bomb pointed..It'll go to powder in one second's time, the whole nation. It'll be completely annihilated. A bunch of heathens...*"[304]

William Branham remained consistent with his visions of 1933 that prophesied communism's demise. In 1962 he reiterates that neither Russia nor communism would conquer the world. As far as a country of military might, he called them "a small pebble."[305] Russia is a small pebble that has an arsenal full of nuclear weapons, the ability to export atomic technology, and an abiding contempt for America.

Hopes of reducing tensions in a post-Bush world were chilled the day after Mr. Obama won. In an address to the Russian Parliament, President Dmitri Medvedev welcomed President-elect Obama with a threat to deploy Russian missiles on the Polish border if the United States put anti-missile systems in Eastern Europe. Leonid Radzikhovsky, a Russian journalist, has said that "the existential void of our politics has been filled entirely by anti-Americanism."

As frustrations mount, it is often easier to blame an external force than the country's own failings. The result is an inferiority complex toward the West and, in particular, the United States. In his November 5, 2008 speech, President Medvedev asserted that "we have no inherent anti-Americanism." True enough, but in recent years, anti-Americanism has been carefully cultivated by official and semi-official propaganda, especially on government-controlled television, which manipulates popular insecurities and easily slides into outright paranoia.

In 2008, Russian television commemorated the anniversary of Sept. 11, 2001, with a prime-time program promoting the conspiracy theory that the attacks were engineered by American imperialists in order to unleash war. A staggering 43 percent of Russians agreed in a poll last year that "one of the goals of the foreign policy of the United States is the total destruction of Russia."[306] With this type of propaganda, and a national belief system that hates America, unleashing its anger and pent up frustration will seem justifiable and make it far easier to press the nuclear button.

I think it is fairly plain to see that America has arrived on the eve of her destruction. The reasons are clear. The method and the agents of delivery are ready and willing. What is left?

Can America change her ways? Can she repent? Certainly America *can* repent and avoid destruction – but will she? That really is the question isn't it? ***Will America change its ways, return to its roots as a Christian nation and follow the moral commands of the Bible? – No, I don't think so.***

Not if this final prophecy of William Branham is unconditional;

"America has become condemned. And what did she do, according to the vision? [The 1933 vision] She elected the wrong person. [This could be Rodham-Clinton as President; it also could be Obama by extension Rodham-Clinton as Secretary of State, or even Janet Napolitano as Secretary of Homeland Security] I don't know how long it'll take it to run out, but it will be someday. THUS SAITH THE LORD. It will. She's on her downward move right now. She'll never come back again"[307]

11 Dangers of Warnings & Predictions

Dangers of Warnings & Predictions

"There is a kind of seesaw of attention between the public and officials," says Dr. Jody Lanard, a risk communications expert. "When everyone is ignoring the problem, officials focus on raising the alarm. When people finally pay attention and start worrying, the officials instantly want to calm them down again. Everybody in the warning business worries that people will accuse them of crying wolf," she adds. "They forget that in the actual Boy Who Cried Wolf story, the wolf finally showed up."[308]

A false alarm, also called a nuisance alarm, is the nonfactual or untimely report of an emergency, causing unnecessary panic and/or bringing resources (such as fire engines) to a place where they are not needed. Over time, repeated false or nuisance alarms in a certain area may cause individuals to start to ignore all alarms, knowing that each time it will likely be a fake. The concept of this can be traced at least as far back as Aesop's story of The Boy Who Cried Wolf, where many episodes of a boy falsely yelling "wolf" caused the townspeople to ignore his cries when a real wolf came. In addition, false alarms have the potential of diverting energy and resources away from legitimate emergencies, which could ultimately lead to loss of life.

One tragic example of the consequences of continued false alarms was at Boland Hall at Seton Hall University on January 19, 2000. Months of false alarms caused many students to start ignoring the fire alarms. However, when an actual fire broke out, three students who ignored the alarms died, and many others suffered injuries.[309]

The Side Effects of Repetitive and/or Numerous Warnings

Shock-tactics in health-promotion campaigns have backfired: new analysis from the Social Issues Research Centre (SIRC) in Oxford indicates that warnings may have hidden psychological side effects. SIRC has monitored media coverage of health issues and public responses over the past three years, and identified several types of adverse reaction to the high "doses" of health-scares and warnings received by the public (points 1-2):[310]

1. Warning-Fatigue

This is the most common effect, in which people become habituated and de-sensitized to campaigns, exhibiting a diminishing response and eventually paying no attention at all. Constant exhortations on healthy eating and exercise, for example, have had little effect on obesity, which continues to rise.

Warning-fatigue is highly dangerous because sufferers from this effect are likely to ignore important genuine information as well as unfounded scares. "That is the danger of crying wolf," said a SIRC Director. "When there really is a wolf, you come up against warning-fatigue: your audience has simply switched off."

2. Forbidden-Fruit Effect

Another very common response to authoritarian warnings is increased desire for the "forbidden" substance or activity. In many cases, the constant stream of warnings, scares and bans has led to deliberate defiance.

This effect was evident in initial public responses to the beef-on-the-bone scare and mad cow disease, when there was a scramble to "beat the ban" and sales of beef increased dramatically.

Rebellious individuals (especially teenagers) seem particularly susceptible to the forbidden-fruit effect: extensive anti-smoking campaigns in recent years, for example, coincide with reported increases in teenage smoking.[311] Heavy-handed warnings about the dangers of drugs and alcohol have been equally ineffective. What is the rebellious individual's approach? Eat, drink and be merry, for to-morrow we may die. (Isaiah 22:13; Luke 12:19, Ecclesiastes 8:15)

The SIRC research indicates that a more socially responsible approach to health promotion could reduce these adverse effects. "The main problem seems to be that health promotion has become a cut-throat competitive industry, with ever-increasing numbers of agencies, charities, politicians and academics vying for media attention and funding," said a SIRC Director.

"The result of all these competing vested interests is that people are bombarded with scary headlines, warnings and often conflicting advice, much of it based on very flimsy or dubious scientific evidence. This is clearly not in the public interest..."[312]

Interestingly, over two thousand years ago a Jewish prophet foretold a time where concerns about current events would create stress so great, that "*men's hearts would be over-charged (Luke 21:34)...and failing* (Luke 21:26)." When I say "concern," I mean worry, anxiety or fear.

Interestingly, over two thousand years ago a Jewish prophet foretold a time where concerns about current events would create stress so great, that "men's hearts would be over-charged...and failing."

Health experts agree that "concern" has negative and often deadly effect upon the body. Chronic stress can be the result of a host of irritating hassles or a long-term life condition, such as a difficult job situation or living with a disease. In people who have higher levels of chronic stress, the stress response lasts longer. Over time, chronic stress can have an effect on: high blood pressure, abnormal heartbeat (arrhythmia), problems with blood clotting, and hardening of the arteries (atherosclerosis). It is also linked to coronary artery disease, heart attack, and heart failure.

A Yale University study recently reported that those aggravating things that go wrong in the day and those irritating things that go bump in the night – disrupting routines and interrupting sleep – all have a cumulative effect on your brain, especially its ability to remember and learn.

The study goes on to say that as science gains greater insight into the consequences of stress on the brain, the picture that emerges is not a pretty one. A chronic overreaction to stress overloads the brain with powerful hormones that are intended only for short-term duty in emergency situations. Their cumulative effect damages and kills brain cells.[313]

Luke 21:34-36; "*And take heed to yourselves, lest at any time your hearts be overcharged with surfeiting, and drunkenness, and cares of this life, and so that day come upon you unawares. For as a snare shall it come on all them that dwell on the face of the whole earth. Watch ye therefore, and pray always, that ye may be accounted worthy to escape all these things that shall come to pass, and to stand before the Son of man.*" and Luke 21:26; "*Men's hearts failing them for fear, and for looking after those things which are coming on the earth: for the powers of heaven shall be shaken*"

Again, the warning comes about "cares" or concerns/worries/fears etc. and an additional warning or prediction about compulsive and addictive behavior. The term *surfeiting* means to do anything in gross excess. It specifically was referring to gluttony or overeating, attempting to supply or feed ones desire for more. It is the increasing tendency to eat to the point where we feel like its Thanksgiving Day, every day. Its broader meaning relates to any compulsion and/or addiction, even to simply accumulating well beyond any necessity. That could be money, collections, even food. Not simply storing up food, but "super-sizing" when it is not biologically necessary for survival.

Surfeiting is that feeling of "needing" when there is no genuine need. For example, collecting insignificant things; in the 1990's there was a *Beanie Baby* craze that swept up many, many people. Not only did people want ALL of them, but were willing to pay large sums of money to obtain rare or missing ones. The net value of some collections was so much, that at one time a collection was used as capital assets to obtain a $200,000 loan.[314] Though retail prices originally listed for less than $5.00 each, one doll *Coral Casino Bear* later sold for $3,550.[315] Online discussion sites that focus on *Beanie Babies*, regularly talk about obsession and preoccupation, even resorting to deception and criminality to obtain the coveted dolls.

The warnings of Jesus were few, and appropriate. They were specific and timely.

Recently I spoke with a relative about the clutter of boxes stacked up in his garage. I was curious, as he usually keeps his house, garage and property quite clean and organized. I asked if he was moving or having a garage sale. He frustratingly responded that his entire garage was completely full of boxes that contained the doll collections of another family member. He said she started collecting a particular type and then just could not stop collecting collections! It went beyond the liking of her own interests, and encompassed a drive to collect, to possess as many as she could. This is surfeiting.

Ask a person that overeats or over-collects if they are satisfied and they will tell you, "NO! I am not." Often the feelings afterward are disgust, despair, sadness, guilt, shame and anger. They feel out of control and anxious – these emotions not only negatively affect mood, but harm the body, particularly the heart.

Jesus warned that this behavior would occur (Luke 21), and that it would be harmful. It was also given as a sign to identify the time of the Last Days and to reflect the feeling of emptiness inside that many attempt to satisfy through buying, drinking, eating or other compulsive behaviors (sex, work, exercise, etc.).

The warnings of Jesus were few, and appropriate. They were specific and timely. They also came at a time when few people were actually warning the people about anything, therefore the people initially "*heard him gladly.*" (Mark 12:37)

But after a ministry that spanned three years, those that did not heed his warnings and change their ways and lifestyles, became hardened and with the hardening came both immunity to the warning and a low-level chronic psychological anxiety.

Warnings were meant to be used wisely and sparingly so they would have a maximum impact and a greater chance of successfully influencing an outcome. Just as refusal to act upon a legitimate warning have harmful consequences, frivolous warnings that upset and frighten are equally dangerous, not only to our physical health but they have a tendency to create immunity to real danger and warning.

Our personal fear alerts are turned on all the time. So we do not, will not or cannot listen to a genuine warning that will save our life or more importantly, our soul.

Unlike mice, we humans can fear events we have merely read or heard about, and so we worry about disasters we may never experience. If we are unable to respond for lack of an appropriate target, the fear accumulates, and we become anxious. Each terror alert, too, triggers a wave of often unjustified fear.

Much of our current external fear still stems from the attacks in the United States on Sept. 11, 2001. Fear and foreboding have become common reactions to terrorism in general and no longer appear limited to particular attacks. There is real danger, but most of what is told on the news is knee-jerk reactions to rumor or overgeneralizations made by uninformed "talking head" reporters whose knowledge of facts or subject matter is confined to what they read on their tele-prompters. [If you want to be frightened for good cause, read the complete report by Anthony H. Cordesman to Senate Judiciary Subcommittee on Technology, Terrorism, and Government Information in 2001.][316]

We have a newfound vulnerability and there is regular ongoing doom-and-gloom in the daily news and in many pulpits. There are physical, emotional and spiritual ramifications of living in a time of pervasive fear, when we are constantly threatened with the prospect of biological and/or nuclear warfare.

Dr. Marc Siegel says *the main problem is that we are all powerful voyeurs.* Rather than learning to be safe by avoiding true dangers, we take what we see on TV and apply it directly to our own lives. We immerse ourselves in the information of the latest terrorist attack, ramping up our own stress levels and planting seeds of fear.[317]

With so much attention paid to that which we cannot control, it is easy to lose sight of, and neglect, behavioral and lifestyle choices that clearly impact the quality of our lives. In addition, important, global health issues tend to get swept under the rug, while hysteria multiplies. Legitimate concerns go unaddressed, and valuable resources are wasted and we are no healthier or spiritually prepared despite it all. That's truly frightening because there is a "wolf" about, but the boy has cried so often no one is listening or they are paralyzed through fear into inaction.

At a time in history when true scourges are quite rare, the population is controlled by fear. Rather than enjoy the safety that our technological advances have provided us, we feel uncertain. Constant and unlikely (e.g. avian bird flu, anthrax in the mail, Russians stockpiling smallpox, etc.) warnings meant to shield us, actually spread panic more effectively than any terrorist agent by sending the message that something is in the offing. Our personal fear alerts are turned on all the time. So we do not, will not or cannot listen to a genuine warning that will save our life or more importantly, our soul.

*A powerful woman...**will** raise up.* Her influence will help bring about the "destruction of America." These prophecies are frightening, yet they only serve to warn us and prepare us for a worse fate.

Focus hard, concentrate on *certain* things, ones that God has said will happen, and then truly be afraid and take action against those things that stand to destroy you both body and soul. Jesus said in Matthew 10:28 "*And fear not them which kill the body, but are not able to kill the soul: but rather fear him which is able to destroy both soul and body in hell.*" Hell; the loss of your soul; separation from God – these are things that should truly trouble and frighten you. I hope this book helps you become convinced, concerned and committed to living differently.

12

The Nature of True Biblical Prophecy

The Nature of True Biblical Prophecy

If we would correctly interpret and apply prophecy which is yet unfulfilled, we should first discern the course or the path which fulfilled prophecy has historically taken. If we would "hit the mark" in our study of William Branham's prophecy, we must first understand the course of prophecy from the Old Testament to the New. From this process, we will establish several governing principles for the study of modern prophecy, principles that should apply to the study of any prophecy.

(1) Some Old Testament prophecy was indirect rather than direct prophecy. This has taken me a number of years to embrace. There are prophecies that were clearly recognized as such at the time they were given. The promise in Micah 5:2 that Messiah would be born in Bethlehem is an example of a direct prophecy. Even the unbelieving Jewish religious leaders of Jerusalem recognized this (Matthew 2:1-6). But Matthew's other "prophecies" in the first chapters of his Gospel are far from direct.

Who would ever have read Hosea 11:1 and concluded this was a prophecy that Jesus would be brought by His parents out of Egypt and back to the land of Israel (Matthew 2:14-15)? Yet Matthew tells his readers that this fulfilled the prophecy of Hosea 11:1. Some prophecies were recognized as such only after their fulfillment. I would call these "indirect prophecies."

(2) While prophecy may be figuratively or symbolically revealed, we can expect it to be literally fulfilled. In type,[318] the Messiah who was to come was portrayed as the bronze serpent, which was lifted up on a pole (Numbers 21:19; John 3:14), and as the Passover lamb (Exodus 12; John 1:29; 1 Corinthians 5:7; 1 Peter 1:19; 2:21-25). In Psalm 22, the passion of our Lord is described by the very terms which David used to portray his personal anguish of soul. In Isaiah 53, we have another prophecy of the atoning work of Israel's Messiah. All these prophetic pictures were literally fulfilled. So, too, the prophecies that Messiah would be born in Bethlehem (Micah 5:2; Matthew 2:5-6) of a virgin (Isaiah 7:14; Matthew 1:21-23) were literally fulfilled. Whether in symbol, in figure, or in direct statement, the prophecies of the Old Testament which have already been fulfilled were fulfilled literally. We should therefore expect that the prophecies which remain unfulfilled, those which pertain to the second coming of our Lord, will be literally fulfilled.

Why is it that Christians today expect that prophecy can be neatly outlined, charted, mapped, and laid out in such a way that we can say with certainty just how the last days will come to a close?

(3) Old Testament prophecy has almost always been fulfilled in a way that no one expected. Peter wrote of the prophets of old who were perplexed by what they had prophesied:

Of which salvation the prophets have enquired and searched diligently, who prophesied of the grace that should come unto you: Searching what, or what manner of time the Spirit of Christ which was in them did signify, when it testified beforehand the sufferings of Christ, and the glory that should follow. Unto whom it was revealed, that not unto themselves, but unto us they did minister the things, which are now reported unto you by them that have preached the gospel unto you with the Holy

Ghost sent down from heaven; which things the angels desire to look into. (1 Peter 1:10-12).

Peter tells us that the prophets themselves could not put it all together. They diligently studied their own writings, but they were not able to comprehend their message so far as the person or the timing of events was concerned (verse 11). In particular, I believe Peter was referring to their perplexity over the two themes of prophecy: (1) the sufferings of Messiah; and, (2) His glory. How could it be that the same person could suffer for the sins of man (e.g., Isaiah 52:13—53:12) and yet reign in power and glory (e.g., Psalm 2)? How could these two things happen at the same time? No one was able to explain before its fulfillment. How could prophecy speak of the humanity of the Messiah (e.g., His birth – Isaiah 7:14; Micah 5:2) and of His deity (e.g., Isaiah 9:6)? [319]

What the prophets failed to discern others did not comprehend either. While the chief priests and scribes knew that the Messiah would be born in Bethlehem (Matthew 2:1-6), they so misunderstood the prophecies about Messiah that they conspired to murder Him. With the exception of a handful of individuals such as Mary, Simeon and Anna (Luke 2), few realized prophecy was being fulfilled before their very eyes. Even Mary, the mother of our Lord, puzzled over what she had seen and been told (Luke 1:29; 2:19). The disciples did not fully grasp the events of our Lord's life as fulfilled prophecy until after they had taken place (John 16:12-24).

Why is it, then, that Christians today expect that prophecy can be neatly outlined, charted, mapped, and laid out in such a way that we can say with certainty just how the last days will come to a close? This kind of thinking flies in the face of what we learn from those prophecies which have already been fulfilled. Divine prophecy will always be puzzling until after its fulfillment. Only then will we see it all marvelously, literally, and meticulously fulfilled. We have a greater grasp of prophecy today because of what has already been fulfilled. An appreciation of the concept of progressive revelation enables us to see more and more truth as time goes on.

We have every reason to expect prophecy to be literally fulfilled, but we have little basis for supposing that we can suggest precisely and dogmatically just how this will take place. Let us be suspicious of every neatly packed prophetic scheme, for why should we think we are better able to predict the specifics of our Lord's second coming when the prophets of old were unable to outline the events of the first?

(4) Some prophecy may very well have multiple fulfillments.

Prophecies may have dual (or multiple) fulfillment, but scriptural evidence should suggest the initial fulfillment and later consummation. Many topics in the Bible lend themselves to illustration of multiple ideas in that they illustrate principles with multiple applications. One known example is God's promise to Abraham.

2 And I will make you a great nation, And I will bless you, And make your name great; And so you shall be a blessing;

3 And I will bless those who bless you, And the one who curses you I will curse. And in you all the families of the earth shall be blessed." Genesis 12:2-3

5 And He took him outside and said, *"Now look toward the heavens, and count the stars, if you are able to count them."* And He said to him, *"So shall your descendants be."* Genesis 15:5

It is clear that Abraham's literal descendants, the Jews, are of sufficient number to satisfy this prophecy. Yet, it also has a spiritual fulfillment, as Paul says.

29 And if you belong to Christ, then you are Abraham's offspring, heirs according to promise. Galatians 3:29

Prophecy may even refer to past events which prefigure future ones. Many are familiar with prophetic types, as when Abraham "sacrificed" his son Isaac on Mt. Moriah, or when Joseph was sold by his brothers as dead only to be made king over them.

Dual (multiple) fulfillments ordinarily take the form of (a) immediate application(s) and (b) consummation. For example, Matthew's prophetic use of Hosea 11:1 in Matthew 2:15:

When Israel was a child, then I loved him, and called My son out of Egypt. As they called them, so they went from them: they sacrificed unto Baalim, and burned incense to graven images.

Was Matthew wrong to quote this as a Messianic prophecy? No, the Messiah, just like Israel, had gone down into Egypt for safety in a time of trouble, only to come back out to the Land God had promised Abraham. It is probable that an omniscient God, Who guided both the Old Testament prophets and the New Testament inspired writers, directed certain prophecies to ancient Israel, but also would have known that a future event ultimately would fulfill the meaning of His words. It surely is possible, and preserves the integrity of the New Testament writers. Let me suggest another example to illustrate this point.

David declared: *"Yea, mine own familiar friend, in whom I trusted, who did eat of my bread, hath lifted up his heel against me"* (Psalm 41:9). During the last supper, Christ quoted from this passage as follows: *"He that eateth my bread lifted up his heel against me"* (John 13:18), applying it to the treachery of Judas and declaring that such fulfilled the statement in David's psalm. The Lord, however, slightly altered the quotation. He omitted, *"whom I trusted,"* from the original source, the reason being, He never trusted Judas! Jesus knew from the beginning who would betray Him (John 6:64). It is clear, therefore, that Psalm 41:9 had an immediate application to one of David's enemies, but the remote and complete "fulfillment" or consummation came in Judas' betrayal of the Son of God.

(5) God reveals prophecy partially and progressively. One reason why the prophets of old could not understand the promises of God contained in their writings is that the plan was only partly revealed. Prophecy, at best, is partial:

For we know in part, and we prophesy in part, but when what is perfect comes, the partial will be set aside. For now we see in a mirror indirectly, but then we will see face to face. Now I know in part, but then shall know fully, just as I have been fully known (1 Corinthians 13:9-10, 12).

We should not be surprised that the prophets had difficulty attempting to harmonize the two prophetic themes of suffering and glory, as Peter tells us (1 Peter 1:11). After all, the revelation the prophets received and communicated to us was partial. So, too, the prophecies pertaining to our Lord's second coming are partial. We know this for certain because Paul has informed us in this Corinthian passage that all prophecy is partial. The prophecies we have been given are like the pieces of a puzzle. There are enough to give us a general idea of what lies ahead, but not enough to reveal the entire picture. Prophecy was therefore not given so much to detail the sequence of future events as it was to underscore the certainty of future events.

The New Testament informs us of certain truths, which are called "mysteries." In its most elementary form, a mystery is a truth which would not be known apart from divine revelation, and which was not known until God did reveal it in the form of prophetic revelation.

As an apostle, Paul was granted the privilege of making known certain "mysteries" (1 Corinthians 2:6-16; Ephesians 3:3). The partial hardening of Israel was such a mystery (Romans 11:15). Since the New Testament informs us of these truths called "mysteries" which were not made known in the Old, we see that the prophecies of the past were partial. Since Paul taught in 1 Corinthians 13 that all prophecy is partial, we must conclude that the unfulfilled prophecies of the Bible are partial prophecies. They provide pieces of the plans and purposes of God for the future, but not the entire picture.

(6) Prophecy is particularly profitable to those who can look back on its fulfillment. Peter wrote in his first epistle that though the prophets of old studied their own works in an effort to understand it, they were informed by revelation that their ministry was particularly intended for the benefit of those who would understand it in the light of its fulfillment. (1 Peter 1:10-12).

Over and over, we are told by the writers of the Gospels that the events recorded were the fulfillment of Old Testament prophecy. The preaching of the apostles was based upon the premise that Christ's death, burial, and resurrection were the fulfillment of Old Testament prophecy (Acts 2). The Book of Revelation, as all other prophecies yet unfulfilled, will be most meaningful to those to whom it can be said, *"These things took place, in order that it might be fulfilled..."* (Matthew 26:53-54)

(7) Biblical prophecy was seldom fulfilled in the lifetime of those who received it. When you stop to think about it, few Old Testament prophecies were fulfilled in the lifetime of those who first received them. For that matter, few prophecies have been fulfilled in the lifetime of those who have read and studied them. Periods of fulfillment are short and infrequent when compared to the periods of expectation.

While men have hoped for the fulfillment of prophecy in their day, few have seen it come to pass. The point I am trying to make is that prophecy would be of little value to the people of God if it were meaningful only to those who lived during the time of its fulfillment. While you and I should hope to see our Lord return, as well as seek to hasten it (2 Peter 3:12), history should teach us that most of those who hoped to see prophecy fulfilled in their day did not.

(8) All prophecy is pertinent to the present. While it is true that prophecy has a particular benefit to those who study it in the light of its fulfillment, prophecy is profitable for all. This is a necessary conclusion from Paul's words to Timothy and to the Romans:

All scripture is given by inspiration of God, and is profitable for doctrine, for reproof, for correction, and for instruction in righteousness. That the man of God may be perfect, thoroughly furnished unto all works (2 Timothy 3:16-17).

For everything that was written in former times was written for our instruction, so that through endurance and through encouragement of the scriptures we may have hope (Romans 15:4).

Peter agrees when he writes:

Seeing then that all these things shall be dissolved, what manner of persons ought ye to be in all holy conversation and godliness, Looking for and hasting unto the coming of the day of God, wherein the heavens being on fire shall be dissolved, and the elements shall melt with fervent heat? (2 Peter 3:10-14)

Prophecy is much more than a mere telling of the future. Prophets are vastly different from fortune tellers. The prophet's role was to incite his listeners to godly living. The reader was urged to remember that God is sovereign over history and that His promises are sure.

Through Biblical prophecy, the godly will be encouraged to live pure and righteous lives and to be willing to suffer and sacrifice in the present in order to participate in the certain blessings of God's future promises. In this way, prophecy is profitable to every reader who will hear and obey God's Word, regardless of whether or not these prophecies are fulfilled in his lifetime. That is why John can say to the reader of the Book of Revelation,

Blessed is he that readeth, and they that hear the words of this prophecy, and keep those things which are written therein: for the time is at hand. (Revelation 1:3).

These are some of the Biblical lessons about true prophecy which we should learn from the examples of the past. Let us not forget them as we seek to study the prophecies which are still future.

13

The Conditional Nature of Prophecy

We now need to examine an aspect of prophecy that is very important, and not well understood by most Christians. When a prophecy is spoken to people about them personally, it is almost always conditional in nature. The fulfillment of the prophecy often depends on the attitude and actions of the one to whom the prophecy is given. This is different from the generally accepted teaching that when God declares something, it is "set in stone." If you are one who has believed that a true prophet of God is defined by the fact that his prophecies always come to pass, you should carefully read this chapter.

Much Prophecy is Conditional

We have seen in the previous chapter that prophecy is giving a message from God or the Lord Jesus to another person or persons, and that the main reason for prophecy is God's love for us. God wants a relationship with us, and He wants to show His love for us and desires us to love Him.

Certainly there are prophecies from God that are "set in stone" and will come to pass exactly as God spoke them, but not all prophecies are that way. Prophecies spoken to individuals or groups about what will happen to them in the future are usually conditional upon the actions and attitudes of the people addressed. God gave us free will, and He responds to the free will decisions we make. What makes the prophecy conditional is there is an unspoken "if" built into the prophecy. In other words, the prophecy has a condition in it.

Another way to look at the conditional nature of prophecy is to remember that prophecy is an expression of God's love for people, rather than just announcing what will happen in the future, so He could then gloat when it happened. Take the prophecy Jonah gave to the people of Nineveh: "*...Forty more days and Nineveh will be overturned*" (Jonah 3:4b). Anyone reading the book of Jonah sees that Jonah's prophecy did not come to pass. Nevertheless, Jonah was a true prophet. Furthermore, had the prophecy been fulfilled as spoken without being conditional, what would have been the point? To tell thousands of people they were going to die in 40 days? No, there is another explanation.

The prophecy of Jonah, and other prophecies to people, often have an unspoken "if" clause.[320] When the "if" is expressed, the prophecy looks like this: "Forty more days and Nineveh will be overturned if you do not change." God is expressing His love via a prophecy that calls people to greater things. The prophecy gives people a chance to rise up and walk in a godly fashion before Him. The people of Nineveh did, and therefore God's prophecy was not fulfilled. Sometimes a prophecy of good is spoken, but the people turn to evil. The good that was foretold to them often does not come to pass either.

There are many times when the "if" of revelation or prophecy is clearly spoken. For example, in Genesis 20, Abimelech of Gerar had taken Abraham's wife Sarah to be his wife. He did this not knowing that Sarah was married to Abraham, because Abraham had told him Sarah was his "sister." God said to Abimelech: "*Now therefore restore the man his wife; for he is a prophet, and he shall pray for thee, and thou shalt live: and if thou restore her not, know thou that thou shalt surely die, thou, and all that are thine.*" (Genesis 20:7).

In this case, God said "if" you do not return her you will die, but how would the revelation have looked were there no "if"? God would have just announced that Abimelech would die because he had taken another man's wife, and then He would have changed the revelation if Abimelech repented and returned Sarah to Abraham.

God can change a revelation or a prophecy, and in this chapter we will see many examples of Him doing so when the people who received the prophecy changed their behavior.

There are two primary reasons why it is important to know that prophecy is so often conditional. The first is to build and maintain faith in God and His prophets. People who do not realize that prophecy is conditional may have their faith shaken if a particular prophecy does not come to pass or if they see a prophecy in the Bible that did not come to pass. For example, a person operating under the premise that true prophecy must come to pass as spoken is forced to say that Jonah was a false prophet. But we know that Jonah was a true prophet of God. If a particular prophecy is not fulfilled, we should examine the prophecy and the situation to see if the reason that it was not fulfilled had to do with a shift in the situation.

People who do not realize that prophecy is conditional may have their faith shaken if a particular prophecy does not come to pass or a prophecy does not come to pass as they may have thought.

The second reason it is important to know that prophecy can be conditional is that people need to know that sometimes their behavior can affect whether or not a prophecy comes to pass. A Christian who is walking with the Lord needs to continue in faith, prayer, and an obedient lifestyle. On the other hand, a disobedient person who receives an undesirable prophecy can repent, in which case the prophecy that he had received may either not be fulfilled (just as Jonah's prophecy to the Ninevites was not), or changed (as we will see in Hezekiah's case).

Jeremiah Sets Forth the Conditional Nature of Prophecy

In the book of Jeremiah, God reveals the conditional nature of prophecy, and He compared His working with people with a potter working with clay. Please read the following section of Jeremiah carefully, because Christians have misunderstood it for centuries.

Jeremiah 18:1-11
"***1*** The word which came to Jeremiah from the LORD, saying, ***2*** Arise, and go down to the potter's house, and there I will cause you to hear my words. ***3*** Then I went down to the potter's house, and, behold, he worked a work on the wheels. ***4*** And the vessel that he made of clay was marred in the hand of the potter: so he made it again another vessel, as seemed good to the potter to make it.

5 Then the word of the LORD came to me, saying, ***6*** O house of Israel, cannot I do with you as this potter? said the LORD. Behold, as the clay is in the potter's hand, so are you in my hand, O house of Israel. ***7*** At what instant I shall speak concerning a nation, and concerning a kingdom, to pluck up, and to pull down, and to destroy it; ***8*** If that nation, against whom I have pronounced, turn from their evil, I will repent of the evil that I thought to do to them. ***9*** And at what instant I shall speak concerning a nation, and concerning a kingdom, to build and to plant it; ***10*** If it do evil in my sight, that it obey not my voice, then I will repent of the good, with which I said I would benefit them. ***11*** Now therefore go to, speak to the men of Judah, and to the inhabitants of Jerusalem, saying, Thus said the LORD; Behold, I frame evil against you, and devise a device against you: return you now every one from his evil way, and make your ways and your doings good."

Many people think that the lesson the potter and the clay teaches is that God can do anything He wants to with people. However, that is not the case. In fact, the lesson is actually the opposite. The potter knew what he wanted to make from the clay, but when he tried to make it, it was "marred" in his hand (v. 4). The clay was uncooperative, and would not take the shape the potter had in mind. The potter did not mar the clay, it was marred in itself. This is a common occurrence in pottery, as every experienced potter knows.

In order for the potter to form his idea out of clay, the lump of clay must cooperate. It is not unusual for a potter to try to make a vase or pot and have the clay seem not to want to form into that shape. In that case the potter simply does what the potter in Jeremiah did thousands of years ago: he collapses the pot and starts over, often with a new idea.

People and clay are a lot alike, and God, the ultimate potter, works with us like a potter does with clay. God has an idea for our lives, but often we are uncooperative, and will not take the shape He desires for us. What does God do? He does His best to work with our free will and make something different out of our lives. The reason God had Jeremiah go to the potter's house was to teach Jeremiah that the way God works with people depends on what the people are willing to do.

After the verses about the potter and clay, verses 7-10 explain the way God works with people as they exercise their free will. In verse seven God gives a prophetic message that a kingdom is to be torn down. If prophecy were inflexible and final as stated, then that would happen: the fate of the nation would be sealed. But wait! In verse eight God says that if, in response to the prophecy, the nation repents and turns from evil, then He will not follow through with what He planned to do.

Similarly, in verse nine, God gives a prophecy that a nation would be built up and "planted," i.e., established. However, if the nation becomes evil and disobedient, like a piece of clay that will simply not take the proper shape, then God cannot follow through with the good He had prophesied about that nation, but has to change His plans. After all, God will not force people to be obedient. Thus is it clear that whether or not a prophecy is fulfilled depends on the people to whom it is given.

The lesson of the potter is applied to Judah and Jerusalem in verse eleven. In Jeremiah's time, God's prophets had been giving prophecies that Jerusalem would be destroyed. There are many examples in Jeremiah alone, but one will suffice.

Jeremiah 4:5-7
"Declare ye in Judah, and publish in Jerusalem; and say, Blow ye the trumpet in the land: cry, gather together, and say, Assemble yourselves, and let us go into the defenced cities. Set up the standard toward Zion: retire, stay not: for I will bring evil from the north, and a great destruction. The lion is come up from his thicket, and the destroyer of the Gentiles is on his way; he is gone forth from his place to

make thy land desolate; and thy cities shall be laid waste, without an inhabitant."

Even though God had prophesied that Judah would be destroyed for her sin, it is clear from the potter example in Jeremiah 18 that God, in His amazing grace, was telling Judah that if they repented they would not be destroyed after all. Sadly, Judah did not repent or change her evil ways. In an astounding show of stubbornness, the Judeans decided to continue in their ungodly ways. They said:

Jeremiah 18:12b
"*...And they said, There is no hope: but we will walk after our own devices, and we will every one do the imagination of his evil heart.*"

We know from both the Bible and secular history that Judah did not repent, and that they were destroyed by Babylon "from the north," just as God had said.

The important thing for us to learn in this study is that if Judah had repented, God would have relented and saved the country, and His prophecies of their destruction would not have come to pass. Thus, in the record in Jeremiah 18, God specifically shows us two types of prophecies that may be conditional: prophecies that foretell disaster, and prophecies that promise blessings. These prophecies are spoken to people, and are usually conditional.

Prophecies That Changed

We are now going to examine a number of prophecies in the Bible that were spoken but not fulfilled. These examples clearly reveal the conditional nature of prophecy, and help us see that God is doing much more than just predicting the future when He gives a prophecy. He is calling people to Himself and working to build the fellowship between God and man.

Saul's kingship - God gave Samuel the revelation that Saul would be king over Israel (1 Sam. 9:17), and that revelation became prophecy when Samuel spoke it to Saul (1 Sam. 10:1). The implied part of the prophecy is that both Saul and his descendants would reign over Israel. There would have been no reason for the prophet to say this, because that was simply the way kingdoms work: after the king dies, a descendant becomes king. Yet Saul disobeyed the word of God, and Samuel delivered a prophecy that modified the original prophecy, stating that Saul's kingdom would not endure. The original prophecy was conditional upon Saul's obedience to God.

1 Samuel 13:13 and 14
"*You [Saul] acted foolishly," Samuel said. "You have not kept the command the LORD your God gave you; if you had, he would have established your kingdom over Israel for all time. But now your kingdom will not endure; the LORD has sought out a man after his own heart and appointed him leader of his people, because you have not kept the LORD's command.*"

Upon receiving the prophecy that his kingdom would not endure, one would think that Saul would have repented in dust and ashes and prayed fervently to have God's blessing restored. Not so. Saul continued to sin, and Samuel confronted him again.

1 Samuel 15:23, 26-28
"*For rebellion is like the sin of divination, and arrogance like the evil of idolatry. Because you have rejected the word of the LORD, he has rejected you as king." But Samuel said to him [Saul], "I will not go back with you. You have rejected the word of the LORD, and the LORD has rejected you as king over Israel!"... As Samuel turned to leave, Saul caught hold of the hem of his robe, and it tore. Samuel said to him, "The LORD has torn the kingdom of Israel from you today and has given it to one of your neighbors—to one better than you.*"

Notice that in verse 28 God had torn the kingdom from Saul "today." This is very important. God is longsuffering. He puts up with a lot of disobedience on the part of His servants, but He has His limits. Saul had disobeyed before, often grievously. But this disobedience regarding the Amalekites was the last straw. God removed His holy spirit from Saul, who then became afflicted by demons (1 Sam. 16:14). Saul still acted as king, but without God's blessing, while David won the hearts of the people. Even Jonathan, the crown prince and next in line to be king, realized that the kingdom had passed from Saul, and said to David, "*...You will be king over Israel...*" (1 Sam. 23:17).

The peace in David's lifetime - David had done many wonderful things for God, and so He sent Nathan the prophet with the following message for David: "*...I will also give you rest from all your enemies...*" (2 Sam. 7:11). There is no doubt that Nathan was a true prophet of God, and if the paradigm of most Christians is right—that a prophecy once spoken will absolutely come to pass, then David would have had rest from his enemies for the rest of his life.

However, we know that prophecy spoken to people is often conditional upon what they do after they receive it, and that was the case with David. He did not continue steadfastly in the ways of God. After David committed adultery with Bathsheba and had Uriah murdered, God changed His prophecy to David. He sent Nathan again, but with a different message: "*Now, therefore, the sword will never depart from your house...*" (2 Sam. 12:10a).

The phrase, "Now, therefore" alerts us to the fact that there has been a change in the prophetic message, and we see that played out through the rest of David's life. He had to fight his own son, Absalom, to keep the throne, squash the rebellion of Sheba the Benjamite (2 Sam. 20), and battle the Philistines (2 Sam. 21:15).

Solomon's kingdom - Another good example of the conditional nature of prophecy can be seen in the life of Solomon. David wanted to build a temple for God, but God told him that Solomon would build the Temple, and also that "*...I [God] will establish his kingdom.*" The prophet Nathan foretold the establishment of Solomon's kingdom.

2 Samuel 7:12 and 13

"And when thy days be fulfilled, and thou shalt sleep with thy fathers, I will set up thy seed after thee, which shall proceed out of thy bowels, and I will establish his kingdom. He shall build an house for my name, and I will stablish the throne of his kingdom for ever."

These prophetic words seem very final. However, Solomon got to the point in his life where he did great evil in the eyes of God and broke commandment after commandment. God commanded that the king not amass horses or get horses from Egypt, but Solomon had thousands of horses, many of them from Egypt (Deuteronomy 17:16; 1 Kings 10:26-29). God commanded that the king not have many wives, but Solomon had 700 wives and 300 concubines (Deuteronomy 17:17; 1 Kings 11:3). God commanded that no Israelite marry a pagan woman, but Solomon married "Moabites, Ammonites, Edomites, Sidonians, and Hittites" (1 Kings 11:1 and 2). God commanded all Israel to stay away from idolatry (which was the first of the Ten Commandments), but Solomon worshipped Ashtoreth and Molech, among other pagan gods (1 Kings 11:5). Solomon "did evil" in the eyes of God (1 Kings 11:6), and after much sin, a different prophetic word came to him:

1 Kings 11:11
So the LORD said to Solomon, "*Since this is your attitude and you have not kept my covenant and my decrees, which I commanded you, **I will most certainly tear the kingdom away from you** and give it to one of your subordinates.*"

Because Solomon disobeyed and turned from the commands of God, the kingdom, which God prophesied He would "establish," was torn from David's line. Only two tribes, Judah and Benjamin, became the kingdom of Judah. The ten northern tribes became their own kingdom, Israel.

Hezekiah's sickness - Another example of God changing His revelation when people act decisively is in 2 Kings 20. Hezekiah, king of Judah, was very sick. The prophet Isaiah came to him and said, "*...Put your house in order, because you are going to die; you will not recover*" (2 Kings 20:1). As final as that prophecy from Isaiah sounded, Hezekiah did not give up. He prayed and wept, and God spoke again to Isaiah.

2 Kings 20:5a

"Go back and tell Hezekiah, the leader of my people, 'This is what the LORD, the God of your father David, says: I have heard your prayer and seen your tears; I will heal you..."

Hezekiah was healed, even as the second word from God said. The original prophecy that Hezekiah would die was not fulfilled, and he lived another 15 years.

Nineveh's destruction - Another good example of the conditional nature of prophecy is in the book of Jonah. The prophet Jonah delivered the following message to the citizens of Nineveh: "...Yet f*orty days, and Nineveh will be overthrown*" (Jonah 3:4). Although the people of Nineveh had been wicked and the prophecy was clear, the king of Nineveh knew not to simply give up, sit back, and await destruction. He knew that prophecy could be conditional, and so he commanded everyone in his kingdom to repent, fast, and "call urgently on God" (Jonah 3:8). The king even commanded that the animals in the kingdom be made to fast. He then gave his reason for these commands:

Jonah 3:9
"*Who knows? God may yet relent and with compassion turn from his fierce anger so that we will not perish.*"

Although the king had no guarantee that his kingdom would be saved if the people humbled themselves, he knew that if they did not, the prophecy would certainly come to pass and Nineveh would be destroyed. Some prophecies, even when given by a genuine prophet, are not the final word. In the case of Nineveh, the word of God spoken in prophecy changed.

Jonah 3:10 (NRSV)
"When God saw what they did and how they turned from their evil ways, he had compassion and did not bring upon them the destruction he had threatened."
The NIV text above is a weak translation. First, the phrase "had compassion" is better translated "repented" as it is in the KJV (the NRSV actually has "changed his mind"). This is very important. We said at the opening of this chapter that, in effect, most prophecies spoken to

people had an unspoken "if" clause. It can be clearly seen here. When God saw that the people of Nineveh repented and turned from their evil ways, then He "repented." God changed His word when the circumstances changed.

Also, although the NIV has the word "threatened," there is no evidence in the Hebrew text that all God did was "threaten" the Ninevites. God plainly stated that Nineveh would be overthrown. The Hebrew is clearly translated in many versions, the King James being one of them, and it is worth quoting.

Jonah 3:10 (KJV)
"And God saw their works, that they turned from their evil way; and God repented of the evil, that he had said that he would do unto them; and he did it not."

It is worth noting, however, that the translators of the NIV have picked up the heart of what God did. Although with words He clearly stated that Nineveh would be overthrown, in His heart He did not want that to happen. His words were a "threat," even though they were not voiced that way, because He intended to change if the Ninevites did. When they repented, He did not bring upon them the destruction that Jonah had so boldly proclaimed. The prophecy of Jonah, that Nineveh would be destroyed in 40 days, was never fulfilled.

Prophecies That Did Not Change

What follows are two examples of people praying to God so that the prophecies they received would be altered, but they were not, and came to pass as spoken. Just because prophecy is often conditional does not mean it always is. Nevertheless, the preponderance of examples in the Word of God teach us that if we receive a prophecy we do not want to come to pass, we should do all that we can to alter the prophecy.

The death of David's child - David committed adultery with a woman named Bathsheba, who became pregnant and gave birth to a son.

While the son was very young, but not a newborn, God gave the following prophecy to David:

2 Samuel 12:14b
... the child also that is born unto thee shall surely die.

After the prophecy was given, the child became sick. David pleaded with God to spare the child. He fasted and "*...spent the nights lying on the ground.*" However, the child died anyway, at which point David washed, went to worship, and then ate. This confused the servants, who wondered why David did not fast and weep after the death of the child, and they asked him about it.

2 Samuel 12:22
"And he said, While the child was yet alive, I fasted and wept: for I said, Who can tell whether GOD will be gracious to me, that the child may live?"

David understood that even though God had given a prophecy that the child would die, there was a chance he might live. He prayed and fasted, asking God to alter the consequences of his sin. The fact that David fasted, wept, and spent the nights lying on the ground, is an indication that he knew that the prophecy of the death of the child was not absolutely set in stone, but might change. In this case, however, the prophecy came to pass as spoken.

Jesus in Gethsemane - One of the most startling examples of the conditional nature of prophecy involves Jesus Christ. On the night of his arrest, he went to the Garden of Gethsemane and prayed three times that he would not have to die. The prayer recorded in Mark is very telling:

Mark 14:36
"And he said, Abba, Father, all things are possible unto thee; take away this cup from me: nevertheless not what I will, but what thou wilt." Jesus began his prayer by saying that everything is possible for God. What he had in mind was obvious from his next statement—that

perhaps God could change what had been foretold about the death of the Messiah. Jesus boldly asked God, "*...Take this cup from me....*"

What was Jesus asking for? He was asking God to change things so that he would not have to be tortured and die. This shows that Jesus clearly understood the conditional nature of prophecy.

He knew that even though his death had been foretold, that did not necessarily mean it was absolutely set in stone, and he prayed to see if there was any way that redemption could be accomplished without his death. The fact that Jesus prayed three times, showed how badly he wanted to avoid being tortured and crucified.

However, in this case, there was apparently no way God could bring about the redemption of mankind except by the death of Jesus, and Jesus humbly accepted that fact and died for our sins. What a Savior!

What God says will indeed come to pass unless there are powerful circumstances for them to change.

It is important to note that God does not desire to be seen as a God whose words have no impact because they change all the time. What God says will indeed come to pass unless there are powerful circumstances for them to change. In that light, although there are many examples showing that prophecy can be conditional, there are many more prophecies (the majority actually) in the Word of God that were fulfilled as spoken.

14 Individuals That Are Born Prophets (a.k.a. Ordained or Called)

Apart from the Gift of Prophecy, another form of prophecy is that which comes from someone who has been appointed, called or a "born" prophet – an individual who is called not just to prophecy but has been specifically given the "office" of the prophet. "*And he gave some, apostles; and some, prophets; and some, evangelists; and some, pastors and teachers; for the perfecting of the saints, for the work of the ministry, for the edifying of the body of Christ*" (Ephesians 4:11-12)

The office of the prophet is to manifest all the things of a gift prophet, as well as bring illumination and further specifics about that which has already been written in the Scriptures. On rare occasions, one within the office of prophet may be called upon to interpret the signs of the times;[321] and on one specific occasion in *The Last Days*, he will be called to broadcast the mysteries once bound up and sealed with seven seals.[322]

Prophesying was a conspicuous phenomenon among the early Christians (see Matthew 21:26; I Corinthians 12:10-28; Chapters 10, 11 etc.), and was not unknown to those circles of the Jewish people who believed in the working of the Holy Spirit (see Book of Wisdom 7:27 a.k.a. Proverbs, and Josephus, Antiquities13:12, § 1;14:16, etc). Thus, it can be regarded that prophesying was and is behavior endorsed by God.

We are exhorted to both believe and respect those that prophesy. It is the only ministry of which God makes the emphatic declaration, *"Do my prophets no harm."*[323] He that curses one of God's true prophets incurs the curse of God. *"He that blesses a prophet in the name of a prophet [has an understanding of what and who the prophet is], receives the same reward as the prophet".*[324] The Lord also says, "Believe His prophets and you shall prosper." (2 Chronicles 20:20)

In the following section we will examine a few examples of individuals that were born seers and considered called or ordained prophets – Samuel, Jeremiah, John the Baptist and William Branham.

Prophecy – forth-telling and fore-telling…the translation for prophecy refers to both meanings. All ministries and all peoples can be forth-tellers, proclaiming God's truth. But not all are called to fore-tell, to speak a word or thought that comes direct from God – whether that word be of past, present or future events or circumstances.

As we have seen, prophecy comes from the Divine Spirit as a message in order to strengthen, encourage, comfort, chastise, correct or warn. However, prophecy is not just speaking human encouragement, it is speaking *divine* encouragement. In simple terms, prophecy is "hearing" from God and speaking what you hear. To prophesy is to hear *from* God and to speak *to* men.

> The office of prophet differs from the gift of prophecy in that it is permanent. It *is* given, but it is more than a gift. It is a calling

In 1 Corinthians 12:8-10, Paul lists nine distinct spiritual gifts. Three of these gifts can be considered revelatory in nature. They are *a word of knowledge*, *a word of wisdom*, and *discerning of spirits*. A fourth, the gift of prophecy, along with these three revelation gifts make up "the prophetic gifts."

These "prophetic gifts" are to be distinguished from the "office" of a prophet and a "called or ordained" prophet. The prophetic gifts are operated when an individual is anointed, moved or inspired by God's Spirit. These individuals are temporarily "possessed" by the Divine Spirit and speak forth the mind of God.

The difference between the gift of prophecy and the office of prophet is a crucial point. We would be wrong to say that anyone who prophesies is a prophet. The Spirit of God is dividing severally His gifts, which God can give in a moment as He wills. That should not, however, be a permanent and abiding distinction or designation.

The Spirit of God can fall on any one of us and we can prophesy. We are operating by the Spirit in the gift of prophecy. The gift is something that the Spirit exercises at His will and it can come to either a man or a woman. It has nothing to do with their calling, their training, their preparation or their qualification. It may be informational, directive or a word of encouragement. However, the office of the prophet is altogether something else.

The office of prophet is a permanent thing and carries an enormous responsibility. Such a one brings the oracles of God. He is standing for God and speaking from God with the authority of God, often in a typically troubled generation. His statements are the statements of God's heart to His people that they may have an understanding of the present time, in view of the things that are future and eternal.

It is the prophet who is alerted. He interprets the event and communicates that interpretation to a church that would otherwise have passed it over. That is his function and that is his call for which he is not necessarily going to be understood nor heard. The true prophet and the words he brings are more often than not going to be rejected or misunderstood.

God has a deep identification with the prophetic, and to somehow touch that is to touch Him, and to abuse that is to abuse Him. It may well be that the greatest enmity of the world against God is visited on prophets for exactly that reason, namely, that to assault a prophet is to assault God. Psalm 105:15, "*Touch not mine anointed, and do my prophets no harm.*"

The world is at war with God. The prophet is the visible, corporeal manifestation of elements central to God's own being, therefore the world has the opportunity both to identify, to hate, to despise and to harm. The testimony of the prophet is the statement of God, not only when he is speaking, but often even when he is silent. His very presence is an abomination and an offense to a world that despises God.

The prophetic man is in himself the offense, as well as his message. In fact, if he is not his message, then we may well suspect that what we have is not a true prophet, but a false one. That is why we need to watch with a jealous urgency, anything that purports to be prophetic and is not, because it destroys the validity of that calling for the church.

There is a great accountability for that gift of God to men, and if it is mistreated, ignored or rejected, then the end result will be judgment. We will suffer when we lightly regard or disregard, let alone violently reject the one whom God sends in that prophetic mantle, because it is so much the essence of God Himself in His own being. Israel repeatedly stoned the prophets that were sent to her, and in so doing, invited and made necessary the devastating judgments that have followed.

A prophet shuns the distinctions and honors that men confer. These things bring a certain aura of prestige and eminence and weight, but the prophetic man, in order to be true to God is the "wilderness" prophet. Wilderness does not just mean physical isolation, but a conscious and willful separation from the kinds of things that are calculated to compromise.

He does not affect any kind of prophetic outward "appearance" to indicate his office. He is unprepossessing in appearance and demeanor and despises what is showy, sensational or bizarre. A prophet's life is used up in the pursuit of turning men to God.

Samuel the Prophet - Who Was He?

Samuel or Shmu'el (Hebrew) is an important leader of ancient Israel in the Book(s) of Samuel in both the Christian and Hebrew Bible. He lived during the 11th century B.C.

His status, as viewed by rabbinical literature, is that he was the last of the Hebrew Judges and the first of the major prophets who began to prophesy inside the Land of Israel. He was thus at the cusp of two eras.

Samuel's mother Hannah was unable to have children and prayed desperately before the tabernacle that the Lord would grant her to bear children to her husband Elkanah, an Ephraimite. Because the Lord heard and answered, Hannah called her son "Samuel," which can be translated "heard by God." This account is in the first chapter of 1 Samuel.

In response to God's love for them, Samuel's parents dedicated him to the Lord's service. He entered sacred service and trained in the house of the Lord at Shiloh under Eli.

God called Samuel to speak for Him in a series of night messages and established him as His prophet. One of Samuel's most difficult assignments came immediately after his call. Eli was allowing his sons to abuse their priestly offices and through the young man, the Lord condemned their behavior and pronounced God's judgment upon them.

Samuel's own life did not always go smoothly. Just as Eli's sons had betrayed their sacred trust as priests, so also Joel and Abijah, the sons of Samuel, became unrighteous judges who "*took bribes and perverted justice.*" (8:1-2) Perceiving this as a problem in God's leadership as well as that of Samuel, Israel demanded that they be given a king such as the surrounding nations had. Samuel warned them that this would lead to even more problems and woes, but when they kept insisting, the Lord told him to do as the people requested.

Samuel anointed Saul to be Israel's first king (10:1). Because of Saul's continuing, flagrant disregard for God's Word, Samuel repudiated Saul's leadership and traveled to the house of Jesse, where he anointed David to be king in place of Saul (16:13).

Samuel's loyalty to God, his spiritual insight, and his ability to inspire others made him one of Israel's great leaders. When he died, "*all Israel assembled and mourned for him, and they buried him in his house at Ramah.* (25:1a)"

Jeremiah - Who Was He?

Jeremiah lived about 2600 years ago. He was the son of Hilkiah and lived in the town of Anathoth in the land of Benjamin in Judah. He was born in a small town just five kilometers from Jerusalem. Jeremiah's father served as a priest in the temple in Jerusalem. In that time, most of the Jews in Jerusalem were still very religious, following the traditions of their ancestors, but they did not heed the Word of the Lord God. Jeremiah, however, was a man who cherished the Word of God and obeyed it; he was looking forward to the day when God would send the Messiah into the world.

The Calling (Jeremiah 1:9-10)

What a memorable day in the life of Jeremiah when God spoke to him, establishing him as a prophet! The calling of Isaiah had been different. Seeing the Lord on His throne in the midst of Seraphim proclaiming His holiness, Isaiah had cried, "*Woe is me, for I am undone!*" But the glowing coal taken from the altar where the victim had been burned provided propitiation for his sins. Then he could answer the Lord's call: "*Whom shall I send, and who will go for us?*" with the words, "*Here am I! Send me.*" (Isaiah 6:1-8)

Nothing like this happened to Jeremiah. God simply spoke to him in his early youth declaring in a few precise statements why He chose to send him: "*Before I formed you in the womb I knew you*" (Jeremiah 1:4-10). This is God's foreknowledge. For us it is connected with His election before the foundation of the world (1 Peter 1:2; Ephesians 1:4).

But to Jeremiah the Lord revealed more, "*Before you were born I sanctified you.*" Like the apostle Paul, Jeremiah was set apart from his mother's womb (see Galatians 1:4, Acts 9:15; 22:14). Then God spoke further to him, "*I ordained you a prophet to the nations,*" and finally "*I shall send you.*"

These passages seem to show that from mankind's genesis, there has been an election on God's part. Furthermore, each servant of the Lord receives a definite call. This is followed by training in "the school of God" through various means before engaged in service.[325]

Jeremiah was not to speak on the basis of what he had in himself, God put forth His hand and touched the young man's mouth saying, "*Behold, I have put my words in your mouth.*" God would reveal things to him which he must faithfully transmit to others.

What a disconsolate message was to be preached by Jeremiah: "*See, I have this day set you ... to root out and to pull down, to destroy and to throw down.*" It was the tragic element of his life to constantly prophesy judgment, destruction and captivity. The essential part of his message consists of warning the people about the unavoidable judgments which they will endure because of their obstinate hearts.

This assurance of God's presence with him encourages the young prophet and gives him boldness to deliver his message. The same promise accompanied Moses the lawgiver (Exodus 3:12-13); Gideon the judge (Judges 6:2); Zerubbabel, Joshua, and the chiefs of the people returned from exile (Haggai 2:4). Likewise, so many others after them, such as Timothy with whom the apostle left this last wish, "*The Lord Jesus Christ be with your spirit*" (2 Timothy 4:22).

Jeremiah ministered for about 40 years during the reigns of the last four kings of the Southern Kingdom. His ministry began during the reign of Josiah, and continued through the reigns of Jehoiakin, Jehoiachin, and Zedekiah.

Jeremiah prophesied in Jerusalem and Judah during the 41 year period from 628 to 586 BC. During that time, the Babylonian Empire had taken control of Jerusalem. The Babylonians took Jews as captives to Babylon as early as 605 BC and 597 BC. Babylon destroyed Jerusalem in 586 BC. Jeremiah lived through the invasions by the Babylonian armies, the deportations of his people, the slaughter of Jews living in Jerusalem, and the destruction of the Temple.

The word came to him "*in the days of Josiah the son of Amon, king of Judah, in the thirteenth year of his reign ... also in the days of Jehoiakim the son of Josiah, king of Judah, until the end of the eleventh year of Zedekiah . . . until the carrying away of Jerusalem captive.*" After the final deportation, he continued his service in relative obscurity among the poor of the country whom Nebuchadnezzar had left. Subsequently he followed into Egypt the remnant of the people who took refuge in that country. Very probably he died there after having given his last known prophecy (Jeremiah 44).

Josiah reigned thirty-one years. It was during the thirteenth year of his reign that Jeremiah began to prophesy. The following eighteen years were a relatively easy period in the prophet's life. The degree to which he felt the king's death is well expressed in 2 Chronicles 35:25, "*And Jeremiah lamented for Josiah.*"

After Josiah's reign, Judah sank into religious and political decadence. None of the descendants of this pious king feared the Lord. Invasions from the north increased in number. Three consecutive times the enemy looted the country and returned to Babylon with their captives and their treasures, including the vessels of the house of Jehovah (2 Chronicles 36:7). Daniel and his companions were carried away into captivity at that time. (Daniel 1:1, 2, 6).

Habakkuk and Zephaniah prophesied in Judah during Jeremiah's time. Daniel and Ezekiel, also prophets during this time, ministered in Babylon. In His grace, God was still speaking to His people despite their sins and hardened hearts. But they did not pay attention.

Jeremiah spoke to all the Jews saying,
"Thus saith the LORD of hosts, Hearken not unto the words of the prophets that prophesy unto you: they make you vain: they speak a vision of their own heart, and not out of the mouth of the LORD...
I have not sent these prophets, yet they ran: I have not spoken to them, yet they prophesied. But if they had stood in my counsel, and had caused my people to hear my words, then they should have turned them from their evil way, and from the evil of their doings."[326]

Thus Jeremiah warned the Jews to beware of the words of those who preached falsehood. Unfortunately, most of the people of Judah did not heed the warning of God's prophet, Jeremiah. Instead they believed the words of the false prophets.

Nevertheless, after it was too late, the king, the priests, the people, and the false prophets found out who had proclaimed the true word of God! They found out because everything that Jeremiah had announced concerning the destruction of Jerusalem came to pass. God's Word always comes true.

Jeremiah warned the people of Jerusalem that they would be punished harshly for their sins. He pleaded with the people to turn away from sin and to turn back to God. In return, Jeremiah was targeted with scorn and persecution. He is known as the Weeping Prophet: he watched his nation decline and finally come under God's judgment.

"Oh, that my head were waters, and mine eyes a fountain of tears, that I might weep day and night for the slain of the daughter of my people!" Jeremiah 9:1

Throughout his life Jeremiah had seen his prophecies rejected and his warnings despised. Now it has happened again. Nevertheless, he follows the people into Egypt and even there warns them by the Word of the Lord (43:8-13). But all is in vain. They reply to him, "*As for the word that you have spoken to us in the name of the Lord, we will not hearken unto thee. But we will certainly do whatever thing goeth forth out of our own mouth*" (44:16-17).

What use is further prophesying, further warning, when no one will listen? *"Oh that I had in the wilderness a lodging place of wayfaring men; that I might leave my people, and go from them!"* (9:2). In other words, I have had enough of it all; I would like to flee to a faraway place and have nothing more to do with these people. David experienced the same feelings when he was being heavily pursued by his enemies: *"And I said, Oh that I had wings like a dove! for then would I fly away, and be at rest. Lo, then would I wander far off, and remain in the wilderness"* (Psalms 55:6-7).

Through all these long and painful years, what is most remarkable is that Jeremiah did not grow weary. Until the end he was faithful to his God, faithful to his prophetic calling, and faithful also to his people despite their rebellion, poverty, and distress. This perseverance is summed up in a few words: *"I have not hastened from being a pastor to follow thee"* (Jeremiah 17:16).

The prophet, rejected and despised like his Master will be, apparently finishes his days in that land of exile. No details are given in the Word. His end is as sad as his lonely life had been. Later, John the Baptist will finish his course in a similar way – put into prison and then beheaded.

Such servants have been eminently faithful, even unto death; they had their moments of weakness, but in the day of rewards their crown will be glorious. To the end, they have answered the call which God addressed to them in their youth.

John the Baptist - Who Was He?

John, son of Zacharias (5 B.C. – 30 A.D.) a.k.a. John the Baptist was an important figure of ancient Israel to both Jew and Christian religions.

We are given the story of the ministry of John the Baptist, called the Precursor or Forerunner of the Lord, with some variation of detail, in the three synoptic Gospels of Matthew, Mark, and Luke, as well as in the Book of John. Luke tells us of the birth of John the Baptist in a town of Judaea, about six months before the birth of the Savior. The attendant circumstances suggest the miraculous and wonderful. The New Testament tells us nothing of John's early years; most which is known about him comes from the Gospels.

He was the son of Zachariah, a Temple priest, and his wife Elizabeth, who was a cousin of Mary the earthly mother of Jesus. He was born when his mother was comparatively advanced in years, after the foretelling of his birth and the choice of his name by an angel. Nothing more is heard of him until he began his mission of preaching and baptizing in the river Jordan around the year AD 27.

When John the Baptist came to the deserts of Judea "*preaching a baptism of repentance for the forgiveness of sins*" he was met with great success. Matthew 3:5 says, "People went out to him from Jerusalem and all Judea and the whole region of the Jordan. Confessing their sins, they were baptized by him in the Jordan River." Luke adds that crowds were coming out to be baptized by him. And, "When all the people were being baptized, Jesus was baptized too." (Luke 3:7, 21).

The Jewish people to whom John's ministry was directed were familiar with the concepts of repentance and forgiveness of sins (1 Kings 8:33-34; Isa 55:6, 7) even though complete forgiveness was not possible apart from the shed blood of Christ (Heb 9:15). But what about baptism? What familiarity did the Jews of the first century have with the practice of baptism?

Baptism as a rite of immersion was not begun by Christians but was taken by them from Jewish and pagan forms. The term mikveh in Hebrew literally means any gathering of waters, but is specifically used in Jewish law for the waters or bath for the ritual immersion. The building of the mikveh was so important in ancient times it was said to take precedence over the construction of a synagogue. Immersion was so important that it occurred before the high Priest conducted the service on the Day of Atonement, before the regular priests participated in the Temple service, before each person entered the Temple complex, before a scribe wrote the name of God, as well as several other occasions.

The rite of baptism, a symbolic act signifying sincere repentance as well as a desire to be spiritually cleansed in order to receive the Christ, was so strongly emphasized by John that people began to call him "the baptizer," and “the Baptist.” His way of life and style of preaching closely resembled those of some OT prophets: his diet was locusts and wild honey, his message one of repentance and preparation for the coming of the Messiah and his Kingdom.

John also denounced the incestuous union of Herod Antipas with his niece and brother's wife, Herodias, and was imprisoned for doing so. His death was brought about by the hatred of Herodias and the weakness of Herod. When her fourteen-year-old daughter Salome had greatly pleased and beguiled the king with her ultra-sensual dance at his birthday feast, he promised she could have from him whatever she liked “even if it is half my kingdom”. Instigated by her mother, she demanded the head of John the Baptist on a dish. Herod, without a trial of any kind, dispatched an executioner to John's prison (identified as Machaerus by the Dead Sea). After John was executed, his head presented to Salome, who passed it on to her mother.

We learn a little more about John from the writings of Josephus, a Jewish historian born shortly after Jesus died. He says:

“John was a pious man, and he was bidding the Jews...to come together for baptism... And when everybody turned to John--for they were profoundly stirred by what he said--Herod feared that John's so extensive influence over the people might lead to an uprising (for the people seemed likely to do everything he might counsel). He thought it much better, under the circumstances, to get John out of the way in advance, before any insurrection might develop, than for himself to get into trouble and be sorry not to have acted, once an insurrection had begun. So because of Herod's suspicion, John was sent as a prisoner to Machaerus, the fortress already mentioned, and there put to death.”[327]

When John began final preparations for his mission, he was probably in his thirty-second year. He withdrew into the harsh, rocky desert beyond the Jordan to fast and pray, as was the ancient custom of holy men. We are told that he kept himself alive by eating locusts and wild honey and wore a rough garment of camel's hair, tied with a leathern girdle (Mark 1:7).

When he came back to start preaching in the villages of Judaea, he was haggard and uncouth, but his eyes burned with zeal and his voice carried deep conviction. The Jews were accustomed to preachers and prophets who gave no thought to outward appearances, and they accepted John at once; the times were troubled, and the people yearned for reassurance and comfort.

He was a man of the wilderness, much like Elijah (1 Kings 17). Since Elijah was taken up to heaven in a whirlwind (2 Kings 2:1-11), the Jews believed that some day he would come back. Malachi, the last canonical book of the Old Testament, promises that God will send Elijah to warn people before the Day of Judgment. People who saw and heard John were reminded that he may very well be the promised Elijah. In fact, Jesus himself thought so (Matthew 11:13-14).

So transcendent was the power emanating from the holy man that after hearing him many believed he was indeed the long-awaited Messiah. John quickly addressed their misconception, saying he had come only to prepare the way, and that he was not worthy to unloose the Master's sandals. Although his preaching and baptizing continued for some months during the Savior's own ministry, John always made plain that he was merely the Forerunner.

His humility remained incorruptible even when his fame spread to Jerusalem and members of the higher priesthood came to make inquiries and to hear him. "*Repent, for the Kingdom of Heaven is at hand,*"- this was John's oft-repeated theme. For the evils of the times his remedy was individual purification. "*Every tree," he said, "that is not bringing forth good fruit is to be cut down and thrown into the fire.*" The reformation of each person's life must be complete – the wheat must be separated from the chaff and the chaff burned "*with unquenchable fire.*"

We read in Acts 19:1-5 that when Paul went to Ephesus, he found a group of people who had been baptized into John's baptism. Apparently there were groups of people who remained loyal to John without necessarily becoming followers of Jesus. Although early Christians saw John as a forerunner of Jesus, the disciples of John and others did not see it quite that way. No doubt some of John's disciples did follow Jesus.

But many others continued in their allegiance to John without ever becoming followers of Jesus. Today in southern Iraq and in Iran there is a small sect of 20 to 30 thousand members known as the Mandaeans (Man-DE-uns) who claim to be followers of John the Baptist. The Mandaeans came from a long line of the Zoroastrians – Chaldeans that blended ancient mysticism and Christian themes. Some think them to have been an offshoot of second century Christianity. They were apparently influenced by Persian ideas and departed from orthodox Christianity. Their allegiance was more to John than to Jesus.

The Scriptures tell us of the day when Jesus joined the group of those who wished to receive baptism at John's hands. John knew Jesus as the Messiah they had so long expected, and at first excused himself as unworthy. Then, in obedience to Jesus, he acquiesced and baptized Him. Although sinless, Jesus chose to be baptized in order to identify Himself with the human race and as a sacrifice that required washing before it was offered. When He arose from the waters of the Jordan, where the rite was performed, "*the heavens opened and the Spirit as a dove descended. And there came a voice from the heavens, Thou art my beloved Son, in Thee I am well pleased*" (Mark 1:11).

The time for John's ministry to decrease came after the baptism of Jesus, the true Lamb of God. Now, John's life rushes on towards its tragic end.

In the fifteenth year of the reign of the Roman emperor, Tiberias Caesar, Herod Antipas was the provincial governor or tetrarch of a subdivision of Palestine which included Galilee and Peraea, a district lying east of the Jordan. In the course of John's preaching, he had denounced in unmeasured terms the immorality of Herod's petty court, and had even boldly upbraided Herod to his face for his defiance of old Jewish law, especially in having taken to himself the wife of his half-brother, Philip. This woman, the dissolute Herodias, was also Herod's niece. Herod feared and reverenced John, knowing him to be a holy man; but he could not endure having his private life castigated. Herodias stimulated his anger by lies and artifices. His resentment at length got the better of his judgment and he had John cast into the fortress of Machaerus, near the Dead Sea.

When Jesus heard of this, and knew that some of His disciples had gone to see John, He spoke thus of him: "*What went you to see? A prophet? Yea, I say to you, and more than a prophet. This is he of whom it is written: Behold I send my angel before thy face, who shall prepare thy way before thee. For I say to you, amongst those that are born of women there is not a greater prophet than John the Baptist*" (Matthew 11:10-12).

Other historians give further testimony of John's holiness and write that he was a man of virtue, who exhorted the Jews to the practice of justice towards men and piety towards God; and also to baptism, preaching that they would become acceptable to God if they renounced their sins.[328] Thus Regarding John, Jews and Christians unite in reverence and love for this prophet-saint whose life is an incomparable example of both humility and courage.

William Branham - Who Was He?

William Marrion Branham (1909-1965) was one of the most influential Bible ministers in the modern era. He was considered by many to be the initiator of the healing and charismatic revival that began in 1947, and from his ministry there sprang a myriad of other ministers who became internationally known.

One historian of that movement stated that William Branham was "a prophet to our generation"[329], and a Pentecostal historian wrote, "Branham filled the largest stadiums and meeting halls in the world."[330] The Full Gospel Men's Voice, (now, Full Gospel Businessmen's Fellowship International), in its February 1961 issue, wrote: "In Bible Days, there were men of God who were Prophets and Seers. But in all the Sacred Records, none of these had a greater ministry than that of William Branham, a Prophet and Seer of God, whose photograph appears on the front cover of this issue of Full Gospel Men's Voice. Branham has been used by God, in the Name of Jesus, to raise the dead!"

From 1947 until the time of his death in 1965, the influential ministry of William Branham was well known and considered unparalleled in the history of gospel meetings. The impact of the supernatural ministry of this one man was felt not only in North America, but also around the world.

William Branham was born April 6, 1909 in a log cabin in the Kentucky hills, the first of nine children of Charles and Ella Branham. Reared near Jeffersonville, Indiana, he knew only a life of deep poverty and hardship, his father being an alcoholic and illiterate. Compounding these circumstances, the young boy was considered "nervous", because from an early age he spoke of "visions" and "a voice" which spoke to him out of a wind, saying, "Don't ever drink, or smoke, or defile your body in any way. There will be a work for you to do when you get older."

William Branham became a Christian and was filled with the Holy Spirit in 1931. From that time, the Bible became the focus of his life and Jesus Christ the center of his very existence. He was ordained to the ministry at the age of 23 years, in the Missionary Baptist Church in December of 1932.

On June 11, 1933, William Branham was baptizing in the Ohio River near Jeffersonville, Indiana, when a bright fiery light suddenly appeared over his head and a voice spoke out, "As John the Baptist was sent to forerun the first coming of Jesus Christ, so are you sent to forerun His second coming!" The next edition of the Jeffersonville Evening News reported the incident with the subheading, "*Mysterious Star Appears Over Minister While Baptizing*".[331]

In May of 1946, he consecrated himself and sought God for the meaning of his peculiar life. As he prayed alone late one night, an angel appeared, saying, "Do not fear. I am sent from the presence of Almighty God to tell you that your peculiar birth and misunderstood life has been to indicate that you are to take a gift of divine healing to the peoples of the world. If you will be sincere when you pray and can get the people to believe you, nothing shall stand before your prayer, not even cancer. You will go into many parts of the earth and will pray for kings and rulers. You will preach to multitudes the world over and thousands will come to you for counsel."[332] This was literally fulfilled in the years that followed, for his ministry took him around the world and many individuals of public influence, including Congressman Upshaw of the U.S.A.,[333] were healed as a result of his prayers.

On the night of January 24, 1950, one of the most amazing photographs (see image) of all time was taken in the Sam Houston Coliseum, Houston, Texas. As William Branham stood at the podium, a halo of fire appeared above his head. This picture was the only one that turned out on the entire film.

George J. Lacy, Investigator of Questioned Documents, and often hired by the FBI in that capacity, subjected the negative to every scientific test available. At a news conference, he stated, "To my knowledge, this is the first time in the world's history that a supernatural being has been photographed and scientifically vindicated."[334] The original of this photograph reportedly is kept in the archives of the Religious Department of the Smithsonian Institute, Washington, D.C.

The spreading news of miraculous healings influenced pastors from various regions to call William Branham to minister for their congregations and pray for the sick. A supernatural sign had been given him for the purpose of encouraging the people to believe. At first a physical sign in his hand would indicate a disease or healing. Later on in his ministry the secret thoughts and needs of individuals were revealed, resulting in faith for deliverance.

While he was alive, it was clear to most objective people that William Branham was a prophet, a man sent from God, and possibly the one to fulfill the many scriptural prophecies concerning the Last Days ministry of Elijah. (Chapters 15 thru 17 explore this topic in further detail.)

15
Elijah was a Man...and a Prophet

James 5:17 – "*Elijah was a man subject to like passions as we are...*"

Elijah was a man. What an odd statement. Why did James (or the Holy Spirit moving on James) feel the need to make this declaration? Is not that an obvious fact, like "water is wet" or "fire is hot?" Of course Elijah was a man! ... Wasn't he?

Hmmm. James goes on to say that Elijah prayed for no rain and there was a drought for three and half years, then he prayed for rain and down it came. He also called fire down from heaven and performed miracles. Those were not the actions of a man, at least, not an ordinary man. Yet, in the opening words of 1 Kings 19 we see LOTS of humanity in the life of Elijah. Here is this famous prophet who has accomplished a lot and experienced amazing miracles. But where does he end up emotionally? In verse 4 he says, "*I have had enough, Lord . . . Take my life.*" This is one prayer God does not answer for Elijah. Instead, the Lord cares for him and helps him out of his despair.

This story has a lot to teach us. What can we learn from it? Well, let's look more closely. Verse 1 says, "And Ahab told Jezebel all that Elijah had done, and withal how he had slain all the prophets with the sword. Then Jezebel sent a messenger unto Elijah, saying, So let the gods do to me, and more also, if I make not thy life as the life of one of them by to morrow."

There is some background that we need to know. Ahab is the king, Jezebel is the queen, and Elijah is the prophet of the true God. Ahab and Jezebel have been leading the nation in worshiping false gods and into worship that included the sacrifice of children. So a huge battle has been going on between good and evil, truth and falsehood, the one true God of the Bible and the false, evil idol god Baal.

God has just used Elijah to perform an amazing miracle that proved the reality of the God of the Bible and sealed the fate of the false prophets. His prayers have been answered. He has seen miracles. He has won a huge victory. The people say that Elijah was right and the Lord is God. Then another prayer is answered, and rain comes. There had been no rain for over three years. The people were suffering, and food was scarce. Now there is rain and hope. Perhaps Elijah is expecting that everything will be different now. Maybe he expects Ahab and Jezebel to change their minds and hearts or at least that the people will rise up and throw them out. But it is not like that. Instead he receives a message that Jezebel is out to get him. Nothing has changed. He has come through all the stress and drama of one crisis only to be faced with a new challenge.

So what happens? Elijah has been brave in the past, but look at him in verses 3 and 4. Verse 3 says he "*was afraid and ran for his life.*" You can be afraid and not fall apart. But Elijah did fall apart. In verse 4 he wants to die. He has had enough. Elijah could have said, "I am not afraid of Jezebel, because God is in control. God has taken care of me in the past, and I can trust Him in this situation too." But it is obvious that Elijah's eyes are not on God anymore. His eyes are on the people and the problems threatening him. He also has his own baggage to deal with - hereditary and environmental influences that shaped his emotions and outlook on life.

> Historically, Elijah and the Messiah are linked together, magnifying & elevating Elijah's status and position

Historically, Elijah and the Messiah are linked together, magnifying and elevating Elijah's status and position. Jewish traditions reinforced this link.

This idea from the Bible that Elijah will come at the time of the Messiah is enshrined in Jewish prayers and rituals. For instance, at the Passover Seder the Jews have a Cup of Elijah. The reason for this cup is because there was a debate by the rabbis, as recorded in the Talmud, of whether they should drink four cups of wine on Passover (for the four terms used to describe the deliverance by God of the Jewish people from Egypt in Exodus 6:6-7) or five cups of wine (for the added expression of deliverance Exodus 6:8). Since the debate is not fully resolved, they pour a fifth cup of wine, which is termed the "Cup of Elijah."

The reason for this ritual is because of the Jewish belief that when Elijah comes with the Messiah, he will answer all questions on Jewish law. Interestingly, the Book of Revelation (Ch.10 vs.1-7) implies that the Seventh Church Age angel/messenger who also will be anointed by the spirit of Elijah will answer all questions and mysteries relating to Gentile scriptures.

But why is Elijah the forerunner, and not Joseph or Moses? Elijah did not even have his own book; why not Daniel or Amos? "Behold, I send Amos the prophet, before the great and dreadful day of the Lord..."

Even Jesus marveled at the power, ministry and life of Elijah as seen in John the Baptist. Luke 7:24, 26, 28:

24: "And when the messengers of John were departed, he began to speak unto the people concerning John, What went ye out into the wilderness for to see? A reed shaken with the wind?

26: But what went ye out for to see? A prophet? Yea, I say unto you, and much more than a prophet.

28: For I say unto you, Among those that are born of women there is not a greater prophet than John the Baptist: but he that is least in the kingdom of God is greater than he." (KJV)

Though all this is helpful in understanding the cult of Elijah, Jesus and James felt it was important to remind both Jew and Christian that - *Elijah was a man...*

John the Baptist as Elijah *Redivivus* (reused)

Elijah (a.k.a. Elias) holds a unique place in Judaism, as Elijah never actually died in the Bible. In 2 Kings 2:11, Elijah is brought to Heaven in a chariot of fire, after which Elisha (anointed with the spirit of Elijah) takes over as the primary prophet for the Jewish people. However, Elijah will return, and his return will be quite special. In Malachi 4:5-6, we read that Elijah will return at the time of the Messiah:

"Behold, I will send you Elijah the prophet before the coming of the great and terrible day of the LORD.

And he shall turn the heart of the fathers to the children, and the heart of the children to their fathers; lest I come and smite the land with utter destruction."

So, we learn from the Book of Malachi that Elijah will herald the coming of the Messiah. Elijah was a man of great austerity and mortification, zealous for God, bold in reproving sin, and active to reduce an apostate people to God and their duty. John the Baptist was animated by the same spirit and power, and preached repentance and reformation, as Elias had done. All held him for a prophet, as they did Elijah in his day, and believed that his baptism was from heaven, and not of men. Note, when God has such work to do he can raise up such men to do it, and can put into a John the Baptist the spirit of an Elijah.

Most Christians believe that John the Baptist was a fulfillment of an Elijah ministry; in Matthew 11:10-14 Jesus stated that John was the Elijah sent to "prepare the way before him" and there would be yet another coming of Elijah "to restore all things" before he returned to the earth for his second coming or what is commonly called *the Rapture (*Matthew 17:10-13).

John the Baptist knew who he was and identified himself as the Elijah of Malachi 3:1. Clearly, John was not actually Elijah. Luke 1:17 implies he was anointed with the power and spirit of Elijah, as Elisha was in 2 Kings 2:9-15 ("*The spirit of Elijah doth rest on Elisha*.").

The writers of the Gospels consistently portray John the Baptist as the fulfillment of Malachi's prophecy (Mark 1:2-3). John dressed like Elijah had done, in camel's hair with a leather belt around his waist (Matt. 3:4; Mark 1:6; 2 Kings 1:6-8). The archangel Gabriel cites the fulfillment of *one* part of Malachi 4:5-6 during his announcement to Zechariah in the Holy Place of the Temple (Luke 1:16-17). Zechariah says that John will be the Elijah that goes before Messiah during his "great day" to turn the hearts of the Jewish fathers to children (Mathew 11:25; Mathew 18:3; Mathew 19:4). This left the second portion of Malachi 4:5-6 yet to be fulfilled – that "Elijah" would come before the "dreadful day" to turn the hearts to the children to the fathers. Make no mistake; men under inspiration say exactly what God wants them to say.

John was a sign, not the destination. Elijah was a sign, he was and is not the destination. These two and future iterations of Elijah are messengers – not the message.

Jesus himself split a scripture verse in Isaiah 61:2, citing only the fulfillment of the first part of it during His ministry – the other part yet to come some two thousand years later. (Luke 4:16-21) Jesus said that He/His first coming "proclaimed the acceptable year of the Lord." NOT "the day of vengeance..."

"1 The Spirit of the Lord GOD is upon me; because the LORD hath anointed me to preach good tidings unto the meek; he hath sent me to bind up the brokenhearted, to proclaim liberty to the captives, and the opening of the prison to them that are bound; 2 To proclaim the acceptable year of the LORD..."(KJV)

Jesus assures his disciples that John was indeed the Elijah who was to come, as the forerunner of His Messianic coming (Matthew 11:10-14; 17: 11-13; Mark 9:11-12; Luke 7:27).

Odd, when John was questioned concerning his identity he denied that he was Elijah (John 1:21, 25). Given Jesus' insistence that he was to be identified with Elijah it is possible that John either did not realize his own significance or was being humble. Possibly he thought of himself only as the forerunner of Messiah (Matthew 3:11; Mal. 3:1-3), not realizing he also fulfilled Malachi's prophecy of Elijah. John was capable of error, as is shown when after being put in prison, he expressed his doubts about who Jesus was and required reassurance (Matthew 11:2-6; Luke 7:20-23). This serves to reinforce the opening statement – "Elijah was a man…"

But it is most probable he knew that the Pharisees were trying to get him to claim that he was the "end-times" Elijah to come before the "dreadful day of the Lord" – which he was not. The Jewish leaders misunderstood the scriptures and the "signs of the times."

They truly did not see Messiah coming as a humble babe in a manger, or that he would be a servant-king, or that he would die sacrificially – they thought (or hoped) Messiah would be a powerful warrior-king, one that would crush Israel's enemies under foot, establish a military kingdom and rule with a rod of iron. John denied he was the Elijah of the second coming of Messiah – it had been revealed to him that Jesus was "the lamb of God that takes away the sins of the world." (John 1:26-36; Genesis 22:8; Exodus 12:5-13; Hebrews 11:4).

Prophets are unique individuals; they are similar in many characteristics and yet very different in presentation, style and demonstration of God's spirit.

It seems a regular phenomenon that we are drawn to prophets that are like us – those that are scared, weak, lonely, confused, and prone to discouragement. The more human they are, the more we hold them in reverence. This point is significant as the life and ministry of Elijah is examined because there seems to be a tendency towards cultishness. The argument about veneration vs. worship applies, as we shall see below.

The Jew was commanded to "have no other god" and to "hear O Israel, the Lord our God is One" and "He is a jealous god and will share His glory with no one" etc, etc – yet, unmistakably their lives and worship is infused with veneration of Elijah. During every Passover meal there is a "cup of Elijah," his name is evoked, songs are sung about him and he is invited into the room and into their presence. Elijah is expected to be ever present, ensuring that the sacred covenants are being kept.

The ministry and anointing of this prophet is so powerful, that many either mistake him for Messiah-Jesus or supplant their worship of God with veneration/worship of a man – this man Elijah. In Luke 3:15 the Jews are shown to be musing whether John Baptist (who performed NO miracles) was Christ, the Anointed One. Such was the spiritual anointing and aura on and about him, after all, he was "*the prophet of the Highest*" (Luke 1:66-80). Think about that: ***the*** prophet of ***the*** Highest.

In John's day, it is said "*that all the land went out to him…*" (Mark 1:5) Great Jewish leaders and earthly kings feared him (Mark 6:14-20; Mark 11:30-32). To be in Elijah's presence when he was anointed would be amazing, frightening, and awesome! Would we also do as Peter, John and James did on Mount Transfiguration and seek to worship him?

Verse 33: "*Peter said unto Jesus, Master, it is good for us to be here: and let us make three tabernacles; one for thee, and one for Moses, and one for Elias.*" (Luke 9:28-36)

It is only in the account in the Book of Luke that Elijah is described as telling the Apostles about Jesus and His ministry. Elijah and Moses are shown here to be instructing the Apostles, teaching them from the scriptures why Jesus was Messiah, why he had to die and what he would accomplish in His ministry. How amazing that instruction must have been, yet God the Father silenced it all and commanded the Apostles to listen to Jesus – "Hear ye Him!"

Peter, James and John were captivated by the life and ministry of the great man Elijah and would have continued to listen to his teachings, but God had a more excellent ministry and pointed them to Jesus. Just as Elijah did in the life and ministry of John Baptist; John taught about Messiah and attempted to send his followers away, and to Messiah.

In John 1:29 *the Baptist (with the spirit of Elijah) said "Behold the Lamb of God, which taketh away the sins of the world.*" Yet, NONE of his followers left and went after Jesus! A few days later the two crossed paths again, and John cried "Behold the Lamb of God!" After this repeated declaration and apparent command to leave him, only two obey – only two leave the cult of Elijah.

Such was his hold on followers, that even after he had repetitively pointed to Jesus, his followers refused to leave his side; they would not leave even while he was in prison (Luke 17:19-20) and confused spiritually and doctrinally (Elijah was a man…). *Unbelievably, after his death (Acts 19: 1-6) John still had followers, yet God's Spirit finally broke the hold on those at Ephesus and turned them to Jesus.*

Few Biblical scholars would debate that mankind is living in *the last days*. The days preceding the Coming of the Lord, the Resurrection of the church, the Great Tribulation period, the return of the Gospel to the Jews and the Battle of Armageddon.

If the Messiah Jesus Christ is about to return, where is Elijah?

Or has he already come and the modern world didn't recognize him?

If the Messiah Jesus Christ is about to return, where is Elijah? Or has he already come and the modern world did not recognize him, just as Elijah came in John Baptist and was unrecognized?

Matthew 17:10-13: *"And his disciples asked him, saying, Why then say the scribes that Elias must first come? And Jesus answered and said unto them, Elias truly shall first come, and restore all things. But I say unto you, That Elias is come already, and they knew him not, but have done unto him whatsoever they listed. Likewise shall also the Son of man suffer of them. Then the disciples understood that he spake unto them of John the Baptist."*

As a person reads the Bible, it would seem a foregone conclusion that Elijah was a man, *and* that he was more than a man. It is clear that Elijah shall come – to forerun/precede the Messiah Jesus' second coming as a sign of warning and to restore all things (clarify doctrinal discrepancies and correct doctrinal error). Both the Old and New Testament declare his position in end-time events. Both Jew and Christian alike are looking for Elijah to come. Identifying the life and ministry of this prophet is crucial for preparedness of the Messiah's appearing.

I Thought Elijah Was to Come First...

Is Wm Branham's Ministry a Fulfillment of Prophecy?

Surely the Lord GOD will do nothing, but he revealeth his secret unto his servants the prophets. (Amos 3:7) God's pattern of dealing with His people has for a long time included the sending of prophets. The prophet Amos informs us that God does "nothing" without a prophetic forerunner, and even a surface study of scriptural history will uncover this to be exactly as stated. Yet, seldom was there a prophet who spoke the words of God who was not greeted with skepticism, rejection and abuse.

Consider the following scriptures:

Malachi 4:5 and 6 is two-fold, fulfilled in part in the ministry of John, the Baptist. He preceded the first coming of Jesus Christ, called the "great" day of the Lord, turning the hearts of the fathers of the "law" to the children of the New Testament era of "grace." One source says, "...John the Baptist was an Elijah in spirit (Luke 1:16-17) but not the *literal* Elijah[335] (John 1:21). This implies that John, referred to by Malachi 4:5, knew by inspiration that he did not exhaustively fulfill *all* that is included in this prophecy: that there is a further fulfillment.

There is a prophet that will fulfill the second part of this scripture, forerun the second coming of Christ and "*turn the hearts of the children to their fathers...*" Literally, a ministry that would turn the hearts of a backslidden generation back to the Word of God and the faith of our "early church" fathers before the "dreadful day of the Lord", the second coming of Christ in judgment.

Again, Matthew 17:10-12 is two-fold. Firstly, "*Why then say the scribes that Elias must first come?*" "... But I say unto you, That Elias is come already and they knew him not ..." speaking of John the Baptist. Secondly, "*And Jesus answered and said unto them, Elias truly shall first come, and restore all things.*" Speaking of a future forerunner to precede Christ's second coming.

The ministry of William Branham involved three distinct stages that he referred to as "pulls" (Like the pulls or tugs a fisherman makes in attracting the fish, setting the hook, and taking the fish).[336] The First Pull: Healing. Second Pull: Prophesying. Third Pull: The opening or revealing of the Word of God with signs still following (Mark 16).[337]

The ministry of Jesus Christ followed exactly the same pattern. First Pull: multitudes flocked to hear his gracious words and to receive His miraculous healing touch. Second Pull: Revealed the secrets of the hearts. (John 4:17-18) Third Pull: His "message," the Word of God which came in strength and contrary to the religious order of the day, caused the multitudes to leave him. *"From that time many of his disciples went back, and walked no more with him."* John. 6:66

This book is to explore prophets and prophecy; as well as the factual basis of William Branham's life events and ministry as the fulfillment of many scriptures - specifically those that relate to the Elijah ministry of Malachi 4:5-6. It is hoped that the readers will respond as the Bereans did in Act 17:11 who "*were more noble than those in Thessalonica, in that they received the word with all readiness of mind, and searched the scriptures daily, whether those things were so.*"

Why does it matter what type of prophesy is being described? Why does it matter whether the prophet says "thus saith the Lord" or "I predict"? ***Remember*** "Elijah was a man…" – A man is subject to error, doctrinal confusion and correction, misinterpretation and personal opinion. This point matters as he is examined in the light of scriptures and given the test of a true prophet.

> There are two categories of prophetic vision and inspiration:
>
> Visions are Literal and symbolic.
>
> Along with visions, a person can have "thus saith the Lord" without vision, and still be Divinely inspired.

Deuteronomy 18:22:
"When a prophet speaketh in the name of the LORD, if the thing follow not, nor come to pass, that is the thing which the LORD hath not spoken, but the prophet hath spoken it presumptuously: thou shalt not be afraid of him."

There are two categories of prophetic vision. One deals with literal events that are foretold and often fulfilled with full awareness. Often times these types of prophecies are preceded by "Thus saith the Lord." The event is clear, like a video or pictorial recording that is simply played out. It is this type of prophecy that does not need any interpretation and leaves no room for speculation. The Biblical prophecy by Elijah concerning the death of Queen Jezebel in 1 Kings 21:20-27 is literal. Though Elijah did not see this prophecy fulfilled, Jehu clearly recognized the exact and precise details after its completion in 2 Kings 9:30-37. Look at this example:

In BC 900 Elijah prophecies concerning Jezebel - 1 Kings 21:23:

"And of Jezebel also spake the LORD, saying, The dogs shall eat Jezebel by the wall of Jezreel."

Six years later in BC 894 Jehu fulfills Elijah's Prophecy – 2 Kings 9:30-36:

"And when Jehu was come to Jezreel, Jezebel heard of it; and she painted her face, and tired her head, and looked out at a window. And as Jehu entered in at the gate, she said, Had Zimri peace, who slew his master? And he lifted up his face to the window, and said, Who is on my side? who? And there looked out to him two or three eunuchs. And he said, Throw her down. So they threw her down: and some of her blood was sprinkled on the wall, and on the horses: and he trode her under foot. And when he was come in, he did eat and drink, and said, Go, see now this cursed woman, and bury her: for she is a king's daughter. And they went to bury her: but they found no more of her than the skull, and the feet, and the palms of her hands.

Wherefore they came again, and told him. And he said, This is the word of the LORD, which he spake by his servant Elijah the Tishbite, saying, In the portion of Jezreel shall dogs eat the flesh of Jezebel:"

Consider the many literal prophesies that King David is credited with in the Book of Psalms, especially those that relate to Jesus Christ. One reference cites 92 prophecies by David.[338] For example:

The Messiah's body would not see corruption (natural decay).
Psalm 16:8-10b – prophecy Acts 13:35-37 – fulfillment

Messiah crucified: Both the Messiah's hands and feet would be pierced.
Psalm 22:16c – prophecy Matthew 27:38 – fulfillment

The Messiah's garments would be parted among the soldiers.
Psalm 22:18a – prophecy John 19:23-24 – fulfillment

The soldiers would cast lots for the Messiah's clothes.
Psalm 22:18b – prophecy John 19:23-24 – fulfillment

The Messiah would ascend back into heaven.
Psalm 68:18a – prophecy Luke24:51; Ephesians 4:8 – fulfillment

The other category of prophecy is the figurative or symbolic type. The meaning of this type of prophecy is not clear and at times the prophet may not even be aware that his words are God's words or that he is even prophesying. There are the many prophets that spoke figuratively, using symbols. Daniel, Ezekiel, and the New Testament Apostle/Prophet Saint John all spoke in symbols and their visions/dreams could not be understood by and within themselves. The Book of Revelation written on the Isle of Patmos, approximately in the year AD 93 is the classic symbolic-type prophecy.

Looking at the Book of Daniel we can see how symbols become reality after God has either provided the interpretation or the interpretation is understood by the vision transpiring – post facto. In Daniel Chapter Two, King Nebuchadnezzar has a series of disturbing dreams, for which he wants an interpretation. He asks his wise men, astrologers and magicians to tell him the dream and the interpretation, none of which can do this. Daniel over the years had gained a reputation for doing this type of work and is called into the presence of the King to help. Daniel is given the interpretation by God and tells the Babylonian King and his court in Daniel 2:19-23, 28:

22: He revealeth the deep and secret things: he knoweth what is in the darkness, and the light dwelleth with him.

28: There is a God in heaven that revealeth secrets, and maketh known to the king Nebuchadnezzar what shall be in the latter days.

Daniel goes on to tell the first part of the dream. He says that the statue with Head of Gold represents rulers and kingdoms, empires that will reign until the end of time. The Head of Gold Daniels says is Nebuchadnezzar. Over the course of Daniel's life, he sees the fulfillment of the second part of that particular vision whereby the "Breast and Arms of Silver" [which is the empire of the Medes-Persians] conquers Babylon. The Third and Fourth Kingdom/Empires would remain unknown to Daniel, though probably he guessed at who they were.

Daniel himself has several symbolic visions of the same world powers that would rise up. In Daniel Chapters 7, 8, 11, and 12 he sees cruel animals, not beautiful statues to represent men and their governments. In Chapter 9 verses 21-27 God sends the angel Gabriel to Daniel with a prophecy concerning the nation of Israel, from that moment in history until the end-of-days. Israel's complete history for the next 2500 years, all in symbols and oblique references, sealed and shut up until the "time of the end." (Daniel 12:4, 9)

These scriptural references are provided to "judge" or test the actions of a modern-day prophet. His life and ministry may be misunderstood, because most will not know how to truly provide an evaluation. What are other tests to identify a true prophet? According to historian Rene Noorbergen, God has regularly spoken to His people through prophets. As we draw closer to the end of time, it should come as no surprise that individuals arise claiming to be a prophet of God. However, nearly all of these fail to meet the scriptural requirements for a true prophet.[339] Noorbergen, has studied a number of psychics and acclaimed prophets including Jeane Dixon, and Nostradamus (*Jeane Dixon, My Life and Prophecies* and *Nostradamus: Invitation to a Holocaust*). In his book *Ellen White: Prophet of Destiny*[340] he lists several biblical requirements for a true prophet. These are:

1) A true prophet does not lie. His predictions will be fulfilled. (Jer. 28:9, "*The prophet which prophesieth of peace, when the word of the prophet shall come to pass, then shall the prophet be known, that the LORD hath truly sent him.*")

2) A true prophet prophesies in the name of the Lord, not in his own name. (2 Pet. 1:21, "*For the prophecy came not in old time by the will*

of man: but holy men of God spake as they were moved by the Holy Ghost.")

3) A true prophet does not assert his own private interpretation of prophecy, he may make predictions but he will not elevate his predictions to "thus saith the Lord". (2 Pet. 1:20, "*Knowing this first, that no prophecy of the scripture is of any private interpretation.*")

4) A true prophet points out the sins and transgressions of the people against God. (Isa. 58:1, " *Cry aloud, spare not, lift up thy voice like a trumpet, and shew my people their transgression, and the house of Jacob their sins.*")

5) A true prophet is to warn the people of God's coming judgment. (Amos 3:7-8, 4:4, "*Surely the Lord GOD will do nothing, but he revealeth his secret unto his servants the prophets. The lion hath roared, who will not fear? the Lord GOD hath spoken, who can but prophesy?" and "Therefore thus will I do unto thee, O Israel: and because I will do this unto thee, prepare to meet thy God, O Israel.*")

6) A true prophet edifies the church, counsels and advises it in religious matters. (1 Cor. 14:3, 4, " *But he that prophesieth speaketh unto men to edification, and exhortation, and comfort. He that speaketh in an unknown tongue edifieth himself; but he that prophesieth edifieth the church.*")

7) A true prophet's words will be in absolute harmony with the words of the prophets that have preceded him, they will line up with Old and New Testament teachings. (Isa. 8:20, " *To the law and to the testimony: if they speak not according to this word, it is because there is no light in them.*" And Galatians 1:8-9, "*But though we, or an angel from heaven, preach any other gospel unto you than that which we have preached unto you, let him be accursed. As we said before, so say I now again, if any man preach any other gospel unto you than that ye have received, let him be accursed.*" And Revelation 22:18-19, "*If any man shall add unto these things, God shall add unto him the plagues that are written in this book. And if any man shall take away from the words of the book of this prophecy, God shall take away his part out of*

the book of life, and out of the holy city, and from the things which are written in this book.")

8) A true (contemporary) prophet recognizes the incarnation of Jesus Christ. (1 John 4:1-3, " *Beloved, believe not every spirit, but try the spirits whether they are of God: because many false prophets are gone out into the world. Hereby know ye the Spirit of God: Every spirit that confesseth that Jesus Christ is come in the flesh is of God: And every spirit that confesseth not that Jesus Christ is come in the flesh is not of God: and this is that spirit of antichrist, whereof ye have heard that it should come; and even now already is it in the world.*")

9) A true prophet can be recognized by the results of his work. (Matt. 7:16-20, " *Ye shall know them by their fruits. Do men gather grapes of thorns, or figs of thistles? Even so every good tree bringeth forth good fruit; but a corrupt tree bringeth forth evil fruit. A good tree cannot bring forth evil fruit, neither can a corrupt tree bring forth good fruit. Every tree that bringeth not forth good fruit is hewn down, and cast into the fire. Wherefore by their fruits ye shall know them.*") How do they live? Are they honest, godly, trustworthy and temperate?

Let's expand two of the more significant passages above:

Deut. 18:17-22. [Moses said to his people] " *The LORD thy God will raise up unto thee a Prophet from the midst of thee, of thy brethren, like unto me; unto him ye shall hearken; I will raise them up a Prophet from among their brethren, like unto thee, and will put my words in his mouth; and he shall speak unto them all that I shall command him. And it shall come to pass, that whosoever will not hearken unto my words which he shall speak in my name, I will require it of him. But the prophet, which shall presume to speak a word in my name, which I have not commanded him to speak, or that shall speak in the name of other gods, even that prophet shall die.*

And if thou say in thine heart, How shall we know the word which the LORD hath not spoken? When a prophet speaketh in the name of the LORD, if the thing follow not, nor come to pass, that is the thing which the LORD hath not spoken, but the prophet hath spoken it presumptuously: thou shalt not be afraid of him."

Isaiah 8:19-22, " *And when they shall say unto you, Seek unto them that have familiar spirits, and unto wizards that peep, and that mutter: should not a people seek unto their God? for the living to the dead?"*

Based on these texts, it becomes obvious that not everyone who prophecies is a prophet of God - for a *true prophet* is not a psychic who performs with the aid of a gimmick, but is someone who has no degree of freedom either in tuning in or controlling the prophetic impulses or prophetic recall. These impulses are superimposed over the prophet's conscious mind by a supernatural personal being, having absolute knowledge of both past and future, making no allowance for error or human miscalculation. Isaiah declares God's omnipotence in Chapter 46 Verses 10-11:

10: "Declaring the end from the beginning, and from ancient times the things that are not yet done, saying, My counsel shall stand, and I will do all my pleasure:

11: Calling a ravenous bird from the east, the man that executeth my counsel from a far country: yea, I have spoken it, I will also bring it to pass; I have purposed it, I will also do it."

A prophet is therefore human, and must rely upon God.

16

One in a Billion Odds - 1932 Vision Foretells Seven World Events

One in a Billion Odds - 1932 Vision Foretells Seven World Events

Just as God revealed to Daniel those things that would take place from then until the end of time, so it was in June of 1933, when a youthful 24-year old William Branham was conducting services in the old Masonic Hall[341] on Meggs Avenue in Jeffersonville, Indiana that he told of Seven Major events that were revealed to him (in 1932) which were to come to pass before the return of the Lord Jesus Christ.

The scope of these events is startling, covering high-profile world leaders, major international military conflicts and natural disasters. Consider the fact the before Roosevelt was even elected to his first term, William Branham had seen he would win and serve an unprecedented three more terms. Or that he described America's destruction by nuclear weapons, before nuclear weapons were even conceived of.[342]

On the above June morning, William Branham spoke of this series of events he had seen by vision in 1932:[343] [344]

"You remember the vision that was read here, 1933? We were having services down here where, I believe the Church of Christ is there now - The old Masonic home; Charlie Kurn's place; at the old orphans home. - as I started to Sunday school I fell into a trance. I'd like to read you a prophecy that was given... 1932, listen to this:

'As I was on my way, as I was getting ready to go on my way to church this morning, it came to pass that I fell into a vision. Our services are being held on Meggs Avenue at the old orphans' home, where Charlie Kurn lives in part of the building.' He lives just across the street, now. 'And it come to pass that while I was in this vision, I saw some dreadful things take place. I speak this in the Name of the Lord.'"

1. "The President which now is, will run into the fourth term, and we will be taken to a second world war.; and the new dictator of Italy, Mussolini, shall make his first invasion toward Ethiopia, and he will take Ethiopia; but that'll be his last. He shall come to his end.

2. We will be in the war with Germany. Watch Russia! Now, that's . . . Communism, Nazism, and Fascism. Watch Russia! But that is not the main one to watch.

3. It shall also . . . has been an evil thing done in this country, they have permitted women to vote. This is a woman's nation, and she will pollute this nation as Eve did Eden." "In her voting she will elect the wrong person.

4. The Americans will take a great beating at a place that Germany will build, which will be a great wall built of concrete,""but finally they will be victors.

5. Then when these women help elect the wrong person, then I saw a great woman rise up in the United States, well-dressed and beautiful, but cruel in heart. She will either guide or lead this nation to ruination." Now, I've got in parenthesis, "(perhaps the Catholic Church).

6. Also, science will progress, especially in the mechanical world. Automobiles will continue to get like egg-shape. Finally they will build one that won't need a steering wheel." "It will be controlled by some other power.

7. Then I saw the United States as one smoldering, burnt-over place. It will be near the end." Then I've got in parenthesis "(But I ***predict*** this will take place before 1977)." [345]

[Note he says *predict* NOT *prophesy,* NOR "Thus saith the Lord" concerning the fulfillment of these visions by the year 1977.]

One in a Billion Odds

Calculating the Probability of the 1932 Prophecies of William Branham:[346] [H]

Reducing and representing the likelihood of a prophesied event coming to pass to a numeric ratio is a subjective undertaking at best. Using an absolutist interpretation of God and His foreknowledge and omnipotence, one can make a convincing argument that the odds of a prophecy uttered by a vindicated prophet coming to pass are always 100%, i.e. there is no possibility that the event will not occur. This thought may be comforting to the believer's mind but is not readily accepted by the secular mind.

Setting aside the *a priori* mindset, we have examined the seven prophecies of 1932 and have used a simple and absolute yes/no test to determine odds of all them coming to pass. This means that we calculated the odds by asking, "Will or did it come to pass or not?" This is the most conservative approach and the easiest to understand and interpret. We did not consider prior trends, mitigating factors, etc, just simply, yes, it did occur or, no, it did not.

When using yes/no criteria, then odds are expressed as $1:2^n$ (one out of two to the ***n***, where ***n*** is the number of events). One of the easiest examples to understand is flipping a coin. When flipped, the coin will either land on heads or tails. Assuming a fair coin, the odds of it landing on heads, for any given flip, is 1:2 or simply 1 out of 2, and the odds for tails is the same.

Things get more interesting when calculating odds for multiple flips. What are the odds of the coin landing on heads two times in a row? $1:2^2$ or 1 in 4. Here are the 4 possible outcomes of 2 flips: HH, HT,

---

[H] Note: The prophecies used for this document are taken from the messages (as presented on Voice of God Message Search Web Site), *Condemnation by Representation (Hybrid Religion)* preached November 13, 1960 at Branham Tabernacle, paragraphs 5-1 and 5-2 and *Why Are We Not a Denomination* preached September 27, 1958 at Branham Tabernacle, paragraph 136.

TH, TT. HH is the only outcome that satisfies the prediction, thus 1 in 4. What are the odds of the coin landing on heads 3 times in a row? $1:2^3$, or 1 chance in 8. One chance in eight? Here are the 8 possible outcomes with 3 flips: HHH, HHT, HTH, HTT, TTH, THT, THH, TTT. The only outcome that satisfies the desired event is HHH, therefore 1 out of 8.

First Prophecy:
The president which now is, President Franklin D. Roosevelt... (Now remember, this is twenty-eight years ago.) will cause the whole world to go to war; and the new dictator of Italy, Mussolini, shall make his first invasion towards Ethiopia, and he will take Ethiopia; but that'll be his last. He shall come to his end. It also said what would take place, and about Roosevelt and them things, how he would run and make that fourth term.

The prophecy has 8 events in it, the odds of all 8 events happening when prophesied is $1:2^8$ or 1 in 256.

1st, 2nd, and 3rd Events: FDR was in his first term in 1932, therefore 3 more election wins is 3 events.
4th Event: "will cause the whole world to go to war"
5th Event: "and the new dictator of Italy, Mussolini, shall make his first invasion towards Ethiopia"
6th Event: "and he will take Ethiopia"
7th Event: "but that'll be his last"
8th Event: "He shall come to his end."

Second Prophecy:
We will be in war with Germany. Watch Russia. (Now, that's...) Communism, Nazism, and Fascism... Watch Russia. But that is not the main one to watch.

This has 6 events (Br Branham explained these prophecies in many other messages which the reader can research): War, Russia, 3 isms, not the main one. This is $1:2^6$ or 1 in 64.

At this point the odds of all elements of the first two prophecies occurring are $1:2^{14}$ or 1 in 16,384.

Third Prophecy:

It shall--also has been an evil thing done in this country; they have permitted women to vote. This is a woman's nation, and she will pollute this nation as Eve did Eden. In her voting she will elect the wrong person.

2 events: Pollute this nation and elect the wrong person. 1:4. Cumulative odds for 1, 2 and 3 are $1:2^{16}$ or 1 in 65,536.

Fourth Prophecy:

The Americans will take a great beating at a place that Germany will build, which will be a great wall built of concrete (The Maginot Line, eleven years before it was ever built.) But finally they will be victors.
4 events: Great beating, Germany will build, made of concrete, Americans victorious. 1:16. Cumulative odds for 1, 2, 3, and 4 are $1:2^{20}$ or 1 in 1,048,576.

Fifth Prophecy:

I seen a great woman rise up in the United States, well-dressed and beautiful, but cruel in heart. She will either guide or lead this nation to ruination. (I've got in parenthesis "perhaps Catholic church.").

5 events: Great woman rise up in US, well dressed, beautiful, cruel, ruination. Odds are $1:2^5$ or 1 in 32. I am not putting cumulative odds on this or number seven until the end, since it is generally agreed among Message believers that this prophecy has not yet been fulfilled.

Sixth Prophecy:

Also, science will progress, especially in the mechanical world. Automobiles will continue to get like egg shape. Finally they will build one that won't need a steering wheel. (They've got it now.) It will be controlled by some other power.

3 events: Science progress, cars egged shape, no steering wheel. Odds are $1:2^3$ or 1 in 8. Cumulative odds for 1, 2, 3, 4, and 6 are 1 out of 8,388,608.

Seventh Prophecy:
Then I seen the United States as one smoldering, burnt-over place. It will be near the end.

2 Events: US burnt over, near the end. (One could make a case for 3 events, i.e. the invention of nuclear weapons to do the "smoldering"). Odds are 1:4.

Cumulative odds for all the events in all seven prophecies are $1: 2^{30}$ or 1 out of 1,073,741,824 (a little over ***One in a Billion***).

Visualization:
Think about a warehouse that has 1 billion Bibles in it stored on bookcases. Each book case is 5 feet wide and has 5 shelves. If the Bibles are 2 inches wide, each shelf can hold 30 Bibles (60 inches divided by 2), and each book case can hold 150 Bibles (5 x 30). It would take a little over 7 million bookcases to hold the Bibles (1,073,741,824 divided by 7). If the bookcases were in rows of 2000 bookcases it would take 3500 rows. Each row would be about 2 miles wide and 3500 rows would make the building about 4 miles long, therefore it would take an 8 square mile building to house the Bibles.

If only one Bible out of the billion had John 5:24 underlined and was mixed in with the other billion Bibles and you were to walk into the 8 sq. mi. storehouse among the 7 million bookcases and could only pick one Bible, your odds of picking the Bible with the underlined passage would be similar to the odds of all of the seven prophecies coming to pass - ***One in a Billion.***

The Seven Events

William Branham provides his own semi-interpretation of these visions and events - *The President we have in now will run even in the fourth term (He's on his first then.)--will run into the fourth term, and we will be taken to a second world war. The first vision was also that Mussolini would invade Ethiopia and that nation would "fall at his steps". That vision surely did cause some repercussions, and some were very angry when I said it and would not believe it. But it happened that way. He just walked in there with his modern arms and took over. The natives didn't have a chance. But the vision also said that Mussolini would come to a horrible end with his own people turning on him.*

The next vision foretold that an Austrian by the name of Adolph Hitler would rise up as dictator over Germany, and that he would draw the world into war. It showed the Siegfried line and how our troops would have a terrible time to overcome it. Then it showed that Hitler would come to a mysterious end.

The third vision was in the realm of world politics for it showed me that there would be three great ISMS, Facism, Nazism, Communism, but that the first two would be swallowed up into the third. The voice admonished, "Watch Russia, watch Russia. Keep your eye on the King of the North."

The fourth vision showed the great advances in science that would come after the second world war. It was headed up in the vision of a plastic bubble-topped car that was running down beautiful highways under remote control so that people appeared seated in this car without a steering wheel and they were playing some sort of a game to amuse themselves.

The fifth vision had to do with the moral problem of our age, centering mostly around women. God showed me that women began to be out of their place with the granting of the vote. Then they cut off their hair, which signified that they were no longer under the authority of a man but insisted on either equal rights, or in most cases, more than equal rights. She adopted men's clothing and went into a state of undress, until the last picture I saw was a woman naked except for a little fig leaf type apron. With this vision I saw the terrible perversion and moral plight of the whole world.

Then in the sixth vision there arose up in America a most beautiful, but cruel woman. She held the people in her complete power. I believed that this was the rise of the Roman Catholic Church, though I

knew it could possibly be a vision of some woman rising in great power in America due to a popular vote by women.
The last and seventh vision was wherein I heard a most terrible explosion. As I turned to look I saw nothing but debris, craters, and smoke all over the land of America.
Wm Branham – *Condemnation by Representation* Jeffersonville, IN 1960-1113; Page 5 ¶1-2

Regarding these *Seven Future Events Foretold* we have read the actual prophecies, and William Branham's description of them; let's take a look at them now after seventy years have transpired.

1st Event - In the first vision, Part One states that the then-sitting president would be reelected to office an unprecedented four times. In Part Two William Branham witnessed Benito Mussolini brutally invading Ethiopia and then coming to a shameful demise.

Part One and Roosevelt's Four Terms - Franklin Delano Roosevelt (January 30, 1882 – April 12, 1945), often referred to by his initials FDR, was the 32nd President of the United States. Elected to four terms in office, he served from 1933 to 1945, and is the only U.S. president to have served more than two terms. Though constitutionally possible, *his unprecedented election to four terms in office will most likely never be repeated; passed after his death, the 22nd Amendment to the Constitution of the United States, denies the right of any person to be elected president more than twice.*

Franklin Roosevelt's Nomination and Election of 1932: In 1932, Franklin Roosevelt won the Democratic nomination for the presidency with John Nance Garner as his Vice President. He ran against incumbent Herbert Hoover. The Great Depression was the backdrop for the campaign. Roosevelt gathered a "Brain Trust" to help him come up with effective public policy. He campaigned continuously and his apparent confidence made Hoover's meager campaign pale in comparison. In the end, Roosevelt carried 57% of the popular vote and 472 electors versus Hoover's 59.

Second Reelection - 1936:
In 1936, Roosevelt easily won the nomination with Garner as his Vice President. He was opposed by progressive Republican Alf Landon whose platform argued that the New Deal was not good for America and relief efforts should be run by the states. Landon argued while campaigning that the New Deal programs were unconstitutional. Roosevelt campaigned on the programs' effectiveness. The NAACP supported Roosevelt who won an overwhelming victory with 523 electoral votes versus Landon's 8.

Third Reelection - 1940:
Roosevelt did not publicly ask for a third term but when his name was placed on the ballot, he was quickly re-nominated. The Republican nominee was Wendell Willkie who had been a Democrat but switched parties in protest to the Tennessee Valley Authority. War was raging in Europe. While FDR pledged to keep America out of war, Willkie was in favor of a draft and wanted to stop Hitler. He also focused on FDR's right to a third term. Roosevelt won with 449 out of 531 electoral votes.

Fourth Reelection - 1944:
Roosevelt was quickly re-nominated to run for a fourth term. However, there was some question over his Vice President. FDR's health was declining and the Democrats wanted someone they were comfortable with to be president. Harry S Truman was eventually chosen. The Republicans chose Thomas Dewey to run. He used FDR's declining health and campaigned against waste during the New Deal. Roosevelt won by a slim margin getting 53% of the popular vote and winning 432 electoral votes versus 99 for Dewey.

Part Two of this prophecy seemed out of step with World politics in 1933, as Mussolini had ruled Italy since 1922 with little or isolated opposition, he had signed a concordant with the Catholic Church four years earlier recognizing the Italian State and an independent Vatican, and he had opposed the rise of Hitler in Germany. It was only after Mussolini's crusade in Ethiopia was opposed by the League of Nations that the Italian-German allegiance materialized. Mussolini and his mistress were finally shot by Italian Communists on April 28, 1945, and their bodies were placed on display on meat hooks in the Piazzale Loreto in Milan the next day.

In September 1934, Italy affirmed its 1928 treaty of friendship with Ethiopia, although the borders between the countries were unclear. At the same time, however, Italian troops began amassing in Italian Somaliland. On October 3, 1935, 100,000 Italian soldiers and a number of Askari attacked Ethiopia from Eritrea and Italian Somaliland without a declaration of war. On October 7, the League of Nations unanimously declared Italy an aggressor but took no effective action.

Mussolini is reported as issuing the following commands to his soldiers:[347]

The use of gas as an ultima ratio *to overwhelm enemy resistance and in case of counterattack is authorized. Mussolini.*

Given the enemy system I have authorized V.E. the use even on a vast scale of any gas and flamethrowers. Mussolini.

All rebels taken prisoner must be killed. Mussolini.

I have authorized once again V.E. to begin and systematically conduct a politics of terror and extermination of the rebels and the complicit population. Without the lex talionis *one cannot cure the infection in time. Await confirmation. Mussolini.*

Besides lacing bombs with mustard gas, the Italians instituted forced labor camps, installed public gallows, killed hostages, and mutilated the corpses of their enemies. Captured guerrillas were thrown out of airplanes in mid-flight, and Italian troops photographed themselves next to cadavers hanging from the gallows, and hanging around chests full of detached heads. The war lasted 7 months, with Ethiopia outmatched by Italy in armaments and brutality. The Italian king, Victor

Emmanuel III, was proclaimed the new emperor of Italian East Africa on May 9, 1937 (which merged Eritrea, Ethiopia and Somaliland into a single state).

The Italians showed favoritism to non-Christian ethnicities (i.e. non-Ethiopian Orthodox and Protestant people) such as the Oromo, Somali, and other Muslims (some of whom had supported the Italian invasion) in an attempt to isolate the Amhara, who had supported Emperor Haile Selassie. With Pope Pius XI silent on Mussolini's unprovoked and terrible conquest of Christian Ethiopia, the bloody Inquisition feared by Emperor Fasilides in 1624 A.D. had finally materialized.

On June 30, deposed Ethiopian Haile Selassie made a moving speech before the League of Nations in Geneva in which he set forth two choices--support for collective security or international lawlessness. He warned that "It is us today. It will be you tomorrow". As a result of the League's condemnation of Italy, Mussolini declared the country's withdrawal from the organization.

In June 1940 Italy entered World War II on the side of Germany. As a result, Britain sought to cooperate with Ethiopian and other forces in an attempt to dislodge the Italians from Ethiopia and from British Somaliland. Ethiopia was finally liberated from Italian control in East African Campaign in 1941.

Mussolini's demise and the fulfillment of Event #1 occurred on April 27, 1945, Mussolini and his mistress, Clara Petacci, were caught by Italian communist partisans near the village of Dongo (Lake Como) while attempting to escape into Switzerland before the Allied armies reached Milan. On April 28, Mussolini, his mistress, and their fifteen-man train (mostly ministers and officials of the Italian Social Republic) were taken to the small village of Giulino di Mezzegra, and shot.

The next day the bodies of Mussolini and his mistress were found hanging upside down on meat hooks in Piazzale Loreto (Milan). The corpse of the former leader became subject to ridicule and abuse by many and therefore, fulfilling the prophecy of Mussolini coming to a shameful end.

2nd **Event** - In the second vision, William Branham witnessed Adolf Hitler bringing the world into a second world war, pounding the Americans at the Siegfried Line, and coming to a mysterious end.

At the time of this prophecy, Adolf Hitler had just risen to power, and Nazi policies were starting to take shape. The rise of Hitler in 1933 created the environment for the fulfillment of this prophecy; however, the world was still years away from the WWII, the build-up of the Seigfreid line, and the death of Adolf Hitler.

The Siegfried Line, called the *Westwall* by the Germans, was a defense system stretching more than 630km (392 miles) with more than 18,000 bunkers, tunnels and tank traps. It went from Kleve on the border with the Netherlands, along the western border of the old German Empire as far as the town of Weil am Rhein on the border to Switzerland. More with propaganda in mind than for strategic reasons, Adolf Hitler planned the line from 1936 and had it built between 1938 and 1940.

Battles along the Siegfried line include the Battle of Hurtgen Forest (Sept. 19, 1944 - Feb. 10, 1945; 33,000 estimated American casualties, 9,000 estimated German casualties), the Battle of Aachen (Oct. 1944, 5,000 estimated American casualties, 5,000 estimated German casualties), and Operation Market Garden (3,500 American casualties, 6,484 British Casualties, and 4,000 - 8,000 German casualties). Other major offensives across the Siegfried Line that did not include the American forces, including the Battle of the Schelt and the Battle of Moerbrugge (both led by Canadian forces), were Allied successes with few casualties and large numbers of German soldiers captured as Prisoners of War (POWs).

One reason so many American soldiers perished in the Battle of Hurtgen Forest was the German method of bombing, and the American soldier's method of defense. Ernest Hemingway, who was there, described the battle as *Passchendaele with tree bursts.*[348] Tree bursts is a technique of using artillery shells that burst in the treetops causing hot metal shrapnel and wood fragments to rain down. Since American soldiers had been trained to fall prone when artillery fired, this technique proved particularly deadly until American G.I.s learned instead to "hug-a-tree" during bombardment. Passchendaele was a reference to a terrible battle in the First World War.

Adolf and Eva Hitler alledgedly committed suicide together on April 30th, 1945 at the Führerbunker in Berlin. Eva was Adolf's long-term mistress whom he had finally married on April 28th, 1945. After much debate, and despite no objective, forensic proof, many historians have concluded that Hitler shot himself in the right temple while simultaneously biting into a cyanide capsule, while Eva died from cyanide. It is said their corpses were doused with gasoline by other Führerbunker aides in the Reich Chancellery garden just outside the bunker's emergency exit, and set alight as the Red Army advanced.

These charred remains were found by the Russians and, to avoid any possibility of creating a potential shrine or rallying point for the Nazis, were secretly buried at the SMERSH compound in Magdeburg, East Germany. In April 1970, when the facility was about to be turned over to the East German government, the remains were reportedly exhumed and thoroughly cremated. According to the Russian Federal Security Service, a fragment of human skull stored in its archives and displayed to the public in a 2000 exhibition came from the remains of Hitler's body uncovered by the Red Army in Berlin, and is all that remains of Hitler; however, the authenticity of the skull has been challenged by many historians and researchers.[349]

German authorities officially released the location of Hitler's bunker in June 2006. The bunker was destroyed by Soviet troops after the war and filled with concrete, however, it was feared that identifying the location of the bunker might provide neo-Nazis and other right-wing extremists with a memorial or rallying point. The bunker lies within a quarter of a kilometer of Berlin's Holocaust Memorial, and currently serves as a parking lot.

While much is known or agreed about Hitler's death, most of the details remained a mystery for years following WWII. Several years after his “death”, reported sightings of Hitler were still coming in. Late in 1945, Trevor-Roper was appointed by British Intelligence in Germany to investigate conflicting evidence surrounding Hitler's final days and to produce a definitive report on his death. In March 1947 Trevor-Roper released his report (later published under the title *The Last Days of Hitler*] of the last days in the Bunker, based on details gleaned from interrogated prisoners and other, less well-placed sources. Despite this report, Hitler’s death, and the events surrounding his death largely remained a mystery.

3rd Event - In the third vision, Fascism and Nazism were swallowed up into Communism. A voice in the vision instructed William Branham to "watch Russia, watch Russia, the king of the North" (rather than "watch the U.S.S.R.") indicating the eventual fall of the Soviet Union and the formation of Russia into a distinct State.

Fascism is an authoritarian ideology that considers individual and other societal interests inferior to the needs of the state. The term Fascism was invented by Mussolini, who was the dictator of Italy before and during WWII. *Fasces*, which consisted of a bundle of rods tied around an axe, was an ancient Roman symbol of the authority of the civic magistrates, and symbolized strength through unity.

Nazism was not a precise, theoretical ideology, but a combination of various ideologies and groups centered on anger at the Treaty of Versailles and what was considered to have been a Jewish/Communist conspiracy to humiliate Germany at the end of the First World War. Nazism consisted of a loose collection of incoherent positions focused on those held to blame for Germany's "weakness": anti-parliamentarianism, ethnic nationalism, racism, collectivism, eugenics, anti-Semitism, opposition to economic and political liberalism, a racially-defined and conspiratorial view of finance capitalism, and anti-communism. As Nazism became dominant in Germany, it was defined in practice as whatever was decreed by the Nazi Party and in particular by the Füehrer, Adolf Hitler.

Communism is a system of political and economic organization where all citizens share in the common wealth, according to their need.[350] Or to paraphrase Frederick Engels, it is the doctrine and actions of liberating the working class.[351]

Communist ideals were first penned by Karl Marx, and instituted by Vlademir Lenin and the Bolsheviks after the Russian Revolution of 1917. By 1956, the U.S.S.R. had grown from a union of four Soviet Socialist Republics to a union of 15 republics. After Joseph Lenin (d. 1924) the U.S.S.R was ruled by Joseph Stalin (d. 1953), Nikita Khrushchev (deposed in 1964), and a collective government from 1964 until Leonid Brezhnev (d. 1982) came to power in the 1970s. In the mid 1980s, the reform-minded Mikhail Gorbachev introducing the landmark policies of glasnost (openness) and perestroika (restructuring) in an attempt to modernize Soviet communism. His initiatives provoked strong resentment among some conservative elements of the government.

The Fall of Fascism: In July 1943, the Italian King Vittorio Emanuele III and a group of Fascist leaders staged a coup d'etat against Mussolini, having him arrested. In September 1943 Italy surrendered to the Allies, but was immediately invaded by Germany. For nearly two years the country was divided and became a battlefield, with a puppet fascist state under Mussolini being reconstituted in the Nazi-occupied part of the country. On April 28, 1945, Mussolini was executed by Italian communist partisans.

The Fall of Nazism: While the German army had initially had great success against the U.S.S.R, the tide turned at the Battle of Stalingrad (August 21, 1942 to February 2, 1943) during which almost 2 million Axis and Soviet soldiers were killed. The German army retreated on the Eastern Front until May 8, 1945 when the Red Army occupied Berlin, and Germany surrendered.

Russia emerges from Communist U.S.S.R.: In August of 1991 an unsuccessful military coup attempted to remove Mikhail Gorbachev from power, but instead led to the collapse of the Soviet Union. Boris Yeltsin came to power and declared the end of exclusive Communist rule.

The USSR splintered into fifteen independent republics, including Russia, and was officially dissolved in December of 1991.

Russia today: On the evening of August 22nd 1991—over16 years ago—Alexei Kondaurov, a KGB general, stood by the darkened window of his Moscow office and watched a jubilant crowd moving towards the KGB headquarters in Lubyanka Square. A coup against Mikhail Gorbachev had just been defeated. The head of the KGB who had helped to orchestrate it had been arrested, and Mr. Kondaurov was now one of the most senior officers left in the fast-emptying building. For a moment the masses seemed to be heading straight towards him.

Their anger was diverted to the statue of Felix Dzerzhinsky, the KGB's founding father. Men climbed up and slipped a rope around the statues neck, and a crane yanked him up. Watching "Iron Felix" sway in mid-air, Mr. Kondaurov, who had served in the KGB since 1972, felt betrayed "by Gorbachev, by Yeltsin, by the impotent coup leaders". He remembers thinking, "I will prove to you that your victory will be short-lived."[352]

Those feelings of betrayal and humiliation were shared by 500,000 KGB operatives across Russia and beyond, including Vladimir Putin, whose resignation as a lieutenant-colonel in the service had been accepted only the day before. Eight years later, though, the KGB men seemed poised for revenge. Just before he became president, Mr Putin told his ex-colleagues at the Federal Security Service (FSB), the KGB's successor, "A group of FSB operatives, dispatched under cover to work in the government of the Russian federation, is successfully fulfilling its task."[353]

Over the two terms of Mr. Putin's presidency, that "group of FSB operatives" has consolidated its political power and built a new sort of corporate state in the process. Men from the FSB and its sister organizations control the Kremlin, the government, the media and large parts of the economy—as well as the military and security forces. According to research by Olga Kryshtanovskaya[354], a sociologist at the Russian Academy of Sciences, a quarter of the country's senior bureaucrats are *siloviki*—a Russian word loosely translated as "power guys",[355] which includes members of the armed forces and other security services, not just the FSB. These people represent a psychologically homogeneous group, loyal to roots that go back to the Bolsheviks' first political police, the Cheka. As Mr. Putin says repeatedly, "There is no such thing as a former Chekist."[356]

By many indicators, today's security bosses enjoy a combination of power and money without precedent in Russia's history. The Soviet KGB and its pre-revolutionary ancestors did not care much about money; power was what mattered. Influential, the KGB was a "combat division" of the Communist Party, an outfit that was part intelligence organization, part security agency and part secret political police.

The KGB provided a crucial service of surveillance and suppression; it was a state within a state. Political power in Russia now lies with the FSB, the KGB's successor. Now, however, it has become the state itself. ***RUSSIA*** is now a neo-KGB state;[357] and with renewed nationalism under Putin soaring, so are hostilities towards Unites States.[358]

The Russian political mindset today is one of "escalating opposition to America" and the spread of Russian influence as a counterweight. Putin has accused America of arrogance and military adventurism, and in a recent speech compared the United States to Hitler's Third Reich.[359]

Recently (2008) the U.S. Senate Select Committee On Intelligence held annual hearings on national security issues, attended by top intelligence officials, including National Intelligence Director, Admiral Michael McConnell; in his 45-page report he listed Russia among chief threats to U.S. national security.

While discussing Russia, senators also touched upon Moscow's relations with Iran. Senator Evan Bayh wondered why Russians supply nuclear fuel for atomic power plants to Iran.

Meanwhile, a source close to the U.S. intelligence said the threats list includes a suspicion that Moscow-Tehran nuclear cooperation might be beyond the framework of current international agreements. The thought of either of these countries (both hostile toward America) armed with nuclear weapons is frightening.

Russia's increasing belligerency is of great concern to U.S. and NATO leaders. The invasion of Georgia comes on the heels of such actions as the resumption of nuclear-armed bomber patrols off the U.S. coast, the planting of the Russian flag under the Arctic ice, the manipulation of natural gas supplies to the Ukraine and a massive cyber attack on Estonia.

The Kremlin also has initiated an enormous arms buildup that includes new ICBMs and ballistic missile submarines as well as advanced tactical aircraft and armored vehicles. It appears the Russians have undergone a near complete reversal of both attitude and military preparedness. All that is left is to once again lift up the statue of "Iron Felix" Dzerzhinsky to its symbolic place in their hearts, minds and its pedestal at Lubyanka Square in Moscow in front of the old KGB building.

But *wait* – that's already been done. In 2002, Moscow Mayor Yuriy Luzhkov proposed that the original statue of *Iron Felix* be returned to his rightful place. And in November 2005 a smaller bust that had been removed in 1991 was restored to the courtyard of the Moscow police.

Felix Edmundovich Dzerzhinsky (1877–1926) was a Polish Communist revolutionary, famous as the founder of the Bolshevik secret police, the Cheka, later known by many names (GPU, NKVD and the KGB) during the history of the Soviet Union. The agency became notorious for large-scale human rights abuses, including torture and mass summary executions, carried out during the Red Terror and the Russian Civil War.[360] [361] In Russia, *Iron Felix* is synonymous with brutal interrogation, death, state terror **and** national pride. Dzerzhinsky himself boasted that: "*We represent in ourselves organized terror -- this must be said very clearly.*"[362]

Watch Russia, watch Russia, the king of the North.

4th Event - In the fourth vision, cars continued to be shaped more and more like an egg and scientific achievement produced a driverless vehicle.

With driver assist technologies being integrated into vehicles today, the promise of a fully autonomous individual vehicle on all or designated roadways are possible. The research for autonomous vehicles began in 1977 by the Tsukuba Mechanical Engineering Lab in Japan. The Bundeswehr Universität München in Europe experimented with video-driven cars in the 1980s, and the U.S. experimented with an automated highway system in the 1990s. Today, however, the most promise is in individually autonomous vehicles made possible by advances in computer technology.

From the sermon **Seventy Weeks of Daniel, August 6, 1961:**

"Science will progress in such a way until they will make a car that will not have to be guided by a steering wheel, and the cars will continue to be shaped like an egg until the consummation," the end time. I seen American family going down the road in a broad way, riding in a car with their ***backs turned towards where the wheel should be; looked like they were playing checkers or cards****. And we got it. It's on television. "Popular Science"--"Mechanics," rather, all have it...*[363] *It's controlled by remote control by--by radar. They won't even have to have any steering wheel in it. Just set your dial like this--like you dial your phone--your car takes you right on to it, can't wreck nor nothing. No other cars--the magnet keeps the rest of them away from you. See? They got it. Oh, my. Think of it. Predicted thirty years before it happened.*

Bob Lutz, Vice Chairman of General Motors[364]

"With radar-based automatic distance-sensing systems, imaging and lane-adherence technology, and the GPS system, we basically have the enablers to do fully autonomous driving.

*It's not out of the question to imagine that someday soon you'll be able to start the car, punch in the appropriate settings, **then swivel the front seats around and play cards** and eat lunch as if you're riding on a train. All in perfect comfort and safety, all the way to that niece's place in Chicago. ...It will help alleviate a lot of traffic congestion and prevent a lot of accidents, assuming the system doesn't break down for any reason. And it's an idea whose time has just about come. If pressed to estimate just how far away that time is, I'd say a working system is ten years out, implementation maybe 20 years."*[365]

There are already many models of "driverless vehicles" - October 8, 2005 a modified Volkswagen Touareg named Stanley beat 23 other robotic cars and navigated 150 miles of Nevada Desert to earn the rights to be called the first autonomous off-road vehicle. Stanley is guided by video, laser, radar and GPS signals, is run by seven on-board Intel Pentiums, and is able to tell the difference between a tum-bleweed and a rock. Stanley was invented by a team at Stanford University. (Visit the GrandChallenge[366] website for more details.)
Based on the success of the October 8, 2005 race, DARPA (Defense Advanced Research Projects Agency) has announced that a second challenge, the Urban Challenge, will take place on November 3, 2007 over a 60 mile mock urban course to be navigated autonomously with-in 6 hours. About 89 teams have already applied to take part in this race.

Parkshuttle - Developed by Frog Navigation (2getthere) and built by Connexion (the Dutch Transit Authority), this bus runs driverless through onboard computers and sensors, together with guiding magnets embedded in the designated roadway. Phileas is already in operation in the Netherlands between the airport and an industrial park.

Not only has the technology for the fulfillment of this prophecy been invented and implemented, for many years so has the "egg-shaped" design. Originating with the Volkswagen Beetle in 1935 as a military-only option, known as the Kommandeurwagen or the KdF Wagen.

Though a VW "Beetle" was produced in small numbers during the late 1930's for the German Nazi elite, it did not go into commercial production and become the "people's wagon" until after the end of WW II. It was popularized in America in the 1960's after a successful marketing campaign.

William Branham's prophecy of the VW "egg-shaped" vehicle still preceded *any* type of production by at least two years. And though it is possible he saw the prototype and/or designs that were held in confidence by Adolf Hitler and Ferdinand Porsche, it is most improbable.

One of the stars of the 2005 Tokyo Auto Show, the Nissan Pivo concept is an electric car with drive-by-wire systems and a revolving egg-shaped cabin.

The Moovie concept vehicle is driven by two large wheels, the center of which serves as doors for the vehicle. The Moovie is an electric car designed by Andre Costa in the third Peugot Design Contest, and developed as a prototype by Peugot.

5th Event - The fifth vision dealt with the morality of America, and the World. Just as scientific advancement was represented by a car in the fourth vision, the decline of morality was represented by women in the fifth vision. William Branham saw women cutting their hair, acting and dressing like men, wearing scant fig-like clothes and finally almost completely abandoning their garments.

The last part of this prophecy began to be fulfilled with the invention of the Bikini by fashion designer Jacques Heim in Paris in 1946. Instead of the U.S.A banning this garment, it was promoted by the film industry, and today is accepted by most Christian Americans as acceptable beachwear. The apron-only style garment at the end of the prophecy is much like the autonomous car of the fourth vision - mainstream production and acceptance of this product has not begun, yet, but it exists and can be seen in magazines and advertisements.

The U.S.A. remains one of the few "Christian" nations not to allow topless bathing (although unofficially acceptable in certain areas). In many European nations and Australia, public topless bathing is common today. William Branham's prophecy suggests that the U.S.A.'s moral laws will go the way of prohibition.

Prior to WWI, the fashion industry was influenced by Paris designers, and the wealthy European class. For ladies, the length of her skirt often indicated her age - knee length for pre-teens, ankle length for early teenagers, and floor length for 18+ women. Innocence and virginity were protected by the community and government, and many adults felt responsible to protect young ladies from premature sexual contact and conduct. Chaperoning was a common social behavior, and the virginity of the mind was just as important as the virginity of the body.

The moral edge of pre-war fashion was the "Gibson Girl", with bare arms, a low neckline, corset-bound body, and floor length dress. Yet even the Gibson-style women did not cut or shorten their hair, but advertized long hair by gathering it in a pompadour.

Pre-WWI men and women were either segregated or swam at different times. Swimwear for women included woolen bloomers and blouse, and black stockings and shoes, and U.S. laws were enforced limiting the exposure of flesh (including the legs).

In 1920, after WWI, women in the U.S.A. were granted the right to vote in federal elections. Shortly after this event, the bob haircut gained popularity among women (where the hair was cut short, but a weighted area was left to fall between the ear and chin), as did the 'flapper' style.

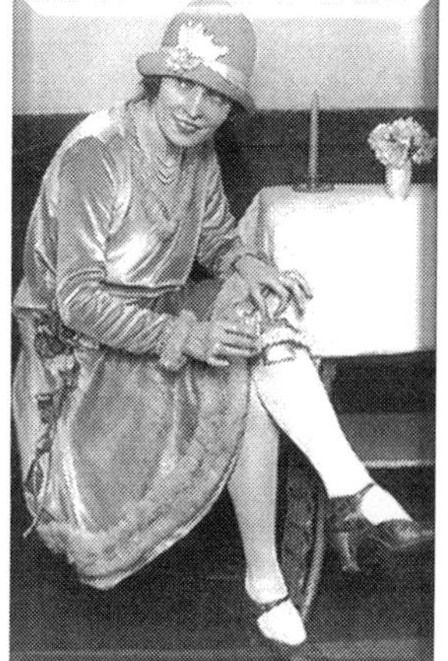

The flapper dress sat on the hips and ended near the knee, and the bust was flattened with a binding to give the woman a boyish look. Flappers also popularized the use of cigarettes, hard liquor, and the distain for "decent" behavior among women. Movie houses gained popularity, and Hollywood stars such as Clara Bow began to influence young people with their styles, flirtatious attitude, and use of make-up.

On the beaches, swimsuits now consisted of figure hugging wool knit with a sleeveless tank similar to the men's swimwear a decade earlier. The depression of the 1930's saw the return of some more modest fashions, and most skirts were again lengthened to the ankles. The uncensored and progressively immoral movies of the 1920's, some including nude scenes, were also curtailed by the implementation of the self-regulating Hays Office so that content-controlling federal laws would not be implemented.

Marlene Dietrich in Trousers

Hollywood's influence expanded during this time (in 1932 Macy's in New York sold 500,000 replicas of the dress Joan Crawford wore in the movie "Letty Lynton"), and photographs of actresses Marlene Dietrich and Katharine Hepburn in trousers helped make pants acceptable for women. New fabrics were developed during this time, and women's underwear changed from corsets and bindings, to form-fitting garments. These garments and designs would become the fashionable outwear of later generations.

As war raged across the world, women were encouraged to help their country by working full-time in the factories. With this change of lifestyle, many children were sent to daycares, and trousers for women (promoted by Hollywood in the 1930s) were integrated into the common-woman's wardrobe. Pin-ups became popular for the enlisted men, showing an overall acceptance by the male population of the glorification of the female body.

Brigitte Bardot, 1953 Bay of Cannes, France

The typical 1950s American girl wore a wide mid-calf length skirt or a poodle skirt, and a modest top. In 1957, Brigitte Bardot wore a bikini in "And God Created Woman" and created a market for the bikinis as swimwear in the United States. The popularity of wide skirts continued, while the same women now wore bikinis on the beach.

In 1964 fashion designers fulfilled William Branham's vision of wearing fig-leaves by creating an evening gown of sheer material with a leaf-like pattern on the lower portion and near-see-through upper.

“And I said, "Then the morals of our women is going to fall in such a degraded things till they're going to be a disgrace to all nations. They're going to wear men's clothes. They're going to keep taking off their clothes till actually they come down like they got their underneath clothes on. That's all. And finally they'll come to wearing just a fig leaf." [367]

For evening, a lining gives the illusion of nudity

Life Magazine July 3, 1964 : Cover - Bob Kennedy at home with his and his brother Jack's children. ***Big fashion fuss over transparent blouses.*** From the article called "The See-Through Look" - these are the pictures that Wm Branham possibly refers to. The caption at the top of the left photo reads: "For evening, a lining gives the illusions of nudity." In the photo in the left, the leaf pattern is distinctive.

Germaine Greer, a prominent and provocative feminist, wrote in 1969 that "*The women kept on dancing while their long skirts crept up, and their girdles dissolved...and their clothes withered away to the mere wisps and ghosts of draperies to adorn and glorify...*"[368]

It's easy to see the unbelievable changes in teen morality by looking at the above icons from two different generations. Betty Boop of the 50's in her long poodle skirt and saddle shoes, and two teen contemporary "ravers" with bair midriff, short-short mini-skirts, mardi gras beads and pacifiers. From fairly innocent sock hops to drug-induced sexual bacchanals, dances and teens are morally worlds apart. Listen to William Branham in 1958, *"their mother was a chorus girl, and... their grandmother, and her mother was a flapper, what's she [a teen girl] today? A rock-and-roll striptease."*

In 1963, prayer was removed from schools in yet another attempt to rid America of any reference to God.[369] President Ronald Reagan recognized the danger of this act when he said:

"Americans . . . [have] for the sake of religious tolerance . . . forbidden religious practice in the classrooms. The law of this land has effectively removed prayer from our classrooms. How can we hope to retain our freedom through the generations if we fail to teach our young that our liberty springs from an abiding faith in our Creator?"[370]

Since 1960, there has been a 560% increase in violent crime; a 419% increase in illegitimate births; a quadrupling in divorce rates; a tripling of the percentage of children living in single-parent homes; and more than a 200% increase in the teenage suicide rate.[371]

Starting in 1970, abortion was legalized in five states. In 1972, as a result of Eisenstadt v. Baird, minor girls now had the right to seek birth control and anything else that related to their bodies without their parents' consent. One year later in the 1973 United States Supreme Court decision Roe v. Wade, abortion became nationally legalized.

Today multiple partners are considered normal for teenage girls. Birth control is widely used and easily available. In 1992 an Appeals court in the state of New York ruled that women have the same right as men to go topless. In 2007 a woman was awarded a $29,000 settlement from the City of New York for being arrested (and being subject to 12 hours in custody and a psychiatric evaluation) after walking topless in New York City in 2005.

America has become desensitized to sex and exposure, and now nothing shocks them except the suggestion that their "liberty" is immoral. Perhaps more than anything else, America's cultural decline is evidence of a shift in the public's attitudes and beliefs. Social scientist James Q. Wilson writes that "the powers exercised by the institutions of social control have been constrained and people, especially young people, have embraced an ethos that values self-expression over self-control." Our society now places less value than before on what we owe to others as a matter of moral obligation; less value on sacrifice as a moral good; less value on social conformity and respectability; and less value on correctness and restraint in matters of physical pleasure and sexuality.

"And God saw that the wickedness of man was great in the earth, and that every imagination of the thoughts of his heart was only evil continually." – Genesis 6:5 (KJV)

John Updike has written: "The fact that, compared to the inhabitants of Africa and Russia, we still live well cannot ease the pain of feeling we no longer live nobly."

The social regression of the past 40 years is due in large part to the enfeebled state of our social institutions (families, churches, schools, neighborhoods) and their failure to carry out their critical and time honored tasks of teaching self-control, compassion, tolerance, civility, honesty and respect for authority. We desperately need to recover a sense of the fundamental purpose of education, which is to engage in the architecture of souls. When a self-governing society ignores this responsibility, it does so at its peril.

6th Event - A powerful woman rose up from America that could be the President or even a cruel, cold Dictator. She was also thought to possibly be a symbol of the Catholic Church. For details see the section in Chapter 1 – *A Woman Dictator? Hillary Rodham Clinton, Or...*

7th Event - In the seventh and final vision there was an explosion, and the nation of America was turned into ashes from coast to coast. Soon after, on September 12, 1933, Leó Szilárd conceived of the idea of the nuclear chain reaction while waiting for a red light in Bloomsbury, England.[372] [373]For details see the section in Chapter 10 – *America – You Will be Destroyed!*

17 Other Amazing Prophecies of William Branham

Other Amazing Prophecies of William Branham

As mentioned in earlier sections of this book, there are different types of prophecy and prophetic modes (vision and inspiration). We have examined conditional and unconditional prophecies. We have also seen that prophecies can be given in the present tense, as well as meant to be fulfilled well into the future. In the preceding section the types of prophetic vision was identified to be of two categories – literal or symbolic.

Finally, it is important to be reminded that though a prophet utters "thus saith the Lord", he himself might not even know precisely what the utterance means. Imagine Isaiah pronouncing "behold, a virgin shall conceive"[374] (meaning a woman that has not had sexual relations shall become pregnant); what might he have thought? What might he have speculated? If Isaiah would have given his opinion or best guess at one of his visions (with a disclaimer to be simply a guess or a prediction), what would he have said? Saint Peter had a vision once and did not know what it meant, he speculated about its meaning, but it took God to give him the specific revelation.[375]

In the life and prophetic ministry of William Branham, he experienced all the different types of prophecy, as well as the types of prophetic mode. He had "thus saith the Lord" with both prophetic vision and inspiration. Unparallel in contemporary times, the sheer scope and number of his prophetic ministry are staggering. Reportedly having tens of thousands of visions, individual "words of knowledge" and specific local, regional, domestic and international prophecies.[376] Not to disparage those individuals that may have provided anecdotal testimony, the prophecies chosen for this book are ones that could be reasonably authenticated by outside, objective sources.

Below are selected highlights from his forty years of ministry, a prophetic ministry that continues to be relevant as we have seen in Chapters One, Nine, Seventeen and Eighteen.

Specific Examples of various prophecies:

a. John F. Kennedy elected as President
b. Bill Clinton elected as President
c. Ohio River flood of 1937
d. Finnish boy hit by car, killed and resurrected
e. The Miracle of Donnie Morton
f. Caribou with 42 inch horns & Silver-tip grizzly bear
g. Marilyn Monroe's death
h. Boxer dies in fight in New York, 1962
i. The invention of iPods
j. "Lay your hat down on the bed."

A. John F. Kennedy Election "Fixed"

"I said, 'Then I seen a... They're going to permit women to vote. And by voting, they'll elect the wrong man some of these days.' And you did at the last election. It was the woman's votes that elected Kennedy. We know that (See?), between the crooked machines and things fixed up, that F--FBI exposed. And how could anybody... Why don't they do something about it? Why ain't something said? Ha, afraid somebody'd lose their job. You see, it's just a bunch of politics, rotten to the core. That's all. Sure."

Wm Branham – Laodicea Church Age. Jeffersonville, IN 60-1211E
Revelation of Jesus Christ Series (ROJC) pgs.493-550 ¶47

A majority of objective historians believe that Republican Vice President Nixon really beat Democrat John F. Kennedy (JFK) in 1960, arguing that Kennedy won due to election fraud in Illinois and Texas.[377]

Kennedy's election in 1960 over Nixon involved heavy fraud in Illinois and Texas.[378] (If Nixon had won those two states, he would have won the presidency.) As examples of ballot box stuffing: In Texas's Angelina County, in one precinct, only 86 people voted yet the final tally was 147 for Kennedy, 24 for Nixon; in Fannin County the 4895 registered voters cast 6138 votes (75% for Kennedy). Discarded spoiled ballots were to be placed by Texas law in "ballot box 4" for later re-examination, but many counties (e.g. Fort Bend County, which had a huge 16% spoilage rate, topping even the worst Florida 2000 County) just discarded them, and did *not* store them, making any biased discarding decisions uncorrectable and improvable. The 100% Democrat Texas Election Board refused to conduct a recount.[379]

Kennedy carried Illinois by 8858 votes thanks to a 456,312-vote advantage in Chicago, whose precincts reported their totals remarkably late. (Compare this with Kennedy's *nationwide* victory margin of 118,574.) The "turnout" in Daley run Chicago was a spectacular 89%. This contrasts with the nationwide turnout of 63%. It also contrasts with the fact that in the 11 presidential elections during 1960-2000, totaling 550 statewide contests, *not once* did any state ever exceed 1964 Utah's 78.4% turnout, and the states with the largest percent turnout were always rural (namely North and South Dakota, Utah, Minnesota, and Maine), not urban.

The fraud in Illinois was partially orchestrated by powerful organized crime elements (a.k.a. the Mob or Mafia) and labor interests. In 1992 mob boss Sam Giancana's nephew and brother wrote a book [*Double Cross: The Explosive, Inside Story of the Mobster Who Controlled America*, Warner books] recounting how Giancana had rigged the Cook County vote for Kennedy as part of a deal, and further stating that when Kennedy reneged on the deal, Giancana had him assassinated. (They claimed they had heard this directly from Giancana himself who also noted "Richard Nixon and Lyndon Johnson knew about the whole damn thing." Sam Giancana was one of the biggest mafia bosses in America and controlled most of the Chicago underworld at the time of Kennedy's election. Giancana was instrumental in the mafia stuffing the ballots in Illinois. The title "Double Cross" is in reference to JFK and Robert Kennedy (US Attorney General) turning around and attacking, rather than supporting, the mafia.

Apart from the influence of organized crime, many voters that challenged the Democratic Party's poll watchers at various voting precinct on Election Day were threatened and beaten up. Much documentation supports the contention that Chicago mayor Richard J. Daley's "creative vote counting had also contributed to the election win for President-Elect Kennedy." After the election Republican groups checked voter lists against addresses in an attempt to find voter fraud. Teams went to poor neighborhood on the South Side of Chicago and knocked on doors, to ask if certain people on their list actually lived there. Clear evidence of voter fraud was found, for example, a young Hillary Clinton had discovered there was a vacant lot in South Chicago listed as the address for a dozen alleged voters.[380]

The GOP's difficulties proving fraud (in the State and Federal courts) does not mean, of course, that the election was clean. Fraud clearly occurred. At least three people were sent to jail for election-related crimes, and 677 others were indicted before being acquitted by Judge John M. Karns. Many of the allegations involved practices that would not be detected by a recount, leading the conservative *Chicago Tribune*, among others, to conclude that "once an election has been stolen in Cook County, it stays stolen."[381]

In 1962, after an election judge *confessed* to witnessing vote tampering in Chicago's 28th ward, three precinct workers pled guilty and served short jail terms. Reporter Earl Mazo, visiting the Chicago address where 56 Kennedy voters "lived," found an abandoned demolished house. He also found a cemetery where all the tombstone names were registered voters. In Ward 27, Precinct 27, the 376 voters cast 397 votes; in the 15th precinct of ward 2, Kennedy beat Nixon 74-to-3 but only 22 people were registered to vote.[382]

Additionally, according to journalist Seymour Hersh, a former Justice Department prosecutor who heard tapes of FBI wiretaps from the period, believed that Illinois was rightfully Nixon's. Hersh also has written that J. Edgar Hoover believed Nixon actually won the presidency[383] but in deciding to follow normal procedures and refer the FBI's findings to the attorney general—as of Jan. 20, 1961, Robert F. Kennedy—"Bobby" shut down all federal investigations into voting fraud, effectively burying the case.

Apart from JFK possibly being fraudulently elected to the Presidency, he was a Roman Catholic. Despite repeatedly reassuring voters that his religion would not influence his presidential action, nor would he become a "vassal" of the Pope – certain aspects of the power structure and dogmas of the Roman Catholic Church have difficulty being compatible with the power structure and ideals of American republican democracy. The traditional position of the Roman Catholic Church, as articulated by Pope Leo XIII before the Second Vatican Council, has been that governments should not only have care for religion, but should also "recognize the true religion professed by the Catholic Church." The chief duty as *Catholic citizens* is to obey their bishops and the Holy See, "As God himself." (See Leo XIII's *Great Encyclical*, page 192). What this actually translates into is submission to the Roman Catholic Church and its supreme leader the Pope.

The concern of this doctrine is not peculiar to those who might be labeled bigoted partisans or Protestant zealots. There are available quotation after quotation from such writers as John Locke (1632-1704),[384] Sir William Blackstone (1723-1780),[385] Lord Francis Bacon (1561-1626),[386] and others who view this question as jurists, philosophers, historians; all maintaining that subjects of the Pope should be excluded from the Government of any Democratic country on the grounds that the Church of Rome is a policy as much as a religion. Adam Smith says: "[The Church of Rome is] the most formidable combination that ever was formed against the authority and security of civil government, as well as against the liberty, reason, and happiness of mankind."[387]

Abraham Lincoln (16th U.S. President -1861-1865) said: "The true motive power (of America's troubles) is secreted behind the thick walls of the Vatican, the colleges and schools of the Jesuits, the convents of the nuns, and the confessional boxes of Rome."[388] [389]

B. William Jefferson Clinton Elected as President

"And now, let me bring something else. I haven't got it written here, but on magnetic tape (And this is taped too.)... In 1956 in Chicago, Illinois, standing at the--that Lane Tech High School (They were there.), I said, "This year is going to be the changing point of America. I've just come from overseas--don't know why I come. Come back; canceled my meetings in Africa and around--come back.

Billy Graham, something mysterious, he canceled his. Tommy Osborn canceled his…I said, "America will either receive or reject Christ this year." Then I said, "When they elected in Indiana, a twenty-two year boy--year old boy to be judge," the Spirit of the Lord came on me and I said, "They'll finally have a president that'll be one of these crew cut, playboy, beatnik-type presidents, a lady's man." Now, them's predictions years ago. See where we're at? It's later than we think."[390] (Wm Branham, November 13, 1960)

Little needs to be said how former President William Jefferson Clinton fulfilled this particular prophecy. President – check. Crew cut – check (see picture below). Playboy – check-a-rooni. Beatnik-type – check. Lady's man – check, check, check.

Young crew-cut high school student Bill Clinton as a delegate to a Boys Nation meeting, with President John F. Kennedy in the White House Rose Garden (1963)

C. The Ohio River Flood of 1937

Sometime during the fall of 1936 while ministering in his church in Indiana, William Branham prophesied of "a flood" that would cause the waters to rise to a height of 22 feet over Spring Street in Jeffersonville. A number of people present in the Branham Tabernacle at the time said *"Get next to yourself Billy. In 1884 it was only was about six inches on Spring Street."* They laughed at him saying, *"Billy, you're just excited."*

But he stood firm and screamed out, *"I'm not excited! It's THUS SAITH THE LORD! I seen a man come down from the skies, and take a measuring stick and put it there on Spring Street, and it measured twenty-two feet."*[391]

As the word spread about William Branham's prophecy, he was mocked. People said, *"You're crazy. You're off at your head."* When he advised the workers at the Falls City Transfer Company, of coming flood they said, *"Ah, Billy, go on home. But less than six weeks from then, twenty-two feet of water measured over Spring Street, just exactly the way it said."*[392] According to historical records, in 1937 the Ohio River indeed recorded its worst flood ever.[393] (See endnote 394 – a photo of Schimpff's Confectionary Store has marks on the left door post that still indicate the 22 foot flood mark.[394])

...g Ohio Inundates Jeffersonville Telepho...

Many a Jeffersonville young man would have liked nothing better than to take Miss West's sage advice even before the waters of the raging Ohio rose to that height. This shot was made Saturday, January [illegible], by M. J. [illegible], who took all the Jeffersonville pictures. The building housing the Indiana Bell office is the first one on the left

D. Finnish Boy to be Raised From the Dead

In 1948 William Branham saw a vision of a young boy being raised from the dead after being hit by a car. Rather than keeping the details of this vision a secret, William Branham retold this vision during his 1948 and 1949 Canadian campaigns, and told people to write the vision down in the fly-leaf of their Bibles.[395]

The vision was fulfilled two years later during a speaking trip to Helsinki, Finland in 1950 at the scene of a street accident near Kuopio, Finland. Reportedly a boy on a bicycle had been struck by a car and killed. Branham's party had come upon the scene and he then asked that the sheet covering the boy's body be removed, as he recognized the boy as the one he had seen in his vision. He then prayed over the child and the child was said to have been raised from the dead. The boy's name is Kari Holma and at last time of contact in the 1990's, he was still alive.

Although Kari Holma readily acknowledged the miracle which took place in April of 1950, he has no personal memories of that day.

William Branham and others arrive in Finland on April 14, 1950. William Branham is at the top of the stairs.

The following is an article by William Branham that appeared in a special overseas edition of ***The Voice of Healing*** magazine, published in June, 1950.[396] (See endnote 397 to listen to a recorded eye-witness that states he heard this prophecy two years prior to being fulfilled.[397])

"One morning at about 3 A.M., I was awakened out of my sleep to find that the angel of the Lord was in the room to show me a vision. By the spirit I was transported in the vision to a scene where an accident had just happened. I saw that a little boy of about eight or ten years of age had been killed. He had light brown hair and his clothes looked very ragged and torn. Some men were taking the child to a hospital or funeral home.

It was at that moment that the angel of the Lord told me to kneel and pray that the child's life would return to him. That I did, and life was restored and he lived. Now this vision is to come to pass in the future. I have told it to hundreds of people all the way from Canada to Florida. Many have written it on the flyleaf of their Bible. About two weeks after the vision appeared to me, I was telling it to a crowd of people at a tent meeting in Miami, Florida. The next evening when I was coming to the service, I was taken to a crowd of people waiting just behind the tent. They had a little boy about five years old that had been drowned that morning in a canal. But when I saw the child I said it was not the boy I had seen in the vision. So I offered a prayer of sympathy for the family.

...It was in Kuopio, Finland, when the Lord Jesus fulfilled the vision that He had shown me some two years before. It was that of a little boy with light brown hair which was raised from the dead. I was with a group of ministers, who were coming down from a mountain where we had been praying and singing hymns.

Among the ministers were Brother Gordon Lindsay and Brother Jack Moore, whom I am associated with. A motor car some 300 yards ahead of us struck a little boy, throwing him to the ground, and then ran over him with such force that it threw him back near the sidewalk.

Brother Jack Moore picked him up and brought him back into the car with us. We saw that he was dead. I looked at the little boy and thought I recognized him. Then I remembered that he was the little boy I had seen in the vision, who was eight or ten years old, with light brown hair and who was poorly dressed. I held him to my body and began to pray. Suddenly his life came back.

Arriving at the hospital, we were surprised to learn that the car had struck another little boy, and had knocked him to the other side of the road. We had not seen him because he was hidden from our view, and another car had picked him up and rushed him to the hospital. After two days he was still unconscious.

The parents of both children came to the hotel to see me. The father and mother of the first boy were so happy because the Lord had given life back to their son according to the vision that He had showed me. But with sadness the other parents looked at me and said, "What about our boy? Is he going to live?"

I replied that I could not say.

But they answered, "You have told the other parents that their boy would live; can't you say something for our boy?"
But I said that I could say nothing until the Lord showed me. Then they began to weep. I then asked the parents if they were Christians. They replied that they belonged to the church but were not saved. I then

asked them if God saved their boy, would they serve the Lord all their days and teach the child to do so.

With tears they answered that they would. Then we all knelt and prayed. I said in my prayer, "Father, please have mercy on us and save their son." Then I returned to my room. The news was brought to me about that time that unbelievers standing by at the scene of the accident, when the boy was killed, had said, "There is the 'divine healer' from America whom they are all talking about. Now let us see what he will do."

When they heard that the dead boy was raised, then they said, "Why doesn't he do something for the other boy who has been unconscious for two days?" That is what my interpreter, Sister Isaacson, reported that the people were telling the parents of the child that was dying in the hospital.

I then said to Sister Isaacson, "I can do nothing until God shows me what to do That is what Jesus said in John 5:19. I can only pray." That night I prayed again for the boy. The report came from the hospital the next day that he was just barely alive, and life seemed to be going fast. The following evening, after returning from the service, I was in my hotel room. The angel of the Lord came into my room. Before me were placed two Easter flowers, one leaning to the south and another to the north. That is just the way the boys' bodies fell when the car struck them. The one toward the north was the one they took up dead, and the Lord healed. The other one to the south was the smaller lad, who was still unconscious these three days.

Then the flower toward the north sprang up at once, strong and alive, but the other one toward the south was fading away and dying fast. The angel made me to understand that the vision represented the two boys.

Then he showed me two pieces of candy which had just been given me before I came into the room. The angel said, "Take one piece and eat it." I did, and it tasted good. Then he said to me. "Take the other piece."

But the second piece did not taste just right, and I started to take it from my mouth. But the angel seemed to say, "If you do that the other boy will die." So I quickly ate the other piece. Then the flower was alive again in the other vision. When the vision was over, I hastened to the room of Brother Lindsay and Brother Moore. I said to my brethren, "Thus saith the Lord concerning the boy."

Then I repeated the vision to the others of the party. I said, "God showed me another vision three weeks before in London, and it came to pass perfectly. So this vision also shall come to pass. The boy shall live."

Sister May Isaacson, the interpreter, tried to call the parents of the boy and tell them what I had said, but they had gone to the hospital, for it had been told them that the boy was dying. But when they arrived at the hospital, they discovered that something had happened. The lad had awakened out of his unconscious condition.

When they reported this to Sister May, she asked, "What time did this happen?" They said, "While we were watching for him to take his last breath, he suddenly became conscious. It was 10 o'clock at the time." When the doctors examined the boy, they reported that he would be all right. After checking the time of the vision, I found that it was just 10 o'clock when the angel of the Lord had come into my room."

E. The Miracle of Donnie Morton

In 1951 both *Reader's Digest* and *Time* magazine carried articles about a boy named Donnie Morton, and how he was healed. Each provide certain details, but none of them include all the facts of this unique miracle.

Time magazine had this to say:
A lot of good doctors had called it a hopeless case: in Pasadena last week, four-year-old Donnie Morton proved them wrong. After three delicate operations for subdural hydroma (water on the brain), Donnie left the hospital and tackled the job of learning to walk and talk again.

Donnie got his chance for life because his father, a Saskatchewan farmer, refused to believe his boy had to die, cradled him in his arms on a six-day bus trip to California, praying for a miracle (TIME, July 2 1951). Brain Specialist William T. Grant (who operated free) seemed to have performed the miracle father Morton prayed for.[398]

The above is correct, insomuch as Donnie Morton's father refused to give up on his child, and went to extraordinary measures to try and save his son. He refused to give up hope and in this instance; God honored his faith and provided a way for the young boy to be healed.

This healing was a joint work; both supernatural and natural elements were involved. Though an actual doctor was used to perform a delicate operation, God used William Branham as an instrument to provide instructions to the father, instructions that once followed led to the healing and miracle of Donnie Morton.

Below is William Branham's account of the healing from his sermon *Demonology*[399]; and after his account is a link to the original *Reader's Digest* article.

E-6 And so the little Donny Morton, he'd set up some kind of a rare brain disease. And the--the people of the--had taken him to be examined, and everywhere, and they'd give him up. They brought the boy to--to my service. Now first, the doctor said the little boy must die. Mayos, Johns Hopkins... They had him in the United States. Everything give him up; there's no operation. Said it'd be impossible: if you operated on the boy's head for that, it would kill him instantly: Mayo Brothers.

Now, of course the "Reader's Digest" didn't say Mayo Brothers, because Mayo's would get after them for that. You have to watch what you're putting in public literature. And so there's... But you can read between the lines and see what it meant, see what it said

E-9 When the little boy... Now, here's the "Reader's Digest," the way they wrote it. The little fellow had been brought from... They had to put him in a sled or something and bring him over ground. He's twisted. His little hands was drawn down in this condition, his little legs up under him, about eight years old; his little head setting sideways; his eyes pushed one, one way and one, the other is a... Oh, it was a pitiful looking sight. And the little fellow shook like this and just smelled terrible.

And the poor little father, the little sled would turn over, nearly, when the horses packing them through the way, bringing them out. And he'd keep patting him on the moonlight night and saying, "Don't fear, Donny, honey. We're not whipped yet." Said, he knowed two people that'd been healed in my meeting, and said, "If I could ever get where that man's at, God will do something for my baby."

So he--they finally got to the airport, him and his wife, and they couldn't--they couldn't--hadn't--didn't have enough money for even one of them to come on a plane. They didn't have enough money to come on a train. So they had to take just the man, and he brought the baby. And they come all the way from Saskatoon, Saskatchewan, to Los Angeles, California, and went into Traveler's Aid for help.

E-10 And then, of course, watch the "Reader's Digest." It said he was searching for the... Said, "A divine what?" A question mark. I'd imagine what they said. And so he said, "Never mind. This man believes this, if the man prays for his baby, he'll get help; so let's see if we can get it." And they dispatched a the paper; put a car, and they took way down in Costa Mesa, forty something miles down to a Assembly of God campgrounds where they had a big school there. And I was speaking to the ministers.

And they brought him in that night. And at--he... They said there was twenty-seven hundred people standing in line to be prayed for when we got there. And of course, everybody had to require a prayer card. And I was praying for the people.

Now, here's where I begin and would know. I seen them. Here he said, when he stepped out of the car, that all those people standing in the prayer line, they just stepped back when they seen that poor little ragged father, that little Canadian cap on, walking with this poor little baby, and coming along." He didn't eat. He had to change it just like a baby: its diapers and everything. And he didn't eat, didn't have time to eat. He'd just run and get a drink of water and get him something to eat and then go on. Oh, it was pathetic story. And so he kept saying,

"All right, Donny, we're not whipped yet, honey. We're not whipped yet." Just keep on like that.

E-11 And when the folks at the place saw, standing in that prayer line, way down through that field, when they saw this poor man coming, they just stepped aside to give him his place. Well, when he come to the platform, Billy Paul asked him for his prayer card. 'Course he didn't have any. He said, "Sir, I didn't even know I had to have a prayer card." Well, Billy and the ushers had orders to--for the people to line up; that's legitimately, and that's right, just exactly what it should be. And I heard him say, "Well, that's all right." Said, "What must I do now to get a prayer card? Where must I go?"

They was holding up the prayer line. I said, "What's the matter?"

He said a--a, "Just a man without a prayer card."

I said, "Well, just have him to step off to one side."

And I looked back and I seen that baby, and something said to me, "Call him now." I never seen the baby. So the "Reader's Digest" gives the whole article of it.

E-12 And I brought the little baby up, said, never asked a question but looked right into the little baby's face and said, "You bring this baby from Canada. And you come here by a bus, a Greyhound Bus. Travelers Aid has helped you." And he'd been there about five minutes. Said, "Traveler's Aid has helped you to get here. And the baby has been to Mayo Brothers and Johns Hopkins. It's got a rare brain disease, and there's no way for them to operate. The baby must die."

And he started screaming real loud. And I prayed for the little baby. He started crying real loud and started off the platform. He turned around. He said, "What about my baby? Will it ever get well?"

I said, "That, I don't know, sir." And while I was speaking to him, a vision broke forth. And I said, "Yes, your baby... Three days from now you're going to meet a woman with a--a brown looking, I guess you call it, coat-suit: it's got a coat here and a skirt beneath. And she's black headed. And she's going to tell you of some country doctor that can operate on that baby; and you won't believe it. But that's the only hope that you have, through the mercy of God, and that operation. You let the doctor operate on the baby."

E-13 Well, he went off the platform crying, and he... Well, the next day the baby seemed to be a lot better after he was prayed for: could move its little arms. Well, he forgot all about the woman; and he was going to go on that way. So about few days after that, he was walking down the street, getting it out, so it'd get in the air (You know?), walking it down the street; and a--or walking down the street with it in his arms, rather. And a lady said, "Well, what's the matter with your baby, sir?"

And he said, "Well, it's a brain disease," he said, "a rare brain disease."

And she said, "You know, I know a doctor that operated on a baby like that one time that was that way and the baby's normal now."

"Well," he said, "But, lady..." Said, "Mayo Brothers said that this..." Said, "Wait a minute: 'a brown coat-suit, black hair...'" Said, "Say, lady, where's that doctor at?" And "Reader's Digest" gives the place, who he was. And he took that baby over there, and the doctor performed the operation absolutely successfully. And the baby come out of it. And so they had the baby around there; it got so he could run, meet his daddy and everything.

The daddy went back to plant his spring wheat or something another. Now, here's what the "Digest" didn't get (See?), what didn't picture. But we had to know behind, because if you did, that a hospital would bring suit against this paper, and there's where it would be; a slip-up come. Somebody left a window up one night and throwed a draft across the baby. And the baby taken pneumonia and lived about two days with the pneumonia, not with the disease, with the pneumonia killed the baby. The "Reader's Digest" give it. Then it goes ahead and gives a nice good write up about--about the miracle was already performed anyhow.

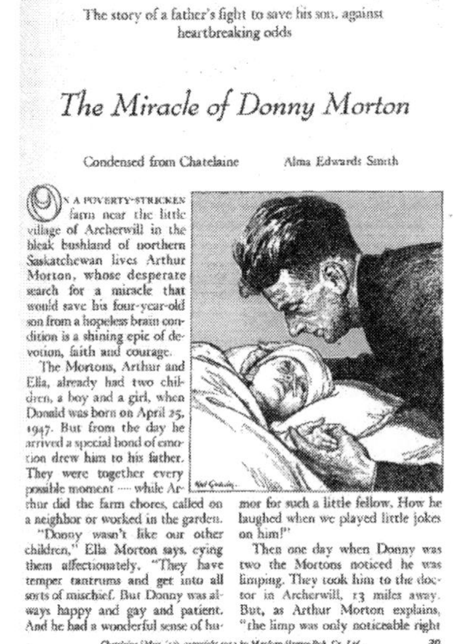

The story of a father's fight to save his son, against heartbreaking odds

The Miracle of Donny Morton

Condensed from Chatelaine — Alma Edwards Smith

On a poverty-stricken farm near the little village of Archerwill in the bleak bushland of northern Saskatchewan lives Arthur Morton, whose desperate search for a miracle that would save his four-year-old son from a hopeless brain condition is a shining epic of devotion, faith and courage.

The Mortons, Arthur and Ella, already had two children, a boy and a girl, when Donald was born on April 25, 1947. But from the day he arrived a special bond of emotion drew him to his father. They were together every possible moment — while Arthur did the farm chores, called on a neighbor or worked in the garden.

"Donny wasn't like our other children," Ella Morton says, eying them affectionately. "They have temper tantrums and get into all sorts of mischief. But Donny was always happy and gay and patient. And he had a wonderful sense of humor for such a little fellow. How he laughed when we played little jokes on him!"

Then one day when Donny was two the Mortons noticed he was limping. They took him to the doctor in Archerwill, 13 miles away. But, as Arthur Morton explains, "the limp was only noticeable right

Chatelaine (May, '52), copyright 1952 by Maclean-Hunter Pub. Co. Ltd., [illegible] University Ave., Toronto 2, Canada — 29

The November 1952 Reader's Digest magazine that features the article "The Miracle of Donnie Morton."

This is a copy of the first page of the article.

(Go to: http://en.believethesign.com/index.php?title=Donny_Morton, for the full article and pages full size)

F. The Caribou with 42" Horns and The Silver Tip Grizzly Bear

Among the many, many specific prophecies and unconscious prophetic utterances, the prophecy about killing two animals is unique. First, it reminds us of how the Prophet Jesus included animals and that such a prophecy has scriptural precedence (Matthew 21:1-3):

And when they drew nigh unto Jerusalem, and were come to Bethphage, unto the mount of Olives, then sent Jesus two disciples, Saying unto them, Go into the village over against you, and straightway ye shall find an ass tied, and a colt with her: loose them, and bring them unto me. And if any man say ought unto you, ye shall say, The Lord hath need of them; and straightway he will send them.

Second, William Branham describes how God allowed him to have visions of animals and hunting, both within a realm he was extremely comfortable in, to build his confidence in the prophetic. As William Branham was not simply a seer, but a "Word Prophet" (A "Word prophet" as being defined as one that was called to correct the doctrinal error of the church, not just to prophesy), he needed confidence to go before the multitudes with *thus saith the Lord* after God had shown him something – anything. He needed boldness and assurance to speak publically, whether it was a vision of animals that he would hunt and kill, humans he would participate with in healing, or correcting and delivering the Word of God.

Finally, the prophecies of the silver-tip grizzly and the Caribou with 42 inch horns[400] would be a lasting testament to the veracity of William Branham's amazing and accurate ministry.

Many men are still alive that can testify to the accuracy of these visions. The artifacts (the bear hide and trophy head of the caribou that still has 42 inch horns) still exist as well, and are displayed in a home owned by the Branham heirs in Tucson, Arizona.

Below is an account of the prophecies by William Branham.[401]

I'm glad this morning, somewhere in the congregation, to have a--a very precious friend of mine, brother, Reverend Eddie Byskal and his wife and children. I suppose they got into the meeting this morning. Eddie, are you here? I thought you... Well, maybe he didn't get to come. Brother, oh, yes, way... Now, that's not the "amen" corner, Eddie. You're welcome up here on the platform with us, the ministers, if you want to come. And then we've been on...

Brother Eddie was along when the Lord gave me the vision about the bear and the caribou. The... How many remembers that when I told you? All right, he was there. He was the young fellow had on the checkered shirt, Brother Eddie Byskal. And he stood there where... and asked... I--I asked them if they had a checkered shirt, any of them. "Nope," no one had it. I said, "Well, it might... It's got to be a checkered shirt. There's going to be a- -a big silver-tip grizzly, and--and some kind of an animal that's got forty-two inches over its horns, like this, looked like a deer." And that was about six months, I said here, you know, before it happened; long about this, oh, earlier than this in the year.

Then I was invited up there to this man, to go hunting. I never been back in that country, back there where we went, and I said it. But the little trail, that's way up on the Alaskan highway, where there's nothing but woods and mountains and animals. And that night at the trailer when I was telling Brother Byskal back there and--and Brother Southwick, he said, "Well I--I... We're going up in sheep country," said, "it won't be up there."

And I said, "Yes," and I said, "it was one of the little fellows was with me had a checkered shirt on." Nobody had a checkered shirt, Brother Byskal didn't have one, none of the rest of us had one.

The second night up, we had seen, spotted a ram way up above timber line. Now, that's way up where timber don't even grow, where's there's nothing but caribou and sheep, and we had spotted some way away. And on the road down that afternoon, Brother Byskal had stumbled into some water and gotten wet.

The next morning we got up early and started after the rams that we thought we were going to get. And on his... We got up there and we was... had eaten our dinner, and we couldn't find the rams, and Brother Byskal had just shot a caribou. So then I, looking around, and we went up, Brother Southwick said to me, said, "I believe we'll... if you want to walk right good, Brother Branham, we'll go over this mountain, down in that draw, them rams might have went over there," which is a long walk. But it don't get dark maybe till real late, it's maybe ten or eleven o'clock sometimes.

And it's a good long walk over them Rocky Mountains. So I like to walk, and so we just standing there with our arms around one another, both of our beards turning gray, with our arms around each other, crying and knowing, I said, "Brother Bud, I hope someday, in the Millennium, I can walk all them mountains there."

He said, "I hope I'm with you, Brother Branham." And we was standing there, just rejoicing in the Lord. And I love the mountains so well!

And then we went down. That's when Brother Byskal there shot the--the--the caribou. That, he's a missionary to the Indians, and he wanted to feed this to his Indians. So we went down, ate our dinner, and dressed the caribou out and come back.

Bud and I were going up across the mountain, and when we happened to look over, and in the distance, with my glasses, I spotted this animal that I had saw, just in a panoramic, like I told you here. Brother Byskal there, standing right by our side. And so I said, "There is that animal."

And he put the glasses on, and said, "It's a great big, old, mammoth bull caribou."

And I said, "I never seen, I thought they had panel horns." But this one had spikes, he was an odd-looking fellow, just like I saw in the vision. I never shot caribou before.

"So, well," he said, "if the Lord's give him to you," he said, "there just..."

I said, "Yes, that's bound to be it. The only thing I'm wondering about is that checkered shirt." And I looked around, and Brother Eddie, his wife must have put it, she was there with him, must have put it in his duffel bag. When he got wet the day before, he had changed shirts, and there was the checkered shirt. I said, "This is it."

When I got over and got the caribou, he, Bud, said to me, said, "Now, Brother Branham, you say these horns are forty-two inches?"

I said, "That's what they'll be."

He said, "Looked to me like about ninety-two."

I said, "No. They're forty-two inches."

He said, "Now, according to what you told me, before we get back to that boy down there with the checkered shirt on, Eddie," (where they was going to meet us down below the mountain, couple miles), said, "you're going to kill a grizzly bear."

I said, "That's THUS SAITH THE LORD."

He said, "Brother Branham, where is he coming from? I can see for fifty miles around."

I said, "He's still Jehovah-jireh. The Lord can provide for Himself, see. He can make squirrels come into existence. If He can make a ram come into existence, if He has spoke it about a bear, a bear can come into existence."

Us trying to pack this heavy caribou down, the trophy, down the mountain, and I packed the rifle part of the time, and then he would pack the rifle, and vice versa. And when we got almost to a big glacier, why, we got under there. It was kind of hot, we get in the glacier of ice, and sit down there a while to cool off. He said, "You know Brother Branham, we're not over about a mile from where Eddie and Blaine, them two boys, be standing. That old bear better be showing up."

I said, "Bud, I believe you're doubting it."

He said "Brother Branham, my brother had epileptic fits for so many years. And you told me once, the first time up here, when we went down to another place, told me what that boy looked like." And Eddie was riding right by my side there, on a horse, when the Lord gave the vision. And I told them what to do with the boy, the fits stopped. And now he said, "I can't doubt it."

I said, "Bud, I don't know where the bear is coming from." But I was about fifty, I'm fifty-five now, so that's been about three years ago. I was about fifty-two or fifty-three. I said, "I've never seen It fail. God will give me that grizzly bear before I get to them boys." And we was almost down to where the small spruce and timber started in.

A little lower down the hill, we was almost into the timber, he sat down. He was the one that was packing the trophy then, I had the rifle. And he said, "That old bear better be showing up, hadn't he?"

I said, "He will be there, Don't you worry."

He said, "I can see every hill."

I said, "I... But I see the promise!" See? See, He promised. I said, "Ever what He..." I said, "Bud, what is that setting right there?"

He looked, said, "It's a big silver-tip grizzly." Said, "That's him." When we got the grizzly and come back... I remembered in the vision I told you, I was scared about the rifle. It was a little bitty two-seventy, small bullets, you see. It's on tape. And I got the bear, just about five hundred yards, like It said. Bud said, "You better shoot that bear in the back." He said, "Did you ever shoot a grizzly before?"

I said, "Nope."

He said, "Oh, they don't know what death is!" I learned that a little later. So he said, "They don't break up from shock," said, "you better shoot him."

I said, "According to the vision, I shot it in the heart."

He said, "Well, if that vision said so, I'm going to stand by you."

And I said, "Here we go." And we got a little closer, and when I raised up, the bear saw me. That was what he wanted, to make a charge. And I--I shot the bear, it didn't seem like it even hurt him. Here he come! And before I could get another bullet in the gun, the bear died about fifty yards from him.

Bud was white around the mouth, he said, "Brother Branham, I didn't want him on my lap." I said, "I didn't either."

Said, "I'm glad that vision said you got him." He said, "Now, if that, if them horns are forty-two inches, I'm going to have a..." I'll say it the way he did, said, "I'm going to have a screaming fit."

I said, "Well, you just have it right now, because that's what it's going to be."

When we got down to Brother Eddie, I said to Brother Eddie... We tied the horses off, they're scared of a bear. And, oh, my, they'd a-had to smell it. We couldn't skin him out, it was too late; had to come back the next day. And then we broke up the string about ten times, and horses running everywhere. So then when we got down there, he said... Went and got the tape measure out of his saddle bag, said, "Blaine."

I said to Brother Eddie, I said, "Watch that little hand now, according..." I thought it might have been Billy Paul, little bitty hand told the tape measure around the horn. I said, "Watch that little hand," punched Brother Eddie. We stepped back. He put it right up like that, exactly on the nose, forty-two inches. See, just exactly. Jesus never fails! That Word will never fail as long as it comes from God."

William Branham had a vision in which he saw himself shooting a silver-tip grizzly bear and a large elk-like animal with 42' horns that turned out to be a caribou. This vision is said to have come to pass; a rug made from this bear now lies in his Tucson home [see adjacent image] and the trophy head [which still has 42" horns – see above image] hangs on the wall in what was once his study.

G. Marilyn Monroe's Death

It remains one of Hollywood's most compelling, and unforgettable, mysteries.

On Aug. 5, 1962, the body of Marilyn Monroe was found in the bedroom of her Brentwood home. The 36-year-old movie star was naked and face-down on her bed.

Former Los Angeles County prosecutor John W. Miner was at her autopsy and was one of those looking into her death. He didn't believe that the actress took her life in 1962 and he doesn't believe it now, and Miner says he's heard secret tapes that Monroe made in the days before she died that prove the actress was anything but suicidal. As head of the D.A.'s medical-legal section when Monroe died, Miner had met with the actress' psychiatrist, Dr. Ralph Greenson. During the interview, Miner says, Greenson played the Monroe tapes, but only on condition that the investigator never reveal their contents.

Monroe gave the psychiatrist the tapes Aug. 4, 1962. According to Miner, Greenson's sole purpose in playing the tapes for him was to help establish her state of mind at the time of her death, "so they were made pretty close to the time she died."

Hollywood columnist James Bacon, met Monroe when she was an unknown in 1949 and would later become a close friend, was at Monroe's house five days before she died.

"She was drinking champagne and straight vodka and occasionally popping a pill," Bacon told The Times. He added: "She wasn't the least bit depressed. She was talking about going to Mexico. She had a Mexican boyfriend at the time. I forget his name. This was the first house she ever owned. She was going to buy some furniture. She was in very good spirits that day."

In 2005 Miner recently gave a copy of the transcript to The Los Angeles Times.[402]

William Branham had this to say about Marilyn Monroe's "mysterious" death:

Setting up in Colorado a few months ago in a--a little cabin, I went and said to my son, my wife, my daughter-in-law, and them: "Last couple of hours something happened. I saw a young lady, a beautiful woman, and she had kind of thick lips, looked like I'd saw her somewhere. And she's--she was trying to get to a doctor, and she died."

And the Spirit that was speaking to me, said, "Now, they will say that she committed suicide, but she died with a heart attack." And said, "It's just a little before four, but you can say it was four o'clock," and the vision left me. I told them, "What did that mean?" I didn't know. "Somebody's fixing to die."

When we come out of the mountains two days later, that movie star (What's that woman's name?), Marilyn Monroe, she was kind of a strip tease or... Or you read her story. She was an illegitimate child. Her mother's in the insane institution. Poor little girl probably had a hard way. And she always hungered for something.[403] *I wish I could've got to her. I know what she needed. I knew what she needed. Yet she'd joined churches and everything. But see, it was just a ritualistic form. She needed the application of the Blood. See?*

Now. I guess there isn't a sex fiend in the country but what knowed her and had her picture. She was supposed the most perfect built woman, as understood, there was in the world. But if that anatomy is so great, then watch... When the life went out of her body, they had to give her a number to lay in a room. And nobody would claim her body. (Wm Branham, November 24, 1962E)[404]

Monroe's body was delivered by ambulance to the Coroner's office at nine o'clock. After the autopsy at 10:30 A.M., her body lay unclaimed on a slab in the storage vault as Coroner's Case No. 81128.[405] As her early life had begun, so it ended – all alone.

A day later, the body desired by so many when it was alive, remained unclaimed in death. Tragically, on August 5th, 1962, orphan number three thousand four hundred and sixty-three at the Los Angeles Orphan's home[406] became Coroner's Case No. 81128.

According to the man from the LA Coroner's office who collected the body, she didn't look like an immortal goddess, she didn't look like "Marilyn Monroe...She looked just like a poor little girl that had died."[407]

A formal re-investigation was initiated in 1982 by the Los Angeles County District Attorney, there was no evidence of foul play uncovered, but the report concluded that the original investigation into her death had not been conducted properly. The officers that arrived at her home had failed to secure the scene, people freely came and went, possibly contaminating or destroying evidence. The re-investigation also revealed that all lab work, tissue samples, and test results from the autopsy disappeared from the county coroner's office immediately after the official ruling had been made public. The report also suggested that Monroe's body may have been moved after death, as bruising had appeared in different parts of her body at different times.

Coroner Dr. Thomas Noguchi, who conducted the autopsy, claims that misplacement of samples has never happened in another case before or since. In his memoir *Coroner*, he also states that it was "highly likely" that Monroe's death was suicide.

He concedes, however, that no trace of the barbiturates Monroe reportedly took was found in her mouth, stomach, or intestines.

Up to four hours passed between the discovery of her body and the phone call to the Los Angeles Police Department. Jack Clemmons, the first officer on the scene, said that Dr. Greenson kept pointing to rows of pill bottles lined up neatly on her nightstand, and saying as if rehearsed, "She must have taken all of these." Simmons said that no typical signs of drug overdose were present, namely foaming of the mouth or twisting of the body due to convulsions.[408]

Most theorists try to make a case for either suicide or murder, but there really is not enough supporting evidence for these claims. Those who spoke with her in the days prior to her death would describe an upbeat, optimistic Monroe. After so much scrutiny and so many high profile investigations there still isn't substantial evidence for murder, death by suicide or even accidental overdose - William Branham said he saw her die of a heart attack.

H. Boxer Dies in Fight in New York City, 1962

E-43 A few weeks ago I was... About eight months ago, or a little more, I saw a vision one night of two fellows, one in one barroom, and one in another, fussing at one another to their congregation that they were talking to. Finally, they met in New York in the middle of a street, dug a hole like, got in there, and one killed the other one. I said, "Somebody's going to get killed." They were nice, tall, young men. About a month after that, them two prize fighters fought the grudge, and one killed the other one. (All Things Are Possible. Shreveport, LA 1962-1124E)[409]

Griffith v Paret was described as one of the great rivalries of all time in a recent 2002 *Sports Line* special. The trilogy between Emile Griffith and Benny Paret was fierce and there was real animus between the two fighters, and unfortunately, it ended in tragedy. In their first meeting -- April 1, 1961 -- Griffith captured the welterweight title with a 13th-round knockout. They met again six months later and this time Paret took back his belt with a narrow split decision.

Paret, from Cuba, failed in a bid to capture the middleweight crown before returning to the 147-pound ranks to meet Griffith a third time. This grudge match took place on March 24, 1962 at Madison Square Garden in New York. At the weigh-in Paret made derisive remarks about Griffith and questioned the New Yorker's manhood, inferring he was gay.

The foes were quite familiar with each other and wasted little time mixing it up. Paret nearly ended the fight in round six, when Griffith was saved by the bell after absorbing a multi-punch combination. Nothing could save Paret from what was about to happen in the 12th round.

Griffith backed Paret into a corner and had him in trouble after landing a series of hooks and uppercuts. Paret was hanging defenseless on the ropes as referee Ruby Goldstein hesitated, allowing Griffith to prolong the attack. [This fight can still be seen on video clip.][410]

Perhaps part of Goldstein's lack of action was due to the fact that Paret often feigned injury, hoping to catch over-anxious opponents on the way in. But this was not an act and by the time Goldstein intervened, Paret was slumping to the canvas. Paret never regained consciousness. He lapsed into a coma and died 10 days after the fight.[411]

I. The Use of iPods and Personal Listening Devices

E-73 They're Yours, Lord. I commit them to You now. And I may never see them. If I'd come back a year from today, there's many sitting here... Next time I meet them will be at the judgment. Let them see, Lord. Let them open their eyes if there's--and see. All these on tape, Lord, that's listened to the voice at this time (many different languages, even be translated), may they understand. Many men and women in little houses, and out in little jungles in Africa, with those little machines with the tubes in their ears, may they hear, Lord, hear. Influence Beaumont, TX 1964-0315[412]

Back when William Branham's generation was listening to his sermons on large, stationary reel-to-reel players the size of small suitcases, God showed him that one day there would be people in remote regions that would hear his voice through a portable delivery system via miniature headphones. [Currently all of his sermons are in MP3 format and are available for download to an iPod.]

It was the arrival of electronics that really changed the world of portable media players. Portable radios were small enough to carry from home to the office; electric record players arrived in the 1930s,[413] and the wind-up gramophone faded away. The invention of the transistor meant portable battery-powered radios, with the first devices appearing in the early 1950s, and commercial sales starting in 1954. Transistor radios ran off a single voltage,[414] and soon became pocket-size. Receivers were initially only for AM, but they soon added support for higher-fidelity FM stations. I.D.E.A. released the very first portable transistor radio. The Regency TR-1 radio measured 3″x5″x 1.25″ and featured an analog AM tuner.[415]

The first popular magnetic recording technology was reel-to-reel tape. Developed in the late 1940s, and popularized by Ampex, the first commercial devices were released in 1948.[416]

The compact cassette was introduced by Phillips in 1963, arriving in the US in 1964. Not widely marketed until the mid 1970's, the cassette eventually replaced the 8-track as the stereo of choice. The Sony Walkman arrived in 1979, introducing the concept of the personal stereo device. Its real innovation was its size, measuring only slightly larger than a cassette tape itself. Featuring lightweight headphones and operating on AA batteries, it ushered in an era of portability.[417]

The very first solid state commercial music player appeared on shelves in the summer of 1998, it did not come from Apple, Diamond or Creative as many think. In fact, it came from a Korean company called SaeHan Information Systems. The MPMan was the very first MP3 player of all time. It featured a whopping 32MB of RAM and held about 8 average length songs (around 32 minutes of music.)[418]

Apple made the original iPod, released in 2001 that combined a 5GB hard drive with a rechargeable battery pack and a paradigm breaking user interface. Marketed by Steve Jobs as "1000 songs in your pocket," this original iPod has evolved over the years into a giant 160GB "classic,"[419] or the very popular "nano," a compact 16 GB, 4000 song/16 hour video player that is less than a quarter of an inch thick.

Several web sites have made over 1000 of William Branham's sermons available for download in mp3 format.[420] His messages are heard in nearly every country in the world, even by men and women *"out in little jungles in Africa, with those little machines with the tubes in their ears..."*

J. "Lay your hat down on the bed" ...

The below incident is included in this section on William Branham's prophecies because it serves to underscore a number of traits that belong to true prophets. One trait is that prophecy is not necessarily designed as a punishment, but rather as a way to bypass trouble - warning before judgment. Another trait is self-discipline, the ability to wait on God to perform his will in the manner and time as He ordains. Obedience to God and personal humility are observed as well. And finally, this vision highlights the nature of prophesy – God knows the end as though it were the beginning, for "*Surely the Lord GOD will do nothing, but he revealeth his secret unto his servants the prophets...*" (Amos 3:7)

"Here some time ago, you might have noticed in the paper at Denver, Colorado. They never did know what happened. The Lord had sent me over there. He showed me a place. He said, "Now, there's a--a--a place where there'll be a car parked this a way," in a vision. He said, "It's a gray car. You'll be going down the street this a way, and there's a white house. And when you look in behind there, there's a gate that opens. And there's hoe laying right down behind the gate."

And [the Holy Spirit] said, "There'll be a man come out and get in a car packing a briefcase. Go at the door." And said, "When you do, there'll be a woman weeping. And when you go in, lay your hat down on the bed, and then she'll pick it up and lay it over here on a television. And there'll be another lady come in with a red sweater on and set down here. Then go lay your hands on this sick baby and say, 'THUS SAITH THE LORD.'" See? I knew what it was….And I--I--I got up, set about it, out of the vision.

And about two or three days after that, telegrams coming everywhere, and, "Come here to pray for this one. Come pray for that one. Come pray for this one, everywhere." You know. And after while I picked up one, and it said, "Come to Denver. A man with TB, dying. Come at once." Something just said to me, "Go."

And I didn't know where the vision was going to be. I went, got off the plane, got a cab, and went to this address, prayed for the man. Never did hear what happened. So it was a little time before the plane was going to leave, so I thought instead of calling the cab, I'll just walk down town. And I won't even think about that vision or nothing. I just knowed it was going to happen."
(Wm Branham – Prince Albert, Canada, August 16, 1956)[421]

"Not long after that, three or four days after the vision, well, I was called to a place in Colorado, to a man that had TB. And I went to pray for him; something told me to go over and pray for him. And I got in the plane and went over. And after praying for that--that man, I don't know whatever happened to him. I was waiting for the plane, and I said, 'I just... He... I just feel like I want to walk.' And I was walking down this street going along, and I seen a doctor with a gray suit on packing a little... I thought 'That fellow looks familiar to me.' And I looked setting here, set--set a little gray Ford. I said, 'It's a vision. That's what come the other day.' See? And I seen--I said, 'If he's... I'll watch him.' He come out; I said, 'Howdy do?' He spoke, got in the car, very polite, and I looked laying behind the gate, and there laid that hoe. I said, 'This is it.' And I went to the door, knocked on the door, and a lady come to the door with the red sweater on. I said, 'Howdy do?'And she said, 'Howdy do?'
And I--I said, 'I'm a minister of the Gospel. Have you sickness?'
She said, 'A baby.'

I said, 'It's laying in a bed to the left as you go in at the door. Described how...'She said, 'Where is your--your parish?'And I said, 'The world is my parish.' I said, 'My name is Branham.' She never heard of me. I said, 'May I have a prayer, for your baby?' She said, 'You may, sir.' She said, 'We are Christians here.' I stepped in.

She took my hat and laid it on the bed. Now, the other lady with the brown coat on hadn't come in. So I waited an hour. The lady wondered what all the waiting about. So it was a hour, the lady had not come in yet. And after while, when she come in she set down in the place where the lady with the red sweater on was supposed to be setting. So that wasn't right, and my hat was still on the bed. I couldn't tell them, but they had to do it. The Angel of the Lord wasn't there yet; that was a sign to me when to pray. And they was working with the baby, after while the--the lady picked up my hat and laid it up on the radio, on the television, then I walked over to the bed, said, 'THUS SAITH THE LORD, the baby will live.' [the baby] Started reaching for its mother and [the family started] taking the covers off of him. That was it. While they were weeping, I slipped out the door. They never knew who I was or nothing about it."
(Wm Branham - Chicago, IL July 22, 1954E)[422]

Like a movie with a script, prophecy must transpire part by part, scene by scene. Though we as observers may not discern the course the film is taking, the director does – it is an expected end.[423] God may take an improvised approach to writing dialogue, nevertheless he has a clear idea of where his "film" will go and a reasonable idea of what his actors will do and say.

The writer James alludes to this concept of actors in a divine play when he instructs early Christians to be "doers of the word." He uses the Greek word *poetes* to convey the thought of divine actors taking on a role and acting out their unique part with enthusiasm and inspiration. Shakespeare wasn't too far from the truth when he said, "all the world's a stage, and all the men and women merely players."[424] Even Jesus recognized he had a role [*"Lo, in the volume of the book it is written of me..."*][425] and performs his part on many, many occasions.

Humans as earthly actors do have the freshness, novelty and vitality that come from the absence of a strict line-by-line pre-determined script. In conclusion, even in an improvised work there is arguably a degree of control that God does exercise. On occasion the director will step in and say "No, I don't want that line or this scene." In the Hebrew Bible, there is much behavior on God's part – intemperate, passionate, demanding, destructive and repenting – that is reminiscent of the best theatre and film directors.

"Lay your hat down on the bed..." This is what William Branham was instructed to do – as a poet, divine actor and prophet – he knew what he was to do, and he did it as scripted. I think of William Branham's vision of Adolph Hitler and how he would "come to a mysterious end." That was the script, Hitler would "come to a mysterious end."

Recently Tom Cruise starred as Claus von Stauffenberg in the film *Valkyrie*, a Coronel bent on the assassination of Hitler. *Valkyrie* can be seen as a comedy of errors, at the end, everything that can go wrong in thwarting the assassination does.

On July 20, 1944 several high-ranking German soldiers sought to assassinate Adolf Hitler by way of a briefcase bomb at the Führerhauptquartier "Wolfsschanze". The bomb, designed to explode indoors, in the enclosed cement bunker of Hitler's command, would have killed everyone either by the shrapnel or concussively. Impulsively (and due to the soaring temperature) the meeting was moved to a normal wooden structure with windows. Von Stauffenberg originally placed the ill-fated device near Hitler, but it was moved behind an obstruction, whereupon with the defrayed detonation Hitler survived. The members of the coup (*Verschwörer*) were eventually discovered and executed.

Von Stauffenberg's plan seems so fool proof, all the right people in all the right places, and yet, at the end Hitler escapes relatively unscathed. Why? Why did Hitler avoid fourteen prior attempts on his life, as well as the von Stuffenberg one? It wasn't because he was Valkyric, simply, it wasn't in the script – had Hitler died this way, his death would have been clear – instead, Hitler's death was to be uncertain and with his demise, he would "come to a mysterious end."

18

Barak Hussein Obama – The Cause of a Million Deaths?

Barak Hussein Obama – The Cause of a Million Deaths?

"I wish I could talk to Martin Luther King. That man, being a Christian, don't know he is leading his people right into a death trap, where there is going to be millions of them killed." [426]

Millions of Blacks killed? Was this a vision or an impression, and what did William Branham see? Did he see civil rights marchers slaughtered in 1963? Did he see future riots in Watts, Los Angeles in 1965 or possibly South African clashes during the 1980's Apartheid era? Did he see the genocides of Africa in the latter part of the 20th Century? Did he see the African AIDS epidemic and the resulting death of millions upon millions? Or could he have possibly seen the slaughter of millions of aborted black children, with the tacit consent and political influence of Barak Obama as both Senator and President?

As we have already shown, any/all prophecy is determined on several factors; is the vision literal or figurative (symbolic), is it conditional or unconditional, and is it immediate or future. For example Psalms 22:16, "they pierced my hands and feet," was literal, unconditional (Jesus had to die to take away mankind's sins), and futuristic (David uttered the prophecy, Jesus fulfilled it 1000 years after the prophecy).

On the other hand, Genesis 37:9-10, Joseph's dream/vision "The sun and the moon, and eleven stars bowed down to me," was figurative (the sun was his father, the moon his mother and the stars were his brothers), conditional (that his brothers would sell him into slavery) or unconditional ("God meant it for good"[427] that many lives would be saved during a famine), and futuristic (74 years after Joseph declared his prophecy to his family).

Before various interpretations are explained, let's look at snippets of the same general 'black leader – people dying' prophecy:

Arkansas - June 28, 1963: *"I wish I could talk to Martin Luther King. That man, being a Christian, don't know he is leading his people right into a death trap, where there is going to be millions of them killed."*[428]

Indiana - June 30, 1963: *One thing, I pray that Brother Martin Luther King will certainly soon wake up. He loves his people; there's no doubt. But if he just only see where his inspiration...*
Just--just like Hitler did, over in Germany, led them right into a death trap, them precious Germans. And they laid by the billions, or millions, piled up there on top one another.
And that's exactly the same thing. And remember, I'm on tape. You'll see it, after, maybe after I'm gone. That's exactly what's going to happen. Them precious people will die down there, like flies. Starts a revolutionary, both white and colored will fight again, and die like flies. And what you got when it's all over? A bunch of dead people.[429]

Indiana - July 21, 1963: *These couple requests. I don't know whether they got the recorders going yet for this, or not. It might be good. Well, I guess it's all right for the outside, the public to hear this, it's a request.*

Did you prophesy that there'd be a--a million Negroes killed on the... or did you just announce that there would be this happening?

Now, see, I've always asked you to be careful what you're listening to. See? There's so much of it that it's just the human side.

It's inspired of the wrong thing, you see, see, they, them people. And that's the reason I say that, not that there is any--any prophecy concerning it. I have nothing on it from the Lord. And be you sure now, if I say anything from the Lord like that, to tell you, it's always... I'm speaking now. But when He speaks, I say "It's not me, it's THUS SAITH THE LORD." And I can't say it until He tells me. I could be al-

together wrong in my thought about Martin Luther King. I don't know, I can't say. That's just my opinion. Anything that rises up trouble, that's what's supposed to be in the last days. And it's all inspired of Satan, to break up our commonwealth and whatever we have, anything that rises up like that.[430]

Indiana - August 15, 1965: *And what are we coming here for? What are we doing? Are we coming here, playing a game? Are we coming here, meeting as a lodge? It's, Christ can't come until that Church is perfectly right. He is waiting on us. I believe we're at the end.*

Look at, in California. Look at the riots. Look at nineteen people being killed, racial. Didn't I tell you, here not long ago, that that Martin Luther King would lead his people to a massacre? How many remembers that?[431]

A Black Man and a Massacre

Were these *nineteen* people the "massacre" William Branham had seen? Or was this event the beginning of a series of events, a social movement that would act like a chain reaction sparking uprisings, riots, revolts, *coup* d'*états*, government overthrows and even genocide? Concerning this prophecy, we'll look at five possibilities: The Watts Riot and the influence Martin Luther King, the Rodney King Riot, an African despot (Idi Amin), the African AIDS epidemic (Thabo Mbeki), and Barak Obama's support and influence of millions of abortions. First, let's examine the life and events of Martin Luther King, Jr. - the man originally thought to be the subject and object of this prophecy.

Martin Luther King – The Original Black Man & a Million Blacks Killed

Martin Luther King, Jr. (1929 - 1968) was a leader of the Black civil rights movement, beginning with the Montgomery bus boycott in 1955. Strongly influenced by the teachings of Mahatma Gandhi, King was a public advocate of non-violence, leader of the Southern Christian Leadership Conference, and the impassioned voice of the Black civil rights movement. He was known for his stirring "I have a dream" speech and for winning the Nobel Peace Prize in 1964.

Thought to be too passive and accepting of the status-quo, his leadership of the movement came under attack by more militant black leaders and from the disillusioned and angry black populace in the mid-1960's. Stokely Carmichael's call for "Black Power" and Malcolm X's call for Black Nationalism directly challenged both King's non-violent message and his role as spokesman for the African-American community.

On August 13th, 1965, a white policeman patrolling the predominantly black Watts neighborhood of Los Angeles, California, stopped a young black man on suspicion of drunken driving. A crowd gathered at the scene, and rumors of police brutality spread throughout the community. Over the next six days, widespread rioting broke out.

According to Los Angeles Times staff writers Valerie Reitman and Mitchell Landsberg, to many, the events that began in Watts during August, 1965, remain a riot, pure and simple — a social breakdown into mob rule and criminality. To others, they were a revolt, a rebellion, an uprising and a violent but justified leap into a future of black self-empowerment.

The riots that summer were sparked by the arrest of a black motorist, Marquette Frye, for drunk driving. When Frye's mother intervened, a crowd gathered and the arrest became a flashpoint for anger against police. The deeper causes, as documented by the McCone Commission, which investigated the riots, were poverty, inequality, and racial discrimination.

After nearly a week of rioting, 34 people, 25 of them black, were dead and more than 1,000 were injured. More than 600 buildings were damaged or destroyed and an estimated $200 million in property was destroyed. The riots spread to other areas such as Long Beach; an estimated 35,000 African Americans took part in the riot, which required 16,000 National Guardsmen, county deputies, and city police to put down. [432] The Watts riots were the first major racially-fueled rebellion of the 1960s, an event that foreshadowed the widespread urban violence of the latter half of the decade.[433]

Watts signaled a shifting attitude among African-Americans. Rioting broke out in the summer of 1966 in New York and Chicago. In 1967 Newark and Detroit were the scenes of deadly riots, and in the spring of 1968, when Martin Luther King was assassinated in Memphis, more than 100 cities across the nation erupted in violence.[434]

King Redux 1992

What did William Branham see? Martin Luther *King* 1965 or Rodney *King* 1992?

On April 29th, 1992, after a year of racial strife surrounding the alleged L.A.P.D. beating of Rodney King, a jury of six men and six women found the officers not guilty. The ensuing rioting that came with the verdict was said to be far worse than the 1965 Watts Riot, and could only be described as "hell" by one news agency.

One witness said that the atmosphere and conditions were reminiscent of those at the onset of the "Watts Riots" that shook Los Angeles following the death of Martin Luther King. One day after the verdict South Central Los Angeles erupted in a violent and deadly outburst of arson and shooting. Local police and emergency medical services officials report the deaths of as many as nine (9) people and injuries to another 138.

Due to the unprecedented violence and social unrest, Los Angeles Mayor Tom Bradley declared a local "State Of Emergency" and requested a California disaster declaration. Mayor Bradley also reported to have issued a "dusk to dawn" curfew which prohibits people from being on the street during nighttime hours. The riot was severe enough that California Governor Pete Wilson initially activated more than 2,000 National Guardsmen to help quell the rampage in Los Angeles.

As lawlessness continued, President George Bush called for calm and a stop to "anarchy" on the streets of Los Angeles. President Bush was said to have monitored the situation closely, eventually activating his plans to provide federal assistance. Eventually 4,000 regular Army troops and 1,000 federal law enforcement officers moved into Los Angeles to quell the violence and restore peaceful order.

An unidentified Los Angeles Police officer provided a concise commentary on the state of affairs in Los Angeles; "Things are totally out of control here... and we expect it to get worse when it gets dark...I hope we all live to see tomorrow".

The death toll had risen following another night of violence and mayhem that is said, by some, to be the consequences for the acquittal of four L.A.P.D. officers in Simi Valley, CA on Wednesday. The three day wave of destruction, which had spread from South Central Los Angeles to Downtown, to Pasadena, to Hollywood, and to Korea-Town, brought the total that had been killed as the result of the fires, riots, and shooting total to thirty-eight.

The current totals of dead, injured and damage done exceeded those that occurred in 1965, when residents of the Watts section of Los Angeles erupted after the arrest of a black man by a white highway patrol officer. Thirty-four (34) people died in the following six-days of chaos, 1,000 were injured, and $200 million dollars in damage was done. Older eyewitnesses say that the most current riots far exceed the days of the Watts riots, both in intensity and level of violence.

As 1,000 federal law enforcement officers, National Guard Units "federalized" by President Bush and supplemented by another 4,000 Army and Marine troops with orders to act as "Light-Infantry" and to "return fire if fired upon" moved into Los Angeles, people began to recognized the severity of this "revolution". The Rodney King Riot found thirty-eight (38) people dead, 1,250 people injured, 3,600 structural fires, hundreds of businesses looted and closed, and more than 3,000 people arrested. At least four (4) police officers and three (3) firefighters had been shot and hundreds of other injured as they attempted to control the fires and lawlessness of this social unrest[435].

Idi Amin Dada – "The Butcher of Uganda"

Idi Amin Dada (1925-2003) died at an age thought to be 78. He was considered one of the most brutal military dictators to wield power in post-independence Africa.

While chief of staff of the Ugandan army, under Dr Milton Obote's civilian government, he seized power in 1971. He made himself president, with the rank of field marshal, and after eight years of power left Uganda a legacy of bloodthirsty killings and economic mismanagement. Parliament was dissolved; no elections were held; secret police - most of them in plain clothes - exercised absolute power of life and death; and the courts and the press were subjugated to the whims of the executive.

The death toll during the Amin regime will never be accurately known. The best estimate, from the International Commission of Jurists in Geneva, is that it was not less than 80,000 and more likely around 300,000. Another estimate, compiled by exile organizations with the help of Amnesty International, put the number killed at 500,000.

For Tanzania's president, Julius Nyerere (obituary, October 15 1999), Amin was "a murderer, a liar and a savage".[436] In the perspective of history he will go down as one who damaged the cause of African nationalism.

Thabo Mbeki – "Nelson Mandela's Successor" or "The Friend of Terror..."

[The South African AIDS Epidemic]

Nationally, African Americans make up approximately 12 percent of the U.S. population, yet half of all new AIDS cases reported in this country are among members of the Black community. AIDS is the leading cause of death nationally for Black women aged 25-34; for Black men aged 35-44, it is the second leading cause of death.[437]

Despite America's staggering statistics, they pale in comparison to many African nations. While most African nations have addresses both the treatment and prevention of AIDS, for the past decade one African nation and one African leader had stood by and allowed hundreds of thousands of unnecessary deaths to occur.

On June 2, 1999, Mbeki, the pragmatic deputy president of South Africa and leader of the African National Congress, was elected president. Despite his initial public support, Mbeki's legacy will be one of infamy. Research from Harvard University indicates that the AIDS policies of former president Thabo Mbeki's government were directly responsible for the avoidable deaths of at least a third of a million people in South Africa.

South Africa has one of the most severe HIV/AIDS epidemics in the world. About 5.5 million people, or 18.8% of the adult population, have HIV, according to the UN. In 2005 there were 900 deaths a day.

From the late 90s Mbeki turned his back on the scientific consensus that AIDS was caused by a viral infection which could be combated, though not cured, by sophisticated and expensive drugs. He came under the influence of maverick scientists known as Aids-denialists. Most notably in April 2000 he defended a small group of dissident scientists who claim that AIDS is not caused by HIV. He and his administration have been repeatedly accused of failing to respond adequately to the epidemic. He described AIDS as a "disease of poverty", arguing that political attention should be directed to poverty generally rather than AIDS specifically.[438]

The present AIDS-HIV epidemic -- against which the Mbeki-regime undertook little action and failed to acknowledge -- the World Health Organization estimates that more than 6-million African South Africans will be dead within the forthcoming decade. And the Mbeki-led ANC regime, which could have undertaken a huge prevention campaign such as Uganda's a long time ago, had done nothing to stave off this terrible death rate.

It was being reported in The Star, that under Mbeki, S. African hospitals were "becoming places of death" and not of healing. It was reported that the cemeteries were filling up so rapidly that upright funerals were being contemplated to save space. For much of 2000-2002, Aids was not being spoken about at funerals, and the silence and utterly unscientific public statements about HIV-AIDS from Mbeki's continued unabated while people died.

For several years Mbeki not only did little to alleviate S. Africa's AIDS sufferers, he and "the South African government acted as a major obstacle in the provision of medication to patients with AIDS," contend Pride Chigwedere and colleagues from the Harvard School of Public Health, Boston, in the Journal of Acquired Immune Deficiency Syndrome.

Only after intense international pressure, did South Africa launch a program for the prevention of mother to child transmission in 2003 and a national adult treatment program in 2004. By 2005, the paper's authors estimate, there was still only 23% drug coverage and less than 30% prevention of mother to child transmission. By comparison, Botswana achieved 85% treatment coverage and Namibia 71% by 2005, and both had 70% mother to child transmission program coverage.

In a recent 2008 paper, Harvard researchers have quantified the death toll resulting from Mbeki's stance, which caused him to reject offers of free drugs and grants and led to foot-dragging over a treatment program, even after Mbeki had taken a vow of silence on the issue. The authors estimate that more than 330,000 people died unnecessarily in South Africa over the period and that 35,000 HIV-infected babies were born who could have been protected from the virus but would now probably have a limited life.[439]

On September 21, 2008 Mbeki was forced to resign. The political landscape in South Africa continues to be volatile. Recent reports are that ousted president Thabo Mbeki and his loyalists, led by former Defense Minister Mosiuoa Lekota (nicknamed "Terror"), were regrouping to retake power. The AIDS death scourge is not over yet.

Barak Obama – The "Renegade"[I] – Surgical Deaths by Abortion [Pro-Choice, Pro-FOCA]

In the summer of 1992, as Bill Clinton solidified his control over the Democratic Party, Robert P. Casey Sr. was banned from speaking to the Democratic convention for the heresy of being pro-life.

The elder Casey (now deceased) was then the governor of Pennsylvania and one of the most prominent elected Democrats in the country. He was an economic progressive in the Roosevelt tradition. But "his Irish Catholic conscience led him to oppose abortion. So the Clintons chose to humiliate him."[440] It was a sign and a warning of a pro-abortion political shift and of a rabid pro-abortionist yet to come.

In 2008 Pastor Rick Warren asked when a baby gets its rights, Obama said, "I'm absolutely convinced that there is a moral and ethical element to this issue." Huh?

If Obama believes there is a moral element of the abortion issue, why does he want to eliminate existing restrictions on the procedure?

For Barack Obama, abortion is not merely a Constitutional right; it is a matter of social justice. He believes it is patently unfair that some women struggle to afford an abortion, or cannot purchase the procedure at all. Consequently, the state (meaning a single federal state) should seize that right and ensure its equitable distribution to every (female) citizen.

[I] *Renegade* – The US Secret Service issued Code Name for President Obama. (From the Medieval Latin renegatus, to deny.) Renegade is a synonym for turncoat; a term for a disavowed Christian or a knight without loyalty or alliance.

Day Gardner, the head of the National Black Pro-Life Union, tells LifeNews.com that Dr. Martin Luther King, Jr., would have been a strong pro-life advocate were he alive today. "I believe if Dr. King were alive today, he would not rest until every unborn child was granted his or her basic right to life," she says.

Gardner laments that the black church is not as involved in the civil rights battle against abortion as it was the civil rights battle for equal treatment under law and in society. "Today, too many churches and black ministers close their eyes to the 15 million deaths of black children slaughtered by abortion since 1973," Gardner says.[441]

"Senator Obama doesn't care that abortion has obliterated the rights of more than 15 million black children since 1973," Gardner said in a statement. "He doesn't care that abortion is the No. 1 killer of African-Americans surpassing deaths caused by accidents, heart disease, stroke, crimes, HIV-AIDS and all other deaths – combined!"

Gardner accuses Obama of hypocrisy, saying he won't make one of his powerful speeches to decry the injustice of abortion providers as they plant killing centers firmly in black communities – making it easier to kill black children.[442]

There's been speculation as to whether President-elect Barack Obama will immediately remove the "global gag rule" that currently prohibits federal funds from going to international family planning agencies that promote or provide abortions. United Nations Population Fund, or UNFPA, had its funding frozen by the Bush administration in 2002. Throughout George W. Bush's two terms, Congress approved funding for the agency, and the president continually put his foot down and would not release the money.

Many believe these agencies will again receive federal dollars with Obama in the White House. The president will have to do nothing; he'll just have to let the will of Congress go through.[443]

The Freedom of Choice Act (FOCA) is a bill introduced in the United States Congress in 2007. It would remove all restrictions on abortion in the United States, both on the state and federal level. FOCA goes far beyond guaranteeing the right to an abortion throughout the nine months of pregnancy; it arrogantly prohibits any law or policy interfering with that right.[444]

Introduced in Congress in April 2007 by Senator Barbara Boxer (D-CA) and Rep. Jerry Nadler (D-NY), the bill was strongly supported by President-elect Barack Obama. Immediately following a speech on July 17, 2007 to the Planned Parenthood Action Fund, Obama was asked what he would do at the federal level, not only to ensure access to abortion but to make sure that the judicial nominees he might pick "are true to the core tenets of Roe v. Wade?" He promised that "The first thing I'd do as president is sign the Freedom of Choice Act. That's the first thing that I'd do." [445] On this fundamental issue of a woman's right to choose abortion during any and all terms of pregnancy, Obama says he will not yield.

And by Obama not "yielding," will he be responsible for the deaths of millions of Black Americans, *and* fulfill a 1963 prophecy? Whether William Branham prophesied this with Obama in mind, *Obama is responsible for millions of deaths* by abortion; placing him in the infamous company of other mass, genocidal murderers such as the Pharaoh Ramses, Adolph Hitler (11 million), Joseph Stalin (40 million), Pol Pot (2 million), and Thabo Mbeki (365 thousand).

I wouldn't want to be Obama or any other person who must stand before God on Judgment Day to give an account of their sinful actions, let alone being responsible for millions of deaths. William Branham recounts horrible incidents where he stood beside people on their death beds that were sinners and not prepared to meet their maker;

"I stood not long ago, by the side of a man that was dying, who refused Christ. He screamed and told, 'Take those demons away from me. They're wrapped in chains. Don't let them get me.'

I stood by a woman's side, who had abortion cases, killing little children. She said, 'Little cold babies hands are running through my hair.'

She said, 'Let that stork away from the window there with those great big head on it.'"[446]

Under current law, approximately 1,876 black babies are aborted every day in the United States. That means over two and half million black babies will be massacred during Obama's first term, under the current law and its constraints. How many deaths will this black man be ultimately responsible for?

Could this be the black man, and the massacre, William Branham saw in 1963?

Planned Parenthood – The Ironic Offspring of Eugenics and the American Birth Control Federation

Planned Parenthood has had a long history of a deadly philosophy and has arguably done far more harm than the KKK, the Nazis, or Segregationists; with the election of Barak Obama, he is poised to be their point man in funding and promotion.

Margaret Sanger (1878-1966), opened up the first birth control clinic in the U.S. in 1916. Margaret Sanger was a life-long advocate for increasing access to birth control. To promote this goal, she began publishing the magazine Birth Control Review in 1917, and founded the Birth Control League in 1922. That organization would later change its name to Planned Parenthood.

Some revisionist historians laud Margaret Sanger as a great social reformer and attribute to her only the best of motives. They want us to believe that Sanger promoted birth control because of her great compassion for women and for minorities who had limited access to contraception.

In truth, Margaret Sanger was an adamant proponent of eugenics. This so-called science postulates that some races are genetically superior and, hence, more fit for survival than others. According to eugenics, the overall fitness of humankind will be enhanced when people with good genes reproduce and people with bad genes don't. Her famous

book published in 1920 *"Women and the New Race"*[447] endorsed eugenics and had a decidedly racist bent. She thought there was a need for *"More children from the fit, less from the unfit."*
Margaret Sanger's writings are laced with her racist views. In her 1922 book, *Pivot of Civilization,*[448] Sanger promoted birth control as the best means for improving the genetic stock of mankind. In this book, she specifically called blacks and Eastern European immigrants *"a menace to human civilization"* and *"human weeds."*

In addition to her own writings, Sanger frequently featured articles in her magazine, Birth Control Review (BCR)[449] from other well know eugenicists and racists. For example, one article contributed by well-known Nazi supporter Lothrop Stoddard was entitled "*The Rising Tide of Color against White World Supremacy.*" Sanger also selected Lothrop Stoddard to serve on the board of her organization.

It is a factual matter that the Nazis actually gained inspiration and methodology from Ms. Sanger and the other influential eugenicists in the United States. Before the German program began, at least seventeen U.S. states (including California) had "forced sterilization" laws. Before 1930 there were 200-600 forced sterilizations per year (in the U.S.A.) but in the 1930s the rate jumped to 2,000-4,000 per year.

The leaders in the German sterilization movement state repeatedly that their legislation was formulated after careful study of the California experiment as reported by Mr. Gosney and Dr. [Paul] Popenoe. It would have been impossible, they say, to undertake such a venture involving some 1 million people without drawing heavily upon previous experience elsewhere.

Who is Dr. Paul Popenoe? He was a leader in the U.S. eugenics movement and in 1933 wrote an article *Eugenic Sterilization: An Urgent Need* in the journal (BCR) that Margaret Sanger started."[450]

Madison Grant, a director of the American Eugenics Society, later merged with Margaret Sanger's Birth Control League to form Planned Parenthood, also influenced Hitler and his racial cleansing policies.

In his 1916 book *"The Passing of the Great Race," Madison Grant* (1865-1937) proposed elimination of the weak and unfit [through sterilization] to curtail crime and disease.

"This is a practical, merciful, and inevitable solution of the whole problem, and can be applied to an ever widening circle of social discards, beginning always with the criminal, the diseased, and the insane, and extending gradually to types which may be called weaklings rather than defectives, and perhaps ultimately to worthless race types."

Hitler thanked Grant for writing *The Passing of the Great Race* and said that "the book was his Bible." Whitney concluded that, following Hitler's actions, one could believe it.[451]

By the late 1930s, growing public hostility meant eugenicists and birth control groups could no longer afford to compete for the dwindling funds from foundations and wealthy donors. As Gordon notes, "In 1938 rivalry in the birth control movement was ended with the reunification of Sanger's friends and enemies in the Birth Control Federation of America (BCFA)."[452]

In 1939, Sanger and her organization launched the Negro Project. Through this project, Sanger sought to convert her philosophical views into social policy. The Negro Project was designed to build clinics in poor black communities so birth control would be made available to keep down the rising black population. To justify this initiative, Sanger explained, "the poorer areas, particularly in the South … are producing alarmingly more than their share of future generations." According to Sanger, birth control would "ease the financial load of caring for with public funds...children destined to become a burden to themselves, to their family, and ultimately to the nation."

Sadly, Sanger persuaded many prominent black leaders that this promotion of birth control in the black community was a sound policy. She shrewdly convinced men like D.W. Dubois and Dr. Clayton Powell that reducing the numbers of African Americans would cause the quality of life to rise for the remaining members of this community.

In January 1940 the BCFA held its annual meeting in New York City. The title of the symposium, "Race Building in a Democracy," showed little had changed. The same title was given to a luncheon speech by Henry Fairchild, president of the American Eugenics Society. At that meeting, the eugenics movement, tainted by public hostility to their Nazi-like ideologies, united with proponents of birth control. In his speech Dr. Fairchild noted, "One of the outstanding features of the present conference is...that these two great movements, eugenics and birth control, have now come together as almost indistinguishable."[453] Planned Parenthood was the product of that union. The luncheon at which Dr. Fairchild spoke also began the 1940 fund drive for "The Citizens Committee for Planned Parenthood."

In a 1942 letter to philanthropist Albert Lasker, Sanger wrote:

"I think it is magnificent that we are on the ground floor, helping Negroes to control their birth rate."

Today, Planned Parenthood openly rejects any adherence to the eugenic philosophies and racist views of Margaret Sanger. In fact, Planned Parenthood's website devotes an extensive discussion about Margaret Sanger trying to explain away what is characterized as anti-choice myths and distortions.

The legacy of Margaret Sanger lives on. The plain and tragic fact is that Planned Parenthood and the abortion industry are effectively carrying out the eugenic policies that Margaret Sanger initiated with the Negro Project nearly 65 years ago.

Planned Parenthood's most prestigious award is the *Margaret Sanger Award*, given in recognition of those who carry on the goals she espoused. If birth control [racial extermination] was her legacy, I'm sure there is a *Margaret Sanger Award* in Barak Obama's near future.

19

Who is "Renegade" Barak Obama?

What Do the Prophecies Say?

On April 2008 Professor Eugene Randell, Deputy Director of the Smithsonian Institution Archives disclosed unreleased Nostradamus information he felt pertained to the up and coming US elections.

The Institute which holds some very rare Nostradamus manuscripts, believes that some of the quatrains written by the 16th century soothsayer are very close to describing the fight for the White House that is happening now.

"We have the only existing fourth edition of Nostradamus' book *Les Propheties* (The Prophecies). There were thought to be only three editions published in 1558, this new edition is from 1559 and includes 20 more quatrains which have never been revealed before -- that is, until now," Professor Randell said on Tuesday, April 8th, 2008.

It seems that with the release of the new quatrains Obama is identified as "the dark one," and he is to wrest control from the Anglo-American dynasty of white rulers. Nostradamus enthusiasts are saying the fight for the White House may have been already written about many centuries ago. Here is the translated quatrain;

243
The great empire will be torn from limb,
The all-powerful one for more than four hundred years:
Great power given to the dark one from slaves come,
The Aryana will not be satisfied thereby.

Boston Globe staff writer Foon Rhee asked: does Senator John McCain's Web ad mocking Barack Obama as "The One" have a darker design?[454]

Outraged Christian supporters of Obama said it does - that it was intended to further Internet-fueled rumors that Obama is the antichrist. Deconstructing and analyzing the ad, they say the images and language play into apocalyptic themes, including those featured in the best-selling "Left Behind" series, fictionalized accounts of the end of the world.

As the ad begins with the words "It should be known that in 2008 the world shall be blessed. They will call him The One" flashing across the screen. The Antichrist of the *Left Behind*[455] books is a charismatic young political leader named Nicolae Carpathia who founds the One World religion (slogan: "We Are God") and promises to heal the world after a time of deep division. One of several Obama clips in the ad features the Senator saying, "A nation healed, a world repaired. We are the ones that we've been waiting for."

Despite Nostradamus' ramblings and McCain's apocalyptic themed tongue-in-cheek proclamation of Barak Obama as "the One,"[456] there are two genuine prophecies describe him as both a "promised warrior" coming to help the Hidden Imam of Shiite Muslims conquer the world, and a Kenyan "son" that will destroy America.

<u>The Muslim Promised Warrior</u> - Is Barack Obama the "promised warrior" coming to help the Hidden Imam of Shiite Muslims conquer the world? This is the question that Amir Taheri asks in an October 26, 2008 Forbes magazine article.[457]

Taheri says the question has made the rounds in Iran since September 2008, when a pro-government Web site published a Hadith (or tradition) from a Shiite text of the 17th century. The tradition comes from Bahar al-Anvar (meaning Oceans of Light) by Mullah Majlisi, a magnum opus in 132 volumes and the basis of modern Shiite Islam.

According to the tradition, Imam Ali Ibn Abi-Talib (the prophet's cousin and son-in-law) prophesied that at the End of Times and just before the return of the Mahdi, the Ultimate Saviour, a "tall black man will assume the reins of government in the West." Commanding "the strongest army on earth," the new ruler in the West will carry "a clear sign" from the third imam, whose name was Hussein Ibn Ali. The tradition concludes: "Shiites should have no doubt that he is with us."

In a curious coincidence Obama's first and second names--Barack Hussein--mean "the blessing of Hussein" in Arabic and Persian. His family name, Obama, written in the Persian alphabet, reads O Ba Ma, which means "he is with us," the magic formula in Majlisi's tradition.

Kenyan Son and Destroyer of America - Is Barak Obama the "Son of Kenya" foretold by the great 19th Century Kenyan Prophet, Johanwa Owalo, the founder of Kenya's Nomiya Luo Church?

Among the Kenyan people of the Luo religion Owalo is believed to be a prophet similar to Jesus Christ and Muhammad, and who in 1912 made this horrific prophecy about the United States: "*So far have they [the United States] strayed into wickedness in those [future] times that their destruction has been sealed by my [father]. Their great cities will burn, their crops and cattle will suffer disease and death, their children will perish from diseases never seen upon this Earth, and I reveal to you the greatest [mystery] of all as I have been allowed to see that their [the United States] destruction will come about through the vengeful hands of one of our very own sons.*"[458]

The Luo (also called Jaluo and Joluo) are an ethnic group in Kenya, eastern Uganda, and northern Tanzania. They are part of a larger group of ethnolinguistically related Luo peoples who inhabit an area including southern Sudan, northern and eastern Uganda, western Kenya, and northern Tanzania. Throughout the 19th Century AD, the Luo migrated from lower savanna grasslands for higher and cooler regions with reliable rainfall. According to the last national population census conducted in 1989, the Luo number over three million people, or about 13 percent of Kenya's total population.

The Nomiya Luo Church (a mixture of Christianity and African tribal beliefs), began in 1912, it was the first independent church in Kenya. The founder of this church, Johanwa Owalo, was believed to be a prophet and leader similar to Jesus Christ and Muhammad. Owalo later teamed up with a Catholic priest and began teaching a new theology that rejected both the Pope and the doctrine of the trinity. It was in the same year that the Nomiya Luo Church was founded, Owalo made the horrific prophecy about the United States.

Of course, it is absolutely true that Barack Obama is the son of a Kenyan. Here is what the official Barack Obama website reported:

Barack Obama was born in Hawaii on August 4th, 1961. His father, Barack Obama Sr., was born and raised in a small village in Kenya, where he grew up herding goats with his own father, who was a domestic servant to the British...Barack's father eventually returned to Kenya, and Barack grew up with his mother in Hawaii, and for a few years in Indonesia. Later, he moved to New York, where he graduated from Columbia University in 1983.

Dreams From My Father - pg 310 *"Inside the stall, an old woman who was stringing glass beads together pointed at me and said something that made Auma (Barack's half sister) smile. 'what did she say?' 'she says you look American to her' 'tell her I'm Luo,' I said beating my chest..."*

President Obama does appear to meet the requirements of this prophecy as he is, indeed, a '*son*' of the Kenyan Luo tribal religion; born on August 4, 1961 in Honolulu, Hawaii to Barack Obama, Sr. (born in Nyanza Province, Kenya, of Luo ethnicity) and Stanley Ann Dunham.

Thus, this potential prophecy concerning Barak Obama was spoken by Johanwa Owalo, and reported by Sister Mary McCrea of the Sorcha Faal Order in her 1915 copyrighted document "Visions of the Great Nyasaye, A Study of the Luo Religion in Kenya". (Go to: www.firststonellc.com/JohanwaOwaloReseach.pdf for extensive research and documentation.)

Who is "Renegade" Barak Obama?

To elect Obama would be "to 'roll the dice' for America," warned former president Bill Clinton ("Obama showing new confidence with Iowa sprint," New York Times, Dec. 16, 2007).

Numerous thinkers have suggested that the office of the presidency has become dangerously powerful. It would be easy to use the excuse of a terrorist attack to proclaim martial law and use the machinery of government to silence critics. Presidents can start wars; Congress was supposed to have this power, according to the Constitution.

Ordinary Americans have dropped out of the political process to the extent that they expect the president to do the hard work of democracy for them (see Dana D. Nelson's excellent "Bad for Democracy"[459] in which she argues that excessive trust in the presidency is a grave problem). The meager extent of American political participation seems to be voting for president -- that's all we do -- and that's not enough. The office is a magnet for the shrewd, for persons with extreme political ambition, and there is real danger that below the mask of any president, even one as apparently good and fair as President Obama seems to be, may lurk a tyrant.

Psychological Profile of Barak Obama

Initially one can ask: why profile President Obama? Is Psychological profiling and personality screening really needed? The answer is yes; understanding a powerful public figure's psyche and psychological motivation are important tools in crisis prevention and risk management, especially when that person holds the codes to the world's most numerous, powerful and advanced nuclear weapons.

A review of Obama's public speeches, campaign materials and especially his writings reflect that Obama's personality has been remarkably consistent from childhood through adulthood.

In his book "Dreams From my Father," Obama lays out the foundation for an examination of his character and personality. That seminal work reveals much, and almost all of what it reveals is truthful and applicable to his presidential prospects.

Obama's life began with loss, hurt, confusion, alienation, frustration. Out of these he constructed a psychological "mask" that still endures.

What the MBTI psychological personality test reveals about Obama.

The Meyers-Briggs Type Indicator (MBTI) was developed by a team that wanted a practical application for the ideas of personality developed by psychologist Carl Jung. By mixing and matching four poles of personal style—extravert and introvert being the best known—the team came up with 16 personality types. Psychologists Otto Kroeger has revised the 16 personality types and David Kiersey sorted these into four overarching categories: Artisans, Guardians, Idealists, and Rationals. (He describes his classifications in the book *Please Understand Me II* and at this Web site, www.keirsey.com.)

Such personality testing is at times derided by academia, but it's used widely by corporations, the military, and government to understand different leadership styles and the dynamics of working in groups. Finding out your personality type requires answering dozens of questions such as, "Do you find visionaries and theorists a) somewhat annoying [or] b) rather fascinating?" and "When finishing a job, do you like to a) tie up all the loose ends [or] b) move on to something else)?" Meta-analysis was used to formulate conclusions.

Barack Obama—no one will be surprised to learn—is an Idealist. His specific type is an ENFP, what Keirsey calls "the Champion." ENFPs, says Keirsey, are "filled with conviction that they can easily motivate those around them." Champions work to "kindle, to rouse, to encourage, even to inspire those close to them with their enthusiasm." Idealists "usually have a tongue of silver" and are "gifted in seeing the possibilities" of institutions and people. Here's Obama on leadership: "[W]e need leaders to inspire us. Some are thinking about our constraints, and others are thinking about limitless possibility."

This ability to move people through imagery and rhetoric carries a danger for the ENFP, says Keirsey—a belief in "word magic." "Word magic refers to the ancient idea that words have the ability to make things happen—saying makes it so." This is the basis of the critique of Obama by his less-soaring opponents. Hillary complains that people ask her to "give us one of those great rhetorical flourishes and then, you know, get everybody all whooped up." (As if she could.) John McCain said, "To encourage a country with only rhetoric is not a promise of hope. It is a platitude."

Nonetheless, having surfed to power on a wave of voter discontent generated by the failures of President George Bush and the Republican Party, and having generated a level of enthusiasm among supporters not seen in decades, Barack Obama has become the 44th president of the United States.

But as he enters the White House, he faces challenges almost unique in modern times.

It has been 40 years since a new president took office in a time of war.

And with the American economy facing what could be its worst crisis since the Great Depression of the late 1920s, Obama will have to act quickly to restore confidence.

On top of all this, add the confused geopolitical dynamics of a world devolving into multi-polarity, at a time when the US' credibility and reputation is at an all time low, and you get a sense of the terrible pressures a young, new president is inheriting.

He may just become one of the most extraordinary leaders the US has had in many years. So extraordinary that many have called him "The One"- as in a *messiah*, a deliverer – or in a negative sense, *the Antichrist*. Obama himself regularly intoned, as if casting a hypnotic spell;

"A light will shine down from somewhere, it will light upon you, you will experience an epiphany, and you will say to yourself, 'I have to vote for Barak.'"

The original quote was removed entirely from CNN articles in later publication, but we offer as evidence this reposting of the CNN article in full on January 28th by blogger 'Fair Proxy Web'; as well as cited by Roberto Davila-Loyola in January 8th, 2008 1:16 PM ET responding to original with this commentary:

"My job is to be so persuasive that if there's anybody left out there who is still not sure whether they will vote, or is still not clear who they will vote for, that a light will shine through that window, a beam of light will come down upon you, you will experience an epiphany ... and you will suddenly realize that you must go to the polls and vote for Obama," the Democrat said in Hanover.

The above words by Senator Obama as reported by CNN are troubling as they show Senator Obama believing that he has the power to cause a divine manifestation to the undecided voters of New Hampshire which will show them that he is the chosen one. Alternatively, he is contemptuously using as political rhetoric the Christian concept of what happened on the Feast of the Epiphany when a divine manifestation (the Star of Bethlehem) announced the birth of the Baby Jesus.

ABC News initially reported the dramatic over-reaction of press and supporters in an article called "Something Stirring in the Air." The article went on to accurately state that based on Obama's actions and his 'a light will shine...you'll have an epiphany' speeches, he evidenced the "makings of a messiah complex."[460]

YouTube, the electronic video pulse of America, aired a negative Obama presidential campaign advertisement created by the McCain camp, it is called "The One."[461] At an August 2008 fundraiser in San Francisco, US House Speaker Nancy Pelosi introduced Obama and said that he was "a leader that God has blessed us with at this time."[462] June 28, 2006, in a speech at *The Call to Renewal's 'Building a Covenant for a New America'* conference, Obama misinterpreted and mocked Old Testament scripture and questioned the wisdom of Jesus' Sermon on the Mount teachings. It was in this speech that Obama provides his prejudice (and indoctrination by Rev. Jeremiah Wright) against using the Bible to lead and guide America and its public and foreign policy.

In the same speech, Obama declares that the United States is no longer a Christian nation. He says, "Moreover, given the increased diversity of America's population, the dangers of sectarianism have never been greater. Whatever we once were, we are no longer a Christian nation; (ed. 'at least not just' added during live speech) we are also a Jewish nation, a Muslim nation, a Buddhist nation, and a Hindu nation – and a nation of nonbelievers."[463]

I understand (at least I think I do) what he is trying to do. On its face, Obama's goals are to unite, and not continue to divide the Nation through sectarian dogmatism. He seems to infer that both religious belief and the use of religious language and metaphor are essential and valuable. Belief in private, except as a social conduit; and religious language and metaphor as a means of a public leader to illicit an emotional connection and inspire the populace.

The overwhelming victory of Barak Obama on a national level, rather than a blue or red state level, seems to reinforce his belief that Americans want peace more than they want doctrinal purity. Obama believes that a literalist reading of the Bible is folly. His personal questioning of Biblical inerrancy also seems to reflect the national uncertainty of Biblical inerrancy – which brand of Christianity is right? As he once asked, "whose Christianity would we teach in the schools? Would we go with James Dobson's, or Al Sharpton's?"[464]

Whose Christianity would we teach? That is an excellent question.

An even better question may be: who is Barak Hussein Obama?

The Salesman of Hope

During his election campaign, Obama sold hope. To get it, you needed only give him your vote. Barack Obama made millions.

"We are the hope of the future," sayeth Obama. We can "remake this world as it should be." Believe in me and I shall redeem not just you but your country -- nay, we can become "a hymn that will heal this nation, repair this world, and make this time different than all the rest."

That was too much for Time's Joe Klein. "There was something just a wee bit creepy about the mass messianism..." he wrote. Klein also said, "The message is becoming dangerously self-referential. The Obama campaign all too often is about how wonderful the Obama campaign is."

You might dismiss The New York Times' Paul Krugman's complaint that "the Obama campaign seems dangerously close to becoming a cult of personality" as hyperbole. Until you hear MSNBC's Chris Matthews, who no longer has the excuse of youth, react to Obama's Potomac primary victory speech with "My, I felt this thrill going up my leg." [Now, that's creepy.]

Obama has an astonishingly empty paper trail. He's going around issuing promissory notes on the future that he can't possibly redeem. The Obama spell will break. My guess is that he can maintain the spell past Inauguration Day, after which will come the awakening. It will be rude.

Obama's combination of confidence, assertiveness, and congeniality fits the profile of a charismatic leader; he is ambitious, dominant, and outgoing, which enables him to advance a personal vision, inspire followers, and connect with people. The outgoing pattern in Obama's personality profile may be key to his meteoric rise to prominence.

Keirsey says Idealist leaders should be called *catalysts* because "[t]he individual who encounters such a leader is likely to be motivated, animated, even inspired to do his or her very best work." *The New Yorker*'s Packer writes, "Obama offers himself as a catalyst by which disenchanted Americans can overcome two decades of vicious partisanship. ..."

Idealists are deeply introspective. According to Keirsey, their "self-confidence rests on their authenticity," which makes them "highly aware of themselves as objects of moral scrutiny." Idealists, such as Thomas Paine, Mohandas Gandhi, and Martin Luther King Jr., tend to be leaders of movements, not office-holders. If Obama is elected, not only would he be the first black president, but according to Keirsey, he'd be the first Idealist president. Idealists are rare in any executive position and within the general population. Because they tend to have a positive outlook, they can be "surprised when people or events do not turn out as anticipated."

The ENFP can have a problem with "restlessness," says Kroeger. "As a task or responsibility drags on and its mantle becomes increasingly routine, the ENFP can become more pensive, moody, and even rigid." Obama himself referred in a debate to his disorganization and dislike of paperwork—and his self-knowledge that "I need to have good people in place who can make sure that systems run."[465] Good people like, say, Hillary Clinton?

More significantly from a profiling approach, his personality lends it-self to planting subtle nuggets of self-revelation in his writings. His earlier writings, moreover, were prepared at a time when the prospects of a presidential campaign were probably not even an idle dream. So these early statements are especially helpful to a personality examina-tion and identification.

He apparently held and still holds Kenyan-American dual nationality, but has scrupulously avoided any discussion of his "dual" status. Dual-ity is not what Obama craves: he craves the singular, the linear, and the straight and narrow, to compensate for his own confused and winding initiation into the hardship of life and family, of creating a personality and mask consonant with his troubled feelings.

But who is Barak Hussein Obama?

a.k.a. Barry Soetoro
a.k.a. Barry Obama
a.k.a. Barak Dunham

Kenyan citizen? Indonesian citizen? United States of America citizen?

Try to find his medical records, you can't, he has not given them out.

Try to find his college papers, you can't and he won't release them or his senior thesis on his views of The Soviet Union and disarmament.

Try to find any article he wrote for the Harvard Law School Law Review, a newspaper, while he was its President.

Try to find any of his records from Occidental College, Columbia University or Harvard Law School, you won't, Obama has refused to release any and all of them.

Actually try and find objective, verifiable "proof" of his birth, and citizenship...none have been provided, despite a formal request for certified documents to Obama and the Democratic National Convention (see the civil complaint filed by Philip J. Berg).

Ask him about his close personal relationship with Dr. Khalid Abdullah Tariq al Mansour, a radical Muslim that prophesied of a black massacre, and powerful influence in his acceptance into Harvard many years ago (Attorney for Malcolm X, and Civil rights activist Percy Sutton said in October 2008 he was solicited by Dr. Khalid al-Mansour to send a letter of recommendation on behalf of Barack Obama); Obama will only say he has had dinner with the man and his family, and leaves it at that.

Obama and Dr. Khalid al-Mansour

[Al-Mansour, whose real name is Don Warden, is a notorious black nationalist, radical Muslim and a sworn enemy of Israel and Christianity.

According to the Social Activism Project at the University of California, Berkeley, al-Mansour was a mentor/advisor to Black Panther Party founder Huey Newton and Bobby

Seale – both violent criminals. In fact, al-Mansour helped establish the Black Panther Party, a violent black-Marxist organization of the 60's and 70's, but broke with the group when it began working with white revolutionaries.

Al-Mansour is the same man, during a speech entitled "Christians Designed Discrimination" stated; "White people…don't feel bad, whatever you do to them they deserve it. God wants you to do it, and that's when you cut out the nose, cut out the ears, take flesh out of their body…don't worry because God wants you to do it."[466]

Indeed the very essence of Obama's personality is the perpetual, eternal promise unfulfilled. Obama's "Hope" is the absence of reality, the unattainable in his own life scaled up to a national fantasy which he hopes to peddle to an unsuspecting populace and especially young people. When he fails, they will feel betrayed.

Who is Barak Hussein Obama? Obama is a liberal, and a rather radical liberal at that.

Barry the Radical Socialist Liberal

Born to Russian-Jewish parents in Chicago in 1909, Saul Alinsky was a Marxist, and the father of *community organizing* who helped establish the dual political tactics of confrontation and infiltration that characterized the 1960s and have remained central to all subsequent revolutionary movements in the United States. Before Alinsky devised his diabolical plan to bring the international socialist revolution to America -- working *within* the very liberal and free system upon which the U.S. was founded -- he was an older fellow traveler[J] and advisor to student radicals of the 1960s.

[J] The term *fellow traveler* (*poputchiki*) was used by Vladimir Lenin and other Bolsheviks to describe those who agreed with the principles of socialism; it has also been used to describe one who sympathizes with or supports the tenets and program of an organized group, such as the Communist Party, without being a "card-carrying" member.

Alinsky was a sort of father figure, to whom many radicals turned in the aftermath of the infamous DNC Convention of 1968 in Chicago. Two of his most notable acolytes were Hillary Clinton and Barack Obama.

What was Alinsky's advice?

"Do one of three things. One, go find a wailing wall and feel sorry for yourselves. Two, go psycho and start bombing -- but this will only swing people to the right. Three, learn a lesson. Go home, organize, build power and at the next convention, *you be the delegates.*" (emphasis in original) - Saul Alinsky; *Rules for Radicals*; p. xxiii

At the time, however, some of the young radicals were still too filled with rage to stop burning and bombing. These fiery revolutionaries continued to wreak havoc on college campuses and in American cities. But the end of the Vietnam War brought a welcome sigh of relief to greater America.

It was time for the radicals to change tactics, and follow Alinsky's advice. They remained convinced of their destiny to be *the ones* to bring the U.S.A. into the fold of the international socialist collective. They began to organize, go to law school, run for public office, whittle away at traditional American institutions, and in all ways prepare for "The One," their closer.

Obama was raised on the mother's milk of socialism. Both his parents were *fellow travelers*, who met at the height of the Cold War in a Russian language class at the University of Hawaii. Obama's grandfather was a close friend of Communist Party member and verified Soviet intelligence agent Frank Marshall Davis, sending young Barry (as he was then known) to him for mentoring.

Obama did everything Alinsky prescribed. He went to Chicago, home of Alinsky and the place where Davis had worked for the communist revolution. Obama trained at the *Industrial Areas Foundation*, an

Alinsky training institute. He organized in Chicago and did voter registration and training for ACORN, a community-based organization tied to fraudulent voter registration.[467] (During the 2008 election season, ACORN gathered over 1.3 million voter registration forms in 21 states, with approximately 400,000 being ultimately rejected as incomplete, duplicated or fraudulent – an astounding 31% error rate.) He went to law school. He built political alliances. He kept a tight lock on his records and his past.

As for Judeo/Christian morals - Forget it, not necessary or wanted. Alinsky trained his radicals in the spirit of no-holds-barred methods. In Alinsky's mind, the American power structure was evil to its core and justified any means necessary to change the "world as it is" into the "world as it should be." Both Barack and Michelle Obama include these Alinsky code words in their speeches, and we should not mistake their meaning. No means are out of bounds.

Alinsky's tenth rule of the ethics of means: "You do what you can with what you have and clothe it with moral garments."

Conclusion

Reading about Mr. Obama, whether autobiographically or not, wasn't what I originally set out or purposed to do. But after a series of emails from the Obama campaign machine prior to his election, I wanted to try and discover who Barak Obama is. I thought, what better way than to discover this information directly from the source.

After reading Obama's *The Audacity of Hope: Thoughts on Reclaiming the American Dream*, I am more uncertain about who he really is. At Amazon.com I rated this book a two star because it is well written, concise and polished - as it should be coming from a former editor-in-chief of a prestigious law journal...but, the content seemed crafted for maximum positive public approval. *Audacity* included all the right stories to elicit pathos, all the right phrases that can be turned into sound bites, etc. It seems believable IF you want a fairy tale and that is what you are desperately looking for and wanting at this juncture in America's history, but it doesn't jive with the reality of the multi-dimensional world we live in.

Mr. Obama has very cleverly and wisely crafted a public persona that seems very, very different from the harsh, autocratic, scandal-ridden lives of some former politicians. He appears to be above the fray, above it all actually. But my experience with his "people" has been quite different, and that was the reason for reading up on Mr. Obama.

Here is what happened:

In an effort to objectively write a key chapter in my last book, *America, You Will Be Destroyed!: Thus Saith The Lord - and Other Amazing Prophecies* I read various Hillary books as a part of my research. Despite what some may think, I was not looking for information about scandals, I was trying to capture the psyche and inner workings of the former First Lady. This work is scientifically called meta-analysis. I did not have a political agenda, nor was/is my goal a financial one. I was trying to see if Hillary's personality and historical/political track record closely matched key identifiers that established her as the possible subject of an astounding prophecy made in 1933.

What my research uncovered was not only data to verify the prophecy, but the means to fulfill it. In a nutshell the prophecy stated that a woman would raise up within America who would become a great leader, the president - and possibly even its first dictator. In 1933, the possibility of a woman president was very remote, let alone a dictator of any gender. But a series of events that happened AFTER the prophecy was announced has created a political and legal mechanism for a virtual dictatorship - this I was not aware of.

As I read it, this new legislation signed on May 9, 2007, declares that in the event of a "catastrophic event", the President can take total control over the government and the country, bypassing all other levels of government at the state, federal, local, territorial and tribal levels, and thus ensuring total unprecedented dictatorial power. By proclaiming and putting into effect Executive Order No. 12919 and Executive Order 12407, the President would put the United States under total Martial Law and Military Dictatorship.

This research concerned me, and I thought that as an opponent of Hillary Clinton, Mr. Obama would be well-advised. I also thought that as a self-proclaimed Christian and lover of America (and all that that implies), he would at least be of some interest regarding a distinct prophecy given by a noted and respected historically recognized evangelist/prophet.

So I went to an Obama web site and signed up, then went to a few support groups and signed up, then I attempted to provide this information to Obama supporters, and that is when I realized that the Obama that is self-portrayed may be very different than the Obama in reality. I received numerous return emails from his supporters, the preponderance which were nasty, vitriolic, and filled with hate, loathing and disrespect to me personally, to Christianity secondarily and to all prophetic-based religions in general (Christianity, Judaism and Islam). I was told that no sane society believes in prophecy, that the foretelling of events by God through human instrumentation was "prophetic crap" or "B.S.", and specifically that Obama was a "secular humanist." (I saved all the emails).

The bottom line? Though Obama has been very careful to historically maintain a moderate persona, who he associates with and what his associates do are at odds with his persona. Mr. Obama states; "there's not a black America and a white America and Latino America and Asian America. There's the United States of America..." It sort of makes you feel all warm and fuzzy hearing that, right? But is that really what he believes? For many years Obama has attended the Trinity United Church of Christ in Chicago, a church that refers to themselves as "African people." Trinity embraces a "Black Values System" that encourages its members to be "soldiers for Black freedom" and states that they are "unashamedly black." Hmmm.

If any other politician chose to attend an ethno-centric church or organization, they would certainly be ripped apart for that association. Obama says he doesn't engage in smear tactics or petty character assassinations, yet the infamous "Hillary as Dictator" YouTube spoof of the Apple 1984 commercial was produced by the Obama support machine. Hillary is, well, Hillary. As an aside, politically, their voting records are nearly the same. In conclusion; regarding Obama, if a person is willing to scratch the surface of his facade, his hypocrisy is eerily identical (from an arms-length) to Hillary. What he has projected in his book, and his presidential campaign is not Obama the person - but Obama the persona.

While Obama claims to be moving along Robert Frost's "road not taken," in reality he is on the same road, seeking the same fund raising contributors (tens of millions of dollars), seeking to stimulate the same media hysteria and ultimately seeking to run a traditional campaign while claiming he is doing precisely the opposite. In short, Obama in his "Mask" is a smoke-and-mirrors artist who is fully capable of convincing himself of the truthfulness of his delusions. The same way children are.

Obama has succeeded largely by his successful concealment at the margins. Obama's natural tendency, his default state of mind, is to evade, conceal, avoid--and escape. He managed to hide his middle name in 2004; he can't any longer. Questions of family background will forever plague him.

All of the inadequacies and frustrations he perceived as a child still drive him and still control his personality. He won't learn how to remove the Mask because he continues to be afraid there is nothing behind it.[468]

20

Los Angeles Earthquake - California "Sinking"

Los Angeles Earthquake - California "Sinking"

Much has been said about the evils of California, especially Hollywood, and earthquakes in general. Though the language used by William Branham in his California earthquake prophesy is not scientific or geologic by definition, it is specific as it is described as he "saw" it by vision. Just as much of the *Last Days* prophecy contained in the Bible sounds peculiar to our modern understanding; it does not negate its truth or reality.

"*And, behold, there was a great earthquake: for the angel of the Lord descended from heaven, and came and rolled back the stone from the door, and sat upon it.*" – Matthew 28:2

It appears that there are times, like this passage from the Book of Matthew, where God intervenes or intrudes into the natural and physical affairs of man. Reading this passage we as mortals are left trying to understand why – was it a result of His beloved being crucified? Or do earthquakes occur as a matter of course when a significant archangel breaks into our space-time continuum?

Though God basically has stepped back and allowed His creation to operate independently of additional divine interference, there are times that He chooses to exercise His prerogative as parent/creator and exert influence when He sees fit. After all, He is the "Lord of the Sabbath... and greater than the temple." (Matthew 12:1-8) Laws, both those that govern man and creation, were designed to maximize health, harmony and functionality. God, and only God can see the big picture and know when, where and how to introduce and event that would not cause a "Butterfly Effect"[469] with irreversible side effects. In 1972 meteorologist Edward Lorenz used the phrase *Butterfly Effect* as a metaphor for apparently insignificant environmental actions that influenced other events in a chain-reaction of global proportion.[470] [471] For example, if God were to turn the waters of Egypt into blood, He would know what to do next to maintain equilibrium in both the short and long term (like create flies and then frogs and then hail and then darkness…).

Storms, floods, and earthquakes are indeed a part of the present world. We sometimes call them "natural disasters," but they are not a surprise to God. Yes, God certainly can control the weather and send deadly storms. Some have concluded that suffering occurs because it is beyond God's control. This is incorrect. God has indeed established certain laws and principles that govern nature, but he remains sovereign over these laws. Psalm 148:8 declares that storms "do his bidding." Concerning Jonah, it was the Lord who "sent out a great wind into the sea, and there was a mighty tempest in the sea" (Jonah 1:4). Old Testament writers did not hesitate to attribute the forces of nature to God: "thy waterspouts ... thy waves ... thy billows" (Psalm 42:7). Today, God's creation is too often depersonalized. He is in control, and has His reasons for all kinds of weather, both fair and stormy.

Natural disasters have been used by God (Genesis 6:5-19) and allowed by God (Job 1:6-19), as well as occurring "naturally" (which is the norm) as an outgrowth or result of weather and geological conditions.

Severe weather had killed Job's sheep, his servants, and all ten of his children. As Job suffered further physical affliction, he asked, "Why is there evil in the world?" His friends were not of great help in answering the question. Finally, after much dialogue, God spoke directly to Job out of a whirlwind (Job 38:1). The Lord made clear that His control over nature and His ultimate purposes are to be trusted. We simply cannot understand all the details of the divine plan.

The Bible *does not* claim that God is behind every disaster. Notice Jesus' commentary on this very subject:

Luke 13:4-5 "*Or those eighteen, upon whom the tower in Siloam fell, and slew them, think ye that they were sinners above all men that dwelt in Jerusalem? I tell you, Nay*"

Jesus denied the idea that how bad a sinner you are is what determines whether you fall into big trouble. Then what was the reason for their end? There had to be a reason, right? Solomon offers further explanation:

Ecclesiastes 9:11-12 "*I returned, and saw under the sun, that the race is not to the swift, nor the battle to the strong, neither yet bread to the wise, nor yet riches to men of understanding, nor yet favour to men of skill; but time and chance happeneth to them all. For man also knoweth not his time: as the fishes that are taken in an evil net, and as the birds that are caught in the snare; so are the sons of men snared in an evil time, when it falleth suddenly upon them.*"

Could it be that the people are just in the wrong place at the wrong time? Yes, according to the Bible that is the general rule. I am not saying that God never intervenes, or that it is not possible in some cases that God is behind the disaster. The Bible tells us God has done these things in the past and I believe there are cases where it is obvious he is doing it today still. He may cause a natural disaster to be worsened or simply timed to punctuate some abomination that men have done. Bill Koenig[472] is an expert in linking up the cause with the effect. He supports his case by using God's own specific claims in the Bible about what he hates and what he will do. For example, Abraham was promised by God that he would forever bless those who bless Israel and curse those who curse Israel (Gen 12:1-3). It can be shown that whenever anyone make plans to divide up Israel's land or pressure her into doing so, bad things happen usually within 24 hours.[473]

I would caution people from making unsupported claims that make God seem out to get people for no reason. The God of the Bible is a logical, rational and reasonable Father (*of course not to the casual ob-*

server, mind you, but only once you study and understand his Word). He does not do things haphazardly, but according to a pattern, according to rules. Everything he does is for a reason and by observing what he does his servants should be able to see how he consistently acts and judges according to his absolute values, building their faith in him.

When God *Does* Allow a Disaster, What is the Purpose?

The question that occurs to most people is not did he do it, but *why did he allow it to happen*. Because it is obvious that he did not stop it. Why does God allow *any* suffering? No one seems to have a good answer for that very big question, even those who read the Bible. God tries through various ways and means to warn humanity to repent from its sinful ways, such as speaking to our conscience, performing miracles and even sending a prophet. This is often not enough. And though the calamity or "natural" disaster is a severe form of warning, it may indeed cause some to look to God. Some disasters may even be selective acts of divine judgment that precede global judgment.

There is an answer to this big question, a very good and reasonable one. We have a clue in the statement of Jesus quoted earlier, if we continue reading.

Luke 13:4-5 " *Or those eighteen, upon whom the tower in Siloam fell, and slew them, think ye that they were sinners above all men that dwelt in Jerusalem? I tell you, Nay:* ***but, except ye repent, ye shall all likewise perish***."

We live in a dangerous, downright lethal world. The world can very easily hand us a situation beyond our limits to survive. But if we choose to go our own way doing what seems right in our own eyes and relying on our own strength, then we cannot expect any help or intervention from God in these crises. We may very possibly encounter a premature death like those in Siloam, or those in other parts of the world that have experienced disasters. But we cannot conclude that this means God did it, although he did allow it for a reason.

God gave us free will to allow us to choose our own way, rather than force his way upon us unconditionally. He allows us to "reap what we sow", or experience the natural consequences of our actions without intervention from him. By doing so He is letting us learn for ourselves, firsthand, what works and what does not work so well. Sometimes these lessons cost us our lives, but God does not seem too worried about that. He already planned for it through the "Great White Throne Judgment" resurrection (Revelation 20; Ezekiel 37) when the billions who died in rejection or ignorance of His way will be taught the truth plainly at last and will be judged by their actions *and* intent.

If we want to be safe from all kinds of disasters, both real judgments from God and also the more common random events, it is up to us. We must realize our strength is not enough and see the need for God and *then act on it*. The action required is to *diligently* search and find out for ourselves what God wants. This is not the kind of thing you should trust someone else to do for you. In other words, you cannot substitute someone else's judgment for your own. You cannot stand before the judgment seat and say you were only doing what your pastor, rabbi or teacher told you was what the Bible or God said.

In case you are not quite there yet, I think you would want to know something that most are not aware of. I want you to be clear that the Bible tells us that more disasters are coming. **In fact, it tells us specifically that an earthquake greater than anything ever recorded is going to come to the entire world**, causing a universal panic. To make matters worse, it will be followed by deep impacts in the ocean and the Earth, great famine and finally the Great Tribulation.

I see the need for there to be better explanations of Biblical and contemporary prophecies

Contemporary disasters are only small forerunners and wake-up calls before similar, yet much worse things that are coming. I see the need for there to be better explanations of Biblical and contemporary prophecies than I have found available in most churches. Later, during the earth's *Great Tribulation* period, there will be nothing anyone can do to help an entire population that finds themselves on their own in a meteorite storm, earthquakes and other plagues, without God and without hope saying *earnestly*:

Revelation 6:16-17 *"...to the mountains and rocks, Fall on us, and hide us from the face of him that sitteth on the throne, and from the wrath of the Lamb: For the great day of his wrath is come; and who shall be able to stand?"*

Modern Occurrences of Earthquake's Predicted by Prophecy

For some time it has been known scientifically that a good portion of the coast of California is just a shell that projects out over the water like a shelf. It is known that one can go out from the shoreline a short distance on the California coast and then it just drops off, there seeming to be no bottom. The largest part of California is washed out underneath. There are only upright supports holding the coastline of California.

Scientists inform us that the coastline of California is moving northwest at the rate of two inches a year. This places a great strain on the San Andreas Fault which extends from lower California to Palm Springs, near San Bernardino, then over to Palmdale and extending up to the San Francisco Bay area and to Point Arena. All this land west of the fault is moving every year. The stanchions or supports cannot move, as they are part of the ocean bed, making it necessary for them to incline or tip.

"One day these supports will tip enough that they cannot bear the weight of the land. This will be at the time of a Great Earthquake. The west side of the San Andeas fault will break off and slide into the sea."[474] This prediction was made in 2002, forty years after modern-day prophet William Branham began to prophesy about the destruction of the West Coast and specifically, the Los Angeles and Southern California coast.

On Thursday evening, 29th April 1965 at the Biltmore Hotel in Los Angeles, California, U.S.A. during his message entitled "Choosing of a Bride," Mr. Branham prophesied:

Thou city, who claims to be the city of the Angels ... remember, one day you'll be laying in the bottom of this sea. You're great honeycomb under you right now. The wrath of God is belching right beneath you. How much longer He'll hold this sandbar hanging over that, when that ocean out yonder a mile deep will slide in there plumb back to the Salton Sea ... Repent Los Angeles!

"That's solemn warning. We don't know what time. And you don't know what time that this city one day is going to be laying out here in the bottom of this ocean. 'O, Capernaum,' said Jesus, 'thou who exalted into heaven will be brought down into hell, for if the mighty works had been done in Sodom and Gomorrah, it'd have been standing till this day.' And Sodom and Gomorrah lays at the bottom of the Dead Sea, and Capernaum's in the bottom of the sea."

"Thou city, who claims to be the city of the Angels, who's exalted yourself into heaven and sent all the dirty filthy things of fashions and things, till even the foreign countries come here to pick up our filth and send it away, with your fine churches and steeples, and so forth the way you do; remember, one day you'll be laying in the bottom of this sea. You're great honeycomb under you right now. The wrath of God is belching right beneath you. How much longer He'll hold this sandbar hanging over that, when that ocean out yonder a mile deep will slide in there plumb back to the Salton Sea. It'll be worse than the last day of Pompeii. Repent, Los Angeles. Repent the rest of you and turn to God. The hour of His wrath is upon the earth. Flee while there's time to flee and come into Christ."
(Wm Branham, Los Angeles, CA, April 29, 1965)[475]

In a later sermon, Mr. Branham spoke about this prophecy. He explained that after making the prophecy, he had no memory of it, or of quoting Jesus' prophecy against Capernaum, implying that it was the Holy Spirit speaking through him at the time. He said:

"And while in there something struck me; I didn't know nothing for about thirty minutes. There was a prophecy went out. First thing I remember, Brother Mosley and Billy; I was out on the street, walking. And It said, 'Thou Capernaum, which calls yourself by the name of the Angels,' that's Los Angeles, city of angels (See?), the angels, 'which are exalted into heaven, will be brought down into hell. For if the mighty works had been done in Sodom, that's been done in you, it would've been standing till this day.' And that was all unconsciously to me. . ."

"And when I understood that, I went; I said, 'There is a Scripture about that somewhere.' And I went and found it was Jesus rebuking Capernaum by the seacoast. That night I looked up the Scriptures. Come home, got the history book; and Sodom and Gomorrah was once a--a thriving city, a Gentile headquarters of the world. And you know that city by an earthquake sank into the Dead Sea. And Jesus stood, and said, 'Capernaum, if Sodom would've had the works done in it that you've had done in you, it would've been standing today. But now you must be brought down to hell.' And about two hundred or three hundred years after His prophecy, with all them coastal towns, every one of them still standing but Capernaum, and it lays in the bottom of the sea. A earthquake sunk it into the sea."
(Wm Branham, *Ashamed*, Jeffersonville, IN, July 11, 1965)[476]

George Davis in his "Bible Prophecies Fulfilled Today" records that "an earthquake destroyed Capernaum about AD 400." Davis explains the situation of Capernaum:

Until recent excavation and partial renovation, for many centuries the synagogue that sat on northwestern shore of the Sea of Galilee lay buried under the earth like the rest of the destroyed sea-side city, many of the great building's stones removed out into the waters. Capernaum was literally sunk, according to the prophecy of Jesus.

Preceding the prophecies about California, Mr. Branham under Divine inspiration prophesied the beginning of the West Coast's destruction, the results of God's judgment against it. During a hunting trip to Sunset mountain in the Coronado Forest on March 25, 1964, William Branham was with his friend Banks Wood walking in a westerly direction when God told Mr. Branham, *"Throw up a rock, and say to Mr. Wood, 'THUS SAITH THE LORD, you'll see the Glory of God'."*

As Moses held his staff in faith over the Red Sea, Mr. Branham's action in throwing up the rock as the Lord had commanded symbolized the whirlwind that would manifest. The following day while Mr. Branham's hunting party was in camp, a powerful whirlwind came down and blasted pyramid-shaped rocks from the mountainsides, it also cut the tops off trees about three or four feet above Mr. Branham's head. This "whirlwind" made three big blasts, and fifteen men ran over asking, "What was that?"

Mr. Branham said, *"Judgment is striking the west coast."*[477] [478] Two days later, on March 28, 1964, an earthquake rocked Alaska;[479] this being explained as an advance warning to his yet-to-be-prophesied California Earthquake.

Below are some statistics that emphasize the power of the 1964 Alaska earthquake. [See endnote 448 for actual post-earthquake film footage.[480]] It was reported that the 1964 Alaskan earthquake actually moved mountains.[481] [482] The ground was lifted beneath such distant cities as Houston, Texas (four inches), and Cape Kennedy, Florida, and the levels of well water jumped abruptly as far away as South Africa.[483]

The reported Richter magnitudes (Ms) for this earthquake ranged from 8.4 to 8.6. The moment magnitude (Mw) is reported as 9.2. The depth, or point where the rupture began was about 14 miles within the earth's crust.

The strong ground motion reported in the Anchorage area lasted about 4-5 minutes which triggered many avalanches and landslides - some being tsunamigenic. Ground deformations were extensive with some areas east of Kodiak being raised by 30 feet and areas about Portage being dropped by 8 feet (Pflaker, 1964). The rise is estimated to come in two thrusts of about 5 meters each. The maximum intensity reported was XI on the modified Mercalli Intensity scale, indicating major structural damage, and ground fissures and failures. This scale is a 12-point one usually given in roman numerals ranging from I, (not felt/no damage) to XII (total destruction many lives lost). From this event, significant damage covered an area of about 50,000 square miles.

The Commerce Department's Coast and Geodetic Survey - more than three years after the Good Friday disaster - is still gathering data on the effects of the *strongest earthquake ever recorded on the North American continent",* states one top researcher.[484]

Some of its findings are incorporated in a technical report issued by the Environmental Science Services Administration. It said some Alaskan mountains subsided because of the quake, and that the sea floor in one area rose as much as fifty feet and a seismic wave was recorded in the Antarctic twenty-two and a half hours after the quake.[485]

"This giant wave", the report said, "had travelled 8,445 miles at 430 miles an hour. The earthquake caused one hundred thirty-one deaths and more than $750 million in damage not only in Alaska but along the US Pacific coast as well."

Here are some additional findings from the report: "The mountains on Kodiak Island and the Kenai Peninsula and the Chugach Mountains near Prince William Sound subsided seven feet or more. Earlier surveys revealed that some Kenai Peninsula Mountains shifted laterally about five feet".

"The ocean floor rose in an area 480 miles by 127 miles with the highest upheaval fifty feet - the biggest ever recorded - between Kodiak and Montague Islands. Shock waves oscillated the water as far away as Key West, 3,968 miles distant."[486]

Tsunamis generated by the 1964 earthquake (and their subsequent damage, loss of life, etc.) were recorded throughout the Pacific.[487] This was the most disastrous tsunami to hit the U.S. West Coast and

British Columbia in Canada. The largest wave height for this tsunami was reported at Shoup Bay, Valdez Inlet (67 meters).

This Alaskan earthquake fore-warned of the massive earthquake William Branham prophesied will sink Los Angeles:

"I remember just my last message in California, where I thought I'd never go back again, when I predicted Los Angeles will go beneath the ocean. And, THUS SAITH THE LORD, it will! She's done; she's washed; she's finished. What hour? I don't know when. But it will be sunk right after that the earthquakes begin to jerk and bound.

You remember, many of you men standing right there, that rock that day when that Angel came down there and that Light and Fire falling from the Heaven around the rock when we was standing there, rocks flinging out of the mountain, and falling across there. And she blasted three times, hard. I said, 'Judgment will strike the West Coast.' Two days after that, Alaska almost sunk.

Remember, that same God that said that, said Los Angeles is doomed. And she's finished. I don't know when, I can't tell you.

I didn't know I said that. But this brother here, I believe it was... No, one of the Mosleys, I believe, had me out on the street out there. I don't know what it was till I looked back. And I looked back in the Scripture, and Jesus said, "Capernaum, Capernaum, how oft . . . You that's exalted yourself (rather) up into Heaven shall be brought down into hell, for if the mighty works had been done in you that'd been done in Sodom, it would've stood today." And about a hundred and fifty years from there - Sodom had already in the earth - then Capernaum is in the water, too, today.

And that same Spirit of God that said all these things and done all these things, It said there, "O city, Capernaum, who called yourself by the name of the angels, Los Angeles. How you've exalted yourself into Heaven!" The very root and seat of Satan. See? "You've exalted yourself." Preachers, it's a graveyard for them. Good men go there and die like rats. What havoc!

"You that call yourself by the name of the angels, if the mighty works had been done in Sodom that'd been done in you, it'd stood today.

But your hour's come." You watch and see. If it ain't, I'm a false prophet. See? There she is, she's laying there." (Wm Branham, The Rapture, December 4, 1965)

"Fifteen hundred mile chunk of it three or four hundred miles wide will sink maybe forty miles down into that great fault out yonder one of these days, and waves will shoot plumb out to the state of Kentucky. And when it does, it'll shake the world so hard that everything on top of it will shake down" (Wm Branham, A Thinking Man's Filter, p. 25:145).

An unrelated, fictionalized account of this earthquake and disaster is recorded by Curt Gentry in *The Last Days of the Late, Great State of California*, published in 1967. In this book a titanic series of earthquakes ruptured the entire length of the San Andreas Fault, resulting in catastrophic loss of life and the first magnitude 9 rating ever given an earthquake (on the Richter Scale as then defined-on the modified version now in use many large quakes have exceeded magnitude 9). South of Los Angeles, a hitherto-unknown fault branched off and curved out to sea just south of San Diego. A few days later the initial earthquake was dwarfed as all of coastal California west of the fault plunged beneath the waves.

Though geologists, seismologists and oceanographers refute the claim that "California will break off and slide into the ocean," they do so based upon the assumption(s) that: A) there are no precedents for such a mass of land being displaced, and B) *ALL* of this land mass will literally *break off*, rather than dip, drop or tilt.

First, according to Louisiana State University geologist Roy K. Dokka, Southern California's coastline ***did*** fall into the ocean millions of years ago as a result of one of the biggest land mass movements known in geology. Within the Trans Mojave-Sierran shear zone, the coastal edge of this fragment was "sawed off."[488] Dokka states,

"If you were to go to Palm Springs and over to Phoenix, you'd find the middle of the Earth's crust sheared like you wouldn't believe. Oil companies have CAT-scanned the terrain, looking for oil in this area, because they think that basins may have formed in which minerals may have collected. In these areas, the crust looks like stacks of overturned dominoes lying on the sheared middle crust. People have never understood the origin of this. It was caused by this mass of land sliding over to the west. In its wake, the Sierra Nevada mountains twisted southward, and with it chunks of the Mojave. Present-day San Francisco was farther south than it is now and coastal California fell into the ocean."

Most people do not realize that California's geological foundation, at least the part that pertains to prophecy, is structurally unsound. These recent new fault discovery reports from petroleum and gas company exploration revealed multitudes of non-solid pockets of both gases and water. Some of these pockets are gigantic, labyrinthine caverns measure from a few feet to thousands of feet, averaging roughly about a 100 cubic feet. Much like dry caverns do, heights and depths vary a great deal and in some cases, two or more caverns or passageways pass over or under each other at different depths.

There are allegedly many subterranean cavities below the western U.S., and they are not limited to California, and many of them consist of very large water-filled aqua-systems. These have been explored via submersible to several hundred miles inland, particularly in the region of southern California and the southern Oregon-northern California area. Most of the entrances to these caverns lie just off the Continental Shelf (i.e. in the Continental Slope), and are said to have been explored by submersible craft and scuba divers for many years. The United States Navy is reported to have explored much of the Western North American continental shelf and many of its subterranean caverns and passageways in vessels as large as nuclear-class submarines.

If You're Going To Sink California, Do It Right, says geologist Steven Dutch

Today, scientific models suggest that it is plausible for a series of large earthquakes along the San Andreas fault line to cause a 1300 mile land mass to drop by one percent (1%), effectively submerging most affected coastal towns in 100 -300 feet of water.

In an article *If You're Going To Sink California, Do It Right*, geologist Steven Dutch theoretically explained how this catastrophe could happen:

"If we can't simply drop coastal California downward [due to the tectonic plates being stacked on top of each other all the way to the sea floor – ed.], that leaves one possible direction: seaward. We'd need a *nearly horizontal* fault plane sloping from near the surface along the San Andreas Fault to the base of the continental slope. That's about 11,500 feet below sea level off California. At the widest, around Los Angeles, we're talking a 1% slope. And is there such a thing? Well, yes, there is. It's called a *listric normal fault*."

"A normal fault is a fault where one of the two opposing blocks drops down the fault plane so the overall length of the crust increases. As the amount of extension increases the fault plane curves to near horizontal. With a simple, steeply dipping fault plane you can get a measly few percent extension, but with a listric fault the extension can be almost unlimited. As the extension increases, a gap opens along the steep segment of the fault and the upper fault block sags into the gap. Also, friction will cause the upper fault block to break up internally along subsidiary faults..."

"Of course, we need a reason for it to start sliding. We can picture the Pacific Plate starting to move more westerly than it now does and thereby relieving compressional stresses along the San Andreas Fault, enabling the block to begin slipping. Confined fluids are great for reducing friction along faults, and major thrust faults in the Coast Ranges are commonly associated with serpentine. Serpentine is a wonderfully slippery rock for fault zones."

"Assuming the deep part of the fault has a 1% slope, then if the upper block slips 10 kilometers seaward, it will drop 100 meters. That will nicely submerge all the coastal cities. Given the way the upper block will sag and fragment internally as it pulls away from the steep segment of the fault, we can probably submerge San Bernardino (300 meters above sea level). The internal breakup of the block will thoroughly devastate the surface. The block will essentially be an extremely large landslide. It will be way bigger than anything known, but not impossible…And the only thing we have to displace is sea water."[489]

William Branham had just finished preaching a series of meetings in Los Angeles in April 1965, when he was asked by the Full Gospel Business Men who organized the meetings to preach just one more service for them. So, on April 29, William Branham stood behind the podium at the Biltmore Hotel in Los Angeles, and preached a sermon called "Choosing of a Bride".

Just before his message that morning, his dear friend Sister Florence Shakarian had just sung a song. [Sister Florence had been sick for a long time and a few months previous, Brother Demos Shakarian had asked Brother Branham to pray for his sister, who was dying of cancer. At that time Brother Branham had been given a word from the Lord concerning Sister Florence. He told Demos that she would not die then, but that she would die before the coming of the Lord, that it would happen between 2 and 3 o'clock some morning, and that he had seen her lying in state.] At the end of her song, Brother Branham, sitting on the platform next to Brother Carl Williams, nudged Brother Carl and said, "Do you hear that?" Brother Carl asked him what he meant, and Brother Branham replied, "She's walking up the Golden Stairs, can't you hear her?"

At about this same time a man rose up and brought a forceful message in tongues, the kind often given in Pentecostal congregations. The interpretation came immediately from the other side of the auditorium: "Oh daughter of Zion, thou shalt not fear, thou shalt not worry, for thou shalt live to see the coming of the Lord." William Branham's son Billy Paul, in the audience that day, was deeply disturbed, for he knew that this message contradicted that which his dad had received from the Lord. The message had come with such force, authority and apparent anointing; yet he knew that the Angel of the Lord had never failed.

No explanation was forthcoming at this time and William Branham went on to deliver his message *Choosing of a Bride.*

Turn again now to the state of unrest that Billy Paul found himself in concerning the conflicting prophecy over Sister Shakarian on that day when the message in tongues had gone forth and Brother Branham had preached *Choosing of a Bride.* According to Rev. Pearry Green[490], as William Branham and his son were walking back to their hotel, he perceived that something was troubling Billy Paul and he said, *"Paul, what's wrong?"*

"Oh, nothing Dad," Billy replied.

After a few steps, Brother Branham asked again, "What's troubling you, Paul?"

"Well, Daddy," said Billy, "You heard that message of tongues and interpretation there."

"So what?" said the prophet.

"But Dad, you know that you said that the Angel of the Lord told you that she would die between 2 and 3 o'clock in the morning." [See Footnote 491 for the fulfillment of this prophecy][491]

Brother Branham did not speak against the tongues and interpretation, yet he replied: *"Well, all I can say is, Paul, that the Lord has not told me any different."*

After making this statement, he turned to his son and said, *"Billy, where are you standing?"*

May Company Building 1960's

"Downtown Los Angeles," Billy Paul replied.

"Where are you standing?" queried the prophet.

"In front of the May Company, downtown Los Angeles," replied Billy.

At this Brother Branham made a prophetic statement: "Billy," he said, "I may not be here, but you won't be an old man until sharks will swim right where we are standing."

May Company today - L.A. Museum of Art

Interestingly, after forty years, multiple renovations and a *Historic Building*[492] designation, the old May Company building is still around (so is Billy Paul Branham). I remember going from LAX to the Korean Consulate at the far end of Wilshire Boulevard in the late 1980's to pick up a travel visa. The drive from the airport to the consulate passed right by the old May Company building, I remember looking at all the large skyscrapers and in contrast this small building seemed so out of place. It struck me that if what William Branham said to his son was spoken as prophecy, the May Company building would have to remain standing that sharks could swim there.

Regarding these California earthquake prophecies, one article describes the event as "pulling the rug out from underneath California."[493] Researchers from Harvard University and the University of California, San Diego, discovered a "new" earthquake fault-line in the Los Angeles area in 1999.[494]

Scientists have for years believed that such faults, called blind thrusts, exist beneath the city. But this is the first solid proof that one is actually present, said Dr. James Dolan, a professor of geology at the University of Southern California.

"Los Angeles is caught in a vise," says John Shaw, an assistant professor of structural and economic geology at Harvard. "It is locked between converging sections, or plates, of Earth's crust, carrying North America and part of the Pacific Ocean floor. As the plates collide, rocks (a.k.a. pillars/stanchions) beneath the city are shattered and cut [sheared-ed.] by faults of many shapes and sizes."

John Shaw of Harvard University and Peter Shearer of the Scripps Institute of Oceanography co-authored the report using a new seismic velocity model based on rarely obtained information from the petroleum industry, including high-resolution, sonogram-like images of the fault itself. These reports show how seismic measurements reveal the land below Central and Southern Californian Coastal to be a vast area of non-solid pockets. This fault's actions describe the mechanism by which the rock pillars or stanchions that hold up much of California [the Continental Shelf] will be sheared off. This shearing process will allow the slight tilting of land mass necessary to submerge that 1300 plus mile portion of the California coast known as the San Andreas Fault.[495]

Though others have predicted California's destruction, many by earthquake, only William Branham has prophesied so plainly and with such graphical detail. Statements like; "You're great honeycomb under you right now. The wrath of God is belching right beneath you. How much longer He'll hold this sandbar hanging over that," so accurately align with very recent scientific descriptions of California's geology. The language is that of a layman, but the insight is divine in nature and the prophecy is of Almighty God. California will be "sunk" and will be the triggering event for the awful End of Days events that will occur during the Great Tribulation period – that's "thus saith the Lord."

21

Decision Time – Repent or Perish

Prophets are a part of God's plan. They have been used to instruct, foretell and to forewarn. Many people live their lives adversely to good health and often need warning before they change behavior. Sometimes the warning is intrinsic and other times extrinsic. Sometimes it takes a sharp rebuke or admonition from a respected individual – a doctor, close friend or spiritual leader. The cartoon character Calvin had it right when he said that everyone he knew needed a good swift kick in the butt!

America's destruction is on its way, and each person also will face judgment someday soon. Most civilized countries will not punish its citizens without just cause, and without warning. For the most part, laws serve as the main "warning" given to people about behavior and actions. Often signs are additionally posted to make sure that "ignorance" of the law is not used as an excuse for breaking the law.

The systems of mankind provide warnings before judgment and punishment. God also provides sufficient warning so that "men are without excuse." God uses humans to remind, to prophecy, to discern the secret details hidden in other's hearts and to live exemplary lives. He also has used the star systems, sacred and other types of writings/text, dreams, intuition and the natural world.

Warning before judgment can be seen within nature. There have been many documented instances of animal life preparing for and/or escaping from the dangers of natural catastrophes.

There is much anecdotal evidence suggesting that some animals have the ability to detect sensory stimuli which humans cannot-- even with our most sensitive technological instruments. That many animals have access to a perceptual range exceeding those of humans is scientifically well-established, but it also appears that many animals have sensory abilities not currently explained by traditional science.

Some people even claim that their pets have precognitive abilities, while others notice their animals act in peculiar ways just before an earthquake strikes.

Since the beginning of recorded history, virtually every culture in the world has reported observations of unusual animal behavior prior to earthquakes (and-- to a lesser extent-- volcanic eruptions, tsunamis, etc.), but conventional science has never been able to adequately explain the phenomenon.[496] [497] It is possible that animals are actually experiencing a form of pre-cognition, or they could be perceiving and responding to stimuli that currently science has no way to measure?[498] [499] [500] [501] [502]

The Scriptures enumerate the signs of the times and of the end of the world in Luke chapter 21. Christ declares that deceivers who claim to be the Son of God shall arise and draw many aside into powerless and/or false religions. There shall be wars and non-stop military conflicts; nation shall rise against nation, and kingdom against kingdom. There will be many great earthquakes, famines, and pestilences that happen with greater frequency and intensity year after year, likened to "birth pains" for the earth.

The signs of the times, and of the end of the world are fulfilling so rapidly and occurring so frequently that instead of professed Christians being awakened and activated to finish God's work in the earth, they are becoming accustomed to, anesthetized by, and blinded to these signs. Because of their love of this world, the very things that should be awakening them are putting most professed disciples to sleep, and into a false security. Jesus says to all such, "O ye hypocrites, you can discern the face of the sky; but can ye not discern the signs of the times." (Matthew 16:3)

Catastrophes are not to just provoke awe, they serve a greater purpose as signs of warning. These signs of our time carry more significance than a present miracle of nature; they point forward to a future disaster of epic proportion. To reemphasize; signs and portents come not to leave observers with mouths open in amazement; having gotten people's attention, they point beyond themselves toward a disastrous future. Each plague holds clues to what lay ahead for a stubborn, wayward population. Their futures will be determined on whether they gave heed to the signs (and the voice of those signs)[503] or not.

Signs/ portents come not to leave observers with mouths open in amazement;

Having gotten people's attention, they point beyond themselves toward a disastrous future. Each plague holds clues to what lay ahead for a stubborn, wayward population

A red light flashes at a railroad crossing when the train is coming; to prevent us from getting killed! A fire engine sounds a siren to warn us of its approach! An ambulance and police car flash lights when there is danger; the wail of their siren warns us to pull over and get out of the way. A fever warns us of sickness and infection.

All of these signals are good, and so are God's warning signs. They are just as effective to keep us from getting killed spiritually as the flashing lights at a railroad crossing are to keep us from getting killed physically! God loves us so much he has posted warning signs just for our protection when they are needed most.

Finally, God has used and continues to use His servants as living, breathing messengers that have cried out in warning to “flee the wrath” that is coming. In the Book of Revelation, its first chapter describes a visage of a glorified and soon-returning King of Heaven and

Earth. In verse 15 Jesus is described as having the "voice of many waters."

His voice was as the sound of many waters, of many rivers falling in together. He can and will make himself heard to those who are afar off as well as to those who are near. His gospel is a mighty stream, fed by the upper springs of infinite wisdom and knowledge and it has been heralded by the ministers of God for two thousand years.

There is nothing more melodious or musical than the babbling brook, or more thunderous than the rush of the cataract over the falls, and there is nothing more fearful to the criminal than the words of the Judge as he passes sentence; but how terrifying will be the sentence when with a strong voice the Son of Man shall say in the Judgment Day, "*Depart from me, ye cursed, into everlasting fire, prepared for the Devil and his angels*." Matthew 25:41.

"Have you never heard the rumbling and booming of ocean on the shore, when it has been lashed into fury and has been driven upon the cliffs? If you have, you have a faint idea of the melody of heaven.

It was "as the voice of many waters." But do not suppose that it is the whole of the idea. It is not the voice of one ocean, but the voice of many, that is needed to give you an idea of the melodies of heaven. You are to suppose ocean piled upon ocean, sea upon sea,-the Pacific piled upon the Atlantic, the Arctic upon that, the Antarctic higher still, and so ocean upon ocean, all lashed to fury, and all sounding with a mighty voice...

Or if the illustration, fails to strike, take another. We have mentioned here two or three times the mighty falls of Niagara. They can be heard at a tremendous distance, so awful is their sound. Now, suppose waterfalls dashing upon waterfalls, cataracts upon cataracts, Niagaras upon Niagaras, each of them sounding forth their mighty voices, and you have got some idea..."I heard a voice like the voice of many waters." Can you not hear it?"
(C. Spurgeon, December 28, 1856)[504]

"203 "Voice of many waters." What does waters represent? If you want to mark it down, turn to Revelations 17:15, and you'll find that the Bible said, "The waters which thou sawest is thickness, and multitudes, and people, and tongues." All right. "Voice..." What a horrible thing for a drifting soul on the sea of life, no pilot to guide him, a-loose, floating with the tides, to hear the roar of the great cataracts, the falls, what a horrible thing it would be to a soul drifting.

"Voice of many waters." What is His voice? It's the judgment; the voice of the ministers through the Holy Spirit, that's cried out to the people in every age, standing there. The voice of many waters cried out, thickness and multitudes. The voice of those seven stars in His hand to every church age, preaching the baptism of the Holy Ghost, the baptism in Jesus' Name, speaking in tongues, the power of God, the resurrection of Christ, the second coming, Divine judgment. The voice of many waters coming forth from this One that looked like the Son of man, many waters.

205 What it'll be to know that you set in meetings and heard that you should get right with God and receive the Holy Ghost, and a drifting soul to hear that voice speak out in that meeting that you set in, and heard the judgments of God preached, and refused it, the great falls just below you, the great cataracts that'll take you to your eternal doom.
...Oh, what will that be on that day when that voice thunders out of many waters, many church ages forming out?

209 Now, I want to ask you something else. Let me say something to you people that's [not] saved, let me say this to you.
Now, you drifting soul, you poor drifter that's drifting over that great cataract yonder, be careful. It'll be a horrible thing when you know that there's no saving for you then. You can't get saved then; you know your doom lays right before you. When you know within a few minutes you'll hear that voice speak out, "Depart from Me, you workers of iniquity, into everlasting fire which is prepared for the Devil and his angels." You'll know when you hear that great falls a-roaring of those voices of those meetings, while you're passing out of this [life]. Oh, what a horrible thing, what a nightmare. Don't let it happen to you, people. Repent, get right with God now, while you can get right."
(Wm Branham, Jeffersonville, IN December 12, 1960E)[505]

God has sent many, many warnings of various types – signs and wonders in the earth and heavens; ministry and even the great Elijah the prophet in these "Last Days"...what will you do? Are you willing to change, turn away from behaviors that violate the commands of God and serve the Living God?

The first step on the path to safety is to commit your life and self-will to Jesus Christ. Why Jesus Christ and not "God" or a "Higher Power?" Why? Jesus Christ is the only way of escape provided by God, *the* Higher Power.

For example, say you were in an industrial fire and needed to be rescued from danger and I was the safety administrator and hazardous materials representative. I would have the knowledge of what best to provide to you for your safety and to put the fire out, thus saving you from danger and possible death. Depending on the type of fire, various solutions might be offered. If I offered a way of escape and you chose not to use it, thinking you had a better plan or idea, you would most likely die.

> The Jewish prophet Daniel said that in the "Last Days" certain portions of sacred text would be illuminated. A prophet would arise to tell mankind about these revelations in order to prepare the world for the return of Jesus Christ and to warn them about the impending judgment.

Likewise, God, in His wisdom knew what/who/when/where to send to you and all humanity for its salvation. There really is not any other way; God provided a way of escape from destruction and damnation in the life and death of Jesus Christ.

After this decision has been made to listen and obey, then the instructions can be studied and followed – the path of safety and health ensured. These instructions are contained in the Bible and have been elaborated on and understanding provided by many individuals throughout the course of time. Some have provided their wisdom as an extension of their ministry and calling, others were called to this job of instruction and clarification. Reformers and prophets – messengers in every period in the church's history, have illuminated God's word, and both reminded and warned as well.

Pascal's Wager - *Memento Mori*: remember mortality.

Suppose you hear reports that your house is on fire and your children are inside. You do not know whether the reports are true or false. What is the reasonable thing to do - to ignore them or to take the time to run home or at least phone home just in case the reports are true? In a nutshell, this is what *Pascal's Wager* is.

Pascal's Wager is the name given to an argument due to Blaise Pascal for believing, or for at least taking steps to believe, in God. Pascal's project was a radical one: he sought to provide *prudential,* rather than *rational* reasons for believing in God. To put it crudely, we should wager that God exists because it is the *best bet*. Pascal maintained that we are incapable of knowing whether God exists or not, yet we must "wager" one way or the other. Reason cannot settle which way we should incline, but a consideration of the relevant outcomes supposedly can. Here is the first key passage:

"God is, or He is not. But to which side shall we incline? Reason can decide nothing here. There is an infinite chaos which separated us. A game is being played at the extremity of this infinite distance where heads or tails will turn up..." [506]

Wagering for God is a hedged-bet: the worst outcome associated with wagering for God (status quo) is at least as good as the best outcome associated with wagering against God (status quo); and if God exists, the result of wagering for God is strictly better that the result of wagering against God. A bet on God if God exists pays out all good things and eternal life; a wager against God rewards the gambler with untold misery (hell).

The Wager appeals not to a high ideal, like faith, hope, love, or proof, but to a low one: the instinct for self-preservation, the desire to be happy and not unhappy. Pascal well knew that it was a low ideal. If you believe in God only as a bet, that is certainly not a deep, mature, or adequate faith. But it is something, it is a start. But on that low natural level, it has tremendous force.

The most powerful part of Pascal's argument is not his refutation of atheism as a foolish wager but his refutation of agnosticism as impossible. “Riding the fence” is not a reasonable option. The agnostic says, "The right thing is not to wager at all." Pascal replies, "But you must wager. There is no choice. You are already committed [embarked]." We are not outside observers of life, but participants. We are like ships that need to get home, sailing past a port that has signs on it proclaiming that it is our true home and our true happiness. The ships are our own lives and the signs on the port say "God". The agnostic says he will neither put in at that port (believe) nor turn away from it (disbelieve) but stay anchored a reasonable distance away until the weather clears and he can see better whether this is the true port or a fake. Why is this attitude unreasonable, even impossible? Because we are moving. The ship of life is moving along the waters of time, and there comes a point of no return, when our fuel runs out, when it is too late. The Wager works because of the fact of death.

Suppose Romeo proposes to Juliet and Juliet says, "Give me some time to make up my mind." Suppose Romeo keeps coming back day after day, and Juliet keeps saying the same thing day after day: "Perhaps tomorrow." To paraphrase *Alice through the Looking Glass'* Red Queen, "Tomorrow is always a day away.”

Eventually, there comes a time when there are no more tomorrows. Then "maybe" becomes "no". Romeo will die. Corpses do not marry. Christianity is God's marriage proposal to the soul. Saying "maybe" and "perhaps tomorrow" cannot continue indefinitely because life does not continue indefinitely – Memento Mori. The weather will never clear enough for the agnostic navigator to be sure whether the port is true home or false just by looking at it through binoculars from a distance. He has to take a chance, on this port or some other, or he will never get home.

If God does not exist, it does not matter how you wager, for there is nothing to win after death and nothing to lose after death. But if God does exist, your only chance of winning eternal happiness is to believe, and your only chance of losing it is to refuse to believe. As Pascal says, "I should be much more afraid of being mistaken and then finding out that Christianity is true than of being mistaken in believing it to be true."

With each passing day I become more persuaded that the Seven Events prophesied in 1933 were meant to be delivered to our world at large. God intended that this generation, which may be the last generation, to be warned one more time before the destruction cycle begins and it is too late to repent or to change your course (or your wager…). Please, dear reader, consider your life before an all-seeing and all-knowing God, who is looking into your heart right this minute.

Once an atheist visited the great rabbi and philosopher Martin Buber and demanded that Buber prove the existence of God to him. Buber refused, and the atheist got up to leave in anger. As he left, Buber called after him, "But can you be *sure* there is no God?" That atheist wrote, forty years later, "I am still an atheist. But Buber's question has haunted me every day of my life." The Wager has just that haunting power.[507]

The betting window is closing very soon. The world stage is prepared, a prophet has come to bring warning, and America's judgment is pending -- are you ready? As "Dirty Harry" Callahan might say; "Ah, I know what you're thinking. Did he fire six shots or only five? Well, to tell you the truth, in all this excitement, I've kinda lost track myself. But being as this is a .44 Magnum, the most powerful handgun in the world, and would blow your head clean off, you've got to ask yourself one question: 'Do I feel lucky?'"[508] Well, do you?

Endnotes

Chapter 1

[1] Dowd, Maureen. *Team of Frenemies*. New York Times, November 15, 2008. Electronic Source.
<http://www.nytimes.com/2008/11/16/opinion/16dowd.html?_r=1&ref=opinion>

[2] Jacobs, Joseph. *English Fairy Tales*. London: David Nutt, 1890.

[3] Jan Thornhill (2002). *A Jataka Tale from India*. Maple Tree Press, Toronto. The story actually originates from the *Jataka Tales* of Buddhist Indian folklore. The basic motif and many of the elements of the tale can be found in the *Daddabha Jataka* (J 322). The *Jatakas* comprise a large body of folklore dating from around Gautama Buddha's time (6th century BCE) to the third century CE. However, this ancient version features a hare as the central character rather than a chicken, and the wise protagonist is a lion (the Bodhisattva or future Buddha).

[4] Aesop, *The Complete Fables*. New York : Penguin Books, 1998.

[5] Andersen, Hans Christian. *Anderson's Fairy Tales*. 1993. Wordsworth Editions.

[6] BBC – Entertainment, Gay Tinky-Winky Bad for Children, 15 February, 1999.
http://news.bbc.co.uk/2/hi/entertainment/276677.stm

[7] Falwell, Jerry. Tinky-Winky Comes Out of the Closet. "Parents Alert" section in the *National Liberty Journal* February1999.

[8] Olbermann, Keith. MSNBC TV – Countdown, Will Sponge Bob Make you Gay? January 21, 2005. http://www.msnbc.msn.com/id/6852828/

[9] The Moral Majority Coalition, *What We Are All About: The Four-Pronged TMMC Platform*. 2007. "The thought of a Hillary Clinton … presidency is simply unacceptable (and quite frightening)."
http://www.moralmajority.us/index.php?option=com_content&task=view&id=12&Itemid=27

[10] Reed, David. Blue Helmets to Jerusalem, Ch.10. 2007. Online Book
http://www.bluehelmetstojerusalem.com/chapter10.htm

[11] Kelly, Reggie. Latest Developments in the Middle East. Ben Israel – The Burning Bush. Online Periodical. 2007.
http://www.benisrael.org/writings/currentevents/Latest_Developments_in_the_Middle_East_Crisis.html

[12] Branham, William. *Why We Are Not a Denomination* Jeffersonville, IN 1958-0927

[13] Every, David K. *Microsoft, Apple and Xerox – The History of the Graphical User Interface.* 1999. http://www.mackido.com/Interface/ui_history.html

[14] Horn, Bruce. *Xerox, Apple and Progress*. 2002. http://www.mackido.com/Interface/ui_history.html

[15] Twain, Mark. Letter to San Francisco *Alta California*, dated May 17, 1867; published June 16, 1867.

[16] Demosthenes 348 BC

[17] Warner, Edward III. Nuclear Deterrence Force Still Essential. (Assistant Secretary of Defense for Strategy and Threat Reduction). http://www.cnn.com/SPECIALS/2000/democracy/nuclear/views/

Excerpts from a prepared statement before the Strategic Forces Subcommittee, Senate Armed Services Committee, March 31, 1998.

[18] Presidential Initiative on Nuclear Arms. The White House. September 27, 1991. http://dosfan.lib.uic.edu/acda/factshee/wmd/nuclear/unilat/sandy.htm

[19] Gerth, Jeff, Van Natta, Don. Her Way: The Hopes and Ambitions of Hillary Rodham Clinton. 2007. Little, Brown.

[20] Carpenter, Amanda. *The Vast Right-Wing Conspiracy's Dossier on Hillary Clinton.* Regnery. 2006

[21] Baker, Peter and Solomon, John. *Books Paint Critical Portraits of Clinton.* Washington Post. May 25, 2007. A01

[22] http://www.ocf.berkeley.edu/~roseying/ids110/MTEST.HTM

[23] http://niwde.blogspot.com/2007/03/history-of-mens-swimwear.html

[24] Montgomery, L.M., *Rilla of Ingleside* (1921).

[25] *Pants for Women. St. James Encyclopedia of Popular Culture.* Thomson Gale. 2006
http://www.bookrags.com/history/pants-for-women-sjpc-04/

[26] Cain, James M. *Mildred Pierce.* 1941. Alfred A. Knopf

[27] Kinnear, Mary. *Daughters of Time – Women in the Western Tradition*. 1983. University of Michigan Press.

[28] The Motion Picture Code of 1930 a.k.a The Hays Code; http://en.wikipedia.org/wiki/Hays_code

[29] IBID

[30] Gallup Poll. (1937). *Would you vote for a woman for president if she were qualified in every other respect?* Roper Poll on Lexis Nexis, Accession #0279248.

[31] Winick, Lyric Wallwork. *Is It Time for a Woman President?*. Parade. April, 2006.

[32] May-June 2003 Gallup Poll; December 2006 Newsweek Poll; July 2007 Newsweek Poll; March 2007 Gallup Poll as cited in *Center For American Women and Politics*. Eagleton Institute of Politics – Rutgers University. 2008.

[33] Branham, William. *God Keeps His Word*. Jeffersonville, IN. April 07, 1957.

[34] Leviticus 25. The King James Version of the Bible.

[35] Exodus 21:6; Romans 6; 2 Chronicles 36:21. The King James Version of the Bible.

[36] Slate, Chuck. *Caution! Hillary: America's First Dictator*. Trafford. 2005

[37] Cox, Ana Marie. *Noted*. The Atlanta Journal-Constitution, 8/27/06 (A Time Magazine writer).

[38] O'Beirne, Kate, Op-Ed, *"Hillary Prepares – With Her Eye On The Oval, The Senator Pretends She's Out Of Center Field,"* National Review, 9/23/05

[39] Williams, Ron, Op-Ed, *"Hillary Ran Through Cash In Easy Race,"* The [Wilmington, DE] News Journal, 11/22/06.

[40] Fox News' *Hannity & Colmes*, October 13, 2006. In a YouTube video clip: http://www.youtube.com/watch?v=AJankEVDsxs

[41] Fox News' *The Big Story with John Gibson, October 16, 2006. In a video clip at Media Matters For America.* http://mediamatters.org/items/200610190002

[42] Noonan, Peggy. *The Case Against Hillary Clinton*. 2000. HarperCollins.

[43] At the Republican National Convention in Chicago in June 1920, the Republicans went through four votes without deciding upon a candidate and adjourned until the next morning. A series of predawn meetings took place in suite number 404 in the Blackstone Hotel. The phrase "smoke-filled room," used to describe the suite is still used to refer to a meeting where political deals are made. The meeting in the original smoke-filled room was controlled by Republican senators, including Henry Cabot Lodge of Massachusetts, Charles Curtis of Kansas, and James E. Watson of Indiana. After consulting with state leaders, the group agreed that Harding should be nominated. The next day the convention proceeded as planned, and on the tenth ballot, Harding received 692.5 votes and was nominated for president.

http://www.brainyquote.com/quotes/quotes/f/franklind164126.html

[44] http://www.theempressproject.com/

[45] Jefferson, Thomas. In a letter to William S. Smith in 1787.

[46] Hatley, Christopher N., *The Empress Project Review*. January 27, 2007. http://www.amazon.com/review/product/1597811238?filterBy=addFiveStar

[47] Hatley, Christopher N., *A True Work of Literary Art*, Amazon.com, January 25, 2007 Electronic source: http://www.amazon.com/gp/product/customer-reviews/1597811238/ref=cm_cr_dp_all_top/103-6551248-4894227?ie=UTF8&n=283155&s=books#customerReviews

[47] Gibbon, Edward. *The History of the Rise and Fall of the Roman Empire*. Macmillan, 1914. Digitized October 21, 2005.

[49] Maranis, David, *First Lady Launches Counterattack,* Washington Post, Wednesday, January 28, 1998; Page A01

[50] *The Political Personality of New York Senate Candidate Hillary Rodham Clinton* by Aubrey Immelman & Aví A. T. Bahadoor. Research paper, Unit for the Study of Personality in Politics, Saint John's University and the College of Saint Benedict, April 2000.

[51] *Hillary as Dictator*, YouTube video spoof, http://www.youtube.com/watch?v=6h3G-lMZxjo&mode=related&search=, 2007.

[52] Weisberg, Jacob. *But Why Can't Hillary Win? Clinton's electability problem.* Slate.msn.com. July 29, 2005.

[53] http://www.asseenontv.com/prod-pages/playpainodvd.html

[54] Goebbels, Jospeh. *Aus Churchills Lügenfabrik*, January 12, 1941. Die Zeit ohne Beispiel

[55] Are Lies More Believable Than The Truth? - Psychological Effects of Lying. Jet Magazine. Jan 22, 2001.
http://findarticles.com/p/articles/mi_m1355/is_6_99/ai_69698454

[56] Sullivan, Bob. *Study: ID Thieves Are Strangers*, Often Women. 10/22/2007.
http://redtape.msnbc.com/2007/10/study-id-thieve.html

[57] Small, Kevonne. *Female Crime in the United States, 1963-1998: An Update.* June 22, 2000. Gender Issues. Transaction Publishers.
http://www.accessmylibrary.com/coms2/summary_0286-1901759_ITM

[58] Crime & Violence - *Perpetrators and types of crime.* Uniited Nations Economic Commission for Europe, Gender Issues. 2007.
http://unece.org/gender/genpols/keyinds/crime/perps.htm

[59] Giddons, Anthony. *Sociology,* 5th Rev. Crime and Gender – Crime Rates. P. 815. 2006. Polity Press.

[60] *Crime in the United States - 2006*. U.S. Department of Justice — Federal Bureau of Investigation (FBI). September 2007
http://www.fbi.gov/ucr/cius2006/data/table_01.html

[61] Griffin, Em. *A First Look at Communication Theory*, 3rd Rev. Ch. 16. 1997 McGraw-Hill.
http://www.csudh.edu/dearhabermas/cognitivediss01bbk.htm

[62] Are Lies More Believable Than The Truth? - Psychological Effects of Lying. Jet Magazine. Jan 22, 2001.
http://findarticles.com/p/articles/mi_m1355/is_6_99/ai_69698454

[63] IBID

[64] Bruck, Connie. *Hillary the Pol*, New Yorker Magazine. May 30, 1994

[65] Immelman, Audrey. *The Character of Hillary Rodham Clinton.* Journal of the Psychohistory Forum, vol. 7, no. 2 (September 2000), pp. 65-66

[66] Branham, William, in an electronic message *God Keep His Word* preached in Jeffersonville, IN. 1957.

[67] Allen, Garland E., *Was Nazi eugenics created in the US?*, Embo Reports, 2004.

[68] Robert Proctor, *Racial hygiene: Medicine under the Nazis* (Cambridge, MA: Harvard University Press, 1988), and Gisela Bock, "Nazi sterilization and reproductive policies" in Dieter Kuntz, ed., *Deadly medicine: creating the master race* (Washington, D.C.: United States Holocaust Memorial Museum, 2004).

[69] An overview of U.S. eugenics and sterilization is in Daniel Kevles, *In the name of eugenics: Genetics and the uses of human heredity* (New York: Knopf, 1985).

[70] On California sterilizations and their connection to the Nazi program, see: Stefan Kühl, *The Nazi connection: Eugenics, American racism, and German National Socialism* (New York: Oxford University Press, 1994); Alexandra Stern, *Eugenic nation : faults and frontiers of better breeding in modern America* (Berkeley: University of California Press, 2005); and Wendy Kline, *Building a better race: gender, sexuality, and eugenics from the turn of the century to the baby boom* (Berkeley: University of California Press, 2001).

[71] George Santayana (1905) *Life of Reason* vol. I, ch. XII Charles Scribner's Sons

[72] Olson, Barbara. *Hell to Pay: The Unfolding Story of Hillary Rodham Clinton.* Page 103. 1999. Regnery.

[73] Rodham, Hillary. Harvard Educational Review, 43, 4, 487-514, 1973.

[74] Rodham, Hillary, “Children’s Rights: A Legal Perspective.” *In Children’s Rights: Contemporary Perspectives*, ed. Patricia A. Vardin and Ilene n. Brody (New York: Teachers College Press, 1979), pp.19.

[75] YouTube: http://www.youtube.com/watch?v=brt4YFnMdZ8

[76] Mathew 24:4-5. The King James Version of the Bible.

[77] Revelation 12:9. The King James Version of the Bible.

[78] Revelation 12:9. The King James Version of the Bible.

[79] Revelation 13:5-7. The New International Version of the Bible (NIV).

Chapter 2

[80] Brown, Dan. The Da Vinci Code (2003) p. 1 [“All descriptions of artwork, architecture, documents, and secret rituals in this novel are accurate.”]

[81] Branham, William. *Why We Are Not a Denomination.* Jeffersonville, IN V-11 N-7R 1958-0927 ¶5-2

[82] Branham, William. *Conference*. Shreveport, LA. 1960-1125 ¶2-6

[83] Branham, William. *Why*. Shreveport, LA. 1960-1126 ¶E-92

[84] Branham, William. *Painted Face Jezebel*. Chicago, IL 1956-1005 ¶E-26

[85] Branham, William. *Condemnation By Representation*. Jeffersonville, IN V-2 N-13 1960-1113 ¶5-2

[86] Branham, William. *The Ephesian Church Age*. Jeffersonville, IN ROJC 131-183 1960-1205 ¶48

[87] Branham, William. *The Seventieth Week of Daniel*. Jeffersonville, IN DA 89-141 1961-0806 ¶206

[88] Author Unknown. *Our Catholic Roots 1492-1865*. Electronic Source: < http://www.cyberfaith.com/examining/roots07.html>

[89] Dinnerstein, Leonard, et.al. *Natives and Strangers: A Multicultural History of Americans*. Oxford University, 2003. Page 90.

[90] Sheen, Fulton J. *Treasure in Clay: The Autobiography of Fulton J. Sheen*. 1993. Page 359, St. Francis of Assisi Books.

[91] Burke, Daniel. *A Catholic Wind in the White House*. Washington Post. April 13, 2008; B02. Electronic Source: <http://www.washingtonpost.com/wp-dyn/content/article/2008/04/11/AR2008041103327_pf.html>

[92] **"Why are there so many Christian denominations?"** To answer this question, we must first differentiate between 1) denominations within the body of Christ and 2) non-Christian cults and false religions. Presbyterians and Lutherans are Christian denominations; Mormons and Jehovah's Witnesses are cults (groups claiming to be Christian but denying one or more of the essentials of the Christian faith); Islam and Shintoism are non-Christian religions. The rise of denominations within the Christian faith can be traced back to the Protestant Reformation, the movement to "reform" the Roman Catholic Church during the 16th century.

There seems to be at least two major problems with denominationalism. First, nowhere in Scripture is there a mandate for denominationalism; to the contrary the mandate is for union and connectivity. Thus, the second problem is that history tells us that denominationalism is the result of, or caused by, one group obtaining divine revelation that creates conflict and confrontation which leads to division and separation. Jesus told us that a house divided against itself cannot stand. This general principle can and should be applied to the church. We find an example of this in the

Corinthian church which was struggling with issues of division and separation. There were those who thought that they should follow Paul and those who thought they should follow the teaching of Apollos, 1 Corinthians 1:12, "What I am saying is this: each of you says, "I'm with Paul," or "I'm with Apollos," or "I'm with Cephas," or "I'm with Christ." This alone should tell you what Paul thought of denominations or anything else that separates and divides the body. But let's look further; in verse 13, Paul asks very pointed questions, "Is Christ divided? Was it Paul who was crucified for you? Or were you baptized in Paul's name?" This makes clear how Paul feels, he (Paul) is not the Christ, he is not the one crucified and his message has never been one that divides the church or would lead someone to worship Paul instead of Christ. Obviously, according to Paul, there is only one church and one body of believers and anything that is different weakens and destroys the church (see verse 17). He makes this point stronger in 3:4 by saying that anyone who says they are of Paul or of Apollos is carnal.

After years of Catholic rule where true doctrine was replaced with dogma, creed and traditions that were not based entirely on the Scripture, Christianity entered into what is known historically as "the Dark Ages." As the truth was gradually taken away from God's people, their lives and faith became corrupted and they were impure. Since God could only marry a "virgin", someone that was faithful to Him, he had to restore His Word (Joel 2:28), so eventually there would be a group of followers that he could marry. Using key figures and movements such as Martin Luther, John Wesley, Pentecostalism and William Branham, God progressively restored His Word (and His Bride by extension) through correct interpretation of Scripture.
Typically, once a man or group received revelation, they stopped progressing and refused further revelation or correction. Once any man or group refused further revelation, they in a sense refused more of God and became both a harlot to Him, as well as spiritually dead. These are the denominations that the Bible calls "harlots." (Revelation 17:5)

Jesus Christ is head or sovereign of both His church and bride. The original usurpation began with Lucifer who had designs to ascend above his station, and ultimately above God. (Isaiah 14:7) To usurp his authority is cause for separation and eventual death. It is sin and unfaithfulness, whether the rebellion and usurpation is overt and direct as it has been with the Roman Catholic church (How much she has glorified herself…I sit as queen and am no widow – Revelation 18:7) or subtle as the denominations ("We will eat our own bread, and wear our own apparel, [we will do as we please] only let us be called by thy name." Isaiah 4:1). Thus we have both the Great Whore and her daughters the harlots. (Revelation 17:5)

[93] *The Catholic Encyclopedia* (Thomas Nelson, 1976), s.v. "Rome."

[94] Karl Keating, *Catholicism and Fundamentalism: The Attack on "Romanism" by "Bible Christians"* (Ignatius Press, 1988), p. 200.

[95] Robert Broderick, ed., *The Catholic Encyclopedia* (Thomas Nelson, Inc., 1976), pp. 103-04.

[96] Thompson, R.W. *The Papacy and the Civil Power* (New York, 1876), p. 82

[97] James, Walter. *The Christian in Politics* (Oxford University Press, 1963), p. 47.

[98] R.W. Southern, *Western Society and the Church in the Middle Ages,* vol. 2., Pelican History of the Church series (Penguin Books, 1970), pp. 24-25.

[99] Cormenin, *History of the Popes*, p. 243, as cited in R.W. Thompson, op. cit., p. 368.

[100] Jeremiah 13:16. Holy Bible, King James Version

[101] 2 Peter 2:12-22. Holy Bible, King James Version

[102] Habakkuk 2:2. Holy Bible, King James Version

[103] Revelation 5:1-5; 10:1-7. Holy Bible, King James Version

[104] 2 Thessalonians 2:7. Holy Bible, King James Version

[105] Deuteronomy 6:1-8. Holy Bible, King James Version

[106] Exodus 13:1-10; Exodus 13:11-16; Deuteronomy 6:5-9; Deuteronomy 11:13-21. Holy Bible, King James Version

[107] Film and transcript of *The Coronation of Pope Pius XII*, March 12, 1939. Electronic source <http://biblelight.net/Coronation-1939.htm>.

[108] *Our Sunday Visitor* (Catholic Weekly). "Bureau of information," Huntington, IN, April 18, 1915.

[109] Electronic Facsimile <http://www.aloha.net/~mikesch/OSV1914.gif>

[110] *Dizionario di erudizione storico-ecclesiastica da S. Pietro sino ai nostri giorni* (Dictionary of Historical-Ecclesiastical Erudition from St. Peter to the Present), by Gaetano Moroni, 103 volumes and 6 volumes of indexes printed in Venice by Tipografia Emiliana between 1840 and 1861.

[111] Electronic facsimile < http://biblelight.net/Sources/Moroni-Vol99-p21.gif>

---

[112] *Catholic Dictionary*, Peter M.J. Stravinskas, Editor, published by Our Sunday Visitor, Inc., Huntington, 1993, pp. 484-485.

[113] Gratian, Johannes. *Concordantia discordantium canonum* (Concordance of Discordant Canons), also known as *Decretum Gratiani* or *Corpus Juris Canonici,* a collection of canon law published about 1140 A.D.

[114] Electronic Source < http://www.aloha.net/~mikesch/666.htm#history> The Bavarian State Library of Germany has a digitized searchable 1879 version of *Corpus Iuris Canonici* available online, including scans of all the pages (page 342 in GIF [low resolution] and PDF format [high resolution]). The relevant section is found under the following headings:
CONCORDIA DISCORDANTIUM CANONUM AC PRIMUM DE IURE NATURAE ET CONSTITUTIONIS - DISTINCTIO XCVI.
- C. XIV. De eodem.
< http://mdz.bib-bvb.de/digbib/gratian/text/@Generic__BookView;cs=default;ts=default?q=uicarius+Filii+Dei&DwebQueryForm=%24q>

[115] Quasten, Johann Dr. *The Vicarius Filii Dei Document*. Washington, DC, 1943. Electronic Facsimile < http://www.aloha.net/~mikesch/quasten.jpg>

[116] Deusdedit cardinals…collection canonum, ed. A P. Martinucci. Oxford, 1869. Page 343. Digitized August 30, 2006.

[117] *The Temporal Power of the Vicar of Jesus Christ*, by Henry Edward Manning, D.D. (appointed Archbishop of Westminster in 1865 and Cardinal in 1875), second edition with a preface, published in 1862 in London by Burns & Lambert, 17 &18 Portman Street.

[118] Martin, Malachi. *The Keys of This Blood.* Simon Schuster, NY 1990.

[119] E. M. Blaiklock, *The Archaeology of the New Testament*, Zondervan, Grand Rapids, 1970, pp. 131, 277.

[120] Timothy 2:9. Holy Bible, King James Version

[121] Carroll, Warren H., *The Building of Christendom*, 1987, Page 11. ISBN 0-931888-24-7

[122] Eusebius, *The Life of the Blessed Emperor Constantine*, Book 3, Chapter 10.

[123] Carroll, Warren H., *The Building of Christendom*, 1987, Page 11. ISBN 0-931888-24-7

[124] Brown, Dan. *The Da Vinci Code* (2003) p. 407

Chapter 3

[125] Patrick T. Reardon, "There are No Sure Bets in Figuring Out Why We Wager," Chicago Tribune, 9 December 1994, pp. 36.

[126] Marfels, Christian. *Gaming Law Review and Economics*. April 1, 2008, 12(2): vii-ix. doi:10.1089/glre.2008.12214.

[127] Dekel, Eddie & Scotchmer, Suzanne, 1999. "*On the Evolution of Attitudes towards Risk in Winner-Take-All Games*," Journal of Economic Theory, Elsevier, vol. 87(1), pp. 125-143, July.

[128] Albert Einstein, *In a letter to Max Born, 1926.*

[129] Grinder, John and Bandler, Richard. *The Structure of Magic I: A Book About Language and Therapy.* Science and Behavior, 1989.

[130] *Willy Wonka and the Chocolate Factory*, 1971. Paramount Pictures. Based on the 1964 Roald Dahl book *Charlie and the Chocolate Factory.*

Chapter 5

[131] Calaprice, Alice. *The Expanded Quotable Einstein*, PUP, ISBN 0-691-07021-0

[132] The Ante-Nicene Fathers; *1 Clement* Chapter 23, ¶99

[133] Electronic source: http://www.ccel.org/ccel/schaff/anf01.ii.ii.xxiii.html.

[134] *Einstein and Religion* by Max Jammer, Princeton University Press

[135] *The Quotable Einstein*, Princeton University Press

[136] Larkin, Clarence. *Rightly Dividing the Word.* Kessinger, 2003. Page 11-12. ISBN 9780766177611

[137] Pember, G.H. *Earth's Earliest Ages*. Kregel, 1987. ISBN 082545331

[138] Genesis 1:1, 28; Isaiah 45:18; Jeremiah 4:23-26; Ephesians 6:12; 2 Peter 3:5-7. Bible, King James Version.

[139] Dalrymple, G. Brent. *The Age of the Earth.* Stanford University, 1991. Page 492.

[140] Psalm 29:10 – Bible, New American Standard Version

[141] Dake, Finis J. *God's Plan for Man*. Dake, 1990. ISBN 978-1558290266

[142] Scofield References Notes online, verse by verse notes on Genesis 1. Electronic source: <http://www.studylight.org/com/srn/view.cgi?book=ge&chapter=001>

[143] G. H. Pember, *Earth's Earliest Ages*, New Edition, edited with additions by G. H. Lang (Grand Rapids: Kregel Publications, 1975), p. 31. (The original work of Pember, under the same title, was initially published in 1876 by Hodder and Stoughton. Later editions were issued by Pickering and Inglis and the Fleming H. Revell Co.)

[144] Isaiah 24:20 – Bible, King James Version

[145] Malachi 3:6; James 1:17 – Bible, King James Version

Chapter 6

[146] Frankl, Viktor. *Man's Search for Meaning*. Pocket, 1997.

[147] Thompson, William I., *The Time Falling Bodies Take to Light*, Page 24-25.

[148] Craig, William Lane. *The Only Wise God.* Wipf and Stock Pub., 1999.

[149] Thomas Flint, "Prophecy, Freedom and Middle Knowledge", in K. J. Clark, ed., *Our Knowledge of God* (Dordrecht: Kluwer, 1992), pp. 151–165. Substantially the same account is given in Chapter 9 of Thomas Flint, *Divine Providence: The Molinist Account*, Ithaca and London: Cornell University Press, 1998.

[150] Shafer, Brian D., *Chronicles of the Host: Exile of Lucifer.* Destiny Image, 2002.

[151] Acts 7:49 - Bible, King James Version

Chapter 7

[152] Ward, Peter and Brownlee, Donald. *Rare Earth*. Copernicus, 2000.

[153] Ross, Hugh. *The Creator and the Cosmos*. Navpress, 1993.

[154] Ross, Hugh. *The Creator and the Cosmos*. Navpress, 1993. pp. 135-136

[155] Robert Jastrow, *God and the Astronomers*, 1992, pp. 117

[156] Michael Denton, *Nature's Destiny* (New York: The Free Press, 1998), pp. 127-131.

[157] Guillermo Gonzales, "Is the Sun Anomalous?" *Astronomy & Geophysics,* 1999.

[158] Walter Dehnen and James J. Binney, "Local Stellar Kinematics from Hipparcos Data," *Monthly Notices of the Royal Astronomical Society 298* (1998), 387-394.

[159] Bienayme, O. *Astronomy and Astrophysics* 341 (1999), pp. 86.

[160] Peter D. Ward and Donald Brownlee, *Rare Earth* (New York: Copernicus, Springer-Verlag, 2000), xxviii, xxvii, 222-6.

[161] Bienayme, O. *Astronomy and Astrophysics* 341 (1999), pp. 137-138.

[162] Achenbach, J. "Life Beyond Earth," *National Geographic,* Jan. 2000, 29.

[163] Ross, H. 1998. *Big Bang Refined by Fire.* Reasons To Believe, Pasadena, CA.

[164] Carter, Brandon . *Large Number Coincidences and the Anthropic Principle in Cosmology* (Boston, MA: Dordrecht-Holland, D. Reidel, 1974), pp. 291-298.

[165] *Cicero,* quoted by Dennett 1995, p. 29, (Gjertsen 1989, pp. 199)

[166] Einstein, Albert. *"Science, Philosophy and Religion: a Symposium", 1941US - (German-born) physicist (1879 - 1955)*

[167] *Voltaire,* From Chapter 2 of A Treatise on Metaphysics, second version, 1736. Translated *by Paul Edwards*

.

[168] Darwin, C. R. 1872. *On the Origin of Species.* London: John Murray. 6th edition. pp. 421

[169] Whewell, William, 1833. *Astronomy and general physics considered with reference to natural theology.* W. Pickering, London, pp. 356

[170] *Richerson, Peter J. & Robert Boyd (2005),* Not by Genes Alone: How Culture Transformed Human Evolution, *Chicago, University of Chicago Press, ISBN 0-226-71284-2.,* pp. 152–153

[171] IBID pp. 50

[172] *Richerson, Peter J. & Robert Boyd (2005),* Not by Genes Alone: How Culture Transformed Human Evolution, *Chicago, University of Chicago Press, ISBN 0-226-71284-2.,* pp. 51–52

[173] Meredith, Lawrence, Meredith, George. *A Spiritual Journey of Mind and Body.* Humanics, 2000. Page 180.

[174] Sonneck, Krumpholz O.G.. *Beethoven Impressions by his Contemporaries.* Dover, 1967. *(page 31)*

Chapter 8

[175] Electronic Source. http://dictionary.reference.com/browse/prophet

[176] Gower, John. *For Want of a Nail.* 1390. Confesio Amantis.

[177] Hebrews 12:1. 2 Kings 6:8-23. The King James Version of the Bible.

[178] Mark 13:20. The King James Version of the Bible.

[179] Note: If time doesn't exist at the Planck scale, and if our souls are creatures of the Planck scale, then wouldn't that make our souls... *eternal?* Wouldn't that mean, in essence, that to describe the nature of reality at the Planck scale might be to describe... *Heaven?*

I only understand this at a very basic, quantum-physics-for-dummies level. Still, from the perspective of an interested if ignorant layperson, I find this notion of "Planck-Heaven," if you will, appealing. As I understand it, physicists believe that structures existing at Planck scales *cannot physically be observed* — not just because of technological limits, but for fundamental theoretical reasons relating to the Heisenberg uncertainty principle and, other suchlike scientific explanations. Therefore, if we postulate that the spiritual realm and the Planck realm are one and the same, we can put the spiritual realm into some sort of physical-world context *without* presuming to "know the mind of God," in Stephen Hawking's infamous words.

[180] Hawking, Stephen. (1988). *A Brief History of Time.* Bantam. pp.193.

[181] Stoner, Peter. *Science Speaks.* Chicago: Moody Press, 1969

[182] *Apologetics – Is the Bible God's Word.* Electronic Media. http://www.truthnet.org/Apologetics/6/

[183] *Scientific Dating of Elephantine Papyrus.* Electronic Media. http://www.harvardhouse.com/prophetictech/new/elephantine.htm

[184] Hosea 6:2, Psalms 16:10, 49:15, Psalms 68:18, 24:3. The King James Version of the Bible.

---

[185] Deuteronomy 11:13-14; Zechariah 12:10. The King James Version of the Bible.

[186] Wilkerson, David. *The Latter Rain!* January 9, 1995.
http://www.tscpulpitseries.org/english/1990s/ts950109.html

[187] The Latter Rain Page; http://latter-rain.com/eschae/latter.htm

[188] Numbers 11:29, 12:6, Deuteronomy 18:8, 2 Kings 20:10, Matthew 14:5, Acts 11:27. The King James Version of the Bible.

[189] Exodus 33:11. The King James Version of the Bible.

[190] Numbers 12:6. The King James Version of the Bible.

[191] Jeremiah 1:6. The King James Version of the Bible.

[192] The church of Christ is by definition the church that is *of* Christ, individuals that have been called out of the world and into Christ.

The church of God has been purchased by the blood of Christ (Acts 20:28). Jesus "gave Himself for us, that He might redeem us from every lawless deed and purify for Himself His own special people, zealous for good works" (Titus 2:14). "But you are a chosen generation, a royal priesthood, a holy nation, His own special people, that you may proclaim the praises of Him who called you out of darkness into His marvelous light" (1 Peter 2:9).

God's people must separate and sanctify themselves: "Do not be unequally yoked together with unbelievers. For what fellowship has righteousness with lawlessness? And what communion has light with darkness? And what accord has Christ with Belial? Or what part has a believer with an unbeliever? And what agreement has the temple of God with idols? For you are the temple of the living God. As God has said: 'I will dwell in them And walk among them. I will be their God, And they shall be My people.' Therefore 'Come out from among them and be separate, says the Lord. Do not touch what is unclean, and I will receive you. I will be a Father to you, and you shall be My sons and daughters, Says the Lord Almighty'" (2 Corinthians 6:14-18).

God's people do not remain in 'Babylon', a representation of false religion. "Come out of her, my people, lest you share in her sins, and lest you receive of her plagues" (Revelation 18:4).

The church is exclusive in the good sense of the word. This exclusiveness is based on God's word, not on human judgment. Salvation by grace is offered to all people

(Mark 16:15,16; Matthew 28:19; Revelation 22:17), but there are conditions: "Truly, these times of ignorance God overlooked, but now commands all men everywhere to repent" (Acts 17:30).

A person is added to the church by God Himself. We read about the establishment of the church: "Then those who gladly received his word were baptized; and that day about three thousand souls were added to them" (Acts 2:41). Peter had commanded: "Repent, and let every one of you be baptized in the name of Jesus Christ for the remission of sins" (Acts 2:38). Only those who believe, repent and are baptized for the forgiveness of sins, are added to the church. "And the Lord added to the church daily those who were being saved" (Acts 2:47). The church consists of those who are saved, who have been added by God Himself.

This is not simply 'joining a group'. It involves a spiritual cleansing, a rebirth, a new creation, a new citizenship. "Since you have purified your souls in obeying the truth through the Spirit in sincere love of the brethren, love one another fervently with a pure heart, having been born again, not of corruptible seed but incorruptible, through the word of God which lives and abides forever" (1 Peter 1:22,23). "Therefore, if anyone is in Christ, he is a new creation; old things have passed away; behold, all things have become new" (2 Corinthians 5:17). "For our citizenship is in heaven" (Philippians 3:20).

About the church at Jerusalem we read further: "And they were all with one accord in Solomon's Porch. Yet none of the rest dared join them, but the people esteemed them highly. And believers were increasingly added to the Lord, multitudes of both men and women" (Acts 5:12-14).

[193] Lindsey, Hal. *The Late Great Planet Earth.* 1998. 25th Edition. Zondervan

[194] *The New American Theology – A Gospel Found Between the Lines.* USA Rei-gious News. September 14, 2007.

[195] Revelation 22:19, Deuteronomy 18:8-22. The King James Version of the Bible

Chapter 9

[196] 1 Samuel 8:5-19. The King James Bible.

[197] Madison, James. *The Debates in the Federal Convention of 1787 Which Framed the Constitution.* Page 181. 1999. The Lawbook Exchange.

[198] Franklin, Benjamin. *Constitutional Convention of 1787. From the original manuscript of his speech.* Electronic source.
http://www.loc.gov/exhibits/religion/vc006642.jpg

[199] Washington, George. September 17, 1796. (Electronic source:
http://www.ushistory.org/valleyforge/youasked/060.htm).
Johnson, William J. *George Washington, the Christian.* Nashville, TN: Abingdon Press, 1919.

[200] Ferris, Robert G. (editor). *Signers of the Constitution: Historic Places Commemorating the Signing of the Constitution*, published by the United States Department of the Interior, National Park Service: Washington, D.C. (revised editions 1975 and 1976)

[201] Lossing, B. J. *Signers of the Declaration of Independence*, George F. Cooledge & Brother: New York (1848)

[202] Electronic Source:
http://www.adherents.com/gov/Founding_Fathers_Religion.html

[203] *Adams, John. In a letter written to Thomas Jefferson, October 11, 1798*

[204] The Chinese call it "ling chi" or the "lingering death." First implemented in 960 A.D., the Chinese torture technique uses slow, shallow, slicing so as to not kill the victim. While no single cut is lethal, the combination of hundreds of small cuts eventually leads to death.

[205] Maier, Thomas. *The Kennedys: America's Emerald Kings*. Page 162. Basic Books, 2004.

[206] Franklin, Benjamin (1706–90). Pennsylvania Assembly: Reply to the Governor, November 11, 1755.—*The Papers of Benjamin Franklin,* ed. Leonard W. Labaree, vol. 6, p. 242 (1963). Electronic source: http://www.bartleby.com/73/1056.html

[207] Kissinger, Henry Dr. Bilderberger Conference, Evians, France, 1991.

[208] Ketcham, Ralph. *James Madison: A Biography*. Page 351. 1990. University of Virginia Press.

[209] Roosevelt, Franklin D. *Requiring Gold...to Be Delivered to the Government.* Electronic source: http://en.wikisource.org/wiki/Executive_Order_6102

[210] Umpenhour, Charles M. *Freedom, a Fading Illusion*. 2005. Page 127. BookMakers Ink.

[211] Branham, William. *Invasion of the USA.* Jeffersonville, IN. May 9, 1954. ¶204

[212] *Emergency Limitations and Restrictions*. Electronic source: http://www.law.cornell.edu/uscode/12/95.html

[213] Reagan, Ronald. *Federal Regional Councils*. Electronic source: http://en.wikisource.org/wiki/Executive_Order_12407

[214] Electronic source: http://www.archives.gov/federal-register/executive-orders/1983.html

[215] Electronic source: http://www.archives.gov/federal-register/executive-orders/1972.html

[216] Electronic source http://www.archives.gov/federal-register/executive-orders/about.html

[217] Electronic source: http://www.fas.org/irp/offdocs/pdd/index.html

[218] Electronic source: http://www.loc.gov/rr/news/directives.html

[219] Electronic source: http://www.law.cornell.edu/constitution/constitution.articleii.html

[220] Electronic sources: http://www.archives.gov/federal-register/executive-orders/; http://en.wikisource.org/wiki/Category:United_States_executive_orders; http://www.presidency.ucsb.edu/executive_orders.php

[221] Electronic source: http://www.archives.gov/federal-register/executive-orders/pdf/12846.pdf; http://findarticles.com/p/articles/mi_m2889/is_n17_v29/ai_14107926

[222] Bennet, James . "True to Form, Clinton Shifts Energies Back to U.S. Focus," The New York Times, 10 July 1998, A10.

[223] Fox, Jeffrey C. *What is an Executive Order?*, Electronic source: Accessed August 7, 2006, thisnation.com, What is an Executive Order?.

[224] Staff Writer. *Chairman Hansen Accuses Clinton Administration of "Abuse of Power."* June 17, 1999. Electronic source: http://www.cnsnews.com/ViewEnviro.asp?Page=%5CEnviro%5Carchive%5CENV19990617b.html

[225] Electronic source: http://www.gpoaccess.gov/nara/index.html

---

[226] Electronic source: http://www.law.cornell.edu/constitution/constitution.articleiv.html

[227] *National Defense Industrial Resources Preparedness*. Electronic source: http://www.archives.gov/federal-register/executive-orders/pdf/12919.pdf

[228] Bush, George W. *The USA Patriot Act*. UNITING AND STRENGTHENING AMERICA BY PROVIDING APPROPRIATE TOOLS REQUIRED TO INTERCEPT AND OBSTRUCT TERRORISM (USA PATRIOT ACT) ACT OF 2001. Electronic source: http://patriotact.com/patriot-act-1.html

[229] Bush, George W. *Justice Enhancement and Domestic Security Act of 2003*. Electronic source: http://fl1.findlaw.com/news.findlaw.com/hdocs/docs/cngrss/jenhact10703s22.pdf

[230] Bush, George W. *National Security and Homeland Security Presidential Directive*. Electronic source: http://www.whitehouse.gov/news/releases/2007/05/20070509-12.html

[231] Thomas I. Cook, ed., *Two Treatises of Government*, by John Locke (New York: Hafner, 947), pp. 203-207; Edward S. Corwin, *The President: Office and Powers, 1787-1957*, fourth revised edition (New York: New York University Press, 1957), pp. 147-148.

[232] 93d Congress, SENATE Report No. 93-549. *Emergency Powers Statutes*. 1973. Electronic source: http://www.givemeliberty.50megs.com/emergency_powers_statutes.htm

[233] Relyea, Harold C. *CRS Report to Congress. National Emergency Powers*. September 18, 2001. Electronic source: http://www.fpc.state.gov/documents/organization/6216.pdf

[234] Sturm, Albert L. "Emergencies and the Presidency," *Journal of Politics*, vol.11, Feb. 1949, pp. 125-126.

[235] Reynolds, Diana. Ph.D. *The Rise of the National Security State: FEMA and the NSC*. 1990. Electronic source: http://www.publiceye.org/liberty/fema/Fema_6.html.

Chapter 10

[236] Moore, R. Walton. George Mason, The Statesman. *The William and Mary Quarterly*, 2nd Ser., Vol. 13, No. 1 (Jan., 1933), pp. 10-17

[237] Murphy v. Ramsey, 114 US 44, 45, 29 L. ed. 57, 6 Sup. Ct. Rep. 747, 1885.

[238] Fernandez, Dominique . *Le Rapt de Ganymède* (Paris: Grasset, 1989), p. 233.

[239] Wittig, Monique. *Paradigm* in George Stambolian and Elaine Marks (editors), Homosexualities and French Literature: Cultural Contexts, Critical Texts (Ithaca and London: Cornell University Press, 1979), p. 114.

[240] Foucault, Michel. *The History of Sexuality*, vol. 1, translated by Robert Hurley (London: Penguin, 1990), p. 42.

[241] Westphal, Carl. *Archiv für Neurologie*, 1870.

[242] Dollimore, Jonathan . *Sexual Dissidence: Augustine to Wilde, Freud to Foucault* (Oxford: Clarendon Press, 1991), p. 46.

[243] Boswell, J. (1980). *Christianity, social tolerance and homosexuality*. Chicago: University of Chicago Press.

[244] *Excerpt from Santorum interview*. Associated Press (AP), April 7, 2004 (posted at USAToday.com).

[245] Missler, Chuck. Prophecy 20/20: Profiling the Future Through the Lens of Scripture. 2006. pp. 245. Thomas Nelson.

[246] Leno, Jay. The Tonight Show. 1997.
http://jokes.maxabout.com/jid0005999/Comedians_Best_Lines_1997.aspx

[247] Anderson, Kerby. *The Decline of a Nation*. Electronic media.
http://www.leaderu.com/orgs/probe/docs/decline.html

[248] The "*Mayflower Compact*," in The Homes of the New World: Impressions of America. Bremer, Fredrika. Pp 183-184. 1853. Harper
http://books.google.com/books?id=jsM9AAAAIAAJ&pg=PA184&lpg=PA184&dq=advance-
ment+of+the+christian+faith&source=web&ots=nrNil_59e7&sig=tsfSeQSulUNRJWFDE47LFsc_q3c#PPA184,M1

[249] *The Mayflower Compact*. 1620. Found in The Avalon Project of Yale Law School: http://www.yale.edu/lawweb/avalon/amerdoc/mayflower.htm

[250] *The Fundamental Orders of 1639*. Found in The Avalon Project of Yale Law School:
http://www.yale.edu/lawweb/avalon/order.htm

---

[251] *The First Charter of Virginia; April 10, 1606.* Found in The Avalon Project of Yale Law School: http://www.yale.edu/lawweb/avalon/states/va01.htm

[252] de Tocqueville, Alexis. Attributed. (1805 -1859)
"I sought for the greatness and the genius of America in her ample rivers-it was not there; in her fertile fields and boundless prairies, and it was not there; in her rich mines and her vast world commerce, and it was not there. Not until I went into the churches of America and heard her pulpits ablaze with righteousness did I meet the secret of her genius and power. America is great because she is good, and if America ever ceases to be good-America will cease to be great."

[253] Rhodes, Richard. *The Making of the Atomic Bomb.* 1995. Ch.1 pg. 1: Moonshine.. Simon & Schuster.

[254] IBID

[255] Dannen, Gene. Leo Szilard – A Biographical Chronology. 1995. Online source: http://www.dannen.com/chronbio.html

[256] Goodstein, Laurie. *Falwell's Legacy in the Pulpit and Politics.* New York Times, May 16, 2007. Electronic source: http://www.nytimes.com/2007/05/16/us/16jerry.html?_r=1&oref=slogin

[257] Falwell, Jerry. Comments About 9-11 Attacks on the "700 Club," Septmeber 13, 2001. http://www.rightwingwatch.org/2007/05/falwells_commen.html

[258] Lela, Wayne. *Is Liberal Propaganda Backfiring?* The Conservative Voice. December 6, 2007.

[259] Eberhard, John. *Liberal Bias in Hollywood.* July 6, 1004. IntellectualConservative.com http://www.intellectualconservative.com/article3576.html

[260] *National Center for Chronic Disease Prevention and Health Promotion,* Abortion Surveillance - United States, 2003. Alan Guttmacher Institute – Abortion Satistics
http://www.guttmacher.org/sections/abortion.php
http://www.cdc.gov/mmwr/preview/mmwrhtml/ss5511a1.htm
http://www.nrlc.org/abortion/facts/abortionstats.html

[261] Judge rules against 'intelligent design' -'Religious alternative' to evolution barred from public-school science classes. MSNBC Technology & Science. December 20, 2005. Electronic source: http://www.msnbc.msn.com/id/10545387/

[262] Schultz, Lynne H. , Summary of Evolution in Public Schools. 2007?
http://www.infidels.org/activist/state/evolution.shtml

[263] Robbins , Thomas. The Religious Right: The Assault on Tolerance and Pluralism in America. *Journal for the Scientific Study of Religion*, Vol. 34, No. 2 (Jun., 1995), pp. 286

[264] The Multiculturalism Tolerance Diversity Movement Is Greco-Roman Paganism. November 28, 2007. http://healtheland.wordpress.com/2007/09/23/the-multiculturalism-tolerance-diversity-movement-is-greco-roman-paganism/

[265] Doolittle, Amy. "Criminalized Thoughts?" *The Washington Times,* December 29, 2004, p. A-2; and "Judge drops all charges against Philly Christians," WorldNetDaily.com, February 17, 2005, at http://www.worldnetdaily.com/news/article.asp?ARTICLE_ID=42905.

[266] Cohen, Helen and Chasnoff, Debra. *It's Elementary: Talking About Gay Issues In School* (video media) 1996. New Day Films DVD 2007.

[267] PBS - Onlne Newshour with Jim Lehrer. *Boy Scout Wars*. May 23, 2001. http://www.pbs.org/newshour/bb/youth/jan-june01/scoutwars_05-23.html

[268] *Internet Pornography*. National Coalition for the Protection of Children & Families. http://www.nationalcoalition.org/resourcesservices/stat.html

[269] *More Sex, Please.* Christianity Today International, Winter 2005.

[270] Whitman, David. *Was it Good for Us?* US News & World Reports, May 19, 1997

[271] Finer, Lawrence B., Ph.D. *Trends in Premarital Sex in the Unted States, 1954-2003.* Public Health Reports, January-February 2007. Volume 122.

[272] Ellwood DT, Crane J. Family change among black Americans: what do we know? *J Econ Perspectives* 4:65 -84, 1990

[273] Donaldson-Evans, Catherine. *'Love Child' the Latest Celeb Must-Have*. Fox News, November 10, 2005.

[274] Iannone, Carol. *The Moral Collapse of the American Family -Review*. National Review, October 15, 2001.

[275] Bennett, William J. The Broken Hearth: Reversing the Moral Colapse of the American Family. Doubleday. 2001

[276] Koppel, Ted & Judd, Jackie. Making *Hillary Clinton an Issue*. PBS Nightline interview with Bill and Hillary Clinton. March 26, 1992.

---

[277] Starr, Linda. *Corporal Punishment: Teaching Violence Through Violence.* Education World, 2002.
http://www.educationworld.com/a_issues/starr/starr051.shtml

[278] Sweet, Laurel. *Bay State Going Slap-Happy – Pols Debate Ban On Spanking.* Boston Herald, November 27, 2007.

[279] U.S. Census Bureau, *Statistical Abstract of the United States: 2006.*

[280] Divorce Rates by State, 1990-2004. Information Please® Database, © 2007 Pearson Education
http://www.infoplease.com/ipa/A0923080.html

[281] Francisco, Wendy. *Why Are Divorce Rates So High?* God's Word to Women, 2005. http://godswordtowomen.org/studies/articles/francisco1.htm

[282] "*Divorce statistics collection: Summary of findings so far,*" Americans for Divorce Reform, at: http://www.divorcereform.org/results.html

[283] *Feminism and Appropriate Roles for Women.* The General Council of Assemblies of God. 2006.
http://www.ag.org/top/Beliefs/contempissues_03_feminism.cfm

[284] Feeny, Jim, Ph.D. Forbidden Fruit is Still Tempting Eve – A Response to Arguments for the Ordination of Women. 2007.
http://www.jimfeeney.org/forbidden-fruittemptingEve.html

[285] Rehwinkel, Alfred. *The Flood: In the Light of the Bible, Geology, and Archaeology.* 1951. Concordia.

[286] The Persian Journal. Iran President Paves the Way for Arab's Imam Return. November 17, 2005.
http://www.iranian.ws/cgi-bin/iran_news/exec/view.cgi/13/10945

[287] Savyon, A, Mansharof, Y. The Doctrine of Mahdism: In the Ideological and Political Philosophy or Mahmoud Ahmadinejad and Ayatollah Mesbah-e Yazdi. June 1, 2007. Iran Press Service.
http://www.iran-press-service.com/ips/articles-2007/june-2007/mahdi_doctrine_1607.shtml

[288] Abedin, Mahan. *Dossier: Hexb al-Daawa al-Islamiya.* Islamic Call Party. June 2003. Middle East Intelligence Bulletin.
http://www.meib.org/articles/0306_iraqd.htm

[289] Yarshater, Ehsan. The Encyclopaedia Iranica. Volume XII – Fascicle 4.

[290] La Guardia, Anton. *Iran May be Seeking Apocalypse Now*. January 16, 2006. The Sydney Morning Herald.
http://www.smh.com.au/news/world/iran-may-be-seeking-apocalypse-now/2006/01/15/1137259944355.html

[291] Ahmadinejad's speech to the 62nd session of the United Nations in September 2007. Carried in the Islamic Republic News Agency. September 26, 2007.
http://www.globalsecurity.org/wmd/library/news/iran/2007/iran-070926-irna01.htm

[292] IBID

[293] Coughlin, Con. *Will the 12th Imam Cause War with Iran?* Telegraph,co.uk September 28, 2007.

[294] Schippert, Steve. Understanding Ahmadinejad. Threats Analysis Center. November 28, 2005.
http://analysis.threatswatch.org/2005/11/understanding-ahmadinejad/

[295] Orlov, Vladimir, Vinnikov, Alexander. *The Great Guessing Game: Russia and Iranian Nuclear Issue*. The Washington Quarterly Spring 2005, Vol. 28, No. 2, Pages 49-66.
http://www.mitpressjournals.org/doi/abs/10.1162/0163660053295185

[296] Deutch, John M., *Testimony Before the Permanent Subcommittee on Investigations of the Senate Committee on Government Affairs*. Central Intelligence Agency. March 20, 1996.
https://www.cia.gov/news-information/speeches-testimony/1996/dci_testimony_032096.html

[297] Pipes, Daniel. The Mystical Menace or Mahmoud Ahmadinejad. New York Sun. January 10, 2006.

[298] *The Encyclopaedia of Islam*. Brill Academic Publishers; Cdr edition (April 30, 2005)

[299] Joffe, Josef. *A World Without Israel*. Foreign Policy. January/February 2005.
http://www.foreignpolicy.com/story/cms.php?story_id=2737

[300] Schippert, Steve. *Understanding Ahmadinejad. Threats Analysis Center*. November 28, 2005.
http://analysis.threatswatch.org/2005/11/understanding-ahmadinejad/

---

[301] Harrison, Frances. Russia-Iran Nuclear Deal Signed. BBB News. February 27, 2005.
http://news.bbc.co.uk/2/hi/middle_east/4301889.stm

[302] Branham, William. *Water from the Rock.* Phoenix, Arizona. February 24, 1955.

[303] Branham, William. *The Handwriting on the Wall.* Jeffersonville, Indiana. September 2, 1956 pp65.

[304] Branham, William. *God Called Man.* Jeffersonville, Indiana. October 5, 1958. pp. 26-27.

[305] Branham, William. *The Greatest Battle Ever Fought*, Jeffersonville, Indiana. March 11, 1962 Pg. 55 pp3, Pg.56 ¶6.

[306] Young, Cathy. *From Russia with Loathing.* The New York Time, Op-Ed. November 21, 2008.

[307] Branham, William. *Condemnation By Representation* Jeffersonville, Indiana. November 11, 1960 Pg.30 ¶6

Chapter 11

[308] Aesop, *The Complete Fables.* New York : Penguin Books, 1998.

[309] Jacobs, Aaron. *Students Say They Learned to Tune Out Siren After Many False Alarms.* New York Times, January 20, 2000.
http://topics.nytimes.com/top/reference/timestopics/people/k/aaron_c_karol/index.html?s=oldest&

[310] The Side Effects of Health Warnngs. Social Issues Research Centre. 2006?.
http://www.sirc.org/news/sideeffects.html

[311] *Growing Up Tobacco Free: Preventing Nicotine Addiction in Children and Youths.* The Institute of Medicine. 1994 pp.73

[312] IBID

[313] Amy F. T. Arnsten, PhD; Patricia S. Goldman-Rakic, PhD *Archives of General Psychiatry.* 1998;55:362-368

[314] Smith, Matt, *Beanie Bubble*, San Francisco Weekly, December 16, 1998

[315] Crews, Barbara, *Your Guide to Collectibles*, July 2004

[316] Cordesman, Anthony H., *The Changing Face of Terrorism and Technology, and the Challenge of Asymmetric Warfare.* Testimony to the Senate Judiciary Subcommittee on Technology, Terrorism, and Government Information, March 27, 2001.

[317] Siegel, Marc. "Profits of fear". *The Nation.* 2001; 273: 5 (#J0112636)

[318] "A type is a shadow cast on the pages of OT history by a truth whose full embodiment or antitype is found in the NT revelation." Wick Broomall, "Type, Typology," *Baker's Dictionary of Theology* (Grand Rapids: Baker Book House, 1960), pp. 533-534.

[319] Jesus put this perplexing question to His detractors: How could David call his son his Lord (Matthew 22:42-46)?

Chapter 12

[320] Schoenheit, John W. Prophesy: Understanding and Utilizing the Manifestation of Prophesy. Christian Educational Services.

Chapter 13

[321] Daniel 9. And Jeremiah 29:10. The King James Version of the Bible

[322] Revelation 10:9-11. The King James Version of the Bible

[323] 1 Chronicles 16:21. The King James Version of the Bible

[324] Matthew 10:41. The King James Version of the Bible

[325] Galatians 2:1. The King James Version of the Bible

[326] Jeremiah 23:16, 21-22. The King James Version of the Bible

[327] Josephus: Vol. XVIII:2. Jewish Antiquities by H. St. J. Thackeray *Antiquities*

[328] "John the Baptist, Saint." Encyclopædia Britannica. 2007. Encyclopædia Britannica Online. 5 Dec. 2007 <http://www.britannica.com/eb/article-3740>.

[329] Harrell, D.E., *All Things Are Possible: The Healing and Charismatic Revivals in Modern America* (Bloomington, IN: Indiana University Press, 1978) pp. 25

[330] Hollenweger, W.J., *The Pentecostals* (Minneapolis: Augsburg Publishing House, 1972) pp. 354

[331] *Mystic Light Appears Over Local Baptist Evangelist While Baptizing At River.* Associated Press. Louisville Times. June 1933. http://www.branham.org/BranhamDefault.asp?Home=Blog_pages&LoadPageDetail=SpringStreet_061507.htm

[332] Branham, William. *Manifestation of the Spirit.* ppE34. Toledo, Ohio. July 17, 1951

[333] *Crippled Congressman Walks from Branham Healing Service.* The Voice of Healing. April-May, 1951. pp. 2. http://www.godsgenerals.com/pdf/1951_APRIL-MAY.pdf

[334] Lacy, George J. *Report and Opinion.* January 29, 1950. http://en.believethesign.com/index.php?title=Image:George_Lacy_Doc2.jpg http://www.biblebelievers.org/glacy.htm

[335] Jamieson, Robert. Et. al. Commentary Critical and Explanatory on the Whole Bible – The Book of Malachi. (1871) http://www.thirdmill.org/files/english/texts/JFB/JFB39.htm

[336] Green, Pearry. *Acts of the Prophet.* Tucson Tabernacle, Arizona, 1969.

[337] Branham, William. *Anointed Ones at the End Time.* July 25, 1965. Par. 262 Jeffersonville, Indiana.

[338] http://biblia.com/jesusbible/2samuel-1b.htm

[339] Noorbergen, Rene. *You are Psychic.* William Morrow. New York. 1971

[340] Noorbergen, Rene. *Ellen White: Prophet of Destiny.*(New Canaan, CT: Keats Publ.Co., 1972

Chapter 16

[341] Historical Note: the Masonic Lodge & Orphan's Home – Originally, Jefferson General Hospital was the third-largest hospital during the American Civil War, located at Port Fulton, Indiana (now part of Jeffersonville, Indiana) and was active between February 21, 1864 and December 1866. The land was owned by U.S Senator from Indiana Jesse D. Bright.

After the hospital closed, the buildings were intended for a soldiers' home, and given to the state of Indiana for that purpose. After two months possession, the buildings returned to the US Government. Until 1874 it was used as storehouses for army materials such as clothing and blankets. Eventually, a man named James Holt came into ownership of the property. At his death he bequeathed the property to his Masonic Lodge, Clark Lodge #40 as a Masonic orphan's home around 1915.

[342] Dannen, Gene. *Leo Szilard – A Biographical Chronology*. 1995. Online source: http://www.dannen.com/chronbio.html

[343] Branham, William. *Faith Once Delivered to the Saints*. May 1, 1955. Par.17 Chicago, IL

[344] Branham, William. *Condemnation By Representation (Hybrid Religion)*. pp. 5-1. November 13, 1960. Jeffersonville, IN

[345] Branham, William. *Condemnation By Representation (Hybrid Religion)*. pp. 5-2. November 13, 1960. Jeffersonville, IN

[346] Knight, Dale. "*RE: Calculating the Odds of Wm. Branham's 1932/33 Seven Event Prophecy*." Email attachment to the author. 5 March 2008.

[347] Giorgio Candeloro. *Storia dell'Italia Moderna*. Feltrinelli. (1981)

[348] MacDonald, Charles B. *The Mighty Endeavor: The American War in Europe.* Page 386. 1992. Da Capo Press.

[349] *Russia displays "Hitler skull fragment"*. BBC News. April 26, 2000. Electronic source: http://news.bbc.co.uk/1/hi/world/europe/725537.stm

[350] Encyclopaedia Britannica Online. http://www.britannica.com/eb/article-9117284/communism

[351] Engels, Frederick. *The Principles of Communism*. Selected Works, Volume One, pp. 81-97. 1969. Progress. First published in 1914 in the German Social Democratic Party's *Vorwarts!*

[352] *The making of a neo-KGB state.* Aug 23rd 2007 | Economist (London), 2007; pp.384

[353] Waller, Michael J. *Portrait of Putin's Past*. (American Foreign Policy Council) Perspective, Volume X, Number 3 (January-February 2000).

[354] Kryshtanovskaya, Olga and White ,Stephen. *Inside the Putin court: A Research Note*. November 1, 20 05. Europe-Asia Studies, 57:7, pp. 1065-75

[355] Zuckerman, Mortimer B. *Has Russia Left the West?* US News & World Report. December 6, 2007

[356] *The making of a neo-KGB state.* Aug 23rd 2007 | Economist (London), 2007; pp.384

[357] IBID

[358] Zuckerman, Mortimer B. *Has Russia Left the West?* US News & World Report. December 6, 2007

[359] IBID

[360] Gellately, Robert. *Lenin, Stalin and Hitler: The Age of Social Catastrophe.* Knopf, 2007. ISBN 1400040051 pp. 46-48

[361] George Leggett, *The Cheka: Lenin's Political Police.* Oxford University Press, 1987, ISBN 0198228627 pp. 197-201

[362] Waller, J. Michael. *Secret Empire: The KGB in Russia Today.*, Westview Press. Boulder, CO., 1994., ISBN 0-813323-231

[363] This work is copyrighted and unlicensed. It does not fall into one of the blanket fair use categories. However, it is believed that the use of this work in the article "Driverless Cars" from the October 1990 edition of Boy's Life: To illustrate the object in question; Where no free equivalent is available or could be created that would adequately give the same information. Within the scope of this book, the use of this image qualifies as fair use under United States copyright law and fair dealing under Canadian copyright law. Any other uses of this image *may* be copyright infringement. See Fair use and Copyrights.

[364] Lutz, Bob. *GM Exec: Driving is Dead - The day of riding in a car that drives itself down a Smart Highway is rapidly approaching*. Fortune Magazine, May 3, 2006. http://money.cnn.com/2006/05/02/Autos/ford_cartech_fortune/index.htm?section=money_topstories#TOP

[365] IBID

[366] http://www.darpa.mil/grandchallenge/

[367] Branham, William. *Broken Cisterns*. Jeffersonville, Indiana. July 26, 1964. Pp. 55

[368] Greer, Germaine in *Oz*, February 1969

[369] *Abington School District v. Schempp*, 374 U.S. 203, 83 S. Ct. 1560, 10 L. Ed. 2d 844.

[370] Reagan, Ronald, et. al. *Ronald Reagan: The Great Communicator*. HarperCollins, 2001. Remarks at a White House ceremony in observance of National Day of Prayer, May 6, 1982.

[371] Bennett, William J. *Quantifying America's Decline*. Wall Street Journal, On Principal, v1n1. April 1993.

[372] Rhodes, Richard. *The Making of the Atomic Bomb*. 1995. Ch.1 pg. 1: Moonshine.. Simon & Schuster.

[373] Lanouette, William. *The Odd Couple and the Bomb*. Scientific American, November 2000.

Chapter 17

[374] Isaiah 7:14. The King James Version of the Bible

[375] Acts 10:9-16. The King James Version of the Bible

[376] Branham, William. *Greater Than Solomon is Here.* Tucson, AZ 1963-0605 ¶E-86

[377] Carlson, Peter. *Another Race to the Finish.* The Washington Post. November 17, 200; page A01 http://www.washingtonpost.com/ac2/wp-dyn/A36425-2000Nov16?language=printer

[378] Bly, Nellie. *The Kennedy Men: Three Generations of Sex, Scandal and Secrets.* 1996. Kensington Books.

[379] IBID

[380] Gerth, Jeff, Van Natta, Don. *Her Way: The Hopes and Ambitions of Hillary Rodham Clinton.* 2007. Little, Brown.

[381] Kusch, Frank. *Battleground Chicago: The Police and the 1968 Democratic National Convention.* 2004, page 8. Greenwood.

[382] Gerth, Jeff, Van Natta, Don. *Her Way: The Hopes and Ambitions of Hillary Rodham Clinton.* 2007. Little, Brown.

[383] Hersh, Seymour M. *The Dark Side of Camelot.* 1997. Little, Brown and Company.

[384] Locke, John. 1632-1704. *Letter Concerning Toleration.* 1998. Prometheus.

[385] Doll, Peter M. *Revolution, Religion, and National Identity: Imperial Anglicanism in British North America, 1745–1795.* Page 86. Madison, N. J.: Fairleigh Dickinson University Press, 2000.

[386] Bacon, Francis. *The Works of Francis Bacon: Volume 8. The Letters and the Life. I.* History of Maryland Page 151. Originally printed in 1862. Longman, Green, Longman, and Roberts, London. Reprinted in 2003. Adamant Media.

[387] Alvey, James E. *Adam Smith: Optimist or Pessimist? A New Problem Concerning the Teleological Basis of Commercial Society*, page 105. Ashgate, Aldershot., 2003.

[388] Various. *Pasquin and Pasquinades.* The Atlantic Monthly, Volume 06, No.36, October, 1860.

[389] Chiniquy, Charles Paschal Telesphore. *Fifty Years in the Church of Rome.* Pg.714. 1886. Revell Electronic source: http://books.google.com/books?id=AhU3AAAAMAAJ

[390] Branham, William. *Condemnation By Representation.* Jeffersonville, IN. November 13, 1960 Pg7 pp3

[391] Branham, William. *Life Story.* Toledo, OH. July 22, 1951. Pp. E-72

[392] IBID

[393] Unknown . *Ohio River Flood of 1937.* Ohio History Central Online – electronic source. http://www.ohiohistorycentral.org/entry.php?rec=528

[394] Schimpff's Candy Store.
http://thumb9.webshots.net/s/thumb1/5/44/54/78254454UKpimE_th.jpg and http://home-and-garden.webshots.com/photo/1030545536014842629QyBMRwIfNT

[395] Branham, William. *Testimony* Cleveland, OH 1950-0814
E-27 Our heavenly Father, coming along down through that Baltic, up along through those hills and seeing those little bitty trains pulling along with those poor Finnish people a few weeks ago, laying burdened, coming walking, packing old bicycles, thousands gathering around... I'm thinking, coming down off of the mountain at Kuopio, seeing that little boy laying on the side of the road, dead, mashed to pieces, helpless, covered his little face over. Looked like life was finished for ever, no breath, no heart. Then remembered the vision of the Lord. Then laying hands upon him and calling in the Name of the Lord, and his life returned, there wasn't a bone broke in his body. How it spared the hearts of those dear people, how they come

from the Lapland. Oh, merciful God, You, Who could take a boy that was mashed to pieces, dead, laying on the road... Now, vision couldn't heal him; It was the Spirit of God.

[396] Electronic Source. http://www.onlybelieve.com/PDF/go_tell.pdf

[397] *Kari Holma*. Electronic Source. http://en.believethesign.com/index.php?title=Kari_Holma

[398] Unknown. "Hopeless? No." Time 3 September. 1951.

[399] Branham, William. *Demonology*. Owensboro, KY. November 11, 1953.

[400] Branham, William. *It Becometh Us To Fulfill All Righteousness* Jeffersonville, IN 1961-1001M

[401] Adapted from the book, published by *Voice of God Recordings*, called "Footprints on the Sands of Time", which is a compilation of excerpts by William Branham, taken from over one thousand tape recorded sermons.

[402] Weikos, Robert W. *Marilyn's Secret Tapes.* Los Angeles Times. August 5, 2005. Electronic source: http://www.latimes.com/news/nationworld/columnone/la-et-marilyn5aug05,1,4091305,full.story?coll=la-headlines-columnone

[403] Original August 5th, 1962 *Los Angeles Times* article about Marilyn Monroe's unhappiness and quest to find self in pdf format- http://www.calendarlive.com/media/acrobat/2005-08/18809448.pdf

[404] Branham, William. *All Things Are Possible.* Shreveport, LA November 24, 1962E pp. E-43

[405] Freeman, Lucy. *Why Norma Jean Killed Marilyn Monroe.* Triumph Books, 1992.

[406] Summers, Anthony. Goddess: *The Secret Lives of Marilyn Monroe.* Onyx, 1996.

[407] IBID

[408] Bell, Rachael.. *The Death of Marilyn* .Courtroom Television Network. Retrieved 28 December 2007. http://www.crimelibrary.com/notorious_murders/celebrity/marilyn_monroe/index.html

[409] Branham, William. *All Things Are Possible* Shreveport, LA 1962-1124E

[410] Emile Griffith vs. Benny "the Kid" Paret III – 1962 video clip on YouTube: http://www.youtube.com/watch?v=StKw0kkJQzA

[411] 12/5/2002 CBS Sports Line (www.sportsline.com) - *Courtesy International Boxing Hall of Fame* (www.ibhof.com)

[412] Branham, William. *Influence* Beaumont, TX 1964-0315

[413] *Brief History of Portable Music Players*. November 2001. http://www.squidoo.com/savingipods/

[414] Branscombe, Mary. *Portable Devices Get Better with Time*. Tom's Guide. March 12, 2007.

[415] IBID

[416] IBID

[417] IBID

[418] Menta, Richard. *iPod Killers for Summer 2007*. MP3newswire.net http://www.mp3newswire.net/stories/7002/ipod-killer-summer2007.html

[419] Tynan, Dan. *The 50 Greatest Gadgets of the Past 50 Years*. PC World. December 24, 2005.

[420] http://www.thefreeword.com/sermons.htm; http://www.biblebelievers.org/messagehub/en/messages.do; http://www.nathan.co.za/sermons.asp

[421] Branham, William. *Workings of the Holy Spirit.*. Prince Albert, Canada. August 16, 1956 ¶ E21-23

[422] Branham, William. *Whatever He Saith Unto You Do It*. Chicago, IL 1954-0722 ¶ E25-26.

[423] Jeremiah 29:11. The Bible, King James Version

[424] Shakespeare, William. *As You Like It*. Jaques (Act II, Scene VII, lines 139-166)

[425] Psalm 40:7. The Bible, King James Version

Chapter 18

[426] Branham, William. *O Lord Just Once More.* Hot Springs, AR V-20 N-10 1963-0628M ¶17

[427] Genesis 45. The Bible, King James Version

[428] Branham, William. *O Lord Just Once More.* Hot Springs, AR V-20 N-10 1963-0628M ¶17

[429] Branham, William. *The Third Exodus.* Jeffersonville, IN V-2 N-21 1963-0630M ¶142-144

[430] Branham, William. *He Cares, Do You Care?* Jeffersonville, IN V-12 N-4 1963-0721 ¶6-7,16

[431] Branham, William. *And Knoweth it Not.* Jeffersonville, IN V-2 N-10 1965-0815 ¶283-284

[432] Los Angeles Times Articles during the Watts Riot period – pdf files. Electronic Source: <http://www.latimes.com/news/local/la-wattsriotspdfs-gallery,0,5804406.gallery?coll=la-home-headlines>

[433] Electronic Source: <www.africanamericans.com/WattsRiots.htm>

[434] Axelrod, Alan and Phillips, Charles. *What Every American Should Know about American History*. Adams Media, 2003. Page 300.

[435] *L.A. Insurrection Surpasses 1965 Watts Riots.* Emergency Net NEWS Service. 1992 Electronic Source: <http://www.emergency.com/la-riots.htm>

[436] Keatley, Patrick. *Idi Amin – Ruthless Dictator*...The Guardian, August 18, 2003. Electronic Source: < http://www.guardian.co.uk/news/2003/aug/18/guardianobituaries>

[437] King County, Washington – Public Health. Tuesday, February 5, 2008 Electronic Source < http://www.kingcounty.gov/healthservices/health/news/2008/08020502.aspx>

[438] Power, Samantha. *The AIDS Rebel.* The New Yorker. (2003).

[439] Bosley, Sarah. *Mbeki Aids Policy Led to 330,000 Deaths*...The Guardian, November 27, 2008. Electronic Source: < http://www.guardian.co.uk/world/2008/nov/27/south-africa-aids-mbeki>

[440] Gerson, Michael. *Obama's Abortion Extremism*. Washington Post. April 2, 2208; Page A19. Electronic Source: < http://www.washingtonpost.com/wp-dyn/content/article/2008/04/01/AR2008040102197.html>

[441]Gardner, Day. *Black Religious Leaders Wrongly Giddy Over Pro-Abortion Barack Obama*. Life News.Com Electronic Source < http://www.lifenews.com/nat3968.html>

[442] World Net Daily.Com – *Black Pro-life Leader Rips Obama*. January 10, 2008. Electronic Source < http://www.worldnetdaily.com/news/article.asp?ARTICLE_ID=59612>

[443] Bedard, Paul, & Schwab, Nikki. *Is Funding for Family Planning Agencies Coming Back Under Obama?* US News & World Report – Washington Whispers. November 12, 2008. Electronic Source <http://www.usnews.com/mobile/blogs/washington-whispers/2008/11/12/is-funding-for-family-planning-agencies-coming-back-under-obama.html>

[444] Kengor, Paul. *Obama's Abortion Socialism.* American Thinker. December 13, 2008. Electronic Source: < http://www.americanthinker.com/2008/12/obamas_abortion_socialism.html)

[445] Starr, Penny. *Obama Supports Freedom of Choice Act*. June 12, 2008. CNS News. Electronic Source < http://www.cnsnews.com/Public/Content/Article.aspx?rsrcid=7882>

[446] Branham, William. *My Life Story*. Cleveland, OH. 1950-0820A ¶E-132

[447] Sanger, Margaret. *Woman and the New Race*. Brentano. 1920.

[448] Sanger, Margaret. *The Pivot of Civilization*. Brentano. 1922. [Electronic Book Available at :< http://groups.csail.mit.edu/mac/users/rauch/nvp/sanger/>]

[449] Richmond, Mike. *Margaret Sanger, Sterilization, and the Swastika.* Tetrahedron. July 1997. <http://www.spectacle.org/997/richmond.html>

[450] Kopp, Marie E. *Legal and Medical Aspects of Eugenic Sterilization in Germany*. American Sociological Review, 1936:763

[451] Whitney, Leon F. *Unpublished autobiography*. Whitney Papers, APS. 1971, pp.204-5.

[452] Gordon, Linda. *Woman's Body, Woman's Right* . New York: Grossman, 1974. Page 351.

[453] IBID. Gordon, Page 290.

Chapter 19

[454] Rhee, Foon. *Some say ad casts Obama as the Antichrist.* The Boston Globe, August 9, 2008.
<http://www.boston.com/news/nation/articles/2008/08/09/some_say_ad_casts_obama_as_the_antichrist/>

[455] LaHaye, Tim and Jenkins, Jerry B. *Left Behind Series*. Tyndale House Publishers. 1984-Present.

[456] McCain Campaign ad vertisement mocking Obama – "The One." YouTube, August 1, 2008. Electronic source:<http://www.youtube.com/watch?v=mopkn0lPzM8>

[457] Taheri, Amir. *Obama and Ahmadinejad.* Commentary, Forbes. October 26, 2008. Electronic source: < http://www.forbes.com/2008/10/26/obama-iran-ahmadinejad-oped-cx_at_1026taheri.html>

[458] McCrea, Sister Mary, Order of Sorcha Faal. *Visions of the Great Nyasaye, A Study of the Luo Religion in Kenya.* 1915.

[459] Nelson, Dana. *Bad for Democracy: How the Presidency Undermines the People.*University of Minnesota Press. September, 2008.

[460]Wright, David. ABC News – Newsline 8 January 2008. "'Something Stirring in the Air' in New Hampshire - Sen. Barack Obama Draws Large Crowds as the Granite State Primary Nears."
<http://abcnews.go.com/Politics/Vote2008/story?id=4099500&page=1>.

[461] YouTube 1 August 2008. "The One."
<http://www.youtube.com/watch?v=mopkn0lPzM8>

[462] Goodwin, Michael. NY Daily News 19 August 2008. "After Barak Obama hype, a backlash." < http://www.nydailynews.com/opinions/2008/08/19/2008-08-19_after_barack_obama_hype_a_backlash.html>.

[463] Obama, Barak. Barak Obama Senate web site 28 June 2008. "Call to Renewal" Keynote Address. < http://obama.senate.gov/speech/060628-call_to_renewal/>.

[464] Obama, Barak. Barak Obama Senate web site 28 June 2008. "Call to Renewal" Keynote Address. < http://obama.senate.gov/speech/060628-call_to_renewal/>.

[465] Yoffe, Emily. *The Supervisor, the Champion, and the Promoter.* Slate.com February 20, 2008.

[466] Carpenter, Amanda. Townhall, August 26, 2008. From a video titled "Christianity Designed Discrimination" uploaded by a YouTube user named IslamStudos.

[467] Falcone, Michael, and Moss, Michael. Groups Tally of New Voters Was Vastly Overstated. *New York Times. October 23, 2008.*
http://www.nytimes.com/2008/10/24/us/politics/24acorn.html.

[468] Editors. *The Mask of Barak Obama: A Psychological Profile.* Contrarian Commentary.com. February 10, 2007.

Chapter 20

[469] Hilborn, R.C. *Chaos and Nonlinear Dynamics.* Oxford University Press, 1994

[470] Washington, Warren. *Odyssey in Climate Modeling, Global Warming, and Advising Five Presidents*. Page 42. Lulu 2007.

[471] Chodos, Alan, Ouellette, Jennifer. *Circa January 1961: Lorenz and the Butterfly Effect.* American Physical Society. January 2003 (Volume 12, Number 1)

[472] Koenig, William R. *Eye to Eye: Facing the Consequences of Dividing Israel.* 2006. About Him.

[473] IBID

[474] Hazlewood, Mark. *Blindsided, Planet X Passes in 2003*, Earthchanges, pp. 83. 2002.

[475] Branham, William. *Choosing of a Bride.* Los Angeles, CA, April 29, 1965E pp. 35 ¶3-5

[476] Branham, William. *Ashamed*, Jeffersonville, IN, July 11, 1965 pp.51

[477] http://alaska.org/videos.htm (under "Other Videos - The 1964 Earthquake [2:07])

[478] Branham, William. *What is the Attraction on the Mountain?* pp.. 22:143-148. 1962. Spoken Word Publications.

[479]Electronic Source. http://www.youtube.com/watch?v=6PRBY4hseO4

[480] Electronic Source. http://video.aol.com/video-detail/alaskan-earthquake-1964-ax7996a/85607776

[481] Shedlock, Kaye and Pakiser, Louis. *Earthquakes*. October23, 1997. U.S. Geological Survey. Electronic Source. http://pubs.usgs.gov/gip/earthq1/earthqkgip.html

[482] Gonzales, Richard. *California Town Still Scarred by 1964 Tsunami*. June 15, 2005. National Public Radio (NPR)

[483] Tvedtnes, John A. *Historical Parallels to the Destruction at the Time of the Crucifixion.* 1994. Pgs 170-186. Maxwell Institute. Electronic Source. http://farms.byu.edu/display.php?id=54&table=jbms

[484] Grantz, A et. al. *Alaska's Good Friday Earthquake March 27, 1964: A Preliminary Geologic Evaluation.* 1964. U.S. Geologic Survey Circ. 491. pp. 35

[485] Unknown. *Shaken Earth.* November 17, 1967. Time. Electronic Source. http://www.time.com/time/magazine/article/0,9171,844104,00.html

[486] IBID

[487] Lander, James F. and Patricia A. Lockridge. *United States Tsunamis*. Publication 41-2. U.S. Department of Commerce. August 1989.

[488] Dokka, Roy K. *Why California's Coast fell Into the Ocean.* USA Today (Society for the Advancement of Education), June 1996. Electronic source: http://findarticles.com/p/articles/mi_m1272/is_n2613_v124/ai_18356777

[489] Dutch, Steven, *If You're Going To Sink California, Do It Right*, in http://www.uwgb.edu/dutchs/pseudosc/sinkcal.htm

[490] Green, Pearry. *Acts of the Prophet.* [Earthquake Judgment]. 1969, page 119.

[491] IBID - *On September 11, 1965, Brother Branham was in Phoenix, preaching a message entitled God's Power To Transform. It was at this time that I personally witnessed the solution to the question troubling Brother Billy Paul. We were at the Ramada Inn when Brother Carl Williams received a long distance call from Los Angeles informing him that Sister Florence had died the night before. Brother Branham was given the message and he immediately asked Brother Williams to find out the time of her death. I was there when the call went through and the answer was given us that she had died at 2:45 a.m.*

[492] City of Wilshire, CA. Monument #566, September 30, 1992. Electronic source: <http://cityplanning.lacity.org/complan/hcm/dsp_hcm_result.cfm?community=Wilshire>

[493] Evander, Alan, et.al. *Fluids in the lower crust following Mendocino triple junction migration: Active basaltic intrusion?* Geology, vol. 26, Issue 2, pp.171, 1998.

[494] Blakeslee, Sandra. *Massive slip-strike fault found from Whittier to LA Downtown.* New York Times. March 5, 1999.

[495] Cromie, William J. *New Earthquake Fault Discovered Under Los Angeles.* Harvard Gazette Archives. March 04, 1999.

Chapter 21

[496] Tributsch, H., *When the Snakes Awake.* Massachusetts Institute of Technology Press, 1982.

[497] Hatai, S. and Abe, N. *The Responses of the Catfish, Parasilurus ascotus, to Earthquakes.* Proc. Imperial Acad. Japan, 8, 1932, pp. 374-378.

[498] Miller, Ted, *Earthquake Prediction Handbook*, Info-Pub, 1996.

[499] Armstrong, B.H, *Acoustic Emission Prior to Rockbursts and Earthquakes*, Bull. Seis. Soc. Am. 59, 1259-1279, 1969

[500] Chapman, S., and J. Bartels, *Geomagnetism*, Oxford University Press, London, 1049 pp., 1940.

[501] Ulomov, V.I. and Malashev, B.Z. "The Tashkent Earthquake of 26 April, 1966." Acad. Nauk. Uzbek, FAN, Tashkent, 1971.

[502] Chalmers, J. A. *Atmospheric Electricity*, New York, Pergamon Press, Chap. 4, 1967.

[503] Exodus 4:1-17. The King James Version of the Bible

[504] Spurgeon, Charles. (1834-1892) . *Heavenly Worship.* December 28, 1856.

[505] Branham, William (1909-1965). *John's Patmos Vision.* Jeffersonville, IN. December 4, 1960E - ROJC pp. 69 ¶130.

[506] Pascal, Blaise. *Pensees*. 1669. § 233.

[507] Kreeft, Peter. *Fundamentals of the Faith: Essays in Christian Apologetics*. Ignatius, 1988. Page 53.

[508] Dirty Harry. Directed by Don Siegel. Starring Clint Eastwood. 1971.

FOR MORE INFORMATION:

Free Downloadable Books:
Nathan Software
http://www.nathan.co.za/sermons.asp

Free Downloadable Audio Files:
Bible Believers
http://www.bibleway.org/wmb/audiolib.asp

Questions or Additional Information:
Dale Knight
Email – wmbinfo@gmail.com

Amazing Grace Fellowship
http://www.amazinggrace-usa.org
Email – agfellowship@msn.com

First Stone Publishing, LLC
http://www/firststonellc.com
Email – admin@firststonellc.com

Made in the USA
Lexington, KY
24 September 2011